Revelations of an Opera Manager in 19th-Century America

by MAX MARETZEK

Crotchets and Quavers
&
Sharps and Flats

(*Two Volumes Bound As One*)

WITH A NEW INTRODUCTION BY

CHARLES HAYWOOD

Dover Publications, Inc.

NEW YORK

Copyright © 1968 by Dover Publications, Inc.
All rights reserved under Pan American and International Copyright Conventions.

Published in Canada by General Publishing Company, Ltd., 30 Lesmill Road, Don Mills, Toronto, Ontario.
Published in the United Kingdom by Constable and Company, Ltd., 10 Orange Street, London WC 2.

This Dover edition, first published in 1968, is an unabridged and slightly corrected republication of *Crotchets and Quavers*, originally published in 1855 by S. French, New York, and *Sharps and Flats*, originally published in 1890 by American Musician Publishing Co., New York. A new Introduction and Index have been specially prepared for this edition.

The publisher is grateful to the Peabody Institute, Baltimore, Md., which lent its copy of *Sharps and Flats* for purposes of reproduction.

Library of Congress Catalog Card Number: 68-19548

Manufactured in the United States of America
Dover Publications, Inc.
180 Varick Street
New York, N. Y. 10014

INTRODUCTION TO THE
DOVER EDITION.

THESE two volumes—*Crotchets and Quavers* (1855), and *Sharps and Flats* (1890)—besides presenting a vivid chronicle of theatrical events, a series of incredible adventures, a gallery of amazing characters, and the multifarious problems, both serious and humorous, besetting an intrepid operatic impresario, also unfold a panorama of cultural life and the level of musical taste in America in the second half of the nineteenth century. Although the action is primarily centered in New York City, the energetic and peregrinating manager, in taking his various operatic troupes to the major cities of the Atlantic seaboard, into the South down to New Orleans, to Mexico and Cuba, gives a colorful portrayal and a highly personal appraisal of the variety and quality of musical activities in the young Republic and in Latin America. Here is the story, enlivened with anecdote, spicy gossip, and "green room" chatter, of persistent efforts—with their accompanying vicissitudes, frustrations, and occasional triumphs—to bring Italian opera, with the outstanding singers of the day, at the lowest price, to the people of America.

Max Maretzek's story is a significant chapter in American musical history, hitherto—with few exceptions (George P. Upton and Henry Edward Krehbiel)—only glancingly noted by our music historians, and not even mentioned in the more recent comprehensive studies. He deserves better treatment, and a more scholarly and objective evaluation. Our present cultural sophistication need not denigrate the stylistic mannerism of a flamboyant romantic—even if it were true, as Krehbiel suspects, that the writing itself was done by another hand—with the inevitable exaggerations and obvious self-adulation. What is of prime consideration is the informative chronicle of American musical life and the events and personalities that have influenced and molded our operatic and theatrical traditions. The dominant role of Italian opera in New York can be understood largely through the efforts of Max Maretzek and others who shared and contributed to the musical scene.

The dazzle and glamour of the Metropolitan Opera House has blinded the general public and obscured Maretzek's contributions. Indeed, the name Maretzek may be quite unknown and come as a complete surprise to many people. However, one must not forget that the musical foundations of "The Met" were, to a considerable extent, laid by the "blood, sweat and tears" of a Maretzek. Of course, there were others who worked before him, with him, against him and after him. The following pages bear ample testimony to their efforts. While Maretzek, typical of many impresarios, will often claim success for a venture solely accounted to his personal managerial magic, credit is not wholly denied to his precursors and co-workers.

The life of a musical manager in the mid-nineteenth century was not an easy one, nor, for that matter, is it today. There was no "Madison Avenue" then, with elaborate, complicated and widespread mass media to transmit the "ballyhoo" on microwaves to all corners of the land. The manager had to be his own publicity agent, and often write his own copy—using P. T. Barnum's "humbug" technique to achieve his goal. And the goal was to survive (and lucky indeed if, at the end of the season, he came out in the black—even if it was only a mere speck on the ledger) against highly competitive attractions. Besides disappointments, frivolities, violent tempers of arrogant *prima donnas* and self-centered tenors, there were endless harassments from subscribers and stockholders, breakdowns in transportation, restrictive local ordinances, limited theatrical facilities, inadequate lighting and collapsing scenery, incompetent instrumentalists and inaudible choristers, and—as if that were not enough—endless court litigations. Of the latter, the most astonishing one, not mentioned by Maretzek in either volume, involved legal action brought against him by two worthy New York citizens seeking to prevent the further showing of Verdi's *Rigoletto* on the ground that it was a lewd and licentious work, and that (according to the court transcript) "by its singing, its business, and its plot, was then and there such an exhibition of opera as no respectable member of the fair sex could patronize without then and there sacrificing both taste and modesty."

It might be very illuminating, if not surprising, to examine briefly the musical and theatrical events at the time Maretzek assumed his managerial duties of the Astor Place Opera House in the fall of 1849. What other attractions were competing for the New Yorkers' attention and purse that season? Utilizing the highlights in the monumental studies and annals of the New York stage by Joseph N. Ireland* and George C. D. Odell,† as well as contemporary programs, playbills, and newspaper accounts, and limiting our survey from September 1849 to January 1850, we discover that the "great white way"—then only lit by gaslight, and mostly situated below Fourteenth Street, chiefly in the area of Broadway and Chambers Street—was a very busy place.

The Broadway Theatre (Broadway and Pearl Street) opened the season on September 17 with *Born to Good Luck*, with James Hudson, popular Irish singer and comedian heading the cast. Other productions that season included *The Irish Lion, A Kiss in the Dark, O'Flannigan* and the *Fairies*. Hudson's success was due not only to his rich, mellow and melodious voice, "exactly suited for the music of Irish melodies, but also to his skill as an actor—chaste, natural and consequently telling." After Hudson's departure, the famous Charlotte Cushman gained attention, to the acclaim of the public and press, with her dramatic impersonations in Shakespearean repertory.

After Miss Cushman's success, the Irish again took over the Broadway Theatre, with titles as these announced in the papers: *The Irish Ambassador, King*

---

* J. N. Ireland, *Records of the New York Stage, 1750–1860* (New York: T. H. Morrell, 1867) vol. 2.

† G. C. D. Odell, *Annals of the New York Stage* (New York: Columbia University Press, 1931) vol. 5.

O'Neill, Rory O'More, The Irish Attorney, and other Hibernian successes.

On November 12, the theatre yielded to a well-known company presenting English opera (that is, opera sung in English: the repertory drawn from the Italian, French, German, as well as those originally composed in English), opening with Donizetti's *The Child of the Regiment*, (a "slight" change from the original, *The Daughter of the Regiment*), Balfe's *The Bohemian Girl*, Mozart's *Don Giovanni*, and Bellini's *Norma*. Quite a repertory was displayed, with some very fine singers who had long been active in singing opera in English: W. H. Reeves, Mr. and Mrs. Seguin, Rosa Jacques, Julia Daly, and the Placides. However, rarely was the work sung as the composer and librettist had intended. Changing the title was the least perpetration. It was common practice to alter the libretto, indiscriminately cut the music, and interpolate tunes and orchestral numbers from other operas and composers; indeed, quite often, any resemblance to the original score and text was purely accidental. As one wit quipped: "What music they did not kill, they cut."

This short season ended November 26, when the great tragedian James H. Hackett took over the Broadway Theatre with Shakespeare and other popular characterizations: *Rip Van Winkle, Falstaff, The Yankee in England, Macbeth*, and *The Kentuckian*. On the heels of the latter, Hudson returned with more of his gallery of Irish impersonations. Among them were *White Horse of the Peppers*, and *The Irish Recruit*, and, to show his versatility, he acted Petruchio to the Katharine of Mrs. Hield.

On December 10, perhaps as a Christmas gift to the "kiddies," as Professor Odell suspects, the Bateman children, Kate and Ellen, were engaged to give their "inimitable" portrayals of Shakespearean scenes and characters. They opened with the fifth act of *Richard III*, with Kate as Richmond, and Ellen as Richard; on another evening, "Ellen as Shylock was cowed into mercy by Kate as Portia." Their success soon led them to Barnum's Museum, where the master showman displayed them among his other freaks of nature.

New artists and repertory kept the Broadway Theatre busy. James E. Murdoch followed the "incomparable child actors" with a more trustworthy presentation of *Hamlet*, followed by *The Elder Brother*, *The Robbers*, and his successful portrayal of Young Rapid in *A Cure for the Heartache*. Charlotte Cushman returned before the end of the year in *The Hunchback*, *The Lady of Lyons*, and the farce *A Bird of Passage*.

Let us see what Burton's Theatre (Broadway and Chambers Street) had to offer for the fall season of 1849. It included such "masterpieces" as the new burlesque *Faint Heart Never Won Fair Lady*, *The Sphinx*, the farce *Turning the Tables*, and the chiller *Temptation, or the Price of Happiness*. The leading interpreters of these gems were Mr. Burton, John Brougham, Miss C. Chapman and Miss E. Barber. On September 17, Mozart's *The Marriage of Figaro* was presented in an English version. Other attractions that tempted the audiences that season at Burton's included *Tis Only My Aunt*, *Dombey and Son*, *Lola Montez*, *The Demon Jester or the Dutchman's Dream*, *The Old Dutch Governor*, *Mammon and Gammon*, and *The Todles*. Burton's efforts that season merited Odell's praise: "he had staged some fine comedies, and had brought out countless trifles, most of which added to the gaiety of the city."

Macbeth opened the busy repertory season at the Bowery Theatre (Broadway and Broome Street) on September 3, with Mr. and Mrs. J. W. Wallack in the leading roles. In rapid succession the audiences were regaled with more Shakespeare: *Othello, Richard III, Romeo and Juliet* (Mr. Wallack as Romeo and Miss Wemyss as Juliet), *Hamlet, King Lear,* as well as such attractions (perhaps in title only) as *Shot in the Eye or the Regulators in Texas, The King of the Commons,* and *The Ragpicker of Paris.* Lester Wallack joined the other members of the family in a number of very successful productions, including a farcical afterpiece to *Othello, The Idiot of the Mill.* The reason for this intrusion, it has been suggested, was to "mitigate the grandeur of Shakespeare."

The most representative aggregate of American theatrical talent was performed that season at the National Theatre (Broadway and Chatham Street). The roster included such luminaries as Frank S. Chanfrau (actor-manager), Joseph Jefferson, Redmond Ryan, and Charles Burke. The repertory was the most representative of American life and folkways (melodramatized, of course, with exaggeration and tall tale): *Rip Van Winkle, Jonathan Bradford, The Murdered Boatman, Mysteries and Miseries of New York, A Budget of Blunders, The Virginia Mummy,* seasoned (if it needed any) with a variety of farces, burlettas, travesties, with Shakespeare making his customary (although somewhat altered) appearance.

The season at the Olympic Theatre (Broadway and

Howard Street), under the management of William Mitchell, began on September 10 with *No! or the Glorious Minority*, followed by a number of other blaring farces bearing such dramatic titles as, *The Lawyer's Practice*, *The Trumpeter's Wedding*, and *Brittania and Hibernia*. For a change of pace and by popular demand, English operatic repertory returned. In their usual truncated versions and, sometimes, unrecognizable plots were presented *Fra Diavolo* (Auber), *Cinderella* (Rossini), *The Child of the Regiment* (Donizetti), *The Barber of Seville* (Rossini), and *The New Lord of the Village* (Boieldieu). Before the year was over Pierce's Minstrels moved into the Olympic. They advertised themselves as "the best Band of Minstrels in the United States, collected from every respectable company in the Union," with twenty-five cents admission to all parts of the house.

A refurbished and resplendent new (after a disastrous fire) Niblo's Garden (Broadway and Prince Street) opened the season, under the well-known John Sefton, with the popular Ravels, a pantomime troupe of twenty-two. These "commedians dell'arte" and balletists alternated with a dramatic company presenting such offerings as *John Dobbs and Jenny* (a parody on the famous Swedish nightingale, Jenny Lind), and an array of vaudeville acts. But even here, Shakespeare could not be kept away. The famous James H. Hackett played again his favorite Falstaff in *The Merry Wives of Windsor*, alternating with *Rip Van Winkle*, *The Kentuckian*, and *Jonathan in England*. Not long after, Niblo's stage yielded to the dramatic and lyrical voices of an Italian opera troupe singing Donizetti's *L'Elisir d'Amore*, and scenes from the same composer's oft-performed *La Fille du Régiment*. It is worth noting that some of these singers were later associated with Maretzek.

Lest we forget, Barnum's Museum at Broadway and Ann Street was, as usual, noisily exhibiting its myriad attractions gathered "from all corners of the earth." However, in the fall of 1849, P. T. Barnum made a notable (if only short-lived) change: he transformed his lecture room with "its ancient freakery" to a regular theater. He set up a dramatic company under the direction of F. C. Wemyss, with some well-known names to lend additional prestige. This foray into serious drama barely got off the board, and quickly expired. Without too much loss of time or money, Barnum went back to his odd assortment of curiosities, in which the Bateman juveniles, portraying Shakespearean characters, held the limelight.

Welch's National Circus, performing at Eighth Street and Fourth Avenue, also competed for the New Yorkers' attention. And not to be undone, the Manhattan Circus, including a band of Negro minstrels, was busy at the corner of Hudson and Thirteenth Street.

Moreover, the Chinese Museum (Broadway and Spring Street), with its large collection of Chinese figures and curios, exhibiting nightly, caught the fancy of many visitors. Macallister's "Temple of Enchantment" in the Assembly Rooms, with its advertised "two dreams of twelve experiments!", attracted its own brand of "worshipers." Barnum's business tentacles soon swallowed up the Chinese curios. Then too, there were Christy's Minstrels cavorting at Mechanic's Hall (472 Broadway). Their popularity continued, drawing large crowds daily. "There is nothing to record," Odell confirms, "but success. The spell of those plaintive plantation ditties, those lively dances, that nimble wit, was irresistible." The New Yorkers' love for the black-faced minstrels was lavished on other groups presenting this form of entertainment: White's Serenaders, proudly displaying Dan Emmett and Charley White, the high priests of minstrelsy; the New Orleans Serenaders, Campbell's Minstrels, and the famous Virginia Minstrels, the latter performing at Lynch's Concert Hall, 237 Bowery, between Rivington and Stanton Streets.

To satisfy a special, but ever-present and persistent taste, there was the Franklin Theatre, Chatham Square, outfitted in the style of Mme. Warton's Walhalla in London, with "a company of ladies not to be equalled in the world for beauty and talent." There were also the captivating and tantalizing Female Serenaders and Arab Girls, a group of "Model Artists" advertised to portray *The Rape of the Sabines.*

To meet the taste of the lovers of concerts, vocal and instrumental, there was the aforementioned Lynch's Concert Hall, where for the modest admission of $6\frac{1}{4}$ cents [!], J. Lynch, the proprietor, furnished eminent artists from "pleasing cantatrices" to juggling acts and magicians. There were numerous other concert halls opening their doors to similar artistic endeavors.

The craze of New Yorkers for panoramas and dioramas kept many ingenious inventors, photographers, and light specialists busy at a dozen exhibition rooms.

They were viewed with awe and bated breath. "They were impressive, with their lights and effects of far distances, and their immovable figures caught in moments of crisis."

There was also the popular attraction of "Readings"—solo elocutionary and dramatic renditions of the works of eminent playwrights and poets (Shakespeare far in front). The leading names in the theater shared in this profitable venture—Fanny Kemble being the most famous and most successful.

For serious music, the classics, and the works of the great masters of Western musical art, the connoiseurs went to the Broadway Tabernacle. After the operatic and concert performances at Castle Garden (Battery Park), the leading vocalists and instrumentalists appeared in solo or ensemble at the Tabernacle, very often for various charitable benefits. Similar programs were heard at the Apollo Rooms (Broadway near Canal Street), at the Society Library, and the Chinese Museum Rooms. And, of course, the *pièce de résistance* of the musical life of this great city was the New York Philharmonic Society, which opened its eighth season on November 24, 1849, at the Apollo Rooms under the baton of Theodore Eisfeld, conducting for the first time in America Beethoven's *Fourth Symphony*.

We have cast a selective and hurried glance at the many theatrical events that held the New Yorkers' attention in the fall season of 1849. The astonishing thing is that there was an audience for all the attractions. Into this maelstrom Maretzek entered, became part of it, shared and influenced it, and left an indelible imprint upon it.

Although a period of thirty-five years separates the publication of the second volume, it really does not continue where the first (whose title, using the English connotation, means "Quarter Notes and Eighth Notes") left off. Rather than a sequel, it amplifies *Crotchets and Quavers*, and fills some of the lacunae with more relevant detail. Of particular importance, among other observations, incidents, managerial headaches and heartaches, and escapades, are the biographical vignettes of the leading singers, the critical and perceptive sketches of the most prominent composers, and the inclusion of photographs.

Out of these informative and breezy letters, addressed to leading European musical personalities (Hector Berlioz, Fiorentino, journalist on the Paris *Corsair*, Luigi Lablache, the famous basso, Joseph Fischof, eminent pianist and teacher in Vienna, Michael William Balfe, composer, Frederick Gye, manager of the Royal Opera House, Covent Garden, London, and Carl Eckert, conductor at the Imperial Opera, Vienna) with whom Maretzek had been associated before his arrival in New York in 1848, emerge suggestive hints, bare outlines, and sketchy information on his early career. But the events of his life after his involvement with the Academy of Music in 1854, until his death in 1897, can not be discerned from these two volumes. One must look for other sources, not all accessible or available. The full story of this indefatigable impresario, gifted conductor, and talented composer has not yet been told. Here we can only attempt to link the main threads of his life. The complete biography must wait for another occasion.

Max Maretzek (né Maximilian Mareczek) was born on June 28, 1821, in Brno, Moravia, Czechoslovakia. After completion of formal education, with strong emphasis in the classics and literature—while pursuing general studies in music and piano instruction—he enrolled in the University of Vienna. His father hoped that he would pursue a medical education, but his first visit to the dissecting room convinced him that medicine was not going to be his chosen field. A brief encounter with legal texts led him to a similar conclusion about the law profession. In his letter to Professor Joseph Fischof, he recounts vividly and passionately the pleasures he found in his musical studies at the University, the encouragement, the youthful enthusiasm, and the sobering advice of his teachers. His major field of study was composition, which he pursued with the eminent composer Ignaz Xaver Ritter von Seyfried.

The most important result of his studies, and the one that was to bring him considerable renown, was the successful performance of his first major work, the opera *Hamlet*, conducted by the youthful composer on November 5, 1840 in his native city of Brno. The opera met with considerable success in other cities. That same year he was engaged as conductor of the opera house in Agram, Croatia. In 1842, after guest conducting for a few months in Bamberg, Bavaria, he occupied the post of opera conductor at Nancy, France, and frequently accompanied the popular singer Mme. Ernst in her recitals, in which she included his own compositions. Maretzek's growing reputation as conductor and composer led, before the end of the year, to an invitation to Paris. There he had the opportunity of personal contact with the musical *élite*, Meyerbeer, Berlioz, Chopin and Liszt. Besides writing ballet music for Carlotta Grisi and Lucille Grahn, he had completed a second opera, *Die Niebelungen*, began work on a comic opera to a text by Vicomte Pinmaigre, and dedicated a collection of songs to the Duchess of Nemours. He conducted opera and ballet in Paris, and at a Concert Vivienne he presented his own works, including the premiere of the overture *Agnes Sorel*.

Maretzek's stay in Paris brought him in contact with the intellectual ferment led by the young Hegelians, who found refuge in the French capital in 1844. These young "revolutionaries," utilizing Hegel's dialectics, critically evaluated and challenged accepted beliefs and traditional concepts. They directed their philosophical polemics with particular force against the Prussian state and Christian dogma. Among the most active "Hegelians of the Left" were Karl Marx, Arnold Ruge, Ludwig Feuerbach, Michael Bakunin, and Friedrich Engels. Heinrich Heine was also deeply involved with them; he shared their ideological position and contributed to their journals. Although there is no evidence that Maretzek was a member of the group, he knew them well enough to speak of "the pleasant evenings he passed with them." In all probability, he listened to their philosophical and political discussions as a contributor to their journal, the *Vorwaerts*, which was founded by Heinrich Boernstein and edited by Adalbert von Bornstedt. Boernstein was really more interested in theatrical and musical matters, and engaged Maretzek to contribute musical *feuilletons* and current reviews. Part of the support for the publication, it was claimed, came from Meyerbeer. It may well be that Maretzek's concepts of music's role in society, and, particularly, the underlying goal that animated his life as manager in America—to bring the best operas, with the greatest singers to the people at the lowest possible price—were, to some degree, influenced by his brief association with the young intellectual social reformers in Paris.

In December, 1844, Maretzek accepted an offer from George Lumley, manager of Her Majesty's Theatre, Covent Garden, for the post of choral director and assistant conductor. The repertory consisted principally of Italian opera. The training and experience he received at Her Majesty's were invaluable: learning a variety of operatic scores and different styles; techniques of singing, articulation, and linguistic knowledge; matters of interpretation, the special skill in accompanying recitative, building up the stretto in finales; and, above all, dealing with singers, choruses and orchestras.

In 1847, Maretzek was engaged as chorus master by Adolphe Jullien, who had grandiose schemes of presenting English opera at Drury Lane. For conductor of this ambitious venture, Jullien secured the services of Hector Berlioz, who was promised an attractive fee and tempting opportunities to conduct and perform his own compositions. Needless to say, Jullien's wild and unrealistic plans collapsed shortly after the opening night, December 6, 1847, when *Lucia di Lammermoor* (sung in English) was presented. As an afterpiece, Maretzek's ballet, *Les Génies du Globe*, was performed. All might have gone well, but the premiere of Balfe's

The Maid of Honor on December 20, gave the enterprise the *coup de grâce*. Berlioz, who characterized Jullien as "a man accustomed to appeal always to the childish instincts of the crowd and to succeed by the most stupid method," left an unforgettable account of this man's wild flights of imagination. This is indeed one of the funniest incidents in operatic history and managerial madness. The occasion was a meeting of the executive committee to discuss plans to bolster the collapsing opera company, and, perhaps, save it from ruin.

Here is a perfect sample [writes Berlioz] of the insane notions that occur to a man who is used to catering always for the puerile instincts of the mob, and succeeding by the most fatuous means. Being at the end of his resources, seeing that Balfe's opera was bringing in no money, and recognizing to a certain extent the impossibility of putting *Robert le Diable* [Meyerbeer] on the stage in six days (even by resting on the seventh), Jullien assembled his committee for deliberation. The committee was composed of Sir Henry Bishop, Sir George Smart, Mr. Planché (author of the libretto of Weber's *Oberon*), Mr. Gye (the manager of Drury Lane), M. Marezzeck [!] (the singing-master), and myself. Jullien stated his perplexities, and spoke of different operas (not translated or copied, of course) which he wished to put on the stage. It was amusing to hear the ideas and opinions of these gentlemen, as the various masterpieces were trotted out.

I listened in amazement. When at last they came to the *Iphigénie en Tauride* [Gluck], which had been announced in Jullien's prospectus (it is the custom of the London managers to announce that work every year, and never give it), the members of the committee, not knowing a note of it, were at a loss what to say. Jullien, impatient at my silence, turned sharply round and said: "Why the devil don't you speak? You must know it?"

"Of course I know it; but what do you want me to say? Tell me, and I will answer you."

"I want to know how many acts there are, the chief characters and their voices, and, above all, the style of the scenery and dresses."

"Well, take a sheet of paper and pen, and write to my dictation: *Iphigénie en Tauride*, an opera by Gluck, as you probably know, is in four acts. There are three male parts: Orestes (baritone), Pylades (tenor), Thoas (a bass going very high), Iphigenia (soprano); another small part, Diana (mezzo-soprano), and several leading chorus parts. The dresses, I fear, you will not think becoming. The Scythians and King Thoas are ragged savages on the shores of the Black Sea. Orestes and Pylades appear in the simple costume of two shipwrecked Greeks. Pylades alone has two costumes; he re-enters in the fourth act with a helmet on his head."

"A helmet?" cried Jullien, in a transport of delight. "We are saved! I shall order a gilt helmet from Paris, with a coronet of pearls and a tuft of ostrich feathers as long as my arm, and we shall have forty performances."

I forget how the meeting ended, but if I were to live a hundred years I should never forget the flashing eyes, the wild gestures, and distracted enthusiasm of Jullien on learning that Pylades has a helmet, or his sublime idea of getting it from Paris, since no English workman could possibly turn out one sufficiently dazzling; or his hope of having forty splendid performances of Gluck's masterpiece, thanks to the pearls, gilding, and feathers in Pylades' helmet. "Pro-di-gious!" as good Dominie Sampson would say, "Pro-di-gious!" I need not add that *Iphigénie* was not even studied. Jullien left London some days after this learned committee meeting, leaving his theatrical undertaking to crash to the ground.*

When Jullien's lofty plans collapsed, the musicians left stranded and unpaid, Maretzek kept himself intermittently busy preparing the choral numbers for the concerts Berlioz was presenting to the English public.

*H. Berlioz, *Memoirs*, (New York: Alfred A. Knopf, 1932), pp. 455–456; Dover Publications Inc., reprint, 1966.

The following announcement of the first concert indicates the character of the program and Maretzek's involvement:

THEATRE ROYAL, DRURY LANE—Under the especial Patronage of His Royal Highness Prince Albert—M. BERLIOZ'S GRAND CONCERT—M. Hector Berlioz begs most respectfully to inform the nobility and gentry, and the public, that his FIRST GRAND VOCAL AND INSTRUMENTAL CONCERT in this country will take place at the above Theatre this evening (Monday) February 7, on which occasion he will have the honour of presenting to an English audience several of those compositions which, during the last few years, have received the most distinguished approbation of His Majesty Louis Philippe, His Majesty the Emperor of Russia, His Majesty the King of Prussia, His Majesty the Emperor of Austria &c.

Principal Vocal Performers:—Mr. Sims Reeves, Mr. Weiss, Mr. Gregg, Miss Miran, and Madame Dorus-Gras.

The Orchestra and Chorus will consist of 250 performers.

The Orchestra will be conducted by M. BERLIOZ, the Chorus directed by M. Maretzek.

The whole of the Music is the Composition of M. Berlioz.

These occasional concerts were hardly sufficient outlets for the energetic and ambitious twenty-seven-year-old Maretzek. When Edward P. Fry offered him the post of conductor of his Italian Opera Company at the Astor Place Opera House in New York City, Maretzek readily accepted. No doubt, he was also fascinated by the uncertainty, the challenge, and, too, the adventurous aspects of his involvement in "the untold possibilities" of the musical life in the New World. He arrived in New York in September, 1848. The narrative of the two books of "Revelations of an Opera Manager in America" chronicles the events from the day of his arrival to the 1860's. The unwritten "revelations" continue the multifaceted story of his managerial and conducting career; with the inevitable occasional successes and more frequent failures, the pleasures and disappointments, the chimerical financial gains and recurring bankruptcy, and the endless movement from one theatre to another. Until his retirement from active managerial duties in 1878, Maretzek was obliged to move, with an ever-changing roster of singers, costumes, scenery, orchestra and chorus, from the following theatres (and this is merely a selective list): the Astor Place Opera House, Castle Garden, Niblo's Garden, the Academy of Music, Grand Opera House, Winter Garden Theatre, and not to mention numerous theatres in other cities, Mexico and Cuba. No wonder he gladly accepted the sobriquet, the "Don Quixote of Opera" in America.

With population increase in the '70s, the competitive struggle became more intense; "kidnapping" of leading singers, especially those that commanded a large following, was the order of the day. Ruinous price-of-admission "wars," with a top price of $1.00, and leading stars receiving as much as $4000 for a performance became prevalent. And then there was the legendary "battle of the Maxes"—Max Strakosch, at the Academy of Music, boasting of the luminous stars, Nilsson, Campanini, Capoul, Maurel and Cary; and Max Maretzek, at the Grand Opera House, proudly announcing a cast headed by Pauline Lucca and the brilliant Spanish tenor Tamberlick and often the two impresarios presenting simultaneously the same opera at both houses. But most of the "battle" was feigned for publicity purposes. One day they fought bitterly, and the next day Max Maretzek might be conducting the other Max's "luminous stars" at the Academy, or, as one observer noted, they might be "walking arm in arm along Fourteenth Street, discussing some prodigious scheme to bring them nearer to bankruptcy than they both already were."

Maretzek brought to the Academy of Music in the '60s and '70s, not only the standard Italian repertory, but also seasons of German and French operas as well, and often in the original languages. Besides bringing the accepted popular opera to the public, such as, *Norma* (Bellini), *Lucia di Lammermoor* (Donizetti), *Il Barbiere di Siviglia* (Rossini), and *Il Trovatore* (Verdi), Maretzek introduced a number of operas for the first time to the American audiences. Among them were: *Anna Bolena, Betly, Don Sebastiano, Il Poliuto, Maria di Rohan*, and *Marino Falieri*—by Donizetti; *Romeo and Juliet*—by Gounod; *Saffo* and *Medea*—by Paccini; *Judith*—by G. Peri; *Carnival of Venice, Duchess of Amalfi*, and *Ione*—by E. Petrella; *Aroldo, Attila, La Forza del Destino, I Lombardi, Luisa Miller, Rigoletto* and *La Traviata*—by Verdi; *Robert le Diable*, and the first complete musical presentation of *Le Prophête*—by Meyerbeer. "The greatest impression on the public [of the last work]," Maretzek informs the reader, "was not the splendid cast, new *mise en scène*, costumes, ballet, but rather a roller skating ballet and electric lights which were introduced for the first time in America . . . only one dollar admission. Artistic success but a financial failure." However, roller skating became the rage in America! Some of the operatic titles listed above mean very little, if anything at all, to a contemporary audience, and have rightly passed into oblivion; yet, some of these works were the novelties of the day and it took some courage to produce them.

In addition to the time- and energy-consuming activities of manager, conductor, publicity and press agent—indeed, he was a veritable "factotum dell'opera"—Maretzek found time to compose. Besides those works mentioned, there is a long list of piano pieces, songs, ballets, and choral works, which were occasionally performed at the numerous operatic and concert programs. None of these achieved any notable success or lasting place in the repertory.

Of his more ambitious compositions, *Baba*, "a spectacular play with music," was presented at Niblo's Garden in September, 1876, with the composer conducting. This spectacle did not invite many repetitions. The work that received favorable comment and some revivals was *Sleepy Hollow; or, The Headless Horseman*, a comic pastoral opera in three acts, with the libretto by Charles Gayler, and founded upon Washington Irving's *Legend of Sleepy Hollow*. It had its premiere in 1879 at the Academy of Music with Maretzek conducting.

His music displays good technical competence, but no noticeable individual or marked personality. It is highly derivative and eclectic, "inspired" largely by the French and Italian grand opera style, but yielding more often, in his arias, ensembles, and orchestration, to the popular cliché and standard devices. His piano pieces and songs are of the Romantic salon type. Since the vocal solos were usually composed for particular singers, they contain all the obvious *molto sostenuto* and *bravura* passages that display the vocal prowess of the performer.

In spite of changing conditions in the operatic climate in New York, and obliged to reduce his pace, Maretzek was still wielding the baton at the Lexington Opera House (at Fifty-first Street—the theatrical area had been gradually moving uptown) in May, 1883, conducting four operas: *Faust, Der Freischütz, Martha* (Flotow), and *La Traviata*. This took place a few months before the fall season witnessed the opening of the new edifice on Broadway, between Thirty-ninth and Fortieth Streets, the Metropolitan Opera House. Maretzek was at the gala opening fully aware that an era had passed and a new one had begun, and modestly conscious of his contributions in helping to lay the artistic foundations for this operatic fulfilment.

A touching portrait of the man, at seeing the world he helped to shape pass him by, is given by H. E. Krehbiel, music critic of the *New York Tribune*. He met Maretzek one evening in the lobby of the Metropolitan Opera House during the early part of the first season. Upon discovering that he had no ticket, Krehbiel offered him his.

But he did not care to accept my offer [Krehbiel relates] and I fancied I saw a rather more serious and contemplative look come over his grizzled face. Naturally, I asked him what he thought of the new house and the new enterprise, adding that I regretted that he was not the manager. He began with apparent solemnity:

"Well, when I heard the house was to be built, I did think that some of the stockholders would remember what I had done for opera. Some of the old-timers, who used to go to the Academy of Music and the Astor Place Opera House when I was manager there, I thought, would recollect what companies I gave them— Parodi, Steffanone, and Marini, and Lorini, and Bettini, and Bertucca [how often I had heard him chant the list, counting off the singers on his chubby fingers!] and Truffi, and Benedetti and Salvi. I thought somebody might remember this and the old man, and come to me and say, 'Max, you did a good deal for us once, let us do something for you now.' I didn't expect them to come and offer me the house, but I thought they might say this and add, 'Come, we'll make you head usher,' or 'you may have the bar.' But nobody came, and I'm out of it completely."

Maretzek's sadness and disappointment is lightened by a puckish sense of humor and a graceful acceptance of the inevitable.

However, he was not "out of it completely." The enthusiasm and acclamation of the distinguished musical and theatrical personalities, and leaders in the cultural and political life of New York, who gathered on the evening of February 12, 1889 at the Metropolitan Opera House to celebrate Maretzek's Golden Jubilee, gave glowing testimonial of the warm appreciation and profound indebtedness to his life-long dedication to music, and to the operatic riches he had brought to the people of America. An appropriate program, reflecting the various facets of his musical interests, was presented that evening in his honor, in which the leading artists shared the stage with him.

It began with a performance of *A Woman's Won't*, by the Daly Company, followed by the overture to *Tannhäuser;* an aria from *La Gioconda* (Ponchielli) was sung by Emily Winant, and a violin solo by Zarzucki was played by Maude Powell. Frank Van der Stucken conducted several numbers of Massenet's ballet music to *Le Cid;* the forge scene from Wagner's *Siegfried* was sung by Max Alvary and Wilhelm Sedlmayer, and conducted by Anton Seidl. Theodore Thomas conducted a selection from Saint-Saens' *Samson and Delilah,* sung by Mme. Fursch-Madi, and Rafael Joseffy played Liszt's *Hungarian Fantasy.*

The second part of the program opened with a play, *Kerry,* an adaptation in one act by Dion Boucicault of Mme. de Girardin's *La Joie fait peur,* in which Coquelin had appeared in New York not long before. The action of the play was transferred from French to Irish surroundings. The veteran actor and author of the play took the title role. Walter Damrosch conducted the tower scene and the "Miserere" from *Il Trovatore,* sung by Mme. Herbert-Foerster and Julius Perotti. Signor Del Puente sang the Toreador aria from *Carmen.* For the finale, Maretzek came to the podium, amidst thunderous applause, and conducted the orchestra in a scene from *Don Giovanni,* with Mme. Fursch-Madi as soloist. He was given a standing ovation, and many wreaths and bouquets were brought to the stage (as reported in the *Musical Courier*).

Maretzek devoted the last years of his life to teaching voice and coaching young aspirants in operatic repertory and acting. There were then very few such competent maestros in New York, or in the United States, who could impart so much vocal and dramatic knowledge, and offer such thorough training in interpretation and *mise en scène* as Maretzek. His more gifted pupils filled the leading roles in American and European opera houses. Having been troubled for some time with a heart ailment, Maretzek passed away on May 14,

1897, aged seventy-six, at his home at Pleasant Plains, Staten Island, New York.

If our music and cultural historians have generally overlooked Maretzek's significant contributions to the development of the lyric theater in America, one of the country's greatest poets, Walt Whitman, has, indirectly, bestowed immortality upon him. Whitman's poems and prose make countless references to the Italian operas and singers he heard under Maretzek's management; he acknowledges the profound influence the Italian voice and music have had on his poems. Indeed, he proudly announced that he shaped his sweeping free verse and exultant poetic line on the dramatic declamation of the Italian operatic recitative. "Oh! those great days! great days!", the poet recollected in his later years, "Alboni, Badiali, in particular, no one can tell, know, even suspect, how much they had to do with the making of *Leaves of Grass.*" Whitman gratefully mentions Maretzek on numerous occasions, the many pleasures he gave him, the great operas and "divine" vocalists he presented; they filled his mind with sounds that inspired his poetic muse. "Have not you, in like manner," Whitman stated, "while listening to the well-played music of some band, like Maretzek's, felt an overwhelming desire for measureless sound." On another occasion: "Then some years later at Castle Garden, Battery, I yet recall the splendid seasons of the Havana musical troupe under Maretzek, the fine band, the cool sea breezes, the unsurpass'd vocalism— Steffanone, Bosio, Truffi, Marini, in *Marini Faliero, Don Pasquale,* or *Favorita.* Realizing the great difficulties managers faced in producing opera, Walt Whitman wished Maretzek "good luck": "Nor can we forego a word of good will for Maretzek, the leader, but hope all sorts of good luck to him including that fortune which opera managers do *not* often, if ever, make."

The great singers he heard, and those that left "the deepest and most lasting effects" upon him were Alboni ("lustrous orb, Venus contralto"), Steffanone ("with her calm and finished style and her delicious voice"), Bettini ("beautiful, large, robust, friendly"), and Brignoli ("that tremulous, manly timbre! The perfect singing voice").

This is only a minute sampling of the numerous references to Italian music, Maretzek, the great singers he heard, the operas he visited, and their effect upon him. All this, and so much more, can be read in *Leaves of Grass* and his *Prose Works*. Of all poems, "Proud Music of the Storm" is, perhaps, his most lyrical and exuberant expression of homage and indebtedness to music of all peoples, and especially Italian opera. Whitman gives a poetic distillation of the essential dramatic action of some of the operas in a section of the poem. In justice to the "Good Gray Poet," the entire poem must be read; here we only quote the relevant lines:

3

All songs of current lands come sounding round me,
The German airs of friendship, wine and love,
Irish ballads, merry jigs and dances, English warbles,
Chansons of France, Scotch tunes, and o'er the rest,
Italia's peerless compositions.
Across the stage with pallor on her face, yet lurid passion,
Stalks Norma brandishing the dagger in her hand.
I see poor crazed Lucia's eyes' unnatural gleam,

Her hair down her back falls loose and dishevel'd.
I see where Ernani walking the bridal garden,
Amid the scent of night-roses, radiant, holding his bride by the
    hand,
Hears the infernal call, the death pledge of the horn.
To crossing swords and gray hairs bared to heaven.
The clear electric base and baritone of the world,
The trombone duo, Libertad forever!
From Spanish chestnut trees' dense shade,
By old and heavy convent walls a wailing song,
Song of lost love, the torch of youth and life quench'd in despair,
Song of the dying swan, Fernando's heart is breaking.
Awaking from her woes at last retriev'd Amina sings,
Copious as stars and glad as morning light the torrents of her joy.
(The teeming lady comes,
The lustrous orb, Venus contralto, the blooming mother,
Sister of loftiest gods, Alboni's self I hear.)

4

I hear those odes, symphonies, operas,
I hear in the *William Tell* the music of an arous'd and angry
    people,
I hear Meyerbeer's *Huguenots*, the *Prophet*, or *Robert*,
Gounod's *Faust*, or Mozart's *Don Juan*.

5

Composers! mighty maestros!
And you, sweet singers of old lands, soprani, tenori, bassi!
To you a new bard caroling in the West,
Obeisant sends his love.

CHARLES HAYWOOD

New York
October, 1967

CONTENTS

Crotchets and Quavers

Sharps and Flats

LIST OF ILLUSTRATIONS

Crotchets and Quavers

Sharps and Flats

Crotchets and Quavers

TO THE PUBLIC.

Since some five months, when the first announcement that I was about to write the present volume appeared in one of the morning Journals of New York, it has been impossible for me to pass up or down Broadway without subjecting myself to a cross-examination respecting it. Did I enter one of the ferry-boats, I was morally certain to meet some acquaintance who questioned me touching my book. If I visited a place of amusement, or sped to a summer-retreat for the purpose of wiling away a few days in forgetfulness of the *baton* I had previously been wielding, I was unable to do so without having the inquiry put to me—

"When my 'Autobiography' was to be published?"

If Napoleon, (the first of the two with whom history has any business) as well as P. T. Barnum, have written their autobiographies; when Jean Jacques Rousseau and Mr. Henry Wikoff have published their "Confessions," while George Sand and Mrs. Mowatt have given, or are giving, the details of their lives to the world, it may not be altogether astonishing, that a belief in a certain amount of self-glorification on my part, should have found an entry into the imagination of my friends and acquaintances.

Let me disabuse them. I am neither a hero, nor have I any pretence to the "principality of humbug." Neither a great philosopher, nor a very small diplomatist, I am equally unable to drape my shoulders with the mantle of an authoress, or to draw the petticoats of an actress around my lower person. Nor have I the self-conceit to eulogize myself for those good qualities which I believe in my possession of, nor the self-knowledge to testify to those weaknesses which doubtless I possess. Some of these last this volume will doubtless, unconsciously upon my part, disclose to you. Should it do so, I feel assured that you will deal gently with me.

Certain is it, that during the first three years of my residence in New York, I carried out four regular seasons of Italian Opera. This alone was more than any one had done in this quarter of the world, since Christopher Columbus first discovered it. My friends and followers, as well as the Press, then dubbed me the "Napoleon" of the Opera. But when in my fifth season, exhausted by previous losses, and the exertions consequent on crushing an opposition at half-prices of admission, I succumbed beneath the attempt to carry it to a close, I received one morning the following lines :

" ' The Napoleon of the Opera' has at last made it evident, that he is simply its ' Don Quixote.' "

The anonymous writer had evidently imagined that

my feelings would be hurt by the receipt of this brief communication.

Let me seize on this opportunity of assuring him that he was completely mistaken. It is with something like pride and satisfaction, that I acknowledge his having struck the nail completely upon the head. In fact, I conscientiously accept the denomination of the "Don Quixote" of the Opera, in preference to the name of its Napoleon, which has been bestowed upon many before, and will most assuredly be applied to so many after me.

Don Quixote, my good friend, if you will allow me so to call you, was in every respect a straightforward, most gallant, persevering and energetic knight, who was willing to shed the last drop of his blood in the cause of honor, truth, and his lady-love, the peerless Dulcinea del Toboso.

Indeed, the noble Don committed only one small mistake. Nor do I pretend to say, but that this error may be very fairly attributed to his maternal relative. He was born too late.

When he made his entry into the world, the fighting for truth, honor, and our lady-loves, had gone completely out of fashion. It was simply ridiculous.

Had his mother not made this grievous error, or, rather, had some "strong-minded" female taken the trouble of his birth upon herself, some two or three hundred years earlier, he would possibly have rivalled the Cid, or have become a second King Arthur.

As far as concerns my operatic and musical Don Quixotism, it can, however, scarcely be said that I

arrived in the United States by any means too late.
On the contrary, little in the shape of Italian Opera
had previously been attempted here. My naturaliza-
tion in this part of the world has, in all probability,
been a trifle too early. At all events, until the advent of my Cervantes, I accept right willingly the
title of the "Don Quixote of Opera" in America.
My Dulcinea del Toboso has been the Art of Music.
As for my Rosinante, who can doubt but that this
was indisputably the patronage of "Upper Tendom"
—a meagre and lazy mare who would not go ahead,
in spite of corn and spurs. My agents were veritable
Sancho Panzas. They looked after their own interests, and while I was absorbed in the dream of my
Dulcinea, kept their eyes wide open and most un-
poetically fixed upon the possible loaves and fishes.
Many first *tenors* were there, whom I had fancied
giants, that turned out to be nothing but wind-mills,
while the *prime donne*, who had been rated by me
as faithful maids of honor to my Dulcinea, proved
too often to be but little better than dairy-maids; and
the enemies whom I had to encounter, not unfrequently exhibited themselves, ere the conclusion of
the combat, as mere Italian barbers or hotel-waiters
in disguise.

Having thus frankly acknowledged myself to be
the identical and original musical Quixote of this
continent, to you, my dear Public, it may very clearly
be seen that I could have had no intention of writing
my autobiography.

The fact is, that only great men write and publish their own memoirs.

According to the verdict of the world, which is in some shape your own, Don Quixote is, in spite of all his good qualities, considered as nothing more than a great fool.

Now, although "The Autobiography of a Great Fool" strikes me as being anything but a bad title for a work, as well as a decidedly original one, my amiable Public, I must confess to you that I do not feel altogether vain enough of my qualifications to undertake it.

You ask me, then—"What is your book, if it be not an Autobiography? Is it an onslaught on the Direction of the Academy of Music? Is it a return to that body for having twice promised you the lease of that House, and on second thoughts, and a re-consideration of the matter, not having kept their promise?"

Most certainly not, my good friends. Such a fancy of retaliation has never crossed me.

Not only have I never dreamed of endeavoring to avenge that breach of promise, but—will you allow me to whisper a word or two in your ears?—I feel an almost unbounded gratitude to the Directors of the Academy for having suffered it to slip entirely from their memories.

Some have insinuated, and this too has been even publicly done, that I had taken the pen in my hand, for the purpose of exposing the operatic *coup d'états* of a certain diplomatic Chevalier, who occupied the post of acting Manager in the Academy during the last season, and with whom I was unfortunate enough not always to agree.

This is, it were almost needless to say, an immense mistake.

The Chevalier has quitted the battle-ground. Consequently there is no further reason for musical polemics. A great Diplomatist has absented himself from the country, but this is to you and myself a matter of small moment. So long as the Princess-Bay Oysters are plenty and in good condition, I think we may rationally and effectually console ourselves for the loss of one Native.

But some reason there must be for writing this book. Custom demands of me a certain explanation touching its appearance.

The fact is, my dear Public, there is an old and well-worn Proverb, which you may possibly recollect. Should you not do so, however, I will repeat it. It is this—

" Money is the root of all evil."

It has so chanced, that there have been several publishers who have applied to me for this identical volume. Moreover, they were willing to pay for its German Anglicism roundly. Who, under similar circumstances, would not have written it? Very few, believe me; and, one of these is most certainly not

Yours, most obediently,

MAX MARETZEK.

FIRST LETTER.

TO HECTOR BERLIOZ, PARIS.

CONTENTS:

mon cher Maretzek

à la répétition générale à Haywood Square Room mardi 27 à 10 h:

Voici la partition de Faust où se trouve le morceau des Sylphes que nous exécutons à mon concert; veuillez le faire répéter dès que vous le pourrez car on doit l'avoir oublié.

Vous avez aussi chez vous la partie de Méphistophélès avec les paroles anglaises; Veuillez la donner à M. Bouché. Il chantera le solo qui précède le chœur des Sylphes.

Mille amitiés et remercîments.

H. Berlioz

AUTOGRAPH LETTER OF H. BERLIOZ

LETTER I.

TO HECTOR BERLIOZ, PARIS.

NEW YORK, *July* 25, 1855.

MY DEAR BERLIOZ :—

WHEN you take up this letter, open it, and turn to the signature, you will in all probability imagine that you are dreaming. You may remember, possibly, that when you quitted London after English opera had terminated for the nine hundred and ninety-ninth time its temporary existence, I promised to write to you. Jullien's management had given that highly respectable musical entity its nine hundred and ninety-ninth burial. As times go, all things considered, it was very respectably managed. You and myself had all the trouble of preparing the corpse for the coffin. Balfe, as the doctor, had penned the last prescription ; Sims Reeves, as a native apothecary, carried off all the glory attendant upon putting it out of the land of the living; while that purely mythical personage, " nobody," would seem to have pocketed the whole of the money its charms had wheedled from its scant admirers. Very certain is it, that none remained.

Over seven years have since elapsed, but, one of your own French Proverbs says, " *Vaut mieux tard que jamais.*" Accordingly, I sit down for the purpose of redeeming my promise.

If you have not yet learned it, which it may be reasonably presumed in these days of almost universal Journaldom (a great traveller informs me, that in Timbuctoo they have already two newspapers) you have, let me inform you that immediately, or almost immediately after you left London, I accepted an engagement in the United States. Shortly afterwards, I myself, Max Maretzek, became a manager. Do not laugh and shake your head incredulously as you hear this, for let me tell you, it is to the full as easy to become a manager in America, as it is in your country to obtain the *Croix d'honneur*. We are all of us in the hands of chance, and either of these is a perverse accident which may befall any human being. But, in order to let you know how this happened, it will be necessary for me to tell you a long story. Be patient therefore, and listen amiably as you were accustomed to do, without chiding.

When I arrived in New York, in the month of September, 1848, I was immediately struck with the beauty of the Bay and its environs. That which principally delighted me, was however its bright, clear and blue sky. Such a sky I had not seen since I last left Naples.

The impression it made upon me was so much the stronger, as in my leaving London towards the end of August, the English fog which seems to concentrate itself upon that city, had already acquired a consistence thick enough to be sliced with a fish-knife. Indeed, to a temperate Neapolitan accustomed to live upon maccaroni, I have always believed that a first-rate London fog would prove no unavailable substitute. See, how Nature maltreats Man. The Neapolitan is born where the rarefied atmosphere only develops instead of appeasing his digestive organs; while the Londoner has a natural appetite for beefsteak and porter, which nothing else can possibly assuage. Do not however imagine, although it were only for a moment, that I intend entering into a philosophical disquisition on the moral, mental or physical variations in Creation; but allow me to say that my determination was at once formed to remain in America, supposing it were possible and (this is for your private ear) profitable.

The Musical Institutions which were at this period to be found in New York, consisted of a Philharmonic Society and an Italian Opera; and the majority of the members of the first of these, were considerably more addicted to the enjoyment of the creature comforts, than they were to the cultivation of Harmony. Their object was rather to make a few dollars by the Annual Subscription for four concerts than to elevate the popular taste. As for the propagation of a liking for Classical Music, this was never even thought of.

Indeed, their *répertoire* consisted always of the same few Symphonies, works of the old composers in our Divine Science, which everybody has heard, although but few have comprehended, since childhood.

The compositions of modern *maestri* had never even been put in rehearsal. Consequently they could not be produced. But I beg pardon, one Overture of yours, there was, " *Les francs juges*," if I remember rightly, which had been proposed for performance. It was accordingly placed in rehearsal, but after a few repetitions withdrawn and condemned. This enlightened Society declared that it was "nonsense." Console yourself, my dear Berlioz, try another—study downward and write in the same manner. With time and perseverance, you may succeed in lowering your musical genius to the level of the musical comprehension of the Philharmonic Society of New York. Perhaps, I ought to tell you that the President of this body is a Mr. Timm, who can scarcely be considered actively responsible for all of their harmonic sins. He is a good and thorough musician, but altogether far too modest as well as too great a lover of peace (you will say that this is singularly unlike a musician), for the position which he holds. He has the talent and capacity, but completely lacks the energy to make of the Philharmonic Society that which a Philharmonic Society ought to be, or at the least to attempt being.

The other musical institution which then existed in New York, was, as I have previously mentioned, the Italian Opera. My connection with music in the New World commenced with this,—an establishment whose "failure" had flourished for the last five and twenty years.

An involuntary smile curls your lip. You inquire how a "failure" can "flourish?"

My dear Berlioz, you were born and have been educated in the Old World. This accounts to me for your smile. You have yet much to learn ere you will be able to comprehend the New one. "Bursting up" is here an old-established rule of the Italian Opera—a rule which admits of no exceptions. Remember, I speak from a long and personal experience. Yet, although continually "bursting up," Italian opera flourished in the United States, and what is more, still continues to flourish.

But the object of my present letter is not to record a history of all these failures. It is, on the contrary, purely personal. Let me, therefore, tell you that are anxious to learn something of the establishment with which I was to be connected, my first evening in New York was passed at the Astor Place Opera House, where, *per interim*, an irregular company was then performing Rossini's "Barbiere."

Most agreeably was I surprised on entering this small but comfortably arranged *bon-boniére*. It contained somewhere

about 1,100 excellent seats in parquet (the Parisian parterre), dress circle and first tier, with some 700 in the
gallery.

Its principal feature was that everybody could see, and
what is of infinitely greater consequence, could be seen.
Never, perhaps, was any theatre built that afforded a better
opportunity for the display of dress. Believe me, that were
the *Funambules* built as ably for this grand desideratum,
despite the locality and the grade of performances at this theatre, my conviction is that it would be the principal and most
fashionable one in Paris.

Now, the Astor Place Opera House had been built barely
a year before my arrival in New York, as the programme
or prospectus issued to the subscribers announced, "for the
permanent establishment of Italian opera" in this city.
Nothing of it now remains save the external walls, internally
containing lecture and reading-rooms, library and stores;
with the above *permanently established* phrase, which printers
keep stereotyped for the programme or prospectus of all
managers and proprietors, whether they be present or future.

But from my admiration of the house, I was aroused by
the first notes of the overture to the " Barbiere."

The orchestra consisted of about thirty-six performers on
their individual instruments. They had a leader, Signor
Lietti, who did not apparently consider it necessary to indicate the movement by beating the time. On the contrary,
he was occupied in playing the first violin part, fully unconscious of the other instruments in the orchestra. But I
wrong him. In order to guide them, he was possessed with
the monomania of playing more loudly and vigorously upon
his fiddle than any of his subordinates. He trampled on the
floor as though he had been determined to work a path
through the deal planking, and made a series of the most

grotesque faces with his nose, mouth and eyes. If you have ever seen a Nuremberg nut-cracker in full operation, you will enter into my feelings as my eyes were riveted on what appeared to me the extraordinary mechanism of this individual. In the mean time, the other fiddlers not being willing to allow Signor Lietti's violin a greater preponderance of sound, exerted themselves with a purely musical ferocity, which you have never seen equalled. I have, (although it must be owned, not often) upon this side of the Atlantic. It was necessary, however, that Lietti should be heard by the wind-instruments. He therefore began to *scrape* his fiddle. For a moment I actually imagined that he had succeeded. But until then, I had not been aware that " diabolical possession" had survived the time of the Apostles. It has, my dear Berlioz, and the players upon stringed instruments are indisputably subject to it. Rossini, had he listened to them, would have been of my opinion. After the first eighty bars of the allegro movement, you would, had you been there, upon shutting your eyes, have undoubtedly believed that you were surrounded by a series of saw-mills in vigorous operation. Under such circumstances, the leader could not of course be heard. They soon came out of time (how could they keep it?) and confusion ensued. Everybody felt himself individually called upon to restore order. A squeak from the *piccolo* would be heard, followed by a loud squall from all the wind-instruments, trying to indicate a place for re-union. Then came a broadside from the trombones and horns, to restrain the already too far advanced violins. It was in vain. The screech from the first trumpet was of no use. Even the kettle-drum player, who began to beat the right time *fortissimo* on his instrument, was totally unable to stay the confusion. Each one went his own way, and made his own speed. Rossini's delicate overture was treated by them, as history tells us that some unfortunate criminals were treated in the Middle Ages. These were tied by arm and leg to the hind-quarters of four wild horses, which were then driven by the scourge in different directions. It will be needless to hint to a man of your erudition, what followed upon this proceeding.

At last, straggling and worn out, one after the other, some few completely distanced, and Signor Lietti by no means first in, they terminated the overture. The audience bestowed upon them a round of applause, and the leader demonstrated by three low bows, his intense satisfaction both with himself and the public.

After having heard *Almaviva*, *Rosina* and *Basilio*, it became unmistakably evident to me, that none of them would ever produce a revolution in the musical world. They will therefore, in all probability, hate me henceforward for neglecting to tell you their names. Such, do I grieve to say, is too frequently musical gratitude. It was but shortly afterwards that I retired, instinctively feeling, rather than knowing, that there were several good musicians in the orchestra, who only wanted purgation and a thoroughly earnest and intelligent conductor to be rendered really available and valuable as its members.

It was my intention on the following morning to look after the choral department, and, on inquiry, I discovered that the rehearsals of this portion of the troop took place in a store-house situated on the East River, in which the carpenters, tailors and painters all worked. This having been arranged by the manager, in order to keep them all under the vigilant superintendence of his *homme de confiance*, who rejoiced in the grandiloquent title of " General-Intendant of E. P. Fry's Opera." Let me assure you that his Intendance was a very general one. He being at one and the same time, secretary, stage-manager, head-carpenter, husband to the first tailoress, and, I was about to say, head cook and bottle-washer to the establishment. This, however, would be going too far, and I apologize for the involuntary injury to his reputation my pen had almost done him.

What was my amazement, when on visiting this store, I found that it contained no more than one large room!

The carpenters were busily hammering in it, the tailors accompanied their labors with nigger-songs, while at the same time, such of the chorus as were inclined for work, were studying and rehearsing their parts. As for the chorus master, he seemed to be an early riser—a very early riser to one who had been accustomed to London and Parisian life, for although it was then barely ten o'clock, he had very evidently been already "laboring in the vineyard." Some of the male members of the chorus, on my arrival, were occupied in a game of cards with the "General Intendant" of Mr. Fry's Opera. It may consequently be presumed by you, my dear Berlioz, that he was evidently a man of decided genius, and had already got through his multifarious and most curiously coupled duties for the day. In the mean time, a few of the ladies employed in the chorus, were dividing their attention with an impartiality of the most praiseworthy character between an operation commonly called mending their stockings and the study of their parts; while others of a somewhat more staid and elderly appearance, were engaged in an earnest conversation with two of the tailor-boys, of which I heard enough, to form an idea that it touched upon the stipulations for a private treaty of commerce, in which the purloined silks and calicoes of Mr. Fry were most certainly destined to play a very prominent part.

On inquiring more narrowly into the condition and consti-

tution of the chorus, I discovered that the " General Intendant," alone, did not rejoice in a curious combination of avocations.

Some few of the choral-singers, such, for example, as a
certain Signor Pauselli, were also engaged in the tailor-
ing department, while a tailoress rejoicing in the euphonious
name of Valvasori, enjoyed the distinction of being secured, in
addition, for the chorus.   This subdivision of personal property was by no means conducive to the undisputed maintenance
of peace.   Occasionally, it would give rise to a serious dispute between such important functionaries as the head-
tailoress and the chorus-master, touching the right which this
one alleged to the throat and lungs, and that other to the eyes
and fingers of these enigmatical beings who were half tailor
and half vocalist.   Need it be said, that having been accustomed to the European school of operatic management, and
being totally unacquainted with the " go-ahead" style in
which theatrical matters were carried on in this country, my
eyes expanded upon all around me with a purely involuntary
amazement ?   Could it be possible that I was really and truly
awake ?   Was it not rather some hideous nightmare which
had taken possession of my sleeping faculties ?   Determined
to prove this, I seized upon a needle which the Signor Pauselli had left in a half-finished doublet, while engaged in looking for his choral part, which had ingeniously been extracted
from between his person and the seat of his chair by some
one who had lost his own, and inserted it vigorously into the
fleshy part of my arm.   This was done, in the positive
hope, my dear Berlioz, of awakening myself from slumber.
Indeed, it was effected with such good-will, that I doubt not,
were my arm curiously examined, the scar of that wound
might be found upon it, even at this long lapse of time.

Suffice it, that I did not awake.   All that was around me,

was but too truly and too indubitably, nothing but fact, and *bona fide* flesh and blood.

Indeed, everything which I had as yet seen, appeared to me to demand a complete and thorough reformation.

But to apply the besom of the reformer to the abuses which existed, demanded the hand as well as the will of the manager. This manager, I had not yet seen. To me, he was at this period, a myth, and I determined accordingly upon reducing him, as soon as possible, to a reality. Making my egress therefore from the *atelier* of the tailors, and the *studio* of the chorus-singers of the Astor Place Opera House, I bent my way to the address given me as that of its lessee. This was Mr. E. P. Fry. When I arrived at the house in question, I sent in my card, and was speedily admitted. He was in his private apartment, and was arranging his wig when I entered it. As he turned towards me, an uncomfortable foreboding of his failure in his present undertaking came over me, which was probably produced by his personal appearance. It would, very certainly, never have induced me to suppose him an operatic manager. He had the general appearance of a gentleman, combined with some degree of oddity; and apparently, none of that peculiar *finesse* which invariably associates itself with our ideas of an unprofessional operatic director. A *finesse*, by-the-by, which had always stricken me as the most evident characteristic of the head of Mr. Lumley, the last European manager with whom I had been connected.

Appearances, however, are very often deceitful in the extreme, and I refrained from at once permitting myself to form a judgment of his capacity.

His reception of me was gracious enough, and we soon entered into conversation, which naturally turned upon the prospects of the approaching season.

He was very evidently a well-intentioned man, my dear Berlioz, and what is infinitely rarer, a well-meaning manager. Unfortunately, he knew nothing whatever of the business he had entered upon, and had but small experience in active life. The principles of operatic management which he ingenuously avowed, were indeed so *naïve*, that they absolutely commanded from me a large amount of sympathy. He exhibited in his plans no symptoms of real and manly energy, although a considerable amount of obstinacy suffered itself to become occasionally visible.

But let me jot down to you the leading portions of our conversation. It may prove to you, that however details may differ, the same main features characterize operatic management in every portion of the world. What these are, you know to the full as well as I do, and consequently, it would here be useless to specify them.

Mr. Fry informed me that he had engaged for his approaching season, Signor Truffi, Signor Benedetti and Signor Rossi, three popular singers, and all of them great favorites with the New York public. He, however, not liking them, had sent his brother, W. H. Fry, to Europe, for the purpose of engaging others. I gently hinted to him, that any favorite artists with the public, whether good, bad or indifferent, are in a managerial point of view, a source of fortune, and should on no account be superseded until the public are wearied with them, or their own demands upon the management become too enormous to admit of a reasonable prospect of profit from their further engagement.

"That may be all very well," was his reply, "as far as regards their merit. But these artists refused to sing under the former management of Sanquirico and Patti, in an opera written by my brother."

In consequence of this, I was left to imagine that the

aforesaid brother was now sent out, to engage such artists as might be able as well as willing to perform his compositions.

At the same time, I learned that my manager had only abandoned his former vocation as book-keeper in a large commercial house, for the purpose of establishing opera through the compositions of his brother. He being then and now fully and completely convinced, that his brother is absolutely destined not only to become the generator of melody, and the harbinger of the golden era in music on this side of the earth, but also the dictator of its present progress throughout the world.

Alas! my dear Berlioz, you might tell him how hard and impossible a work this is, after Art has once taken its first *impetus* in its true direction. How much genius and how large an amount of love have you lavished upon a somewhat similar object! You have begun to make the downward descent in life, and, haply, when you are over-ripening on the far side of sixty, the public may begin to feel that a great master is slowly passing away from them. Such are the earthly chances of a reformer, and such you have, in a certain shape, been. Such are the worldly prospects of an inventor, for such in music you undoubtedly are. Mr. Fry then knew, and even now, suspects not that it is so. Will his brother ever learn this secret?

Speaking at some length upon the public and the press, my manager further declared himself a personal and implacable enemy of James Gordon Bennett, the Editor of the *New York Herald*. In saying this, he also seized the opportunity to inform me, that he not only intended to exclude him and any of the staff of his journal from the Opera, unless they paid at the door, but also announced his determination of never advertising in any paper with which James Gordon Bennett might in any manner be connected.

Now, at this period, the *Herald* was to New York almost that which the *Times* is to London. It was, in point of fact, a necessity.

" Oh ! miserable man," I thought to myself, as he mentioned this ; " what are you thinking of ? Do you wish to undermine the very artists that you tell me are favorites with the public, by not announcing their performances in a paper which you admit has a larger circulation than any other which is published in this city, or indeed which may be published in the Union ?

Whatever the intrinsic merits or demerits of the journal in question might be, this seemed so extraordinary, that even while restrained by courtesy from expressing my disapproval of such a course, I could not avoid asking him what might be the reason for his entertaining such a decided enmity as he then evinced.

Upon my putting this question, he told me that some time since, Mr. Bennett had written, or caused to be written, some severe critical notices of his brother's opera of " Leonora," which had been produced in Philadelphia.

You know, my dear Berlioz, that half a drop of Croton oil will for a time completely disorganize the digestive faculties. In like manner the meanest trifles will at times produce the most violent effects ; and, causes which appear to be harmless, may not unfrequently bring about the most terrible results.

Some four thousand years, more or less, since, a fashionable lady dwelt in Greece, who was a great beauty. Her name was Helen. Now this Helen took it into her head, being already a married woman, to get up a private flirtation with a dashing young Trojan scamp named Paris. This common, although immoral, proceeding upon her part, has resulted in one continuous chain of events, calamities and catastrophes up to the present day, which catastrophes, events and calamities will in all probability continue for four thousand years to come, should this round world last so long.

I seem to feel your laugh. It encourages me to continue my parallel.

Without this flirtation, there would very certainly have been no abduction. Abductions at all times have had evil consequences.

Had the abduction never taken place, the Greeks might never have besieged Troy. Now had Troy never been besieged, it would very certainly not have been taken. Untaken, Æneas would never have run away from it with his paternal progenitor on his back. Had he not run away, as fast as he could, thus burdened, the pious son of Anchises would never have dreamed of establishing himself in a foreign land, to which he had no title, as a colonist; and, consequently, his descendants could not possibly have founded Rome.

Without the existence of the seven-hilled city, it is more than probable that we should have had no universal empire.

But for the existence of that universal empire, what chance would the past have presented for the establishment of a Roman Catholic and Apostolic church? Had that Roman Catholic and Apostolic church never been begotten in the womb of Time, the world would neither have had popes, nor the Inquisition, *auto da fés*, cardinals, archbishops, nor Jesuits. Without Jesuits and archbishops, what, you must permit me to ask, would have possibly become of the Irish? But for the existence of the Irish as a nation, we might never even have heard of the name of Archbishop Hughes. In his absence, is it not clear that Know-Nothingism would speedily have died a natural death, that is, if we presuppose it ever to have been born?

Who, therefore, can tell what in the next four thousand years may be the united consequences of popes, Irish, archbishops, Jesuits, Know-Nothings and Young America?

Permit me to call your attention, my dear Berlioz, to the progressive influence which Helen's most immoral escapade has had over all our affairs, religious, social or political, upon this side of the globe.

Now, precisely and exactly in the same manner as that in which Helen's *faux pas* had operated to cause such an aggregative amount of trouble, had the development of his musical taste in the brain of W. H. Fry, scattered the seed of what has turned out a very pleasant and agreeable musical quarrel, to those by-standers who have either nothing, or have had nothing at all to do with it.

His opera of "Leonora" was most undoubtedly the sole cause avowed by his brother for rushing into management. *Par parenthese*, I may observe that his management offered me the "engaging" inducement which led to my quitting Europe. This operatic management originated a new series of operatic quarrels, (you shake your head and say with sorrow, "We have already had enough of these,") inaugurated a succession of assaults and batteries, law-suits, judgments and executions, libels and defamations, literary and musical *émeutes*, as well as gave birth to a newspaper war of some nine years standing, in which angry broil, more ink has been spent and more brain been used up, than all the blood which was shed, and the lives which were sacrificed in the wars of the Greeks and Trojans. Indeed, the battle was waged with such virulence upon either side, that New York itself was divided into parties. One class of society in it which consists of "upper tendom," and bears a spurious sort of consanguinity with the *Faubourg St. Germain* and the West End upon your side of the ocean, was taught to regard the opera, or I should say, any opera so long as it was Italian, as one of the paramount necessities of life. Another and a larger class remained, who were more democratic in their tendencies. Partly because the opera was an expensive amusement, suiting more particularly those who have long purses, and largely influenced by the tone of the *Herald*, these look upon it as an anti-republican institution, and unhesitatingly condemn it. It would therefore seem, that after nine years of quarrels, lawsuits, and public and private warfare, only the first act of this drama has as yet been completed. Musical speculation has suffered, and operatic taste has been nipped in the bud, simply because W. H. Fry chose to write an opera which he placed upon the stage, and James Gordon Bennett had not musical knowledge enough to appreciate it, or lacked that musical ignorance which alone could have enabled him, as I have been told, conscientiously to puff it.

Yes, my friend, in this part of the world we have made one very decided advance upon your ancient half of it. A conscientious puff may be met with here, as a man may occasionally meet with a conscientious "smashing." An acquaintance has more than once suggested to me, that this is because musical criticism is entirely unknown as a science amongst us. Indignantly, do I repudiate this suggestion. Are we not, by several inches, the tallest nation under the sun, and is it to be for one moment supposed, that critically we do not understand everything?

But I presume that you would like to know something about James Gordon Bennett. You mutter to yourself, "What a devil of a fellow he must be." You are about to question me respecting his mental, moral, and physical nature.

Allow me to tell you, my dear Berlioz, that such questions would be very difficult for so unintellectual an individual as myself to answer. Some imagine him to be a moral ogre who digests reputations, artistic or political, as a *bona fide* one would make his meal of a *ragout d'enfans*, or a *potage des jeunes Anglais*. There are others, however, who assert him to be a totally misunderstood and infamously underrated Christian philosopher. One would say that he enjoys little, so keenly, as the pulling to pieces public character, while a second praises the courage with which he has applied the knife to a moral ulcer upon the body politic. Here, he is possibly accused of the wanton destruction of private happiness; and, there he is warmly hailed as the undaunted advocate of popular liberty. This man will accuse him of having violated the secret sanctity of the domestic hearth, while the other will congratulate him upon having uncapped a hidden moral baseness. Some have named him the " Satan" of the New York press, while others have styled him its " Napoleon." These assert that he takes " black mail" from everybody who fears his pen. Those, it is well known, have been turned out of his office for having simply attempted to bribe him.

Should you still wish to have my opinion of this man, I am ready at present to give it to you.

You say that you do. I therefore prepare to jot it down. It is this. James Gordon Bennett is neither more nor less than the New York " Diogenes."

You laugh, but let me assure you that there is no jest in this opinion respecting him, upon my part. Bennett is, in this comparatively new American Republic, and almost as modern New York, precisely that which the philosopher of the Cynic school was in the old Greek Commonwealth of ancient Athens. The only differences which mark the two men, are the differences of time, place, progress, and circumstances. Had the first-named preceded the last, in point of time, and been born in Athens, he would have taken up his lodgings in the classical cask now hallowed by the memory of Diogenes. He would have excluded himself by that very act from fashionable society, for how could fashion tolerate the man who lived in a tub? With a lamp in his hand, in broad daylight, he would have wandered through the streets of Athens in search of an honest man, always a somewhat difficult article to find. In a word, Bennett would have been the genuine and identical Diogenes.

But the last-named, if he had come to New York some twenty years ago, would have done nothing of all this. No! Berlioz, I feel positively convinced that he would simply have started a newspaper.

He would most indubitably have selected a corner-house in Nassau or William-street for his business domicile. Consequently, the fashionable world would exclude him from their society. "Upper Tendom" would know him not, nor would he have cared two straws for knowing "Upper Tendom." Lifting his rod over their backs, he would have castigated their sins. Taking his paper in his hand, he would have gone forth in search of money. Believe me, when I say that he would have done right. Money at the present day outvalues a dozen honest men. Therefore is it, that I tell you the Diogenes of the New World is most undoubtedly the identical and genuine James Gordon Bennett.

Nature has undoubtedly refused him an advantageous personal appearance such as she bestowed on the Admirable Crichton, D'Orsay or Beau Brummell, but in return for her penuriousness in this respect, she has gifted him with a rare talent for observation. Quick and penetrating in his judgment, he has of course discovered in the human race amongst whom birth and the will of God had chanced to cast him, much more to censure and to ridicule than to praise and to admire. Have you and I not made the same discovery, my friend, long since?

On starting the *New York Herald*, he undertook singly and unaided to sweep away the whole of that filth and mud which had for so many years gradually accumulated on politics, arts, commerce and fashion in this section of the world. Scarcely, however, so fortunate as the son of the Thunderer, who managed to cleanse the Augean stables, he, on the contrary, bears some resemblence to the daughters of Danaus. The more that he sweeps from the one side, the larger amount of moral filth rushes into, and, perforce fills the other.

Sometimes it may also have happened, that in his toil, after a day's hard sweeping, a remnant of dirt and some bad odor might remain about him. Such accidents, my dear Berlioz, will happen to every reformer.

This feature of direct antagonism to every abuse, as well as his constant and most successful labor to acquire the earliest news ere steamer and telegraph had placed it within the reach of all, have by degrees ensured his paper a prodigious circulation. His enemies buy and read it to see whether they have been attacked. His friends do the same, that they may get for two cents, a shilling's worth of fun; while the great bulk of the population, invariably the most acute judges of that which is really good, secure an early copy for the sake of learning all the current as well as acquiring the earliest news.

Now, this was the man whom my manager had with a sublimely heroic pugnacity, selected as his enemy. It would almost seem, as though Destiny had called me across the water to New York, to view their encounter.

You must now allow me to tell you something of the

artists whom Mr. Fry was preparing to undermine, and who therefore must naturally become his enemies.

The Signora Truffi was a lady singularly prepossessing in her appearance, and of the most distinguished manners. Had you looked on her abundant fair hair, and sunned yourself for a moment in the glance of her bright and azure eyes, you would rather have believed her some sentimental maiden from Northern Germany, than an Italian *Prima Donna*. Judged simply as an artist, she was one of that kind which seldom palls upon the ear, but never electrifies the soul of the listener. She rendered certain parts which do not admit of a *fiasco*, such as *Elvira* in the "Ernani," and *Lucrezia Borgia*, well, carefully avoiding all she imagined might not suit her capacity. In quality her voice was a rich *soprano*, and she had considerably augmented its register by a careful musical cultivation.

Benedetti had a manly and robust figure. Indomitable, energetic, quarrelsome as a gentleman who has recently come from the South of Ireland, conceited with the inevitable self-approval of a first *tenor*, and cunning as either a monk or a weasel, he possessed a strong voice. Its degree of cultivation was extremely mediocre. Did he chance to sing a false note, or commit an error in intonation, he would look daggers at some unoffending member of the orchestra, or if the humor seized him, publicly rebuke an innocent member of the chorus, for the purpose of inducing the public to believe that one or other of them had dragged him into a false key. Whenever he could not keep time, he had the trick of beginning to beat it himself, although he literally never knew the difference between a six-eight and a two-four movement. This was for the purpose of showing the audience that the fault, supposing they discerned it, lay with the conductor. You may imagine that such a vocalist was an almost priceless *tenor*. Yet he, for so **Mr. Fry** had told me, was a favorite with the public.

The *basso*, Signor Rosi, was a big man, standing, at the least, six feet in his stockings. He measured some thirty inches from one shoulder to the other, and trod the stage with all the dignity of a great artist. His greatness, however, was in the extent of his person, rather than in his vocalization. Before he commenced singing, he would draw a long breath, put himself in a fighting attitude, and then rush to the footlights. Your expectation would have been raised to the highest pitch. Alas! my good Berlioz, his singing realized the ancient Latin proverb, *"parturiunt montes, nascitur ridiculus mus,"* which is so admirably translated by the philosophic inhabitants of Dutchland, into *"nix komm, raus."*

Now, it so happened, that I imagined Mr. Fry had confided to me a great secret in telling me his intentions to render these three artists *disponibles*. Never was a man more completely mistaken. Like many would-be managers, my present one neglected the first principle of diplomacy, and by no means retained his secrets locked within his own breast. In consequence of this unpardonable mistake upon his part, the artists speedily became well acquainted with the nature of the musical mission which he had intrusted to his brother. Indeed, they were as thoroughly cognizant of the whole of its details, as the manager himself was.

A triple league was accordingly formed between Truffi, Rosi, and Benedetti, against the gentleman who was, at this time, at the head of operatic affairs in the Astor Place. At the head of this tripartite alliance, Mr. Bennett kindly consented to operate. This was for the purpose of defending the legitimate rights of his allies, against the aggressions of one who, although advertised as their ally and manager, was in truth their secret foe.

Soon after, having gradually become conscious of their in-expugnable strength and value, these three powers, greatly reinforced by the support of the *Herald*, determined upon going further. Their object was apparently to establish a new religion, of which Truffi, Benedetti, and Rosi, were to be the Musical Trinity. A post was kindly kept open by them for Mr. Bennett, under the nomination of their prophet, although it may reasonably be considered, more than doubtful, whether he was ever aware of their design to inaugurate him into such a distinguished position. Vocalists, as you well know, my dear Berlioz, are generally intolerably vain.

The first opera which was placed in rehearsal, was the " Norma" of Bellini. Delicate Truffi, who by no means felt herself strong enough to render the part of the Druidical priestess to the satisfaction of the public, begged at rehearsal my influence and interference with the manager, to induce him to substitute another opera for her *début*. It was proba-bly concluded by her, that as a new man and one mixed up with the intrigues of neither party, for or against the manage-ment, my representations might have some effect. Such a mission was flattering enough. I accordingly repaired to Mr. Fry, and represented to him the risk which he ran in suffer-ing any doubt to rest upon the success of his opening night.

It is impossible for me to say, whether he would really have relished a *fiasco* on the part of Truffi, but very certainly, his eyes twinkled ominously behind his spectacles, as he lis-tened to me.

The circumstance, however, that his general-intendant had already disbursed $800 for the bear-skins of the Gallic soldiers, with other cogent pecuniary reasons, may have forced him to " go-ahead"—as we say, with a classic energy, my own Teutchland and your France are lamentably deficient in.

Certain it is, that "Norma" remained upon his *programme* for the opening night. Nevertheless, like a prudent captain, he thought over my application, and prepared for the worst, engaging, upon my advice, Madame Laborde, who had just arrived, for one or two months, until his brother should bring out a new cargo of operatic stars.

This lady was a capital *prima donna*. She possessed a flexible voice of great compass, had an astonishing execution, and was in every sense of the word, a finished artist.

Our first night was announced for Philadelphia, for in this country, my friend, at the time I am speaking of, New York was by no means its musical capital. This position was, indeed, jointly held by three cities, Boston and Philadelphia being the other two, who severally assigned and ratified the position to be held in the United States by any vocalist. Nay, a fourth large city lay in the extreme South, whose judgment declined conforming with any of these. This was New Orleans. A French opera pretty constantly existed there, in the season which was free from yellow fever, whose artists were never, or at any rate, very seldom heard in the Northern States.

You say that this was too republican a style for cultivating musical taste, as thoroughly as it should be cultivated. Believe me, that in entertaining this opinion, my dear Berlioz, you are wrong. All Art is republican in its nature, and Music made a more rapid and early growth in the United States, when it was thus diffused, than it has lately done, since it has gradually become more centralized.

Meanwhile, the chorus and orchestra had undergone much of that reform which I had found absolutely necessary, and had been brought into a tolerably fair condition. You are aware that whatever amount of material is at your disposal, an orchestra such as Habeneck's was, or a chorus equal to the one at the German opera in Vienna, are not the chance formation of a day.

Printed orders had been sent to all their members, to meet at a certain hour and place, for the departure to Philadelphia.

Now, these orders were headed thus:—" General Intendance of E. P. Fry's Grand Opera of the United States," and had a splendid aspect to those who received them. This aspect was however doomed to dissolve, which it did very speedily after our arrival in the " Quaker City," as it is here called.

On the road, we were all excitement, in spite of the discomfort of the railway cars. You are astonished to hear one who has become a citizen of this "glorious" country, speaking thus of anything in it. But, my dear Berlioz, I have heard many Americans affirm that New Jersey is no part of this Union. This railroad runs entirely through New Jersey, and I therefore feel completely at liberty to censure it, without at all rendering myself amenable to the censure of a want of due patriotic feeling.

We arrived at length at our destination, and the day announced for the performance of " Norma" dawned upon us.

But there are some few impossibilities in this world, which cannot be overcome. Amongst these, may be reckoned the attempt to make an elephant execute a *pas seul* upon the tight-rope; the endeavor to make a vessel sail in the teeth of a sharp north-easter (the Flying-Dutchman always excepted; or the idea of stopping a cannon-ball when once discharged from the tube that held it, on the application of a match to its priming) with a sheet of blotting paper. All of these are simple impossibilities. But, there is one which is

more impossible still. This is the belief that you can make
a *prima donna* sing, when her mind is made up not to do so.

The house was full; the overture had been played by the
orchestra; the *tenor* had sung his *cavatina;* and the *blonde*
and bewitching Truffi appears upon the stage. A tremendous reception is awarded to the *Norma* of the hour, who
receives it as a really savage *prima donna* invariably receives
applause, with a tender grace that is truly touching. She
sings a few bars of the recitative, staggers, and falls upon
the stage, fainting. Druids, call-boys, and Roman soldiers,
rush towards her. *Oroveso* brings a glass of cold water, and
Adalgisa applies a smelling-bottle to her nose, but she does
not move. *Pollio* calls on his Italian gods in no very choice
Italian; a cockney carpenter vents an oath such as are sworn
upon the banks of the Thames, and nine-tenths of the male
chorus swear as lustily in German as the *lanz-knechts* were
wont to do. As for the parquet, it shrieks with laughter;
from the boxes breaks a storm of hisses, while the gallery
hoots in wrath or yells with delight at the unwonted spectacle.
Mr. Fry is about to rend his hair, but thinks better of it as
he remembers that he wears a wig. The curtain comes
down, and the manager walks before it, announcing that "in
consequence of Signora Truffi's sudden (he lays an ugly emphasis upon this word) indisposition, the money (here, I
thought I heard him groan) would be returned, or the tickets
(in saying this, his face recovered from its previous gloom)
might be retained for the next performance."

So ended the first night of the season in Philadelphia.

On the same evening, a rehearsal of " L'Elisir d'Amore "
is ordered; and, by the most unremitting exertions on the
part of all, excepting the delinquent Truffi, was produced on
the following day. Madame Laborde appeared in it, and
achieved a triumph. Indeed, this artist, alone, might be said

to have carried through the remainder of the brief season, which only lasted some four weeks.

Several weeks slowly elapsed after we had returned to New York, without bringing our manager any intelligence from his missing brother. Poor houses but ill supplied the treasury, and salary-day was an artistic festival that occurred but twice in one month. Positively convinced that nothing but W. Fry's " Leonora," or the "Norma" of the luckily dead and buried Bellini, could revive the drooping fortunes of the establishment, Mr. Fry, therefore, ordered the latter composition once more into rehearsal. This time, my good Berlioz, to use a common and somewhat vulgar saying, he danced " out of the frying-pan into the fire."

There is an anecdote which so strongly illustrates his position, that I am unable to refrain from calling it to your memory. Moreover, although it has been translated into and adapted by all languages, it is, I believe, specifically a French anecdote.

Once upon a time, (the old-fashioned style of commencing a tale actually deserves veneration), a French, not a Parisian vocalist made his *début* in a provincial city. Those who were in the *Loges*, received him with an ominous silence, while the denizens of the *parterre*, as well as the more elevated portion of the house, amused themselves with aping his acting, and imitating his very peculiar style of singing. This endured some time, when they began to call him all sorts of names. " Leather-lungs" and a "cracked pair of bellows," were among the mildest which they offered to him. The wife of the miserable vocalist was standing in the wings, and near her was the stage-manager. This official seeing that the aforesaid wife was very good-looking, was, in consequence thereof, filled with commiseration for her feelings.

" My dear madam," he said, in a tone of the most profound

pity, as he took her white hand in his own, "you must take courage."

"Why must I, monsieur?" was her unexpected reply.

"You know that an artist cannot succeed everywhere."

She smiled in the most engaging manner, and the stage-manager consequently continued.

"Our public has the most absurd pretensions to taste and critical knowledge." Here he squeezed her taper fingers. "You must take it pleasantly."

"Oh! don't be alarmed for my nerves," replied the spouse of the ill-treated *tenor*. "I am more than satisfied with your public."

"Indeed!"

"I am even touched by their most exemplary politeness."

The stage-manager opened his eyes, and was so astonished that he forgot to admire her.

"In every other city where my husband has sung, he has been pelted with rotten oranges or kicked off the stage. Here, on the contrary, he is allowed to sing. I assure you, that to me, the change is perfectly delightful."

Now, in precisely the like manner, would the "Norma" in Philadelphia have been "delightful" to Mr. Fry, supposing that it had followed the results of the "Norma" in New York.

No sooner was the rehearsal for this opera ordered, than Signor Benedetti became violently sick, while the amiable Truffi positively refused to sing the part for the first time in this city (neither is she greatly to be blamed for so doing) with the supplementary *tenor*, Signor Arnoldi. But Madame Laborde, who was not simply a clever singer, but an astute and crafty diplomatist, had in the meantime been occupied in closely studying the principal *rôle* in this opera. Determined to take advantage of the chance given her by Truffi's refusal to play it, she immediately volunteered to take her part with the supplementary *tenor* included.   Mr. Fry immediately accepted her offer.

Only imagine the *tapage* which ensued when this became known.   The musical Trinity had been more than completely outwitted.

Upon the first notice that Laborde would sing in the " Norma," Benedetti forgot that he was sick, and appeared in the operatic world again.   He was ready to rehearse his part.   With a wisdom that I confess I should scarcely have given him credit for, the Manager fearing his propensity for mischief, politely invited him to remain sick until further orders.   Benedetti growled, but was perforce obliged to obey. The result of the first performance was that Madame Laborde created a perfect *furore* as the Druidical priestess, while the *supplemento* very narrowly escaped the fate of the French *tenor*, whom I a few moments since recalled to your remembrance.

A repetition of "Norma" was accordingly loudly demanded, but with Benedetti in the part which Arnoldi had filled. The fair Truffi was for the moment completely forgotten.

It was on a stormy evening in December, that the operatic Napoleon entered the dressing-room of *our* king of modern *tenors*.   He found him painting his face.   In the first place, the two monarchs glanced at each other.   Their glances were such as a lion and a tiger might exchange, in measuring each other's strength.   The Napoleon of the Opera exulted, like a successful Machiavel, over his last demonstrable success, that of having vanquished the queenly Truffi.   On the other hand, the prince of *tenors* was literally burning with indignation, and panting to avenge his *blonde* ally.

After a moment of awful silence, the Napoleon of the Opera said, with that laconic brevity which distinguishes him—

" Friday, "*Norma.*"—You, *Pollio !* "

These four words were pronounced very slowly, and with an expression which would have caused a tremor in any other than the king of *tenors.*

Passing quietly a damp towel over the *rouge* upon his cheeks and the lamp-black upon his eye-brows, he calmly responded—

" Never."

" Never ?"

" Neve-e-e-e-e-r ! "

" Why ? "

" Arnoldi has taken the part. It is, and must remain his property."

" He took it, simply because you were sick."

" Only at your request. I was sick, simply to oblige you."

" But the public wishes specifically to hear you with Madame Laborde."

" Have the kindness then, to inform the public that the principal *tenor* of this operatic troupe only sings with the queen of *prima donnas.*"

" That, sir, shall certainly be done."

Having registered this declaration, the Napoleon of the Opera rushed out of Benedetti's dressing-room, and dashed upon the stage. He appeared before the astonished audience as unexpectedly as the ghost of *Banquo* rises through the trap at *Macbeth's* banquet, and, *apropos des bottes*, announces to the public who had assembled in the Astor Place Opera House, to hear and quietly enjoy " Lucretia Borgia," that Benedetti had positively refused to sing in " Norma" on the Friday following.

Before any one could understand what this extraordinary announcement might mean, he has vanished from the stage, and again stands before Benedétti.

Waving his hand, he grandiloquently exclaims, "I have now given you your deserts."

"Then I will now give you yours, you puppy and liar," replies the incensed royalty.

So saying, he draws his sword, and attempts with the flattened side of it (the edge was as blunt as stage swords invariably are) to castigate the Manager.

A fierce struggle ensued. Unhappily, my dear Berlioz, (remember that I say this as one of the unlucky race of Managers), the prince of *tenors* soon found the Napoleon of the Opera entirely in his power. Turning him round, he administered a kick to his enemy. It took effect in that part of his body where the completed dorsal bone terminates, and the leg has not yet begun. With its force, he was sent three or four paces beyond the limits of Benedetti's dressing-room.

His equilibrium had been so forcibly disturbed, that he plunges out of it, and falls upon the boards. He is totally unable to resume the offensive with so powerful an opponent, and Benedetti remains the victor.

A committee of the subscribers who had heard the statement of the Manager, then repaired to Benedetti to inquire into its truth; and what think you was his response?

With true Italian subtlety, he informed them that he had never dreamed even for one moment, of refusing to sing the part of *Pollio*. "Oh! dear, no!" he only required that some sort of apology should be made to Signor Arnoldi, "who was a very admirable singer." I leave you to imagine the spirit in which this last observation was made by Benedetti. You, who know, even better than I do, the hatred with which an Italian vocalist looks upon all who in any way supplant him or her, even for a moment, will be at no loss in divining this.

Satisfied with the expression of willingness to sing, upon

the part of Benedetti, the committee retired, and left Mr.
Fry to enjoy the fruits of the declared enmity which he had
so wantonly provoked.

The public, however, are invariably the supreme judges
in all matters of this description, and they were by no means
so readily appeased. They had not heard the *tenor's*
Italian and soapily improvised explanation. Simply did
they understand, that the Manager as well as the vocalist
were both in the wrong. The Manager, very decidedly so,
by his perverse interruption of the quiet and orderly performance of the "Lucretia," for the purpose of making an
accusation of insubordination against one of his principal
singers. This was when, be it remembered, he had yet
eight and forty hours before him. In this period of time, he
might very certainly, had he so chosen, have exhausted the
various diplomatic means of persuasion which were at his
disposal, before adopting the harsh and compulsory measure
of appealing to the public. The error of the *tenor* was at
the least as obvious. He had no right, upon his first impulse,
to positively refuse singing at the side of an excellent and
most estimable artist, whom, with a purblind insolence only
to be found in Italian vocalists, he believed not equal to his
own degree of merit.

Accordingly, upon the Friday evening in question, three
distinct parties were to be found in the Astor Place Opera
House.

These were the personal friends of the Manager, those
who supported the refractory *tenor*, and the public.

The first of these came simply and purely for the purpose
of hissing Benedetti and sustaining Mr. Fry in his attempt
to control him. This was, it must be confessed, my good
friend, a very praiseworthy example of private friendship.
The second of the three parties were the friends of the

culprit. These appeared on this night with the purpose of doing precisely the contrary. This, you must grant, was at the least, to the full as praiseworthy. But the public also chose to be present *en masse*. A part of them undoubtedly came with the simple view of enjoying the row which was expected by all, a virtuous pleasure which is in general keenly appreciated by them. The remainder had, however, paid their money solely to have the satisfaction of giving a lesson to each of the belligerents.

Plans for the evening's campaign had been arranged beforehand by either of the two first parties.

Benedetti, who would be exposed to the primary outbreak of the popular indignation, artfully fomented by the friends of the management, was prepared with a lengthy speech. In it, he would touch upon every possible point of accusation against him. He would explain, modify, denounce, entreat, bully, and apologize—appealing to the well-known generosity and kindliness of the public, while he announced his thorough good will, and asserted his at the least as thorough good faith towards the management. In fact, it was a very commonplace, every-day sort of theatrical speech, with which he had primed himself—a sort of oration which the public, friend of mine, ought long since to have known by heart, but by which it is still content to be deceived on almost every occasion.

Thus read the programme issued from the camp of the Manager.

Benedetti was by all means to be hissed off the stage. Then, when the confusion had reached its highest point, Mr. Fry was to appear before the audience. After a flattering reception, he was to address the audience, and request, as a personal favor, their pardon for Benedetti. Was it not at once obvious, that all who were present would say, " What a noble-hearted, fine and generous fellow we now have for a manager!" After this, he would give utterance to a few modest remarks, composed expressly for this occasion, and then retire, followed by a sedulously prolonged and deafening cheering.

Now, let us see what really chanced upon this evening.

The house was crammed from the top to the bottom. Every seat was taken. The avenues in the parquet were thronged by those who had been attracted by the scandal. It was another proof, my dear Berlioz, that Art is by no means the principal thing to be cultivated by a management that would rejoice in attracting large audiences.

When the introduction was over,* Benedetti appeared. He was immediately greeted by a storm of hisses, which were as quickly broken in upon by thunderous acclamation. This at length stilled, and he began to sing. That man, however, who would have heard a note after he had touched the first *bar*, must have had good ears. Screams, whistles, clapping of hand   hisses, trampling of feet, roaring, menacing outcries and gesticulations of every kind filled the theatre. You might have imagined that the inmates of some half a hundred mad-houses had broken loose, and crowded it upon this occasion. To catch a note from the Orchestra, was as impossible as to listen to the singing. After a brief time, chaos having roared itself hoarse, began to shape itself into some intelligible form, and a few cries of "Order! order!" were occasionally heard.

"What order?" retorted the friends of the manager. "Off the stage with the rascal!"

"No! no! Go on, and give us a tune," roared the public. "Order! order!"

"Off the stage with him! He wouldn't sing when we wanted him. He shan't sing, now."

* The Opera on this occasion was of course the *Norma*.

"Apologize to Fry."

"Fry be d—d! Apologize to Madame Laborde."

"Never mind Laborde! Apologize to the public."

"The Public does n't want an apology."

"Give us a song."

"Yes! yes! 'Yankee Doodle!'" shouted a portion of the public.

"We don't want 'Yankee Doodle.' 'Carry him back to Old Virginey.'"

"Order! Order!"

For some time, Benedetti stood all this very quietly. Occasionally, he would open his mouth with the attempt to sing. It was perfectly hopeless, and his lips would close again almost as quickly as they had separated. At length, he advanced a few steps, and performed a curious specimen of pantomime, supposed to be expressive of his desire to speak. As you and myself both know, the public is at all times a curious animal. Its curiosity at present, therefore, restored order. But this order menaced Mr. Fry's programme of proceedings with the destruction of its utility. He and those of his friends who were with him, behind the scenes, trembled, lest by these means their own tactical arrangements might be turned by their astute enemy against themselves.

"Ladies and gentlemen!" said Benedetti, "I came here to sing —"

"So you did!"

"Why the deuce don't you, then?"

"Give us 'Yankee Doodle!'" roared out a voice from the gallery.

Benedetti gazed on the audience with an air of unabashed majesty, as he mildly inquired—

"Shall I sing or withdraw?"

" Sing !"

" Withdraw !"

" Yes !"

" No !"

" Yes ! Yes !"

" No ! no !" were the cries and screams that broke from every part of the theatre, while in the same roar from the gallery—

" Give us 'Yankee Doodle !' " was again heard.

" No ! No !"

" Yes ! Yes ! Yes !"

Now, whether this " Yes ! yes !" applied to singing or withdrawing, or the vocalization of " Yankee Doodle," it would be impossible to say, and Benedetti stood for a moment completely nonplused.

To correct his misappreciation of their desires, he therefore repeated the question; and, drawing himself up in a graceful and expressive position, was preparing to proceed with the rest of his previously prepared speech, when the acuteness of one of Madame Laborde's friends frustrated his intention. This was Monsieur Nourrit, an old stager and old Stage-manager, who, seeing the turn matters were about to take, pulled the wire and gave the signal for dropping the curtain. Down it at once came, between the internally irate and externally most pacific *tenor*, cutting short any further colloquy between himself and the public.

With a brief compliment to Nourrit for his strategic skill, Mr. Fry settled his new pair of spectacles securely upon the bridge of his nose, and rushes out to the foot-lights.

But what was his astonishment to find that the flattering reception indicated in his programme was by no means accorded him ! There must have been some unaccountable error committed by those to whom his arrangements had been entrusted.

He gazed wildly around the house, but hisses, cat-calls, and objurgations couched in the most derogatory terms, were all that could be afforded him. In his horror, he would not even have endured it as long as Benedetti had done, but for the suggestions of some of the members of his Orchestra. These, with a keen relish for his most unmistakable nervousness, encouraged him not to leave the battle-ground. At length, agitated and trembling, he was permitted to stammer out his speech, hissed by the friends of the *tenor*, applauded by his own, and laughed at by the public, after which the performance was allowed to go on.

Never, possibly, had Benedetti or Laborde sung better, and very certainly, never was there a greater amount of merriment elicited from its hearers by any farce, than was then called forth by the lyrical tragedy of " Norma."

Nay! It would have seemed that on this evening scarcely an American was present who did not understand Italian. The slightest bearing upon the private affairs of the vocalists, into which the words of the Opera, or the acting might be tortured, was immediately taken up by the audience. Witty commentaries were passed from one to the other upon it, and received with unbounded merriment. In the scene in which *Pollio* speaks about *Norma*, in the *finale* to the first act when *Norma* reproaches *Pollio*, and in the *Duo* when she tells him that at length he " is in her hands," the most ludicrous exclamations were heard from the gallery, and immediately caught up by those who were in the parquet and boxes. But, when in the last scene, *Pollio* implored *Norma* to pardon him, and the exclamation—

" *Ah! troppo tardi, ti ho conosciuto*," bursts from him, the merriment of the public could no longer be repressed, and the Opera concluded amidst a general outburst of laughter from the public, the Chorus, and the Orchestra, in which, even Fry's and Benedetti's personal friends were, almost against their will, obliged to join.

The former gentleman made money upon this evening, but it brought the Opera House into bad repute, while he himself incurred a large amount of personal discredit, even amongst his own friends. Bennett, also, consecrated a certain amount of space in his columns, daily, to the abuse of the Opera. It may safely be affirmed, my dear friend, that this was the only thing which induced the public to visit the establishment. Such things, you and myself have seen, Berlioz, even in Europe. Indeed, had our Manager answered and attempted to refute the daily charges brought against him by the *Herald*, I entertained, and still entertain not the slightest doubt, but that he could have turned the excitement caused by these articles greatly to his own advantage. However, he preferred to keep his wrath smouldering, and was wont to say, in answer to my hints upon the advisability of entering upon a more retaliatory course,

"Never mind. Mr. Bennett shall pay the piper, and I will dance. I shall sue him for heavy damages."

Thus, with an amount of nerve and a degree of equanimity for which you ought to award him a large degree of moral credit, he suffered himself to be daily abused and ridiculed. While doing so, he nevertheless jotted down each truculent jest or aspersion in the note-book of his memory. Bitter words and savage sneers were rated by him as so much cash. It was an agreeable mode of rectifying the balance-sheets of a speculation which had undeniably turned out ill. An imaginary twenty thousand dollars turned the scale of operatic chances greatly in his favor.

In the meantime, the season was advancing rapidly. Nothing, however, had yet either been seen or heard of W. H.

Fry and the new vocalists, with whose importation from Italy he had so obligingly charged himself.

Not a single day passed, but his expectant brother sent messengers, or should I not call them envoys, down to Castle Garden, to scan the Bay and bring him the first intelligence that could be obtained of these long-desired artists. But alas! it was useless. Nothing was either to be seen or heard of them.

Like the ultimate wife of the ferocious "Blue-Beard," who stationed her sister on the top of "Blue-Beard's castle," to inform her of the first glance she might catch of her long-expected brothers, demanding every moment—

"Sœur Anne! ne vois tu rien?"

and receiving to every question the invariable answer— "Rien!" he waited in daily increasing doubt and agony for tidings of his relative.

Seriously, my good Berlioz, it appears to me that in his short career as an operatic Manager, he had already paid more than enough of heart-burning and more purely physical evils for the calling which he had so rashly entered upon.

At length, in the last week but one of the season, Mr. Fry received a letter. It brought the long expected and grievously delayed intelligence. Success had crowned the efforts of the Manager's musical brother. As for the time which had been employed in the selection of the desired artists, it, combined with the reputation of the agent as a musical critic of the first water, as well as the object which he had in view, the performance of his own operas with these artists, admitted of no doubt with regard to their excellence.

If any one, animated by a very pardonable degree of curiosity, inquired the names of the new vocalists, the

Manager would purse up his lips, and with a look of the most vigorous mysification, say—

" That must remain a secret until their arrival."

The knowing smile which followed this diplomatic announcement—for you see, my good friend, that the Chevalier Henry Wikoff was by no manner of means the first diplomatist in the New York managerial market—indicated that New York should very certainly be surprised this time. Daily, therefore, did this subtly nurtured secret increase, until it was a full-grown and full-blown mystery. Rumors were sedulously circulated that Mr. W. H. Fry had actually been successfully employed in inducing Rubini and Persiani to visit America. It was obvious that the *blonde* Truffi became perceptibly paler as she listened to these ominous reports, while the king of *tenors* quivered in his boots as he brooded over his possible dethronement.

However, the duration of this mystery was but brief. It was solved by the arrival of the proximate steamer, upon which, the daily journals announced the arrival of the following new artists for the Italian Opera.

Your ears, I intuitively feel, my amiable Berlioz, are widely distended.

You wish to know the names of those vocalists, under whose skill a new and native composer was to be ushered upon the boards before a New York public. Can it be possible that you have not yet heard of them? Nay! I know you have. Is not Paris one of the centres of musical Europe? Such names as those of the Signori Ferrari, Taffanelli, and Castrone, as well as that of La Signora Fascioti, cannot be unknown to you. These were the fair artists destined to close the first operatic season with which I had been connected in New York, with *éclat*. In addition to this, our Manager counted, by producing the whole of the new vocalists on one

3

and the same night, the last of the season, upon exciting an enthusiasm which would justify him in announcing a *new season*, with the prices of admission raised, at the least, fifty per cent.

My advice was, it is true, proffered to him. Singularly enough, it very considerably differed from that which his deeper and more profound skill in the science of operatic management had determined upon. I actually thought, my friend, that it was unadvisable to produce them all at once upon the same night. Consequently, I recommended him to arrange their *débuts* to take place in succession. By this means, at the least, so it appeared to me, he would in all probability, have secured four good houses instead of one. Moreover, he would, in addition to this, have avoided the inevitable nervousness of four *débutants* unacquainted with the public and in a strange country, as well as unaccustomed to sing with one another.

Convinced of his infallibility, the Manager announced to me that I was decidedly wrong, and I of course immediately believed him as completely as any of his *employés* could believe in such a Manager.

Consequently, " Ernani" was announced for the last night of the season, and for his own benefit, the four principal parts being confided to the above-named four artists.

The house was crowded almost to suffocation, when the curtain drew up. In order not to appear too late, I should presume, upon the stage, the *tenor*, Signor Ferrari, appeared full five minutes before his cue was given. Here he waited. Exposed to the scrutinizing gaze of the public, his fright momentarily increased. He trembled, as a mouse does between the paws of a benevolent cat who means to have some sport with him, before she puts him out of this world. When he attempted to sing, his throat refused him its service; the perspiration washed out his painted face, and trickled over it in red and brown drops; he grew terribly pale, and exhibited rather the appearance of a suffering martyr in his last agony, than that of the bandit-chieftain who was the successful rival in love of Charles V., on whose wide kingdom the sun never couched, and consequently could never rise.

In New York, my friend, we have ordinarily a far more gentle and generous public than you have in Paris. It is indulgent to a degree with almost any novelty.

In the present instance, therefore, it allowed his attempt to sing to pass in silence. Their judgment, however, was only postponed.

The Signora Fasciotti appeared in the next scene. Self-possessed, in striking contradistinction to the *tenor*, she appeared arrogantly conscious of her merit as well as of her beauty. Such was, at any rate, the first impression she produced. But when she sang, all this was unmercifully knocked upon the head. Her voice produced a precisely similar effect upon the ear, which an edgeless razor might produce upon the skin. Scarcely had she ended her *cavatina*, than a certain rumor was distinguishable in the gallery, which might, by an attentive student of nature on a larger scale, have been compared with that rolling of the waves which is said by those who study such matters, (you know that I do not, my dear Berlioz), to be the precursor of a storm. But the acting and singing of Taffanelli, the *barytone*, calmed down the moving elements, and all might yet have gone on smoothly, but for the appearance of the new *basso*. This was the vocalist rejoicing in the name of Signor Castrone. Very evidently had he never before been upon any stage. On his entrance, he tumbled over his own sword, and rolled into a terrified group of chorus-singers. After this, he managed to get his spurs entangled in the dress of the *prima donna*, and when released by the intervention of her lady in waiting, found his way to the prompter's box. Thence, no incident of the plot and no suggestion of the conductor could induce him to move. Beating his time with one hand and one leg, and counting the rests in his music audibly enough to be heard by the whole audience, there did old *Sylva* remain until the curtain fell upon the first Act, amidst general laughter, far worse for *debutants* than hisses.

The second and third Acts followed, in the same way, and with the same result.

Ferrari trembled and was inaudible. Fasciotti screamed in a mode that would have rendered her invaluable, in breeches, as a shepherd in the Pyrenees, while the poor Castrone met at every step with some new and unforeseen difficulty. Had he his sword to draw, it stuck in the scabbard. Would he sheath it, he could never find the aperture through which he might pass its point. If he was to enter upon the right side of the stage, and those who were on the scene were looking in that direction, it was morally certain that he would appear behind them. Did they prepare for such a chance, then he might be seen coming on from the right entrance. When he knelt down, some part of his dress was certain to crack ; and had he to rush out sword in hand, he would find all the doors of the stage closed. Then, after running to all of them in a devil of a hurry, he would with a remarkably Parisian shrug of the shoulders, subside into quietude, and walk coolly off through the wings. Taffanelli was the only artist of the four that might have come off, creditably.

But, unfortunately, the worst, or should I not say the best, for it ranks in my memory as one of the grandest musical farces, I have ever seen and listened to, my dear Berlioz, was reserved for the last Act.

This capped the events of the evening with a climax. But I feel compelled to beg of you to believe that I am inventing nothing which I am recounting. The whole of it is undeniably too true.

Ernani had at length been united with *Elvira*. Lapped in dreams of future happiness and bliss, they were retiring from the festival, when the fatal horn is heard from the other side of the painted canvas. That sound recalls *Ernani* to the memory of his oath. For a brief period, almost does he believe it the mere effect of his excited imagination. Then for the second and third time its note rings upon his ear, and *Sylva* rushes upon the stage to demand the fulfilment of the vow which he had sworn.

I have intimated that *Sylva* rushed upon the stage. But can you imagine in what guise the unhappy Castrone brought him before the audience? No! you cannot. The decency of your imagination altogether disowns such a possibility, and I feel that I shall be obliged to tell you.

As I prepare to do so, although alone at my writing-table, a crimson blush overspreads my modest face.

It creeps across my body, and along mine arms, until it even dyes my fingers. They involuntarily redden like newly-pulled radishes, as I recall that incident to my memory.

He (could I hide my face I would do so, Berlioz, did I not luckily remember that you cannot see it) had forgotten what the Erse or Northern Scotch, though which it is I have suffered myself to forget, call their "gallygaskins." In our own more fastidiously refined language, upon this continent, they are most generally and generically classified as the "unmentionables." There he stood, representing the Spanish idea of an Inexorable Fate, clad in a black velvet doublet, but with a pair of flesh-colored and closely-woven silk inexpressibles upon his nether man. The horn, that fatal horn, hung from his neck, in a position which it would be absolutely impossible for me consistently with propriety to indicate upon paper. Certainly, it was in anything but its right place. Some of the ladies who were present, rose and quitted the theatre. Others shrank back in their seats, and veiled their eyes with the feathery ridges of their fans, or the delicate lace of their handkerchiefs. Even the self-possessed and resolute *prima donna* reddened through her well-laid-on rouge, and dropped her eyelids over her bold eyes, while the Conductor for once forgets the impassibility imposed upon him by his position, and hurries up the Orchestra to the end. At length *Sylva* offers to *Ernani* the dagger. In his eagerness to put an end to himself, and escape the ridicule of which he felt conscious, the latter clutches at it. But, alas! the blade remains in *Sylva's* hand, and the lucklessly unconscious *Ernani*, a martyr to misplaced confidence, is obliged to dispatch himself with the scabbard. After this, the curtain falls where it always does, leaving *Ernani* without its drapery, and close to the foot-lights. The dead body sits up, and gazes around it in speechless consternation. An universal and irrepressible titter is heard throughout the whole house. In its agony it rises, and runs off from before the audience.

Nor yet, my good Berlioz, have the mischances of the evening fairly terminated.

A few of his personal friends insist upon calling Mr. Fry out, as is ordinarily the case at the close of a season. In consequence of this, the Manager makes his appearance before the curtain. Unfortunately, he was not gifted with that presence of mind which is, I may safely say, a theatrical Manager's most paramount necessity, and was unable to compose a speech upon the spur of the moment suitable to the occasion. He had, however, acquired a very graceful speci-

men of oratorical writing, by rote, which he forthwith de-
livers, talking about the "excellence of his new artists" and the
"intelligent enthusiasm of the public," as well as "the heavy
expense which he had incurred to secure vocalists of such
unapproachable merit." Here the public laughed. After
this, he wound up by promising the lovers of music generally, and his subscribers in particular, a new season, (!)
with advanced prices of admission, (!) in order to enable
him to recompense the unrivalled merit of such great artists
(!) as those whom he had now placed before them.

Your experience scarcely needs the information, that this
was very necessarily the last of Mr. Fry's management. He
was, beyond doubt, a well-meaning Manager, yet his obstinacy
and brotherly love, for the time, ruined him.

But one thing worse, my dear friend, can there possibly
be for any Manager than the having a brother who writes
Opera. This is, the writing it himself.

Possession was now taken of the Opera House by the proprietors and shareholders. Applications for the lease and
directorship of it were invited. Many of the *habitués* of the
Opera encouraged me to put in an application. At the first
I steadily excused myself, on the grounds that my means
were far too limited for such an enterprise. Induced, however, by a direct hint from the Committee who had the management of the property in their hands, and, let me own it
to you, with my ambition somewhat awakened, as well as in
no small measure deceived by the assurances of aid and support which were on all sides volunteered to me, I one day
declared myself a candidate for the lesseeship, and in a few
days more had forgotten having done so, or at any rate had
almost permitted it to slip from my memory.

In the meantime, the house was leased by Messrs. Hackett
and Niblo for a short season, with the intention of playing

the legitimate drama, as tragedy and comedy are called here and in England, although wherefore has invariably passed my comprehension. Opera, farce, melodrama, and even pantomime, being in my opinion to the full as *legitimate* entertainments. Macready was the "star," upon whose reputation these gentlemen intended to form their season.

At this time, Macready the Englishman had a difference of opinion, or controversy of some description, with Edwin Forrest the American.

This purely personal quarrel eventually threw into shade the Fry and Bennett row, assuming a proportion which endangered the peace of New York, while it proved that the Americans will always as a body stand by and enforce peace and order. Indeed, in my opinion, I have always regarded it as a valuable lesson, (although its necessity was greatly to be deplored) to much of the rowdyism which was and is somewhat too prevalent in New York. You ask me what "rowdyism" is, my dear Berlioz, and had I faith in your retention of this letter, I would tell you; but were it to pass out of your hands and find publicity, my explanation of this term might prove detrimental to me, as the "rowdies" generically fear nothing and care for nothing. Therefore, I conscientiously feel that it would be far wiser for me to hold my peace. The reason of this difference between Forrest and Macready was as ridiculous as the cause of the Fry and Bennett controversy. It was alleged by Edwin Forrest that Macready, or Macready's friends, had hissed him during his engagements in England. Therefore, he expected that his friends should hiss Macready now. It was a pure deduction from the *lex talionis*. Statements and counter-statements had severally appeared. Appeals and counter-appeals to the public had been published. In fact, a terrible war (in vulgar English, it might, with the greatest possible propriety, but for its results, have been called a "shindy," with which term, you, my friend, can of course have no acquaintanceship) raged upon this matter in nearly all the newspapers of the Union, amounting, as I have been very credibly informed, to something more than a hundred thousand in number.

Supposing, my dear Berlioz, that the two artists had been Italians, the difficulty would have speedily been settled; but it seemed that the members of the "legitimate" drama had a "legitimate right" to kick up an "illegitimate row." They did so.

The Astor Place Opera House was selected by them for this inspiriting diversion. Like two giants, who prove their strength by thrashing a third and innocent party, this theatre was selected by Messrs. Forrest and Macready, to suffer for their sins.

On the first appearance of Macready, he was most unmistakably hissed off the stage by those who identified Forrest's grievances with national injuries. A portion of the public, called by the "Upper Ten" the "Lower Class," declared that they would permit *no* English actor, *no* Italian Opera, and *no* aristocratic theatre in New York, they being a free and enlightened people. That portion of the public, however, who were called by the "Lower Class" the "Upper Ten," being likewise a part of that free and enlightened people, declared that they would have whatever amusement they chose to pay for, whether it might consist of English actors, or of Italian Opera. In accordance with which determination, a number of gentlemen, of high standing in society, invited Mr. Macready to perform once more, taking the whole of the seats in the house, and consequently refusing admission to the mass of the general theatre-going public. This proceeding was regarded by them as a positive defiance, and on the evening in question (May 10th, 1849), more than 15,000 of them surrounded the Opera House, and attempted to storm it during the performance. The police-force which had been provided, was not strong enough to resist so overwhelming a force, and the military were therefore called out. That is to say, the volunteer companies which constitute, under a different name and with a different organization from that in Paris, our National Guard. After vain efforts to restore peace, it was unfortunately obliged, in order to save the building and protect the audience collected inside of it, to fire upon the crowd.

After several volleys, a few pieces of artillery were stationed at the different corners of the Astor House, and this led to the gradual dispersal of the mob.

The audience were then permitted to leave, (Mr. Macready, as I afterwards heard, had already fled,) and immediately after, the Temple of Harmony was transformed into a Morgue for the dead and a hospital for the dying, upon either side.

Had the slain and wounded, my good Berlioz, been the victims of political ambition, or religious fanaticism, the authors would have paid heavily for this outrage upon the public peace. As it was, everything remained or rather merged into quietude during the following week. Macready escaped to England, where he enjoys his money and his laurels. Had he but done so two days earlier, how many a life, to the full as valuable to the world as his, would have been spared! On the following evening, Edwin Forrest appeared at the Broadway Theatre, where his appearance was hailed by three cheers. To ensure him that triumph, how many lives as valuable to the world as his, had been sacrificed! The people on that morning had gone to their work, and save, in rare instances, where their affections had sustained a personal loss, thought not of their fellows slain to satisfy the "illegitimate" differences between two "legitimate" tragedians. The citizen-soldier cleaned his musket, and thought not whether its ball had been one of those which was plumbed with death.

As for the poor Opera House, its doors were riddled with balls, and its windows broken. Moreover, it was rebaptized in blood with an ominous surname, having been nicknamed, the "Massacre" Place Opera House.

It was upon the morning following this gloomy and terrible disturbance, that a communication from the Committee was handed to me. This communication informed me, that I was the "successful candidate for the lease and direction of the said establishment." Under such circumstances, my dear Berlioz, did I become its Manager. The blood of those who had been borne into it, the night previous, had not yet been scrubbed from its boards when it passed into my hands.

Believe me yours, most truly,

M. M.

PALMO'S OPERA HOUSE

THE ASTOR PLACE OPERA HOUSE

SECOND LETTER.

TO FIORENTINO, PARIS.

New York Fashions and Fashionables—James Foster, Jun.—Henry A.
Coit and others—Re-organization of the Opera—New York Critics
and Criticisms—N. P. Willis—R. de Trobriand and others—Fancy-
Dress Balls—Mozart's Don Giovanni—The first successful Opera
Season in New York.

MARIETTA ALBONI.

LETTER II.

TO FIORENTINO, PARIS.

NEW YORK, *July* 28, 1855.

OLD FRIEND OR ACQUAINTANCE:—

FOR which name I am now to give you, I am scarcely able
to decide. Separation and silence have, it is more than probable, done their work. So long, indeed, is it, since we last
set eyes upon each other, that it appears to me somewhat
dubious whether you will now recognize that Moravian
appellation, whose perverse consonants seemed, when we
were accustomed to meet daily, ever too difficult for your
Neapolitan tongue to shape into sound. Besides, Paris may
lay claim more than any other capital to be considered the
city of the moment. You live through ages in it, while other
portions of the green earth are counting only years. Dynas-
ties and revolutions bud, blossom, and die; liberty is fought
for, acquired, and then put in the breeches pocket of some
successful operator upon the *Bourse* of society, while another
people are only dreaming of the changes which they need, or
another individual is only imagining that which he might
possibly attempt, in some far corner of the world. Charles
X. has long been forgotten. Nay! he has passed entirely

out of remembrance. Memory can scarcely recall the period when Louis Philippe received his " walking-ticket." Lamartine is heard of no more. The Republic is defunct, and Cavaignac rules not. Louis Napoleon has been replaced by Napoleon III. You have almost suffered Algiers to slip out of recollection, and are engaged in dreaming about Sebastopol. How, then, can I possibly have the consummate impertinence to imagine that you retain the Moravian name of Max Maretzek in your Gallicized Italian memory?

Yet, if you will allow me to recall to your recollection the period at which you wielded the stiletto of musical critic upon the Parisian *Corsaire*, a dim memorial, of one who was then your friend, may float across your mind.

My pen was then employed upon the German *Vorwaerts*, in a similar capacity.

A vague *souvenir* may be awakened of M. Boernstein and his amiable family, as well as his partner, M. Bornstedt, its two editors. You will, perchance, recall the pleasant evenings which we have passed with them, in the society of such men as Heine, Marx, Rugge, and Marc Fournier, with others of the would-be Reformers of society. Or, haply, you may remember our mutual friend, the Marquis de Brême, with his adorable *blonde*, Pauline, who had so charmingly *naive a penchant* for getting married, and suffer your memory to fall dimly back upon the little *danseuses Viennoises*, whose music I wrote, Bernard Latte being verdant enough to buy it from me, while yourself were amiably conscientious and actually affixed your critical imprimatur to it. If you can do so—if these memories have, in your Italian heart, bid defiance to Parisian mobility, you will perhaps manage to remember the writer of this letter.

Its object is to renew, if possible, my acquaintance with yourself. You shake your head doubtingly, and ask me, whether this is really its only object. My very amiable Fiorentino, doubt is an exceedingly unfriendly proceeding upon your part. You say—" why is it that I have so long been silent?" Are you determined, then, to give me no credit for the possession of any friendly feeling? Again you shake your head, and your obstinacy compels me to make a clean breast of it, owning that I wish, through you, to give the artistic world a portion of " My Confessions." This will comprise, my doubting and inquisitive friend, a narrative of part of my own experience, and a description of taste as well as fashion, in that part of the New World called the United States.

The most conflicting opinions are circulated abroad, and more especially among artists, concerning America. Some believe it to be a literal *El Dorado*, the Land of Musical Promise running with rivers of milk and honey, instead of streams that. like those in old Europe, contain nothing more than clear water and a few speckled trout, admirable things in their way, but somewhat few and far between. These plant the land of their imagination with cities, like the Tharsis of King Solomon, filled with gold, and silver, and ivory. Their inhabitants are wealthy, confiding and generous, in the extreme ; modern Crœsuses, with the open heart and free hand of some ancient Arabian patriarch. In fact, the wealth, opulence, and prodigality of republican America, has become proverbial with many of the inhabitants of Europe. Recently, the old English " *Deus ex machina*" of writers of Comedy, who used to appear, in moments of extreme need, and settle all difficulties by inserting his fingers in a prodigious purse, or unclasping a plethoric pocket-book, has been wiped out of theatrical existence by a retired American railway-speculator, or a returned Californian gold-digger.

Others are there, however, to be found in Europe, who regard America in a very different light. These believe it to be inhabited by a set of savages, barbarians, and Red Republicans. In their opinion, it contains a race of people who eat raw meat and devour uncooked vegetables, who chew tobacco, and void their rheum upon ladies' dresses and Turkey carpets, who drink unheard of quantities of brandy, schnapps, ale and Monongahela whiskey, while, instead of having been provided with a delicately palpitating heart like other races of mankind, Nature has in its place inserted simply a silver dollar, coined in their own mint.

My good friend, this last opinion is most decidedly false, whilst the first one is by no means accordant with truth.

Believe, my amiable Fiorentino, neither the one nor the other. Calmly and discreetly survey and weigh us. Then, take the *juste milieu*, and say—

       " *C' tout comme chez nous.*"

Yes! all things here, are as they are everywhere else. More or less modified by Nature are they, or developed by chance and circumstance. But I am wrong. There is no such thing as chance. Let me correct myself, therefore, and say they are more or less developed by circumstance.

Here, as elsewhere, society has fallen into its two natural divisions, Aristocracy and Democracy, a *quasi* refined upper portion, and the *Plebs*. However, American aristocracy is not such as the English is, and the French was ere France became progressive ; an aristocracy purely of birth, with some slight and almost imperceptible admixture of talent. Neither is it the purely poetical aristocracy of Art, Science and Intelligence, such as the old Grecian was, nor one of Protection, exclusively, like the antique Roman Patriciate. It is, simply, an aristocracy of Money. Money is its *Lettre de noblesse*. Money is the diploma of science and intelligence. By money, you are protected and pushed on in the world, and in a purely monetary ratio is the value of an American aristocrat to be computed. You will undoubtedly perceive that this simplifies in an extraordinary manner the value of an individual's stand- ing amongst the " Upper Ten" on this side of the ocean.

The Democracy (pray observe, that I am here speaking in the purely social, rather than the political sense of the term) has not the slightest difference in character from the so-called *Plebs* in any other portion of the known world. Vary, it may, in manners and decorous observances, but not in its radi- cal nature. It is the same fine-hearted, noble-minded, hard- working and stubborn race of men. Not rejoicing in the full blood of the high-mettled racer, as it is far removed from the dull and thistle-eating vitality of the donkey, it may be likened to the laborious, but at times, impracticable mule.

To the American aristocrat, the most important matter, after money, is fashion. After his daily bread, to the Amer- ican democrat, the only desirable thing is amusement. Their life may be summed up in three words. These are—" *Panem et Circenses.*"

You will agree with me, Fiorentino, that the world, in its democratic portion, has not changed much in the last eighteen hundred years of its existence.

Fashion in America obeys the immutable law which has been bestowed upon it from its first birth, when Eve, at the instigation of the serpent, clothed herself in fig-leaves. It is originated, kept up, quitted, resumed, revolutionized, restored, put out of the way, found again and re-baptized by the ladies !

Be quiet, my amiable Fiorentino, and allow me to write to you in my own way. You ask me to give you some informa- tion about the American ladies. How will it be possible for me to impart any to you, which you would think reliable ? You well know that I have always been conspicuous for my bashfully retiring disposition. My internal modesty is so great, whatever others may please to say of me, that it has always been with profound difficulty that I have constrained myself to regard a female in the face, when I am forced to talk with her. The compulsory nature of my professional career has necessitated me in many instances to do this, but, as yet, my bashfulness has remained invincible.

Besides, my friend, you have asked me an unpleasant question. Let me assure you, that in my experience of life, one woman is a more dangerous enemy than twenty men. Should I chance in my modest ignorance to offend the female half of the American nation, all would at once be over with me in this portion of the world. Nothing would remain for me to do, but to pack up, take my berth in the next steamer, and return at once to Europe.

You still insist upon my giving you an answer. How is it to be done, Fiorentino, by one who has never relished putting forth his opinion on politics, woman, religion or cookery?

One man prefers a damsel with flowing auburn ringlets, a blooming cheek, and deep blue eyes, swimming in pearly moisture. Another relishes, with an even keener delight, a plump turkey stuffed with pistachio-nuts. This man cleaves to a religion which 'spunges out the whole of his sins in the confessional-box, and allows him, if he so chooses, to begin a new score with a well-cleansed breast. That individual possesses a quiet and gustatory relish for the government whose liberality permits him a respectable share in its spoils. On the other hand, here is one, who never having by any chance participated in the delight of drawing one red cent from the public purse, anathematizes that government with a truly picturesque delight. This Calvinist heartily abominates the Confessional, and all that appertains to it, in any shape or way. Here is a feeder in a more homely fashion, who gloats upon a broiled rump-steak with fried onions; while his friend is possessed with the chastest of admirations for raven locks and black eyes, gazing in whose slumberous depths he can dream of a life of love and joy.

It must be obvious to you, that he who pretends to dictate to these, is liable to be ostracized by all who do not agree with him.

In order, if possible, therefore, to save myself from such an unpleasant fate, I had scarcely attained the age of eighteen than I shaped my creed, my political belief, and my taste to suit everybody. In other words, I resolved to belong to all tastes and creeds, political or spiritual, in a general way, but to none in particular. Therefore, I believe in God, and endeavor to do my duty, without calling myself Roman Catholic, Episcopalian, Member of the Greek Church, Lutheran, or Presbyterian. In cookery, I make a point of relishing all the delicacies of the season, or of either half of the earth which is at present amenable to the laws of civilization. Halibut, prairie-hen, and bear-steak, are as warmly delighted in by my inner man, as turbot, styrian, pheasant, and a haunch of English venison were wont to be. To me, my dear Fiorentino, all governments are highly respectable, although I own a shadowy preference for that one which gives the slightest sign of its existence. And as for the ladies, let me own to you that but for my invincible modesty, I should consider all of them, without any distinction of nationality, ranging between blushing fifteen and ripened thirty, worthy of my most particular attention.

Do you still insist upon my writing to you as I really think? "Yes!" Do I hear you rightly? Well, then, I suppose I must do so; but in intrusting you with my opinion, remember that I pledge you to the strictest secrecy.

In general, as far as a retiring and bashful man like myself is able to form his judgment, the American lady, saving in her language, assimilates more to the French than to an

English beauty. The *femme comme il faut*, in New York, lacks the physical consistency and solidity, as well as the artlessness of Albion's daughters. In revenge, however, for this, she exhibits all the ease and grace, while she possesses all the consummate taste and elegance of the Parisian dame from the Faubourgs St. Germain, or St. Honoré. Artificially instructed, it has occasionally appeared to me that her ignorance is real. Full of elevated sentiments, she too often sacrifices them to the claims of etiquette and worldly formality. Rather infatuated in favor of an artist or an author, than enthusiastic in her love either of Art or of Literature—imprudent in the first place, afterwards reflecting—she is deliciously coquettish at all times and in all places. In a word, the American lady has a young heart when she has attained the ripe age of forty, but carries an old head upon her shoulders when she yet counts no more than sixteen years upon them. Capable of the greatest sacrifices, nay! of heroism for the man she has honored with her love, she is unable to speak well of another woman. Her life is an admirable concentration of passions, virtues, ambitions, jealousies, loves, mysteries, flirtations, hates, disoppointments, and pleasures. These produce a sort of poetic confusion in her own conscience, and render her not only a problem to others, but an enigma, even to herself. After years of internal struggles, therefore, worn out by the doubt which has proved itself unable to afford her a solution for the intricated and Gordian-like riddle of her own existence, in nine cases out of ten she becomes religious, and in the tenth instance sinks into literature. Whichever it may be, from that moment she exhibits an open contempt, and feels a secret dislike for the younger being, who is then doing what she was wont to do, in her own person.

Two qualities, however, it would seem to me that the American lady almost invariably possesses and retains.

These are a sound common sense in all questions which the heart does not touch, and, at the same time, a natural appreciation for the really grand and beautiful, which would seem to be born actually in her nature.

To this circumstance is it, that the Americans, as a people, are indebted for whatever has been done in this country for artistic cultivation and progress, or for the refinement of life. Hence it is, that up to this very day, the male portion of society visit only in such houses, and patronize such artists and productions as the ladies, in this respect very decidedly the better half of them, have thought proper to seal with their approbation and declare "fashionable." It is little matter whether the gentlemanly section of New York society likes this or that artist, whether it appreciates at all, either music or pictures, or whether it thinks highly of this or that "lion." Scarcely, even, is it necessary that the aforesaid "lion" should have a mane or a tale, or that this picture or the melody in question should be indisputably excellent. Sufficient it is, that Mrs. T—— or the Misses B—— declare them to be worth attention. Some exceptions may occasionally be met with. There are gentlemen who have studied the world as thoroughly, as a man with means and time at his command can always do, but these do not govern taste. The ladies alone do this, at any rate, so far as my limited experience, controlled by my unfortunate modesty, has given me the means of judging on such a subject.

Indeed, beyond the principal cities, it is the ladies alone that patronize and love the Arts. These, alone, know anything about them.

As an illustration of my opinion, you will allow me, my dear friend, to give you an anecdote which actually occurred under my own experience.

Some few years since, I sent two *prima donnas* of reputation, a clever pianist, and a celebrated *basso*, on a concert-tour. On arriving in a city in New England, the agent who preceded them, found that the estimation accorded to these artists in New York, Boston and Philadelphia, had not yet travelled there. They were comparatively unknown. After some reflection, he therefore determined to make the names of the composers, whose pieces were selected for the evening of the concert, a larger feature in the programmes and posters than those of the artists themselves. Consequently, the names of the last-mentioned appeared in small type at the head of the bills, while those of Handel, Bellini, Beethoven and Mozart, occupied the most conspicuous places in them, and rejoiced in the most sizeable letters that the printing-office of the little town was enabled to furnish.

The trick, if trick that could be called which was intended to impose upon no one, and very certainly imposed upon none of the female half of the inhabitants, succeeded.

Two-thirds of the audience were ladies, but the other third of it, which would decidedly not have come to hear anything that anybody could sing, provided that anybody was unknown to them by reputation, consisted of gentlemen. But imagine, my good friend Fiorentino, what was my agent's intense astonishment on the following morning, when, on wishing to settle the hotel-bill for the artists, he found these strange items on that which was handed to him by the very gentlemanly official standing behind the desk of the principal hotel in the place :

"Mr. *Mozart*, Room, Meals, Wine, &c. &c. . . $5 75
Mr. *Handel*, Do, Do, Do, ... 7 50
Mrs. *Bellini*, Room, Meals, Bath and Carriage, 9 00
Mrs. *Beethoven*, Room and Meals, ... 4 50."

Believe me, my dear Fiorentino, when I tell you that this

bill has existed, does exist, and will be, barring accidents, in existence for many years. When we next meet in Paris, I promise you that you shall see it.

But on another occasion, when your correspondent was travelling with the renowned Violinist (for, be assured that in this section of the globe, he ranks as a most distinguished fiddler) Ole Bull, and several other eminent artists, a concert had been advertised in one of the largest of our western cities. It was in the course of being given, and indeed was almost over, when I was standing at the door of the concert-room in close conversation with my treasurer. You may readily enough divine the verbal skeleton of this peculiarly interesting colloquy. As it was going on, a highly respectable and well-dressed individual, who proved to be a western farmer, but who might have been anything else that was doing well in those " diggings," issued from the door of the hall, with both hands plunged into the pockets of that garment which it is impossible for me to name. Looking round him, his eyes lit upon my face, which he seemed to imagine might be the property of one who was an inhabitant of the city for that night only. So, striding up to me, he placed his broad hand, drawn for that purpose from one of his capacious pockets, upon my shoulder, and thus addressed me—

" Look a-here, stranger, do you belong to this show?"

" I have the honor to do so, sir. Can I be of any use to you?"

" Ah! yes. Can't yer let a fellow know when all this confounded fiddling" (what would Ole Bull have said, Fiorentino, could he have heard this?) " will come to an end?"

" Don't you like the music, sir?" I blandly inquired.

" Wall! I guess I do like the music, too."

At this I smiled pleasantly, and made him a graceful bow.

4

In those younger days, my friend, I was not considered altogether devoid of grace.

"But it has lasted quite long enough." Here the treasurer laughed. "I say, what's that darned fellow grinning at?" At my questioner's indignant look, the official's face relapsed into an aspect of the most stolid inanity. "I've a great mind to 'lam' him." The treasurer walked off, quaking in his boots. "Wall! he's gone. All the better for him. But, stranger! why don't yer begin with the show? I would just like to see the 'Bull,' that's sartain, and then I'd to home."

Matters are, however, far otherwise in those cities which border on the broad Atlantic. Here the public is now, musically, exceedingly intelligent, and will no longer endure anything which may be considered artistically second-rate. In New York, more especially, Italian Opera is not only well understood, but it is one of the "fashions;" and when it was beginning to take its place in the world of American Art, I was selected by the proprietors of the Astor Place Opera House to become its Manager. This was in the midsummer of 1849.

Then, very young, very unwise, very enthusiastic, I was, in spite of that natural modesty to which I have elsewhere alluded, *un homme à la mode*. Fortune, in spite of her bandaged eyes, seemed to smile upon me.

Now, alas! it is quite different. My years are in their wane, and my body is becoming stout and widening into heaviness. Somewhat wiser, and considerably more phlegmatic, I am no longer "in the fashion," and find I have something about ten years more to work, in order to repay my losses of time, and, consequently, of money, when I stepped forward as the destined generator (such, Fiorentino, was my absurd idea) of musical taste in my adopted country.

You will lift your eyes in reading this, and demand how it can be possible? Full of your exclusively Parisian ideas on management, you will inquire whether I did not receive the Opera House free of rent? You will ask what has become of my *subvention* of half a million of francs per year? whether I have not been secured by " privilege " against all opposition; and, if at my retirement from the dignity of directing the Italian Opera, the subscribers, the government, or my immediate successor were not obliged to make good my losses?

Fiorentino, musical matters may be managed in this way at Paris and in other places in Europe. In America, their management is a purely different thing. Here, every business or undertaking, whether an Opera or slaughter-house, a soap-factory or a public library, a railway or a monument to Daniel Webster, is a private speculation. The success of an enterprise depends upon one of two features,— the general utility of the work, or the amount it realizes. In the one case, he who has inaugurated it, may possibly starve. In the last, should he know how to preserve as well as he has made his profits, he will die wealthy. The merit of a speculative man is estimated by the rate of discount at which his notes are taken. His qualities, excellencies and errors, are valued in relation with the balance of his account in a Wall Street Bank. His merits are simply estimated by the amount of specie in his possession. Should he be able to draw a cheque for one or two hundred thousand dollars, every body will decide favorably with regard to his *talent*. Could he call for double this amount with the certainty of finding it, he would undoubtedly be regarded as a man of genius. Were he puzzled to find a dollar of his own for immediate necessities, beyond any suspicion, he must be a fool.

Divine, Fiorentino, in which class of estimation your correspondent is held? Perhaps not in the last, but very certainly in neither of the two first.

However, to return to my subject, the lease of the Astor Place Opera House was mine, not free of rent, but at the rate of something near twelve thousand dollars *per annum*, which sum was either payable in advance, or to be taken from the first 152 subscribers for the season. Instead of a *subvention* to assist the speculation, it was arranged that each proprietor should take ten seats for the whole season—gratis: —there are, as a general rule, dear friend, many benevolent proprietors to one house. So far from insuring the Director against all opposition, it was determined that the amount of subscription-money beyond the rent, for the season, should remain in the hands of a trustee until the fulfilment of all promises on the part of the said Director and Manager.

One of the proprietors, by name Mr. James Foster, jun., a gentleman of fashion, benevolently undertook this task. It may be presumed that during the season, he made a quarter *per cent.* every day out of it, by accommodating his mercantile friends or "shaving" notes.

Should the Manager, however, be in need of more than his fortnightly share of it, he had to run down to Wall Street. Here, he would have the satisfaction of ascertaining that the pecuniary success of his enterprise stood at a low figure in the market, by the peculiarly high rate of discount *imposed* upon his note in more senses than one.

But, at least, you say to me,—" The operatic *habitués*, those who loved music, did something to enable you to bring over a good company."

Yes! They gave me many promises; but no money.

However, I am mistaken. Amongst them there was one real lover of melody, not for the sake of fashion, but for the sake of Art itself. This was Mr. Henry A. Coit, a *virtuoso* of the right stamp. Indeed, could twenty-four more like him have been found in New York, the Opera would long since have been an established fact in this city.

He took my part when I complained to the Committee of the proprietors who had expressly promised pecuniary aid, although they would not insert it as a condition in the lease, and headed a subscription-list for my support with his own name for several hundred dollars. His example was followed. But, what Mr. Coit may probably have considered as a *gift*, they regarded as a *loan*, which was made payable from the first receipts of the Opera House.

Had not several artists been already engaged by me, it is more than probable I should have at once thrown up the speculation.

Let me also ask you, how much you may imagine was the amount of this loan, given under such conditions, which should enable me to bring out a new company from Europe? Judging from those fabulous sums which private speculators have secured and paid to single artists in America, you will imagine that I needed an infinitely larger one, to induce a whole company to visit these shores. The reports of the liberality of the middle and lower classes in this country, will have induced you to believe that the " Upper Ten," the *crême* of fashionable society, the *fleur des pois* of taste and refinement in the New World, now distinguished themselves by at the very least as prodigal an outlay. Do not suffer your imagination to be too highly exalted, my amiable Fiorentino. My patrons liberally handed me, on leaving New York, a letter of credit for £540 (!) payable in London, sixty days after sight, (this was very nearly the time at which it was to be repaid by me, here,) and took from me, in exchange, a transfer of the reciepts until the re-payment of the afore-said £540.

Several weeks after this, £50 more, as a second *loan*, were received by me, when in London, with a kind and encouraging letter.

In this most remarkable document, the belief was expressed, that the "large sums" then at my disposal, would enable me to bring over Grisi and Mario (!), or afford a strong inducement for Jenny Lind and Lablache to visit this country.

Need I say to you, that I made not the slightest attempt to persuade these artists to do this? The means in my hands absolutely forbade this satisfaction to the proprietors of, and subscribers to the Astor Place Opera House. To Cruvelli I however did speak. At that period, she was ready to visit America, with her sister, the *contralto*, for the paltry sum of ten thousand francs *per* month. She, however, demanded an engagement of ten months and the usual advance of one-fifth. This was too much for the large means which had been so liberally placed at my disposal. However, let me candidly confess that I did not dare expose my pecuniary condition to a leading *soprano*, although she was an old acquaintance of mine. Ashamed, both of my own position and for that of the prodigal proprietors and subscribers, sooner than compromise my own reputation or injure the future prospects of Opera in New York, I preferred leaving the charming Cruvelli without any definitive answer. Should any one now wish to engage her to visit this continent, he must pay five times as much as she then asked. The whole amount of the salary must be secured her. Servants, hotel expenses, and carriage hire, will also have to come out of the pocket of the enterprising *entrepreneur*. Yet, I candidly believe, Cruvelli was at that period to the full as great an artist as she is now.

Another vocalist was then offered me through the agency of Bonola of Milan.

This was Raffaelle Mirate, the *tenor*, who asked six thousand francs *per* month.

Believing him too dear at this price, although he was then young and fresh, this offer was declined by me. Yet, six years later, he managed to get an engagement in New York at eighteen thousand francs *per* month, with one clear benefit, and this when he has added six years to his age, and, in great measure, used up his voice.

But, there was another acquisition of immensely more importance which I could at this time have made, had I chosen so to do.

This individual, or acquisition, was no other and nothing less than that man of many talents, the Chevalier Henry Wikoff.

The opportunity of securing his co-operation in management was offered me at the Hotel de Bâde, where he introduced himself with surpassing suavity and ease of manner, proposing that I should either secure his services as a partner in the concern, general diplomatist in its affairs, or more specially as the Manager of the New York Press. Under the seal of the most profound secresy (believe not that I should violate it, my dear Fiorentino, had he not himself removed the veil for all who would listen to him) he confided to me that he was, at that time, engaged in arranging the preliminaries of a marriage for one of the principal members of the Buonaparte family, as well as in settling the monetary affairs of a personage of high standing in the political world. At the same time, he graciously gave me to understand, that having formerly been mixed up with musical matters, through the toes of Fanny Ellsler, he should feel a very decided preference for the operatic line of business. Indeed, he hinted, that through his then influence with the Prince-President (now the Emperor Louis Napoleon) he might, could, and would in time, obtain the privilege of managing the Grand Opera at Paris for him and myself. Consequently, he should feel not the slightest hesitation in abandoning the marriage which he had then on the *tapis*, and suffering the monetary matters to arrange themselves for the well-known personage in question.

This, you will at once confess, my friend, was a truly captivating offer of alliance to one who had such a slight personal experience in management as myself.

However, I naturally required some little time to weigh it in my own mind, before coming to any determination, and declined giving him a response at the moment. Luckily, I was induced to make some inquiries respecting the Chevalier, and learnt from the very best authority (this was, as I presume there will be no harm in my mentioning the name, Dr. Conneau, who was, or had been, the private physician to the Prince-President) the real position and occupation of the Chevalier.

His advice was clear in the extreme—" that it would be best for me to have nothing to do with the man."

Was it not natural for me to believe, therefore, that the marriage preliminaries on which the Chevalier was then engaged, were those of some princess of the *Treizième Arrondissement* with the *valet de place* of one of his intimates, and that the pecuniary negotiations in which he was interested, might in all probability lie between himself and the director of a *Mont de Pieté;* while, it was by no means improbable that his acquaintance with the Prince-President, might resemble that of the English peasant with his Grace the great Duke of Marlborough.

This individual, my amiable Fiorentino, was standing at the gate of his lordship's house, anxiously waiting to see the renowned General leave it, and enter his carriage.

His curiosity somewhat interfered with his politeness, for you know that all Englishmen are by nature most excruciatingly polite. Nay ! he actually impeded his Grace's movements, whereupon, the Duke spoke to him.

His words were these: " Can't you get out of the way, you d—d jackanapes ?"

Overwhelmed with joy by this gracious specimen of Ducal condescension, the peasant was accustomed all his lifetime to brag of this distinction. And in the long winter evenings, he would narrate to his children and grandchildren, as they sat around the brick fireplace, and the log of freshly cut wood smouldered and crackled before them into flame, how, in his younger days, he had the honor of being spoken to by the great Duke of Marlborough.

It may be considered as no improbability, that in some way or other, the Chevalier learnt money was not at all so plentiful with me as he had at first supposed.

At the least, it may be supposed so, from the circumstance of his soon afterwards retiring from his previous application to me, and starting upon that Gamble-ing speculation which secured him such a pressing invitation from the officials of the Castle of St. Andrea, in Genoa. Indeed, this invitation was so imperative, that it admitted no possibility of declining it, by any exertion of his diplomatic skill and subtlety.

It was fully six years later, that he obtained the situation of Acting Manager at the Academy of Music, under Messrs. Phalen and Coit, which I had so carefully avoided giving him at the Astor Place Opera House. But, let me, my dear Fiorentino, to my shame confess, that had I then been fully aware of his managerial capacity, and myself known as much of management as I have since learnt, it would have, beyond a doubt, been far better to have taken him when he offered himself to me. So admirably did he manage for these gentlemen, that in three short months, crowded houses lost them more money than I had myself done in six years. It would have been infinitely better for *me*, and more lucky for *Mr. Wikoff* and the *public*, had I been then as wise as now, and associated him in my enterprise. With his aid, my managerial career would have ended after three months instead of six years of struggles, and in that case *I* should have saved more than five years of my valuable time. Mr. Wikoff would have avoided the troubles attendant upon " His Courtship," and the public have escaped the annoyances of reading " Its Consequences."

You will therefore see that I was actually obliged, through my ignorance of the future, to manage my business alone. This I did, and ultimately brought together a highly respectable company. Considering the small means at my disposal, it might fairly be considered a very creditable one, consisting of Mademoiselle Bertucca, Signora Truffi, who had figured in the Fry management, Signora Borghese, Signori Forti, Guidi, Beneventano, Novelli, and others.

At that time, when the public of New York had not yet been accustomed to the Jenny Linds, Sontags, Albonis, Grisis, Marios and Lagranges, who have since bewitched them out of their dollars, it was a decidedly good Operatic Company, and compared with the Fasciotti and Castrone *troupe*, brought over by Mr. W. H. Fry, it might safely have been called an immense one. Moreover, they gave satisfaction to the public, and under my direction, this Company, consisting mostly of Italians, gave sixty consecutive performances without a single postponement, and even without one solitary alteration in the bills announcing the evening's entertainment. This will, I know, appear almost incredible to you, but, nevertheless, Fiorentino, it is a fact.

As regards the positive standing of the artists themselves,

they were good, without approaching the planetary proportion of modern stars. Of Signora Truffi, I have already spoken, in a letter which Berlioz will show you. With Mademoiselle Bertucca, there is one little circumstance connected, which permits neither eulogy nor criticism upon my part. In spite of that unconquerable bashfulness which is mine by nature, she has become my wife. It would be useless upon your part, Fiorentino, to ask me how this chanced. Such, she undoubtedly is. At the first a favorite, she lost her primary *prestige* with the public by marrying her Manager. Nevertheless, in your ear, my friend, I may whisper my conviction that she is an excellent artist, and one that can always be depended upon. Were I to say more, you might bid me refrain from eulogizing the better portion of my individuality; wherefore, it may perhaps be best for her that I should remain silent.

Our first night was in the month of November, 1849, and was very successful.

The entire press, with one solitary exception, supported me. They seemed determined upon giving me a fair trial. Had I, indeed, received the tenth part of the aid and support given me at this period by the press, from the proprietors and subscribers, I might possibly have avoided all pecuniary loss, and established, through my own proper efforts, a sound and critical musical taste in America.

You will observe that I have mentioned one solitary exception in the press, and you will be astonished to hear that this was the only journal which exclusively lays claim to a "fashionable" position in New York. One of its editors, Mr. Nathaniel P. Willis, was at this time the "fashionable" writer. He embroidered his articles in the *Home Journal*, with peculiarly graceful English, and served the female world as its paid professor of *etiquette*. His weekly contributions dictated their fashionable duties. Shining as an instructor in deportment, and a preceptor in manners, he also endeavored to grasp at the rank of a Master of Ceremonies. In a word, he attempted to dictate to them on matters of taste, and felt the task of teaching them how to pose their feet on entering a ball-room, or how to sink their eyes when a gentleman might "pop" the all-important question, much too small for his ambition. Like himself and his occupations, are his writings. He possesses a highly refined language, a style of extreme elegance and finish, but a wonderful paucity of striking ideas. Like the banquet set before the Barmecide, there are splendid China dishes and gold spoons. Vases of silver and a profusion of flowers abound, but unfortunately there is *no* meat. Mental starvation is a necessity for him, who would sit down and enjoy a feast of the soul, with N. P. Willis.

Fortunately for me, the ladies of New York were not disposed to be hoodwinked by their self-elected Master of Ceremonies, or my fate must have been a woeful one. I was more bitterly persecuted by this dapper mosquito, than ever the unfortunate Fry had been by Bennett. Vatel never suffered as much from you, Fiorentino, as I did from N. P. Willis. Jules Janin's persecution of Roqueplan was not to be named with this untoward visitation.

What could I do? I might have sued him for damages accruing to me from his libels, as Mr. Fry had done with the Editor of the *Herald.* He had charged me with robbing the subscribers of their money, when, it was only by superhuman exertions, I was enabled to carry on the season. From an excellent lawyer, therefore, did I take advice, but to my astonishment he asked me where the *Home Journal* was published, and assured me the verdict would be for so small an amount, being proportioned in all probability to the standing of the journal, that it would fail to pay him his expenses.

"As for you, my dear Max," he said with a courtly smile,

"it would, I feel certain, altogether depend upon the results of your season."

On leaving his office, deeply chagrined to find my vague prospect of twenty thousand dollars damages (!) melting away, a bright idea occurred to me. Why not imitate Roqueplan? Fascinated by the thought of a newspaper duel, which possesses all the charms of a personal rencounter, without any of its dangers, I rushed home. My letter was written and published. War was begun. At it we went, and, in a short space of time, the laughers had changed sides.

Neither one nor the other of us sustained any great amount of damage from the interchange of our paper pellets. Materially, I candidly believe we have both been benefited.

The whole of the Opera-*habitués* of the middle classes, all of its *employés*, from the *prima donna* and leading *tenor* to the call-boys and supernumeraries who had never before so much as heard of the existence of the *Home Journal* and the "fashionable" notoriety who wrote upon it, purchased and read it. They naturally relished the verbal insolence to which their Manager was weekly, with a consistent regularity of the most exemplary order, exposed. On the other side, all of the readers of N. P. Willis's operatic diatribes, who had never yet dreamt of visiting me, before the curtain, now came. Their object being simply and solely, to get a sight of the unfortunate monster, weekly knocked down and laid out for inspection by the agreeable and accomplished journalist.

It is possible, that had Mr. Willis known the circumstances, and the real amount of means placed in my hands to carry on the Opera, he might have transposed his critical disquisitions into a less bitter key, and managed to keep in time and tune with the other journals. Let me own to you, my dear friend, in a quiet way, that if this had chanced to be the case, I should most deeply have regretted it.

But to you, more especially, beloved Fiorentino, a few jottings upon musical criticism, and those who deal with it in the New World, may, possibly, not be devoid of interest. You shall have them.

First, then, let me tell you we have a real live French Baron amongst us, M. R. De Trobriand, who writes in the *Courrier des Etats-Unis*. Ordinarily, he is a warm friend to the Opera, and a kindly adviser to artists. However, should the *prima donna* forget to smile on him, or the *primo tenore* not raise his hat sufficiently, in salutation, he will grow a trifle savage, and forget (even as you and I have sometimes done, Fiorentino) the first duty of a professional critic —impartiality. M. De Trobriand is a Baron by birth, a musical critic by necessity, and a *barytone*-singer by inclination. It may further be said, that he writes as good French as any Baron can be expected to do, and sings as well as may be desired from any musical critic. His style, as a *feuilletoniste,* may be considered verging on the *Rococo*. *Bon-mots* from the *Epoque de la Régence*, with refrains from old *Operas Comiques*, sprinkle his criticisms. Nevertheless, he uses the pen with sense, a great deal of wit and truly Parisian ease, while he was the first successful transplanter of the *Revue-feuilleton* in America.

The *Courier and Enquirer* gives cleverly-written and generally dispassionate notices on Music and the Drama. These only appear at rare intervals, and on great occasions.

In the *Daily Times*, impartial reports are to be found, spiced with witty remarks, and mingled with acute and shrewd observation.

One daily paper alone attempts to give anything like theoretical criticism. This is the *Tribune*. But its critical disquisitions may be said, my dear friend, to be rather anatomical dissections of the form, than psychological observations upon the spirit of music. The present musical critic of this journal, for, at the time of which I am speaking, it had not yet taken so scientific a position, uses in every ten or a dozen words some four or five technical expressions. By this simple means, he has the satisfaction of rendering his writing unintelligible to the general reader, while it is of no service to the practical musician. You and I know, Fiorentino, that what may be good for the mere student, is useless to the composer, and incomprehensible to the amateur. In short, the mathematical rules of music are not the music itself. They are simply its physical conditions, in the same way as the theory of distributing and balancing color cannot be esteemed the art of painting.

Correct judgments upon Art are generally given in the *Albion* and *Weekly Dispatch*, but in some of the other scores upon scores of papers published in New York, you may occasionally discover that "'Lucrezia Borgia' is a sparkling comic Opera, written by Rossini," that "the 'Barber of Seville' is the best thing Verdi has ever given to the musical public," or, that "the ladies of the Chorus in 'Rigoletto' (which contains no female Chorus) were dreadfully out of tune." Perhaps you will be informed, "that the magnificent *contralto* notes of Jenny Lind constituted the secret of her triumph," or, that "the *Ut de poitrine* of Benedetti rivals, in its power, that of the huge Lablache." Only figure to yourself, my good friend, the despair of that Titan of all *bassi*, past, present, and to come, should he ever conceive that there are musical critics actually in existence, who believe in his physical possession of a mythical *Ut de poitrine*.

But, let me return once more to my narration of those events which were connected with my *début* in American Musical Management.

Although the sixty performances of the season took place

without the slightest disappointment to the public, it must not be presumed that they could be given, without difficulties and annoyances of the most serious description to the Manager.

Was there ever any Manager, whose luck saved him from annoyance and difficulty?

No! Fiorentino. That man who is destined to be a Manager, is, most indubitably, not born with a silver spoon in his mouth. It was only my enthusiasm for the Art, and a lying confidence in the future, which gave me the energy and the capacity for perseverance.

Let me detail to you one of the numerous mischances, on which I can now pleasantly lay the finger of my recollection.

At the last rehearsal but one of the "Maria di Rohan," never before placed upon the stage in this part of the world, great carelessness was evinced by some of the members of the Orchestra. Indeed, matters went worse with them at this than they had done at the first rehearsal. Growing nervous for the consequences of this unwonted negligence upon their part, I rebuked the offending portion with considerable asperity. The last—a Dress Rehearsal—was to come off upon the same evening. More than a hundred of the subscribers had received invitations to attend it, and were already in the house. But, on entering the Orchestra, I found myself alone there, with some two or three only out of its forty-two members. It was evident that a conspiracy had taken place, and I at once hastened upon the stage. Here, a messenger met me from them, who informed me, that the absent members had determined neither to attend rehearsal nor performance, until a public apology had been made by me, for the intemperate expressions I had made use of, that morning. At the same time, with a *naïveté* peculiar to the musical profession in this country, he invited me to step round to a bar-room near the theatre, in which they were assembled, and register that apology.

You know me of old, my friend, and may consequently divine what answer was given to the mutineers.

Pulling out my watch, I told them that if they had not determined on returning to their duties, unconditionally, in fifteen minutes, they might one and all consider themselves discharged.

Had the offended parties themselves personally spoken to me, immediately after the morning rehearsal, the difficulty might have been settled long before evening, but it was impossible to offer them any apology under such circumstances as the present. The next day, the Chorus would have hoisted the flag of insurrection—the tailors and tailoresses would have gotten up a charming little *émeute*—the firemen would have determined upon striking; and, as for the three *prima donnas*, Heaven only knows what they might have done. It was clear to me that the difficulty had to be overcome, and my course was therefore determined upon. Fifteen minutes had passed, and none of the refractory fiddlers appeared. In consequence of this, I was obliged to adjourn the rehearsal, and declare the whole of the malcontents discharged, on account of their wilful breach of contract.

So far, Fiorentino, so good. But, "Maria di Rohan" was announced for the following evening, and, at that time, it was believed by me, that the postponement of an Opera would terminate my career as a musical notoriety, and that my pecuniary death was involved in the protest of a note.

You laugh, my good friend. Alas! what strange illusions we are subject to, in our youthful advance upon a knowledge of this world!

Keenly alive to this idea, I began immediately to revolve what was to be done, and in half an hour more, the only two remaining members of the Orchestra, the Stage-manager, Orchestra-librarian, and every available personage in the theatre, had started with myself in search of musical recruits. They were impressed everywhere. We seized them in the streets. Descents were made upon the highly moral dancing-houses. Fiddlers were taken from the vessels of war in the harbor. That night, no musician was secure. He was enlisted wherever he might be found. At *five in the following morning*, we had collected a new Orchestra. At *seven o'clock*, the first rehearsal was called, with closed doors. The key was in my breeches' pocket. There was not the slightest possibility of escape for any one of them. When *ten had stricken*, breakfast, prepared by my orders, was served in the green-room. At *eleven*, we had the second rehearsal. Dinner was ready at *two o'clock* for every body. The third rehearsal was called on, at *three precisely*. When it had concluded, at *a quarter after six*, the doors were unlocked, and they had permission given them to retire for one hour. At *eight o'clock*, the performance of the Opera of "Maria di Rohan" had commenced. When *eleven* struck, a complete triumph over insubordination in the ranks of my Orchestra had been achieved, and at *midnight* I was in bed and sound asleep, after forty hours of unremitted labor and continuous anxiety.

You may divine, my friend, the wrath of the discharged fiddlers. Suffice it to say, that it actually beggars the attempt of my imperfect English to describe it.

All was, however, useless, and my mode of dealing with so flagrant a case of insubordination, had, I am happy to say, a subsequently most salutary influence over the Orchestras in New York generally, and, perhaps, more especially with those over whom I had the honor to preside.

After this occurrence matters progressed very smoothly,

and the benevolent proprietors and subscribers, touched by the visible harmony that reigned this year, so far as they might see, (for when, Fiorentino, was there ever a real harmony amongst the sons and daughters of Melody?) in the Astor Place Opera House, and which caused them no trouble whatever, determined at last, so they said, to do something for my advantage.

Touched by the unanimity of this determination, one of the proprietors of the Opera House to whom I have elsewhere alluded, sent for me, and the following conversation ensued. He also was determined to *do* for me. Should there be anything equivocal in this expression, remember, my amiable Fiorentino, that I am not writing in my native Teutonic. Consequently, you must ascribe me a wide margin in my English phraseology.

" My dear Max !" he said in the most affectionate of manners, on seeing me ; " do you know that you are very poor in good scenery ?"

" I have quite enough to do, sir, in paying my salaries, and procuring dresses, music and properties."

" Well, I am inclined to help you," he continued, with one of the blandest of truly benevolent smiles upon his countenance. " Listen to me. There is some splendid scenery in the Opera House, which has been painted by Allegri."

I nodded my head in answer to this observation, for I knew it.

" It formerly belonged to Mr. Fry, but has been mortgaged."

My reply was, that I was well aware of this fact.

He looked sharply into my face, but was apparently satisfied, by its immobility, that I knew no more. Accordingly, he continued. " In default of the payment of the mortgage, the whole of this scenery will be sold to-morrow by the

Sheriff. Now, supposing that I should lend you the money necessary for its purchase—"

" Upon what conditions?" I immediately inquired.

You must allow, my friend, that this was an exceedingly natural question upon my part.

" Conditions!" he repeated after me. " Oh! they shall not be hard ones. I presume that you might get it for something close upon two thousand dollars. It is worth five," he parenthetically observed. " Now, if you choose to transfer to me the first hundred dollars of your receipts for the ensuing twenty performances, you shall have the money. *Or, possibly, it might be better for me to pay it, myself, to the Sheriff.*"

" I will think over the matter, sir, and, should it appear advisable, I shall certainly avail myself of your kind offer."

So saying, I left him, firmly convinced in my own mind that this gentleman, and nobody else than this gentleman himself, was the mortgagee. Or, rather, that he was the mortgagee on behalf of the proprietors, who, instead of benefiting me by allowing my management the use of this scenery, actually wished to make me pay in the above manner the debts of Mr. E. P. Fry. Fortunately, my suspicions had been aroused by his unwonted familiarity, and I was consequently prepared for him.

On the morrow, I accordingly sent my head-carpenter, Mr. Tunison, a true and confidential friend, to the auction, with the order, upon my account, to bid five hundred dollars for the scenery, and on no account to go beyond this figure.

Nobody appeared at the auction, save Tunison and the Sheriff.

Tunison offers one hundred dollars, and the Sheriff himself caps the offer with double that amount. Tunison, then, says three hundred, and the Sheriff makes a bid of four. Matters are progressing very rapidly. Five hundred is offered by Tunison. "Six hundred!" says the Sheriff.

Tunison, then, takes up his hat and leaves the room.

For a moment, the Sheriff looked decidedly astonished. But he had his private instructions not to sell, save at a certain amount. What was he to do? This did not require a very lengthy consideration. Obedient to his instructions, and with the keenest of noses for his own *per*-centage, he proceeded with the sale.

"Seven hundred dollars!" he ejaculated. "This lot of truly splendid scenery, painted by Allegri, in a style that completely rubs out the English scene-painter Stanfield, and leaves his rival, Turner, nowhere, is going at seven hundred—"

"Eight! did you say, sir, for these magnificent works of art? Eight hundred dollars! Going—going—going. Does nobody bid more?"

"One thousand!" he interrupts himself with, bowing to an imaginary individual in a far corner of the room. "On my honor—not as a Sheriff, but an auctioneer—" he in all likelihood prudently added, "it is dirt cheap. Fifteen hundred! Ah! we are now approaching the real figure. Going— going. It completely whips Delacroix out of the field. Horace Vernet couldn't touch it. Does nobody say more than fifteen hundred? Going—going. Two thousand dollars! Two thousand for the first—for the second—for the— Will nobody bid more? Two thousand dollars for the third time! Gone—to ——!" Here, he named my kindly adviser, who had so benevolently offered to advance me the money necessary for the purchase.

"Not altogether a bad half-hour's work!" said the Sheriff, as he sat down and made out a bill of sale and of his *per* centage, which, it is to be presumed, he presented to his employer, with his congratulations.

Half an hour afterwards, I again saw this gentleman, at his request.

"How is it," asked he, "that you have let such an opportunity escape you?"

"I have changed my mind. I shall have new scenery painted."

"This scenery is perfectly new. Now I will make a bargain with you, and sell or hire it to you."

"Well! sir," said I, "let us make a bargain. First of all, let me ask you whether you have been paid the rent for the house?"

"Certainly!" he replied. "The hundred and fifty-two subscribers have all paid."

"Then," I rejoined, as coldly as a cake of ice sliced in winter from the Wenham Lake, "the house is mine until October next. Therefore, I request you to remove your property in the next twenty-four hours, or to pay me storage for it."

He immediately flew into a wild passion, but I coolly told him, that unless he had the whole of his scenery removed by twelve o'clock on the next day, Mr. Tunison would be instructed to have it all placed in the middle of the street.

The next day, he, in his turn, called upon me, and it was then agreed that the scenery should remain in the Opera House, and that, instead of storage-money, I should have the right to use it.

He never forgave me this trick, my dear Fiorentino, and used to say that—"it was suggested by a Yankee, as no foreigner would have had sufficient wit." It must be said, my friend, that in uttering this opinion he most prodigiously overrates his own skill, and underrates that of the Yankees. Unfortunately, Teutonic as I am, I certainly proved one too many for him, in this instance, and that, unassisted.

As has been previously mentioned, the subscribers to the Opera House wished to demonstrate to me their satisfaction with my management, and to do something for the Manager. They accordingly proposed to give three Fancy Balls, or more, if successful, for my benefit. But, you must not imagine that a fancy ball in New York bears any resemblance to the tumultuous thronging and headlong gaiety of a *bal masqué* at Paris. Masks are here prohibited, and at fancy balls in this city, the visitor may appear in the dress that pleases him best and becomes him least, with the full consciousness of the awkwardness of a novel costume written upon his bared face As a natural consequence of this, he moves as stiffly, and dances as awkwardly as the wooden figures in front of the instrument of a Piedmontese organ-grinder, until his limbs begin to be loosened, and he forgets the strangeness of his unwonted attire, under the influence of a flask of Champagne, or the stronger and fuller body of a Burgundy. Moreover, fancy balls come with sufficient rarity to tempt no great amount of variety in the costumes. The same *Julius Cæsar* and the same *Vestal*, in dress at least, appear at all. *Don Juan* and *Zerlina* are always to be found together. The French Vice-Consul will make his entry as a *Bedouin*, and the Gambler figures there as a Gentleman of the old school. Mrs. B— displays her curls and diamonds as *Madame Pompadour*, which character she must have assumed some dozen times. The lovely Mrs. W— and her two even fairer sisters, shine there as the *Three Graces*, while you might chance even to light upon Mr. C—, doing the character of *Adonis*, stereotyped upon memory, by his persistent appearance in its remarkably tight unmentionables.

Sufficient be it, that my faith in fancy dress balls was of

the most homœopathic character. It was obviously impossible that three of them could succeed.

In consequence of this conviction, which I entertained, young as I was in New York life, and which is still entertained by me, I requested as a favor that these balls might be simply full dress ones. This favor was granted me, and then, a dozen of the most fashionable gentlemen formed a committee, and took the business in their own hands. Nothing was required of me, except the preparation and decoration of the Opera House for the occasion. These were, it must be confessed, sufficiently onerous in the matter of expense. Firstly, a new flooring had to be provided for the house, and six hundred dollars were demanded for this alone. The decorations for the stage required an expenditure of four hundred. Then, one of the committee spoke with me. He wished to have two Orchestras, as one would scarcely be heard in the buzz and movement of the enormous crowd which was expected by them. Another suggested that I might as well procure new carpets for the lobbies; while a third intimated that ranges of flowers (it was then, Fiorentino, in the month of January) should be placed on either side of the principal staircase; and a fourth kindly advised that refreshments should be provided gratis, for the ladies. To all this, need it be said, that I, in my innocence, unhesitatingly assented.

The day of the ball at length drew near, and no advertisement of it was to be seen. Upon my inquiring the reason of this, I was informed that nearly the whole of the tickets had been already disposed of, and that advertising would, most certainly, be an unnecessary expense.

It is superfluous to say that such a result of the labors of the committee delighted me, and that this delight, upon my part, actually ordered more flowers and refreshments.

But two days previously, some of my personal friends had

applied for tickets to some of its members, and could obtain none. It was moreover told me, that strangers stopping at the principal hotels had offered large prices to secure an admission. It was, however, too late. When informed of this, although filled with regret for the disappointment of my friends, I was overwhelmed with joy upon my own account. Rubbing my hands warmly together, I executed a *pas seul* in my own room, which would most certainly have astonished St. Leon, and dispatched orders for a larger quantity of flowers and more refreshments. Experience, Fiorentino, had not yet taught me, how little dependence it was prudent to place upon those whose labors we do not pay for.

At length, the long-expected evening arrived. In order to enjoy the *coup d'œil* on entering the crowded ball-room, I repaired thither tolerably late.

Judge of my astonishment, my friend, when, on entering the wide *salon*, mine eyes fell on no more than some two or three hundred persons. It is true that these were the *crême de la crême* of New York society. But was this any consolation, to one whose pockets had been emptied to afford them an evening's amusement? There they were, a select little party of intimate acquaintances, amusing themselves upon my premises, ordering waltzes and polkas from my two Orchestras, eating my refreshments and destroying my flowers, after having excluded from the ball not only my personal friends, but that trusting, generous, and sympathetic friend who, alone, has ever tendered me an unwavering support, and whenever I have trusted to it alone, has rarely, ought I not to say, never failed me—the New York public. Suffice it, that I left the ball-room, annoyed with their callous egotism, but far more angered with myself for having in the slightest degree trusted them.

Of course, the expenses of this ball very far overrun the

receipts from it; but no one dreamt, for so much as one moment, of making up the difference between them, to me. They seemed to imagine that it was my speculation, and carried their indifference so far, as not even to hint their regret that it had failed, or offer me their acknowledgments for the hospitality which I had offered them. Need you be informed, that the other two balls did not take place?

This untoward result, combined with the everlasting outlays in music, dresses, and properties unavoidable in a Manager's first season, brought me considerably in arrear in my pecuniary affairs. My pockets were not only empty, but I was in debt to an amount of many thousand dollars.

Not despairing, however, and believing that the turn must be well at hand, I placed the " Don Giovanni" of Mozart in rehearsal.

Promises had been made of its production, regularly, by all Managers, for the last fifteen years. Some twenty years previously, it had been rendered by the Garcia *troupe* when in this country. This time, I had made up my mind not to depend on the proprietors, and in a measure, to abjure any dependence upon the " Upper Ten." Those to whom I appealed, were that public which I had hitherto been managed into a neglect of. Nor did they fail me.

The Opera of " Don Giovanni" brought me support from all classes, and attracted persons of all professions and every description to the Opera House. Fourteen consecutive evenings was it played to crowded houses. This Opera, alone, enabled me to conclude the season and satisfy all demands made upon my exchequer.

Nor is this the first time Mozart's matchless master-piece has saved some poor devil of a Manager from ruin. It is truly wonderful how, not only the music, but the mere plot of this Opera, interests the public, in all and every country in which it may be performed. Indeed, there is no tale which, under forms so multiple and various, has so often been employed by poets in almost every land, as the "Don Juan," if I possibly except the more mystical and absurd fable of the "Faust." These two subjects would seem never to lose their attraction or to fail in the interest which they attempt to excite, in whatsoever shape they may be presented to us. As Romance or Tragedy, Ballet, Poem, or Opera, they have, in turn, for more than two hundred years, exercised their influence over all mankind. "Don Juan Tenorio" is the title of a drama by a Spanish author, whose name is Zorilla, that supplied Molière with the plot of his "Don Juan." The Italian poet Da Ponte wrote the *libretto* for Mozart's Opera. In Germany, Grabbe and others have adopted the same fable, while the English "Byron" has stolen the name and married it immortally to his own verse as a "Don Juan" of his own. Still more, has the weird imagination of Faust's thirst for the secrets of Infinity offered an inexhaustible mine to all poets and musicians. Even in 1587, a certain Johann Spies had published in Teutchland, the romance of "Faust." In 1594, a Dutchman named Toleth Shotus edited a tale called "Faustus," which he admits having translated from the Spanish. Theophilo di Adama, a Sicilian writer, composed somewhat later an Italian legend with the title of "Faust." The French, in the olden time, played mysteries which were known under the name of "Faust." Contemporary with William Shakspeare, was an English dramatist called "Marlow," who wrote a play upon the same subject. Spohr founded his well-known Opera upon this fable. Ballets almost innumerable have been welded upon this subject. Scarcely a writer of dance-music, to a consistent plot, but has felt it incumbent upon him to treat *Faust* to a few *pas* in some shape or other.

Goethe has consecrated the myth by adopting it to his own subtle and quaint intelligence, while Byron has impudently seized upon it, as he had done upon the name of *Don Juan*, and converted it into a shape bearing no more than a faint resemblance to the original, in his own " Manfred."

But, why is it that these two fables have so strongly and decidedly excited the curiosity of the masses? Is it not that these two mythic characters (for the character contains the fable, more than the fable contains the character) represent, in the pursuits and trials to which they are exposed, the two horns of that dilemma in which human nature is placed?

Faust is employed upon the pursuit of knowledge under difficulties, while *Don Juan* is engrossed in the pursuit of pleasure.

Faust would search into and examine the origin of things. He is curious about the real purpose of his existence. *Don Juan* entertains the idea that he has been placed in this world simply to enjoy it, and that it is to be reckoned by him as so much material for his own pleasure.

Both of them are philosophers. While *Faust* is a disciple of Socrates, *Don Juan* has a decided touch of Epicurus in his nature. Both of them are religious. The latter blindly believes his dogma, like an excellent Roman Catholic ; while the first is ready to believe, but wants PROOF to wipe away his doubts. Is not the same the case with many, otherwise, very admirable Protestants? Both are determined to act, *coute que coute*, as they think, and consequently both have " to pay the piper." *Faust* makes a pact with Satan, and goes to hell. *Don Juan*, as a homicidal reprobate and libertine, has the satisfaction of travelling upon the same road, and by as short a cut. Connected with this portion of their personal history, Fiorentino, there is one very remarkable circumstance. The first author of "Don Juan," Zorilla, and the last author of " Faust," Goethe, entertained very strikingly different ideas from all other writers, touching (" Manfred's" *finale* is altogether a most dubious one) the exit of their heroes from this sublunary sphere. They both dispatched them, in a remarkably off-hand manner, to — Heaven. Here, they both obtain the pardon not only of their first lady-loves, *Gretchen* and *Donna Inez*, but of One who is at the same time far more mighty and infinitely more forgiving!

But, I must beg the pardon of Theophilo di Adama. He also inclines to the merciful view of the question, and frustrates Satan's views upon the soul of his *Faust*, through the intercession and interference of the Holy Virgin.

Poetic, most certainly, this solution of their enigmatic careers is. A man who does wrong, in following out the bias imprinted upon his perceptions by Nature, ought not, as it will seem to you, to go to the inferior regions which human vanity persists in conceiving the place of final retribution. Still less ought he to be consigned thither, if, intending to do right, he has simply mistaken one road for another. While that man who thirsts through his whole life after truth, can really, as you will say to me, have nothing to fear from Satan. When his spirit is at last capable of seeing clearly, he is not condemned to eternal darkness, but is rather summoned by a Higher Power into the regions of living day. Common justice sends them to grill below, but poetic justice lifts them into the light of perpetual love. Now, my dear Fiorentino, your creed shocks me, and obliges me to tell you that I cannot agree with it. As a good Christian, I have not the slightest doubt but that *Don Juan* and *Faust*, with their earthly representatives, are in, or if not, will finally go to Tophet.

But while I have been discussing the nature of the two Fables, I have suffered Mozart's wonderful music to pass me without a word.   Fortunately, it is music which asks us for no description, music which literally needs no analysis from the critic, music which demands only a feeling heart to understand its marvellously individual character, music which at once seizes upon the hearer's soul and steeps it in a distinctive joy, music which—

My dear Fiorentino, I am forgetting myself.   To write a critical disquisition upon Mozart's miraculous musical genius, to you, would be a gratuitous insolence, only to be paralleled by the individual who would graciously sit down to teach Janin the theory of writing French.

Pardon me, my friend, and permit me to tell you, that for the moment I was lost in one of those vague dreams which at times will seize upon all of us, the most as well as the least worldly.   Believe me, when I say that forgetfulness of you and myself shall not again come over me.   To prove this, let me tell you that the " Don Giovanni" had the greatest success of any Opera which has been brought forward, in my time, in America.   This argues, as you must admit, well for the public taste in this portion of the world, and promises even more for their future musical development. Everybody was delighted. Even a little mercantile acquaintance of mine, who was an enthusiastic admirer of Opera, and had a positive standing among amateurs, as a man of recognized judgment in musical matters, was literally carried away. Upon the first night, when the Opera had come to an end, he scarcely seemed to know whether he stood upon his head or his heels.   My step was not heard in the lobby, ere he rushed up to me like a diminutive madman. Grasping both my hands in his, and shaking them with a very painful fervor to myself, he there and then gave me his opinion about Mozart.   It was delivered by him in these terms:

" My dear Mr. Max ! That music of Mozart's ! A-h-h-hh ! Oh-h-h-h-h !   Indeed—I nev-v-v-ver !"

This was all. And yet, I am mistaken, for there and then did he invite me to dine with him.

" Come to dinner," he said. " We will talk about Mozart, and you will find at my table the heaviest silver spoons and forks, from one end of the United States to the other. I assure you, you will. Now, pray come."

It was with the greatest difficulty I excused myself. You ask me, why? my amiable Fiorentino. Was I not a poor Manager, and had I no reason to be afraid of that temptation which he offered ?"

As you have been earlier told by me, the Opera of " Don Giovanni" ran up to the last night of the season. At its close, the committee of the subscribers offered to give me a benefit as a proof of their approbation of my management. In other words, they meant that I should prepare and outlay everything, and that they would direct it. With most exemplary courtesy, I politely returned them my thanks, and declined their munificent offer, having already determined to take a benefit and *manage it myself*. Therefore, on the last night of the completed season, it was announced, and I had the satisfaction of seeing the house crammed from the top to the bottom, not by the friends of the subscribers, but by the veritable public. The public of New York, Fiorentino, are like no other public in any city of the Old World. If you knew them as well as I do, you would, I feel convinced, agree with me. Gentle and *inexigeant* in the extreme, when they find a servant who treats them fairly, who exerts every effort to please them, and who has sufficient talent or knowledge to do so, they become his personal friend. Mine, they have now been for six years. You smile, and ask me whether it is on the score of my knowledge or talent? Candidly, Fiorentino, I do not know, but I am grateful to them for their unwavering and consistent kindness.

Shortly afterwards, the artists and the Dramatic Fund Society presented me with valuable tokens of their esteem, and were I not writing to one whose mouth involuntarily curls at every attempt I make to speak kindly of myself, I might say of their appreciation for all that which had been done by me for Art upon this continent.

You ask me—" What did the committee of subscribers?"

Well! They did their share. They had taken me upon trial, and they were tolerably well satisfied. On the morning after the benefit, the venerable Dr. G. S. Pattison, an excellent old gentleman, called upon me and presented me with a paper of the following tenor :—

"Astor Place Opera House, *Feb.* 16, 1850.

" At the Annual Meeting of the Five Years' Subscribers to the Italian Opera, held at the Astor Place Opera House, on the evening of Saturday, the 16th Feb., 1850, the Meeting was organized by appointing Thomas E. Davies, Esq., Chairman, and Henry A. Coit, Esq., Secretary.

" The Committee appointed at the last Annual Meeting, consisting of Victor de Launay, Robert Emmet, and Granville S. Pattison, Esq's, having made a full Report to the Meeting of the affairs of the Opera, the following Resolutions, being regularly moved and seconded, were passed unanimously :

" *Resolved*, That the Report of the Committee be approved of, and accepted.

" *Resolved*, That the thanks of the Meeting be given to the Committee for the faithful and successful discharge of their duties during the past year.

" *Resolved*, That the members of the Committee of last year be re-elected to manage the affairs of the Opera for the ensuing year.

"*Resolved*, That that portion of the Annual Report, in which the Committee recommend the re-leasing of the Opera House to the present lessee, Mr. Max Maretzek, for next year, meets the approbation of the Five Years' Subscribers.

"*Resolved*, That the Five Years' Subscribers to the Italian Opera consider it due to Mr. Max Maretzek to express their entire and unqualified approbation of his conduct as Manager of the Astor Place Opera House.

"*Resolved*, That the admirable manner in which an unprecedented number of new Operas have been performed, during the season, now drawing to a close, is the best evidence which could be furnished of the high musical qualifications of the artists selected by the Manager.

"*Resolved*, That the excellence and superior execution of the Orchestra and Choruses, prove the indefatigable industry, zeal, and ability of Mr. Max Maretzek, as the Musical Conductor.

"*Resolved*, That the great gratification afforded to the subscribers and patrons of the Opera, by the Manager, demands from them a substantial expression of their appreciation of his praiseworthy efforts.

"*Resolved*, That a Committee be appointed to tender to Mr. Max Maretzek a Complimentary Benefit ; and that the subscribers and patrons of the Opera be solicited to co-operate with them in making it a profitable one.

"*Resolved*, That a copy of the five last Resolutions, signed by the Chairman and Secretary of this Meeting, be enclosed to Mr. Max Maretzek.

"*Resolved*, That the Committee be authorized and instructed to take such steps as they may judge most advisable, to carry out the suggestions made as to securing a bumper Benefit for Mr. Max Maretzek.

"*Resolved*, That the proceedings of this Meeting be printed, and a copy sent to each of the Five Years' and Annual Subscribers.

"The Meeting then adjourned *sine die.*

> "THOMAS E. DAVIES, *Chairman.*
> "HENRY E. COIT, *Secretary.*"

In handing this paper to me, the old gentleman said:

"We had intended to give you a benefit, but you have preferred giving it yourself, and I am most pleased to know that it has turned out so well. We ought to have given you a more substantial testimonial, but, at all events, take this paper. If it does nothing else, it will give you credit."

"Credit! That is the very thing that I need most of all," I replied, receiving it from his hands.

So, I immediately hurried down with it to the house at which my banking account was kept, in Wall Street, and handed it across the counter to the Receiving Teller, with the request that he should enter it in my folio, and give me credit for it.

He looked at it, turned it over, (a habit with banking clerks that means nothing,) smiled, and then handed it back to me.

"The signatures are doubtless good enough, but the wording, my dear Mr. Maretzek, is not in the ordinary business style."

"Then, you won't give me credit for it?"

"We can't, my good sir. Have you any other commands for us?"

I shook my head, and he turned away to a gentleman who was standing at my elbow.

Several other institutions were tried by me with a precisely similar result. None of them would take this paper and give me *any* credit. It was, therefore, stored away in a corner of my iron safe, (I have one, Fiorentino, although there is but little in it,) like an over-issue of the New Haven Railroad Stock, with a dim and vague expectation that something might possibly, although not probably, turn up from it.

My next care was to look over the accounts of my season's management. Its balance-sheet, when everything had been carefully wound up, stood thus:

DR.		CR.
My debts during man- agement, ... $3,600		Property on hand in music, dresses, &c., $6,000

The properties—it being observed, having been used already—would not have sold at auction better than Mr. Fry's scenery had done.

What could I do, my good friend, but make up my mind to manage another season? So, I remained silent, and kept up appearances.

This, Fiorentino, is the faithful and correct history, with the actual result of the *first successful season* of operatic management, which had occurred for twenty five years in New York

Believe me, dear friend, most faithfully yours,

M. M.

THE ITALIAN OPERA AT CASTLE GARDEN.

THIRD LETTER.

TO L. LABLACHE, LONDON.

Jenny Lind—P. T. Barnum—Teresa Parodi—Humbug, Merit, Curiosity, Enthusiasm—Jenny Lind's Concert Tour, and Barnum's Autobiograpy.

GIULIETTA GRISI.

LETTER III.

New York, *August* 28*th*, 1855.

Lablache!

Præclarum et venerabile nomen! for such it certainly is
in the annals of contemporary Music, to you I address my
present letter. But a wide change has come across me and
my intentions, since I penned the first of this series. No
sooner was it known, illustrious *basso profondo*, that I had
commenced writing an account of my various Operatic Expe-
riences, than I have literally been besieged by publishers.
My friends have enjoined publication upon me. Fair dames
and blushing damsels have appealed to me, to know when
my volume would come before them.

It was not of the slightest use to tell them, that the intention of publication had never entered my brain. Unhesitatingly they laughed, and said I was one of the most prudent
of authors.

"But I am no author!"

"Very true. We know that," was the answer. "But you
will soon be one."

"How can I write pure English?"

"You can talk it well enough, our good Mr. Maretzek. Besides, we do not want ' pure English.' We only want to hear your ' Confessions.' "

What was to be done? With the publishers I remonstrated, but in vain. They were determined to employ my pen. Offers were made to provide me with a literary *cicérone*, to introduce my penmanship to the public, and a gentle force was employed upon me to compel my decision. Then it was that I rushed from the world, secluded myself in Staten Island with an English Grammar, an English Dictionary, and an English friend, who has expatriated himself to become a citizen of this free and " enlightened Republic," and made up my mind, with the assistance of these three indispensable necessaries to my task, to attempt its completion.

It is under these circumstances that you will receive this letter, no sooner than the rest of the public. If you reply to it, Lablache, I shall be most happy to hear from you. Should you not do so, I shall console myself with the idea that my trouble is more than repaid, by the kindly smiles of those fair ones, to gratify whose charmingly feminine curiosity I have taken up the pen.

You must certainly remember that memorable evening, when the Swedish Nightingale first struck a note before a London audience.

It was in the spring of 1847, and all London, which you will agree with me is a tolerably large city, was excited to the highest pitch of curiosity touching the result of her *début*. This was not, that her artistic reputation was then so great as it afterwards became. On the result of that evening, however, depended a musical question which was shaking the operatic world of London to its centre. This question was two-fold. First, whether Grisi should abdicate or divide the throne which she had occupied for some fifteen years in that capital, as the acknowledged Queen of the Lyric Drama.

While, secondly, it was to be decided whether the recognized *impressario* of Her Majesty's Theatre in the Haymarket, Lumley, was to secure the rank so long indisputably held by it, or if the insurgent vocal forces under the command of Delafield, the son of the great brewer, were to do battle successfully with him on behalf of Italian Opera newly domiciled in Covent Garden. It must be confessed, Lablache, that it was a very pretty quarrel as it then stood.

On the one side were the musical Tories of Operadom, the friends of Giulia Grisi, Mario, then in his very prime, the almost worn-out Persiani, and Tamburini, no more than the memory of that which he had been.

On the other side were the Radical Reformers and Whigs of Music, who had found a Cobden in Jenny Lind, while they patted you upon the back, as a proof that their change was not intended to be destructive.

Those contributed as much by their opposition to raise the public excitement, as these did by their puffing, diplomatizing, biography-writing, and eulogizing.

Two hours before the commencement of the Opera on that evening, Her Majesty's Theatre was crowded. Every class of society, from crowned and coroneted heads to the shopkeeper, on whom their existence was built up, was represented in that audience. In the first tier of boxes, on the right from the stage, the second box was occupied by Victoria and the Prince-Consort. In that next her, sat the old Duke of Cambridge, with his bald head glistening in the shining gas-light. Beside him was the Queen-Dowager. But I implore the pardon of these distinguished personages. They were *not* in the house two hours before the commencement of the Opera. Other boxes were occupied by the "Iron" Duke, as he was called, and his charming daughter, the Marchioness of Douro, since his death the Duchess of

Wellington; the kindly-hearted Duke of Devonshire, and the leading members of the British aristocracy, with the representatives of foreign courts, until the last box to the left of the stage. In this, almost exactly opposite the Queen, sat a thin, small, pale-green gentleman, with a magnificent pair of huge moustaches. He was almost looked upon as an intruder in that range of royalty and aristocracy. This was no other than the fugitive from the Castle of Ham, the Prince Louis Napoleon, at the present moment Napoleon III., and one of, if not perhaps the most powerful of the European Sovereigns. It has even been hinted to me, that this box was a token of courtesy from Mr. Lumley to the then little-distinguished stranger, which his means did not allow him to pay for. In the second tier sat many of the *noblesse* and leading members of the fashionable world, with a fair sprinkling of the moneyed autocracy of London. In the third and fourth, were the usual varieties of the wealthy *Plebs*, while in the pit-tier a few of the editors of the leading journals might be seen, mingled with the bachelor scions of the nobility, and not a few of their *chères amies*, whose flashing jewelry, beauty, and bare white arms, might well have shamed those of the more respectable, though, in many cases, not a whit purer portion of the audience.

The Orchestra-stalls were filled by a mixture of the musical bachelordom of the aristocracy and wealth of England, while the pit was tenanted by people of all and every class. Half a guinea, a black dress-coat, and white cravat, being the necessary passports to this location.

You, yourself, venerable Lablache—such you are now, although you scarcely were then—were placed in a proscenium-box on the second tier, in such a position that you could be seen by, at least, two-thirds of the audience. Of the fact, whether this was purely accidental, or had been

so arranged by Mr. Lumley, I am obliged to confess myself
ignorant. The truth is, that I never remember questioning
him upon the subject. It must, however, be owned, between
ourselves, Lablache, that it was a most admirable arrangement, and demands our approbation on account of its apparent forethought.

The Opera of the evening was " Roberto il Diavolo." Jenny
Lind, the new *debutante* in London, was to appear in the part
of *Alice*, while the remainder of the principal parts were supported by Castellan, Fraschini, Gardoni and Staudigl.

Perhaps, the three Italians were not altogether fitted to cope
with the comparative mysteries of German music, while the
one German was not too well versed in the amenities of the
Italian language. However, who in the whole audience cared
two straws for this? The only object of popular attention
upon this evening, was the Swedish candidate for an Operatic
immortality.

When she appeared, I was standing in the first wing to the
left of the stage, and never before in Germany, or afterwards
in England and America, have I heard her sing so exquisitely
as she did in the delivery of her first *Romanza*.

Applause of course marked the pauses of the vocalist, but
it was somewhat sparse and scattered. The public was evidently pleased, but, as evidently had it determined to judge
her carefully, before it placed her on a par, in its estimation,
with its long-established favorite, Grisi. In addition to this,
it was not familiarly acquainted with the music of Meyerbeer,
while the style of the Swedish Nightingale, as she was subsequently named, was essentially new. On these accounts, the
public seemed determined to hold back in its decision upon
her merits. Like a cautious judge, it wished not to compromise its opinion too early. Knowing how much is dependent
upon the first impression made upon it by an entirely new

artist, I frankly own to a feeling of some regret, that her first appearance in aristocratic London should have been made in an Opera which could allow the public no means of comparison. Her vocal inches could not be computed at the side of Persiani, or rated against the stature of Grisi. At this time, neither of them knew the music of Meyerbeer. Again, had she come out in a well-known work, with you, my dear Lablache, at her side, success, as I reflected, would not so long have been dubious. You would most infallibly have put the public into a pleasant humor. It would have forgotten its judgment, and been alone disposed to admiration. These reflections were suddenly dispersed by a long and most beautiful shake from the Swedish vocalist, in the *cadenza* of the Romance. The next note would have been its concluding one, but this she never reached audibly. Scarcely had the shake terminated, than one madly enthusiastic, roaring, thirty-six-pounder-like " Brava-ah-ah" interrupted her.

This was immediately followed by a prolonged and deafening storm of applause, which was mingled with laughter and outcries.

" That was Lablache. · Did you hear him?"

" Yes! it was his voice."

" Look at him.   There he is in the proscenium-box."

The audience had recognized your potent lungs, my white-haired friend, and, in a moment, the spell was broken.   Critical judge as it was, it had laughed, not at her, although upon her account. It had laughed at you.

Your " Brava" fell like a bomb-shell into the camp of the coalition of Covent Garden. It ruined Persiani, Delafield, Hasland and Webster. Your " Brava" made the fortune of Jenny Lind, as well as that of Lumley (who unfortunately could not keep it) and of Barnum. Great as a vocal artist as you are, never before had your vigorous lungs produced such a startling effect as they did upon that evening. It settled the standing of Jenny Lind as a vocalist in public estimation, while it saved Lumley from the bankruptcy that threatened him, and averted from Her Majesty's Theatre the immediate ruin which was staring it in the face.

At all events, whether you were really carried away by Jenny's delicious singing, or whether your thundering " Brava" was a preconcerted explosion, it must candidly be admitted that the spoiled child of fortune owes a great deal to it.

The look of grotesque astonishment which you summon into your face, my large friend, for most certainly if you have continued on the increase, you must be indubitably large at the present moment, is altogether useless. It is in vain that, with a merry twinkle in your gray eye in spite of your astonishment, you ask me wherefore I call her " the spoiled child of fortune?" Fruitlessly, you tell me that she had to struggle with unheard-of difficulties in her early years, and that her first singing-master in Stockholm advised her to abandon a profession for which she had not that most necessary of materials—voice. You may, if you so will it, remind me that by her indomitable energy and continuous studies, she at length found that voice which she felt must be somewhere hidden within her chest ; but, in spite of this, that she was obliged to appear and sing in small and secondary parts, to secure a living ; and then, when after long and wearisome struggles she had at length arrived in Paris, through the intrigues of Madame Stolz (the Egeria of the managerial Numa, Leon Pillet) that even a trial was refused her.

All this, my respected friend, may, or may not be true, in a purely literary point of view. This I shall not, for a moment, take upon myself to determine.

But every artist, my good Lablache, has had, as you can judge from your own personal experience, his or her time of

difficulties, and his or her period of good fortune. When
Jenny's moment of chance came, she had fortune enough for
any half dozen of vocalists.   When it broke upon her, it was
with no modest and unpretendingly shadowy twilight.   No
sooner had it done so, than one of the greatest composers of the
age (I allude to Meyerbeer) took her by the hand, and
pushed her before the world as one of the chosen exponents
of his own genius.   Not only did he recognize her talent, but
he wrote for the almost unknown aspirant for vocal distinction, his Opera of " Vielka," now re-baptized by him as
" L'Etoile du Nord."

When, subsequently to this, she had to make her German
reputation an European one, she found one of the greatest
impressarios of the period, whose only chance of saving himself from ruin, lay in her engagement.   To struggle against
the opposition of the insurgent Italians at Covent Garden,
Benjamin Lumley was obliged to throw his money, his credit,
his influence, and his undoubted talent for management into
the balance, in her favor.   Nay! when she decided on quitting the stage, yet still hankered after the golden price her
notes had previously brought her, she had the luck to discover
one of the greatest " humbugs" of the day, as he has himself
avowed with a candor of the most ingenuous fashion, who,
finding himself for the moment rather short of work, felt
somewhat inclined to dabble in Music, with the innocently
speculative view of making money.   This individual was, it
it is needless for me to say, the singularly simple-hearted and
guileless P. T. Barnum.

In fact, scarcely had Jenny Lind undertaken her arduous
peregrinations in search of the *toison dorée* of artistic reputation, than a Mentor presented himself to her in the person of
Giacomo Meyerbeer.

When she had succeeded in her first toil, and had shred a

fair portion of it with his assistance, she became more ambitious. Wishing to seize on the diadem of the then reigning Queen of Song, a Talleyrand stood at her elbow. This was Benjamin Lumley.

Then having gained both reputation and position, her wish was simply to pull the pocket-strings of the world. The *Robert Macaire* offered himself in the form of Phineas Barnum.

Under the protecting tutelage of Meyerbeer, she was as the unconscious nightingale who sings for the mere sake of singing. When in the guardianship of Lumley, she became the mere peacock of vocalism, airing her many-colored notes in the mid-day sun, for the purpose of deafening us to the song of others. And at last, with Barnum, she displayed herself as the Syren whose delicate tones warbled the American gold-finches into her outstretched fingers.

Now with Meyerbeer and Lumley you are well acquainted. Of the amiable Barnum, my dear Lablache, I should suppose that you know next to nothing, unless indeed your literary studies have induced you to read a volume which, with a sublime and happy audacity, he has named his Autobiography. In this curious work, he candidly owns that he first gave himself the name of the " Prince of Humbugs." Now "γνωθι σεαυτον" is a maxim, and a very capital one, first laid down by Socrates, or Plato, or some other of the Greek philosophers; and nobody who knows or has known Barnum, will deny that he has shown a strange amount of self-appreciation, although a scanty amount of republicanism, in awarding himself this title.

But—" What is humbug?" you ask.

Exhibiting a fly through a microscope and passing it off as an elephant to one who pays, would, my dear Lablache, be a very decided humbug.

"*Per Bacco!*" you exclaim, "but such a proceeding would come, in Europe, under the head of obtaining money by false pretences."

So it would here, my venerated friend, if it, or something similar to it, took place in the commercial world. In the world of amusement, it is altogether different.

Thus, Barnum exhibited an aged negress as the nurse of George Washington, and proved the truth of this assertion by documents. It was discovered that the assertion was false. In his Autobiography, he serenely admits that the affair might be a hoax, but states that he purchased woman and documents from a Mr. Lindsay. Is it at all probable that the "Prince of Humbugs" could have been "humbugged" by a Lindsay?

In a similar way he made money from a *real* mermaid, manufactured from a monkey and a fish-tail; displayed a black spotted with white, and a woolly horse, with many other curiosities of a similar kind.

"And do the people of America patronize him?" you inquire of me, with a look of sublime wonder mantling over your face.

Of course they do. At first, they flocked to his exhibitions in scores, because they believed all that he announced. Now, they rush there, or would rush to anything he introduced, in hundreds, simply to ascertain in what manner he is about to "humbug" them this time.

Should he once attempt not to "humbug" them, and dare to represent what he exhibits as it really is, he would be a lost man, or rather should I say, a lost manager. His *prestige* would be gone forever, for his reputation as the "Prince of Humbugs" would be forfeited.

Yet the man is a genius. With his extraordinary talent for combination, had he received a better education, and been thrown by those chances, which are Destiny, into a higher sphere of action, he would have made a first-rate minister of finance, and have retired a "millionaire," as he is now, according to his own accounts. As it is, he is contented, provided you will only coincide in the justice of the title he has bestowed upon himself. For one, let me confess that I do, and very fully.

Now, when Barnum engaged Jenny Lind, he had very decidedly but a scanty faith in the taste and discrimination of the American Public. In the power of music over it, he had next to none. His creed was "humbug," and, consequently, the real merit of Jenny was no guarantee with him for her success. Her visit to this country might have exercised the most salutary influence upon the taste and development of Art in the New World. Blind by nature to every consideration of this character, he took the knowledge of a rail-road conductor* as his best authority in musical matters, and came to the conclusion that, as an artist, the fair Swede would be at the best a very uncertain speculation. In consequence of this, he determined upon working her as a *curiosity*, as he had done with the Feejee Mermaid, and other of his pseudo-irregularities of nature. It was purely a matter of the most perfect indifference to him, whether she produced any enthusiasm as a songstress, provided she excited curiosity, as angel, woman, or demon. No sooner, therefore, had he ascertained the extent of knowledge respecting her upon the part of a railway-conductor, than he went to work at the enlightenment of the people.

Reputation was manufactured for her, by wholesale. It was not merely made by the inch, but was prepared by the cart-load.

* See page 303 of his Autobiography.

Letters from England were written in New York anterior to the arrival of each steamer, and by the highly moral Phineas were passed into the columns of the newspapers as genuine epistles from the other side of the Atlantic. These letters were received and published by the New York press, with a *bonhommie* and readiness to oblige which I have never seen manifested by any other press in the world.

After six months continuously employed in this manner, Barnum had done what he counted upon doing. The letters had been copied in every portion of the country. Public curiosity had been so industriously stirred up by him, that out of every five persons one would have been glad to hear, but four were restlessly desirous to see her. In consequence of this, the candid Phineas, my good friend, at a serenade given to Jenny in Philadelphia, presented her chambermaid on the balcony of the hotel to the crowd as the genuine article; while at church in Baltimore, those who were present, were enraptured with the singing of Barnum's daughter, in the firm conviction that she was the *bona fide* novelty which he had fathered upon the hour. Everywhere, the curiosity to see her was stronger than the enthusiasm after hearing her, and great as her merit most unquestionably was, the "humbug" of her manager was by far the most powerful attraction to her concerts.

It was in September, 1850, that Jenny Lind arrived here. Now, my good Lablache, the Opera season was to begin about the middle of October. It was my second season.

Figure to yourself the position of a luckless *impressario* with a company of Truffis and Beneventanos upon his hands, and the lease of the Astor Place Opera House upon his shoulders, with Jenny Lind and Barnum, real genius and undoubted "humbug," in a strange copartnership, staring ominously in his face. Of how quickly and decidedly the

Swede had eclipsed Grisi, Viardot-Garcia, Persiani, and Alboni, in London, I had been a witness. What could I expect to do with my second-rate artists? But that my hands were tied by my arrangements, and that I had not, as I must honestly own, the means to do anything else, I will confess that I should have been glad enough to give up the whole concern. However, there was one decided consolation. This was, that I had nothing to lose except my theatrical properties.

It was, however, necessary to do something. My old artists were impossible cards, for me to attempt playing in Barnum's manner. They were, alas! too well known.

At the same time, it appeared almost impossible to induce a first-class reputation to come to America, at the same period as Jenny Lind. Necessity, however, urged me to try, and if successful, to enter upon the contest with the "Prince of Humbugs," using his own weapons.

My choice fell upon the Signora Teresa Parodi.

She was an artist of sufficient talent to realize the expectations which I might raise upon her behalf. I had heard her at Her Majesty's Theatre, in London, as *Norma*, *Lucrezia Borgia*, and *Donna Anna*. I knew her to have been Pasta's favorite pupil, and had heard you, my dear Lablache, express a favorable opinion of her undoubted merits. As soon, therefore, as my choice was fixed, I wrote to my old friend and employer, Lumley, and to the energetic and busy Madame Puzzi, in London. I told them my situation, frankly, and asked material aid from the former, in the person of Teresa Parodi.

By return of mail, I received the intelligence that upon receipt of a *bonus* of 20,000 francs, Mr. Lumley would be ready to transfer his engagement with Parodi into my hands.

The money was raised, by my transferring the first receipts

of the Opera House until full payment, and sent over the water to him.

Then, for the first, and I am proud to say, the only time, I went to work in the same manner I had seen practised by Barnum. Foreign letters, puffs, portraits, biographies, were manufactured under my supervision, and distributed by means of the journals and the music stores throughout New York. All was of no use. Public attention was absorbed by Jenny Lind. Whatever I did, was against the pyramidal puffing of Barnum. It was no more than the murmuring of a garden streamlet as compared with the roar and thunder of Niagara. In my distress, I had, however, remarked that the great showman's gigantic system of eulogy had, by no means, any particular *rapport* with Jenny's qualities as an artist. He exaggerated her virtues *a la Munchausen:* he proclaimed her a ventriloquist, romanced about Victoria's adoration of her excellencies, and fabricated charities by the bushel-full. Now, as one of our German proverbs says—"when among wolves, it is very necessary to yell as they do." It is true, no one had vouched to me for its having saved him from their jaws, yet, in this instance, I determined upon obeying its injunctions to the letter.

One morning, therefore, I dispatched a confidential friend to the office of one of the morning newspapers, and the following dialogue took place between him and one of the editors, with whom he was acquainted.

" Poor Maretzek !" said my friend, with a woeful shake of the head.

" Why ! What is the matter ?"

" Well ! I suppose I ought not to tell you," he answered, looking as lugubrious as a man who is hired to weep at a funeral. " But he is ruined."

" Eh ! What ?"

"This season will finish him."

"How is that possible? Everybody says Parodi is very great."

"Yes. Parodi would carry everything before her."

"What is the matter, then?"

"She need not be afraid even of Jenny Lind."

"Explain yourself. What is it that has happened, my dear sir?"

"If I do, you must promise me the most implicit secrecy."

"Most assuredly, I do."

"Poor Max would scarcely outlive it, if it were known."

"Well, I never will mention it."

"Under your pledge of the most sacred secrecy"—

"Certainly!"

"I think I may tell you."

"Pray, continue."

"The truth is, that the old Duke of Devonshire has long been in love with her."

"The deuce he has!"

"And when he heard that she was to visit New York, he made up his mind, rushed to her feet, and offered her his fortune and coronet."

"You don't really say so?"

"But the worst of it is, that such a chance for the establishment of a vocalist does not occur every day—that is to say, her establishment in life as a married woman of high rank."

"I should think not, indeed. The Duchess of Devonshire!"

"Therefore, she has consented to marry him."

"And this is true?"

"It is certain. The letter came by the last steamer. But, for Heaven's sake, do not say a word about it. Remember poor Max Maretzek with the Astor Place and a large company on hand. He is decidedly ruined."

" Really, it is provoking !"

" Is it not ?"

" Most undoubtedly !"

" Mind ! You have promised me to be strictly silent."

" As the grave."

Having received this promise, Lablache, my friend then quitted the office of the daily journal in question, impressed with the serenest of possible convictions that the luckless editor had swallowed his bait, hook and all.

And so he had. Anxious to have the first of this peculiarly piquant piece of intelligence, he suffered his promise of the most implicit secrecy to slip entirely from his memory. Next morning, the whole story appeared, with additional embroidery, in his journal. Upon the following day, it was repeated by every daily paper in New York. In something less than three weeks, it had found its way into almost every newspaper from Maine to Texas, and in a fortnight more, had completed its travels by one huge stride from New York to San Francisco.

Biographies, portraits, and anecdotes about her, which had dropped still-born from the press, were now republished, admired, and listened to.

Some of the country editors even went so far as to adopt Barnum's plan, and described the very *trousseau* with which the Duke of Devonshire had presented her, in a foreign correspondence of decidedly home-manufacture. A few of them even published verbatim copies of the assumed contract of marriage. Numberless applications were received by me from musical agents, who offered to arrange my difficulties with the Duke upon amicable terms. Letters from lawyers came into my hands, which stated their writers' readiness to start for Europe and commence a process against the new Duchess. These asked only for a share of those damages which they felt certain of obtaining.

My part was very clearly marked out for me, my venerable friend, and it is needless to say that I stuck to it. This was to answer not a single letter, and to correct no newspaper. So I quietly opened my subscription list, and shortly afterwards commenced the season, without the name of one of the artists who formed my company having been previously announced.

As may be reasonably supposed by you, my subscription list was thin, nor were my houses much better. But after some two weeks more, the supposed Duchess of Devonshire arrived from Europe, in the Pacific, and was completely astounded to find such a report in circulation.

From the day of her arrival, I announced that I should accept of no more subscriptions for the season, and raised the prices of admission exactly one hundred *per* cent. This last fact dispelled all doubts of her superiority, as it was supposed that I could not have dared to do this, with such a rival attraction as Jenny Lind in the market, if I had not been morally certain of her success. Well, she appeared as *Norma* to a crowded house, and as you know, she had talent enough to sustain that reputation which my agents and friends had manufactured for her. To the end of the season she continued to draw excellent houses, and, instead of being ruined, as I myself had predicted, with a full determination were it possible to falsify my own prophecy, I carried three operatic seasons in New York, Philadelphia, and Boston to a triumphant close, being enabled to pay the debts of the anterior season, and to close my campaign with some profit.

In the mean time, Jenny Lind, under the management of

the excellent Barnum, had made the most successful musical *tour* on record.

Indeed, if any reliance can be placed upon the statements given in Mr. Barnum's Autobiography, the proceeds of the ninety-three concerts given by her while with him, amounted to some $700,000. But as the romantic fiction which purports to contain the details of his life is full of contradictions and improbabilities, it may also be presumed that the above figures are slightly exaggerated.

It is, at any rate, astonishing how a man of such marked shrewdness as the worthy Phineas, could have been guilty of so many blunders as he has perpetrated in his biography.

But it would be too wearisome, as well for myself as for you, did I expose all the contradictions which even I can detect in it, in those portions that relate more exclusively to his Jenny Lind musical campaign. Two or three examples may suffice. Thus on page 313 you may read as follows :—

"Jenny looked at me with astonishment. She could not comprehend my proposition. After I had repeated it, and she fully understood its import, she grasped me cordially by the hand, and exclaimed, ' *Mr. Barnum, you are a gentleman of honor. You are generous. It is just as Mr. Bates told me. I will sing for you as long as you please. I will sing for you in America—in Europe—anywhere !'* "

which is, upon the same page, almost immediately succeeded by this :—

"Upon drawing the new contract, a condition was inserted, by Miss Lind's request, that she should have the right to terminate the engagement with the one hundredth concert, instead of the hundred and fiftieth, if she should desire to do so, upon paying me $25,000."

Now, how is it to be understood, that Jenny wishes to sing for her skilful *entrepreneur* " as long as he may please," when almost immediately afterwards she stipulates with him for the possibility of breaking her engagement before it comes to an end? And, indeed, at page 339, you will read, or have already read, the following :—

" At about the eighty-fifth concert, therefore, I was most happy to learn from her lips that she had concluded to pay the forfeiture of twenty-five thousand dollars, and terminate the concerts with the one hundredth."

Allow me to inquire how or why he was " most happy" to learn this from her lips? Have the concerts not been altogether so profitable as he would have the American public believe, or is it, that Jenny herself is not *au fond* that " angel" which he had in his first moment of enthusiastic certainty dubbed her? Was she capricious, self-willed, or difficult to manage, like any other *prima donna?* This he does not confess, although it would seem that the disinterested Swede, who had in her angelic nature *promised to sing for him as long as he pleased, in Europe—America, or anywhere else*, did not particularly relish finishing even the first hundred concerts with Barnum at the head of affairs. At all events, page 340, there is a copy of a letter from Jenny which reads thus :—

" To P. T. Barnum, Esq.

" My Dear Sir :—I accept your proposition to close our contract to-night, at the end of the ninety-third concert, on condition of my paying you seven thousand dollars in addition to the sum I forfeit under the condition of finishing the engagement at the end of one hundred concerts.

" I am, dear Sir, yours truly,

" Jenny Lind.

" *Philadelphia, 9th* of June, 1851."

So that we are forced to conclude the able Manager, who had dealt in Giants, Orang-outangs, Dwarfs, Generals, Elephants, Bearded Women, Boa Constrictors, Feejee Mermaids and Alligators, was unable to manage one little "angel" of a *prima donna*.

And what is the reason assigned by him for the abrupt termination of her engagement after the ninety-third concert? Can the readers of his volume, my good friend, really believe that Jenny broke it, and paid him $7000 more forfeit than that which she had determined to pay him for not concluding the 150 concerts, originally stipulated upon, simply because he had forced her to sing in a "horse-circus," which, as he says, had been cleansed and fitted up before for Italian Opera by myself?

Had not the divine Jenny sung before, and that without expressing the slightest objection, in a pork-house in Madison? Why is it, that she now prefers to pay $7000 to singing in a horse-circus?

Here is, evidently, some mystery, which the great Autobiographer ought to have explained.

As he did not do so, my amiable friend, you will, I should presume, not be offended with me for volunteering an explanation for him.

Shortly before she was called upon to sing in the horse-circus in Philadelphia, Mr. Barnum's great Asiatic Travelling Menagerie arrived in New York, and made its triumphant progress through the streets of this metropolis. When the elephants, ostriches and monkeys paraded through Broadway, preceded by bands of music, tawdry inscriptions traced upon banners, and other mummeries, in order to excite the curiosity of those who passed it, it so happened that Jenny Lind was standing at her window, and observed the procession. There, she seemed to remark the same faces in the

crowd which had greeted her own arrival, the same enthusiastic brows which had followed her carriage on that memorable occasion, and the same demonstrations which had taken
place upon her advent in New York.

Is it not possible that, upon this morning, Jenny found
out, in Barnum's eyes she was no more than his Woolly
Horse, or one of his monkeys? Would it be astonishing,
that the Swedish Nightingale felt hurt in both her womanly
and artistic pride?

If, within a few days afterwards, Barnum forced her to
sing in a horse-circus, which had *not* "been cleaned out and
fitted up by Max Maretzek," my dear Lablache, inasmuch as
the aforesaid Max Maretzek never played there at all, until
some three months after Jenny Lind had inaugurated it for
musical entertainments, can it be marvelled at, that she should
become entirely disgusted with the management of the
"Prince of Humbugs," and preferred paying $7000 addi-
tional forfeit to staying another moment under his guidance?
What a striking contrast is presented between the mutual
sentiments of Jenny and P. T. B., at the time of their separation in Philadelphia, and those which they had experienced
towards each other in Havana and Charleston!* Especially
in Havana, would it seem, that their life had been purely
patriarchal in its cordiality. They there sported and amused
themselves, like shepherds and shepherdesses in the age of—

"Tytyre, tu recubans sub tegmine fagi"—

or, in a German Idyl of Gessner.

You may, indeed, see a woodcut somewhere about page 330,
which may be regarded as a singularly close representation
of one of these Idyllic scenes. The gentle Swede had consented to receive the tight-rope dancer Vivalla and his learned
dog. In this cut, she is represented as a young girl, having no

* See pages 324-25 and 326 of Barnum's Autobiography.

more than some seventeen or eighteen summers, kneeling on the floor in front of the fire-place, (in Havana, who has ever seen a fire-place?) fondling a large dog. The Signor Vivalla stands on one side with his cap in his hand, and a large hook-nose, looking amiable, while the agreeable P. T. Barnum figures behind the group with a marvellously benevolent regard in his physiognomy. Anything more deliciously patriarchal it would literally be impossible to conceive. Nothing, perhaps, is here lacking, save a portrait of Joyce Heth and the Mermaid, with a slight hint of the Woolly Horse in the background, to give it the look of a veritable " Happy Family."

But, in addition to this, my most friendly *basso*, you will find it actually upon record in this precious Autobiography, that the Historiographer of the Lind-mania wept—indeed, that he positively could not restrain his " tears of joy." Oh! my amiable Lablache, what a chance was here lost! Could he but have perpetuated those diamond-drops, which he speaks of, what an invaluable addition would his own person, in its weeping state, have made to his museum! You may also see, somewhere near this, how Jenny Lind also *" cries with joy,"* and how she actually (so Barnum at any rate says) kisses that Royal Slip of " Humbug." Really, all this is too affecting, my excellent friend!

Such real, such true, and such genuine emotion, expressed in such a candid and natural manner, makes me also overflow with tears.

Yes! I weep, Lablache, with *tears of joy*, in merely speaking of it. The page blisters with them. It is about to produce the same effect on you, and I refrain from prolonging my observations, lest you might melt into a tarn of something the same size as the Dead Sea, and London or Paris, whichever city you are now in, might be swallowed up in it as Sodom and Gomorrha were in that Lake.

Yet still, in spite of their mutual exhibitions to each other of weeping sensibility, that fine-hearted, benevolent, and admirable old "humbug," was unable, efficiently, to harmonize in Philadelphia with the amiable, meek, and charitable "Angel," who embraces the "learned dog," as we see, and *kisses* Barnum, as we are told. Nay! when Jenny offers him a glass of wine, and requests him to drink it to her own happiness and prosperity, he replies thus :—

"Miss Lind, I do not think you can ask any other favor on earth which I would not gladly grant; but I am a teetotaller, and must beg to be permitted to drink your health and happiness in a glass of cold water."

Yet, upon nearly every second page in his book, you may see how he performed his practical jokes in bar-rooms, saloons, and country-taverns, for the bet or payment of "drinks all round."*

Now, should you, good Lablache, wish to know more of the contradictions in this work, if by any chance you should not have read it, let me advise you to procure it, which you may now probably do at half-price, inasmuch as, with a much keener appreciation of its value than he formerly had, P. T. B. has knocked off seventy-five cents from the dollar and a half he had affixed to it. It abounds in invention and improbability, sufficient to satisfy the travelling *Quack* in the Opera founded upon the old tale of the "Maid and the Magpie." He talks about everything which interests himself, and tells his readers nothing about anything which interests them, save as much as they have already known. You will find descriptions of his grandfather and his Shanghai-roosters, of

* See pages 73, 79, 89, 145 (application to become a bar-keeper) 147, 185, 187, 249, 278, &c. &c.

Ivy Island and Iranistan, of Lottery schemes and Buffalo hunts. Rules how to make a fortune will be given you, which are very certainly not the rules by which his own was made. You will learn how to palm off a Negro-woman on the public, as the nurse of Washington, and have a faithful description (at the least so it must be presumed) of the ceremonies at his birth, his marriage and his—

No! no! I was about so say even of his—obsequies.

Yet Charles V. dictated the terms of his interment, himself, and rehearsed it during his life-time. In order to make his Autobiography complete, ought not Barnum to have given us the *programme* of his funeral rites?

You may imagine, my large friend, for I know you have a superabundance of the *vis comica* in your imagination, a group of young "Mermaids," crowned with myrtle, opening the procession and scattering *immortelles* upon his path to eternity. Six "Halifax Giants" should bear the sarcophagus of the great showman. The tassels of the pall (made of six Jenny Lind "posters") should be supported by six "Fat Women." Behind the coffin should be led his "Woolly" battle horse, by the "Negro" who had consented to *turn white*, once more, expressly for this occasion. Funereal hymns might be screeched out by those youthful vocalists who had taken the prizes at the "Baby Show." "Faber's Automaton" should follow, for the purpose of pronouncing his funeral oration, while a regiment of the "Sons of Temperance" should file after it, headed by the venerable General "Tom Thumb." His "Wax Figures" might melt away in an unavailing sorrow, while the "Bearded Lady" would pull the black bristles from her chin, in sublime despair. Stockholders of the "Crystal Palace" and the original "Proprietors of the Fire-Annihilator" might be weeping bitterly, and a deputation of his colleagues, the moral, honest and pious "showmen' of America, could bring up the rear, in deep mourning, and doing their utmost *not to laugh*.

This would make a truly magnificent exhibition, my dear Lablache, and, I trust that I may live to see it—of course upon the payment of 25 cents admission. Believe me, that I remain,

   Yours, most truly,

        &c. &c. &c.

BINA STEFFANONE.

FOURTH LETTER.

TO PROFESSOR JOSEPH FISCHOF, VIENNA.

Recollections of earlier years—Successful Opera-Managers—Barbaja, Dr. Veron, Don Franscisco Marty y Torrens—The Havana Opera-Troupe, Steffenone, Bosio, Tedesco, Salvi, Bettini, Lorini, Marini, Badiali, Coletti, Bottesini—Glances behind the Scenes—Opera at Castle Garden.

ANNA LA GRANGE.

LETTER IV.

TO PROFESSOR JOSEPH FISCHOF, VIENNA.

NEW YORK, *August*, 1855.

EXCELLENT FRIEND :—

IN taking up my pen and drawing before me the sheet of paper with the purpose of, at present, addressing you, I am unable to suppress the many remembrances which throng upon me. Albeit, this letter is destined, in spite of its German-English, for publication, and consequently the public will claim the right of becoming my *confidant* in all which I may herein say to you ; I cannot entirely stifle the recollections of my earliest years. Memories, even as I trace your name, come struggling back into my mind. Youth and boyhood are too powerfully welded into all our lives, to be brushed entirely away by the subsequent chance and change of our existence.

Therefore is it, that my pen places upon the paper an acknowledgment of my gratitude for all your kindness ; and registers its remembrance of the encouragement which you, the well-known *maestro*, gave the unfortunate *tyro* in his passion for melody.

Through your interference in my behalf, I was allowed to embrace a musical career. To your kindness do I owe it, that my parents permitted me to become an artist. Possibly, my dear Professor, it was a rash longing upon my part and an unwise benevolence upon your own, which enabled me to do so. But not being one of those discontented individuals who are never happy save when quarrelling with their destiny, I chide neither at you, nor censure my own determination. Sufficient is it for me to know that I have embraced the most arduous of professions, and that I am now perforce obliged to pursue the career of an artist.

Then, no more than a beardless boy of some seventeen years, at College I had swallowed the Greek and Roman classics without doing any harm to the digestive faculties of my brain. As a proof of this, it may be mentioned that they are now almost completely forgotten by me. If my memory tells me that there was such a historian as Thucydides, such a romanticist as Hesiod, and such poets as Catullus, Juvenal, or Terence, believe me that it is all it can do. The Lectures on Philosophy, Metaphysics, Geometry, Logic, and the Common Law, were attended by me. These have served me but little, although they were destined by my father to direct me in my course of life. He had already mapped it out for me. The truth is, I was to be either a *doctor medicinæ*, or should I chance to prefer it, a *doctor juris*.

In the mean time, I had imbibed a strong dislike to fighting out the quarrels of other people in a black gown, and had contracted an invincible repugnance to scalpels and dead bodies.

Living only for Music, my youthful fancies reverenced nothing but Art.

Already in the last two years of my collegiate experience, the works of Mozart, Weber, Rossini, and the older masters, had more charms for me than the mathematical problem first worked out by Pythagoras, and called by the vulgar, the *pons asinorum*. My musical enthusiasm venerated Mendelssohn and Meyerbeer, far more than my studious nature respected the metaphysical dogmas of the Romanist priest who was one of our professors. Indeed, often when our admirable instructors endeavored to make us comprehend their Tables of Logarithms, or logically argued the necessity for an origin of the World, trying to prove the existence of a God with algebraic figures (which argument and proof never said as much, I may be permitted to observe, as does the first line in the Book of Genesis,) my wandering ideas had strayed far from the lecture-room, and were occupied in the composition of an *andante grazioso*, or in modelling the concluding bars of some *allegro furioso*. Nevertheless, I always managed to squeeze myself through the difficulties of an Examination, until, at length, the critical moment had arrived.

It was determined that I should be a surgeon. Consequently, I had to enter the dissection-room.

At this moment in my life, my nervous feelings at the thoughts of that which must be undergone, were by no means soothed on my introduction to the locality, hallowed, as my Professor had told me, by the first blush of Science.

On entering the well-ventilated Hall, the Beadle of the University had just put up to auction the mortal remains of some poor fellow who had hung himself, thereby placing his body within the legal reach of a dissecting-knife.

It was the first dead body I had ever seen. Such a frightful impression did it make upon me, that for weeks afterwards were my waking thoughts and sleeping dreams haunted by that blue and livid face with its ghastly and open eyes.

Two old students, who, during the auction, had been eating their breakfast, consisting of cold sausages and bread and cheese, were fortunate enough to become its enviable proprietors. When knocked down to them, they had finished their meal and rushed up to their prize. They turned it over and handled it, playing with it as babies play with their dolls, while my flesh was creeping over my bones with a painfully unmitigated disgust. Then, they sold out portions of it in a carefully modelled imitation of the auctioneering capacity of the Beadle. At last, they removed it to the dissecting-table. Imagine then, my good Professor, the indescribable loathing and horror which seized upon me, when I saw one of the identical knives which had operated in dividing the sausages, and cutting up the bread and cheese, thrust into the dead man's body. Had it been thrust into my own flesh, the emotion could not have been one whit more horrible. I felt that knife passing through my very soul.

Leaping up, I rushed from the hall. What passed between me and my parents, I have no distinct remembrance of, but it was decided that Max Maretzek should no more return to the Surgical College.

After this, it was determined that I should devote myself to Music. The life of an artist, at that time, seemed to me the only reasonable and honorable existence for any man.

Consequently, instead of frequenting lecture-rooms and colleges, I sat down to complete an Opera which had been already commenced. What young composer does not write an Opera? In the innocence of my youthful belief, the said Opera was to carry me straight along the road to Fame and Fortune. The more my work advanced, the more evidently did it become, in my opinion, a *chef d'œuvre*. It was bound (so, at least, did I believe) to make a profound sensation, and earn for me an equality with the greatest composers. Dreaming, even in my waking hours, of those honors which perforce awaited me after its production, and seeming to compose even as I slumbered, at length, I completed that stupendous work.

Possibly, my dear Fischof, you may not remember this sublime exhibition of my youthful genius. Far as we are apart, I feel that you shake your head in answer. Yet it was to you

I ran with my first Operatic score. It was to you that I first began to play it over. Your observations I well recollect. What were they? After listening to several pieces, you very coolly advised me to continue my studies, and to persevere in my determination to *become* a musician! Professor! how could you be so cruel? You told me that melody and imagination were abundantly manifested in the score, and these you considered sufficient guarantees for the *future* development of my musical talent. This, my dear Fischof, was the bitterest cut that you could possibly have administered to the over-weening vanity of a mere boy.

Let me confess to you, that for the moment, disappointment overmastered me. I was indeed sadly hurt. My expectation had been that you would have hailed me as a genius. I had supposed that you would have been thunderstruck to discover what enormous talent had suddenly come to light. In my day-dreams, I had seen you, with my score under your arm in a huge brown-paper parcel, hurrying off to the administration of the Imperial Opera. Nay! in my fancy, I had listened to you while urging its immediate performance.

It is needless to say, that I left not my Opera for a moment in your hands, after your opinion had been expressed.

Resolved, however, not to abandon my chance of immortality, I hurried off to Doctor Ignaz Jeitteles, the celebrated Professor of Æsthetics, and with less modesty than that which had been displayed towards you, laid the score before him. My request was, and sooth to say, it was made, if my memory serves me, in a remarkably determined manner, that he would use his influence in proposing my Opera for performance at the Imperial Opera. After a few questions which he addressed to me, he in all probability ascertained that I could not be easily dismissed. He therefore requested me to leave my score with him and to return in a few days.

The minutes and seconds of those few days were eagerly counted by me. They seemed to me so many centuries. On the appointed day, I accordingly presented myself again.

"I have sent," said the worthy Doctor, "your Opera to our Maestro, the Chevalier Seyfried, who, as you know, is the greatest musical theorist of our days."

"Well!" was my answer, "and the result?"

"He gave his opinion in writing upon its merits. Shall I read it to you?"

"Most certainly!"

"Then listen!" Here he took out a letter, unfolded it, and began reading :—"The Opera which you have sent me, has, after its perusal, actually made me feel forty years younger!"

Here, I jumped up in a perfect ecstasy, and completely wild with delight, as the Doctor, looking at me with an ironical smile on his intellectual features, asked me whether I would listen to any more?

"Yes! yes! continue by all means, my dearest Doctor!" I stammered out.

"Because, forty years since, I was unfortunately in the habit of writing just such nonsense as this Opera is!"

A blow with a feather would at this moment have felled me. I sunk back into my chair, like an automaton, whose wheels and watch-springs have done their appointed labor

"Will you hear the remainder?" asked the professor.

"No! This is more than enough."

"Never mind what he has said—" continued Dr. Jeitteles.

I hid my face in my hands.

"Take courage, and be attentive to what follows;" and then, resuming the letter, he thus continued: "However, there are such keen modulations displayed in portions of it, together with such a plentiful supply of melody, that it may be permitted me to believe, if the unknown young gentleman were to begin his theoretical studies *anew*, he might, in some two years, become an accomplished *maestro*, and as such, would promise well for the future. In such a case, I should not be altogether disinclined to take charge of his musical education myself!"

Mute with disappointment, all my hopes had vanished from me.

All the pictures of Fame and honors (not yet had I began to think of money, my old friend) which my imagination had painted, were at once dissolved. All the castles which I had reared in the morning-skies of my fancy, had melted into the unsubstantial heavens.

Old Dr. Jeitteles, however, viewed the affair in a widely different light. He assured me that this reply from Seyfried, seemed to him flattering enough.

" Flattering enough!" I groaned with an involuntary echo.

For his part, he had not expected half as complimentary an answer.

" Half as complimentary!" Was the kind-hearted old wretch not adding positive insult to injury ?

He, consequently, advised me to take advantage of the honorable offer which the Chevalier had implied at the conclusion of his letter, and to obtain permission from my parents to terminate my musical studies under his care. Leaving the Doctor, I went homeward, however, with the resolution to abandon the profession of my choice, and rush into bone-setting or process-serving, or anything else to which it might please my parents to call me. Old as I was, I do not feel ashamed to say, that, on this night, my feelings sobbed themselves to silence upon this determination. It was evident that, as yet, although fancy had dubbed me a man, fact still ranked me as a child.

But with the following dawn, Fischof, when I arose and

dressed myself, all things had changed to my perception. What it was, I know not. Certain is it that I had not dreamed, yet my first waking reflections were widely different from those under whose influence slumber had come upon me.

Cool thought treated my childish presumption, now, at its right value.

Returning again to you, I begged your interference with my parents, and through your intercession was it, with them, that their consent was given to my boyish ignorance of music, being placed under the tuition of the Chevalier. With what ardor and perseverance I worked under his guidance, and how, some time afterwards, an Opera was actually produced by me, with more than the mere success generally awarded by public courtesy to a first production, is known to you and most of my countrymen who understand and relish music. What German is there that does not do so ?

Sixteen years have passed over me since that period, and although I again tell you how thankful I was and am for your kindness, the thought has occasionally passed through my mind whether it would not have been better for me to become either a doctor or a lawyer.

Had my father's will made me the first, perchance my imaginative faculty might have developed itself in some Universal Medicament " good for all kinds of diseases, and very wholesome to healthy persons," like *Dr. Dulcamara's* in the " Elisir d'Amore." By this time, I might have been a *millionaire* like Professor Holloway, of London, or have emulated the glories of Dr. Townsend's palatial mansion in our own Fifth Avenue.

Had he made me a lawyer, a single year of study would have fitted me for practising at the Bar in my new country. The money of my clients would, in the first place, have been paid me for commencing and not carrying on their suits ; while the money of their opponents would have rewarded me for suffering them to go by default. Perchance, I might have *concertized* with political Lectures, and have ultimately obtained some fat slice at the division of the spoils ; or, could I not even have supplied families and hotel-keepers with opinions on the Maine, —or rather on the New York Liquor-Law, *pro* or *con*, in every style, at the shortest notice ; terms—cash.

But as a simple musician, after sixteen years of hard labor, and as a Manager after a musical war of seven years' duration, my dear Fischof, where am I ?

The *baton* has been wielded by me, now as a *maestro*, again as a Conductor, and afterwards as a Manager, in various cities, from Agram near the Black Sea to Mexico almost on the borders of the Pacific Ocean. Here, I have been almost starving. There, I have been entertaining a host of guests in a style that was well nigh princely. Occasionally, my request has been made in vain for employment as a musical copyist. At another time, employment has been given by me to somewhere about three hundred persons. Now, I have been forced to borrow a few score of dollars from particular friends, and then, compelled to lavish hundreds (or as it might truly be said, thousands) upon professional enemies. As a reward for the first necessity, my friends were invariably lost to him who dared make use of their pockets ; and, as a return for the last, my compulsory profusion has ever managed to retain my enemies. Sometimes hissed by the public ; at others, I have been the object of the most flattering ovations. But, my old and dear friend, the object of my younger ambition, the writing and the production of Operas, has been neglected until the present.

You will naturally enough ask me why this should be ?

To this, only one answer can be made. Circumstances have thrust me into my present path, and have not, as yet, allowed me for one moment to diverge from it. As a necessity, almost, was management forced upon me.

This, you will tell me, was an admirable position for a young composer, to bring out his own Operas.

But do you not know that a Manager is nowhere the absolute ruler of his own artists.   In America more especially, is he their slave, while they are his tyrants.   No rules and regulations are enforced by the law, in this land of freedom, which these sons and daughters gotten by caprice upon whim, are forced to obey.   It might possibly have been managed, but the example given me, by my predecessor in the Astor Place Opera House, frightened me.   Mr. Fry had ruined himself by his predilection for his brother's Operas.   Consequently, my reasoning was this.   If a brother's Operas are so dangerous, how much more must the Operas of a Manager himself be.   Therefore, not only my time and labor, together with my own money and that of others, have been risked and staked in the establishment of Opera in America, but the real object of my whole life has also been sacrificed to it.   You inquire of me, wherefore my Operas were not produced in other theatres than those which I was managing ?   Blushing with shame, a confession, which cannot be avoided, rises to my tongue.   Mine, my respected friend, was the only operatic Company in the United States, if the French Opera at New Orleans (only some 2000 miles distant) be excepted !   In Germany or Italy, not a town is there of twenty thousand inhabitants, which has not its own Opera House and its own operatic Company.   A city which possesses 60 or 100,000 inhabitants, generally has two or three well-sustained and well-supported musical theatres. We in the United States (there are more than 25,000,000 of us) have but two.   Even with this small number, failures are the general order of the day.

The Grecian, Roman, Florentine and Venetian Republics not only encouraged Art, but were in fact the hearth and harbor of all Art and Genius.

Yet, it would seem that our new and young Republic, which in point of commerce, wealth, industry, and the genius of invention, has in such a brief space of time surpassed and out-flanked your old Europe, is not willing to acknowledge the wholesome and useful influence of Art over the education of youth and in the culture of Manhood.

Beyond a doubt, a really creative genius in Poetry, Music, Painting, or Sculpture, must starve in America, should he de-cide on confining himself to that calling for which his Maker has pre-eminently gifted him. Bryant, whom you of course know by his Poèms, edits a daily journal. Would it be possible to say more than is said in this single sentence ? The greatest poet in the New World deals in daily politics and the price of stocks.

Yes ! my old friend, cities such as Boston, Philadelphia, Cincinnati and Baltimore, with populations as large as those of Vienna, Naples, Berlin and Milan, cannot or do not choose to support a regular Opera.

Indeed, the only regular Italian Opera in the Northern half of that part of the world in which I am now residing (admire, my dear Fischof, the extent of that last phrase,) save our own in New York, was located in the city of Havana and the island of Cuba.

It was under the direction of Don Francisco Marty y Torrens.

Señor Marty, like Barbaja in Naples, or Dr. Veron in Paris, belongs to the class of successful operatic Managers. The reason of this is, that, like Veron or Barbaja, Marty has by no means made it his principal business. With either of the three, it is only an accessory or secondary affair, kept up with a view of palliating the principal one, for which service the cloaked concern, in its turn, makes good the losses which may be in-curred by the Opera.

Thus, as you well know, Barbaja has the privilege of all the gambling-houses in the kingdom of Naples placed in his hands, together with the management of the Opera. His position as its *impressario*, necessarily brought him into connection with every class, strangers and natives. Consequently, after having animated his acquaintances with music and singing, and after having diverted their eyes with the silk fleshings and short muslin *jupons* of his *corps de ballet*, he fleeced them at his gambling-houses, and soon became more wealthy than the king of Naples himself. Report says, although it may be a matter of question with me and most other Managers, whether report ought always to be implicitly believed, that the said Barbaja used to be extremely polite with those individuals who won at his gambling tables, and regularly sent them home in his own carriages. His politeness used to be accurately proportioned to the amount which they bore away with them. Those who lost, he did not even notice. They were allowed to find their way to their dwellings upon their own legs.

Once, an acquaintance who had been winning, asked him the reason of this.

Barbaja smiled.

" My system," said he, " is a very simple one. The lucky gambler, loaded with money, may be robbed in returning home. But I consider the money in his pockets as still mine. Barring accidents, he will return and lose it to the last *scudo*. I have to take care of him. The unlucky gambler, on the contrary, having been already " cleaned out," cannot be robbed. His passion and the desire to retrieve his losses, will bring him back to try his fortune once more. There is no necessity for extra care or politeness with him."

Barbaja again smiled pleasantly, as his acquaintance buttoned up his pockets.

How it was, that the great gambling-house proprietor had

made such a mistake, I know not, but the gentleman never again played at one of his tables.

As for Dr. Veron, it is generally known that he was the inventor of the celebrated *Pate Pectorale*.* What position could be more admirably calculated, than his was, as Manager of the French Opera in Paris, to advertise that *Pate* through the whole of Europe ?

But, now, you will ask me about the business of the very worthy Don Francisco Marty y Torrens. My personal knowledge of him is very small. If I state to you what is said about him, remember that I am very far from vouching for its scrupulous exactitude. It is said, then, that in his younger days, the Havanese *impressario* was the mate of a most formidable Pirate who infested the Mexican Gulf and the seas more immediately adjacent to it. The Spanish government offered a large recompense for the capture of this pirate. Immediately, the youthful Francisco felt it his duty to serve his government. The rover fell into a trap, which was very neatly laid for him, and was taken. He was, of course, "garoted," this punishment being a peculiarly agreeable and expeditious way of throttling a prisoner in public, which is in vogue in Cuba.

As his recompense, the amiable Francisco received the privilege of all the fish-markets in the island.

Nobody in all Cuba had the right of selling a single fish, without paying certain dues to Don Francisco Marty y Torrens.

In addition to this, he had money. How much or where acquired, no one knows. This loose cash he invested in building or chartering some hundreds of fishing-boats. He was therefore enabled, after a short time, to supply his own markets.

* A lozenge adapted to dispel hoarseness, and used alike on the stage and in the pulpit.

This business, in which he could encounter no opposition, soon afterwards took under his management such colossal proportions, that, some years since, its annual profits were estimated at 10,000 ounces of gold, or something equivalent to 800,000 francs. Still retaining a certain predilection for everything approximating to his old profession (you note, I should presume, the delicate name with which it is characterized), he fitted out several large vessels to carry on the slave trade. His baits were now fire-arms, doubloons and kegs of brandy. His hooked fish were negroes from the coast of Africa, and Indians from Yucatan. These, the bribed authorities of the island permitted to be landed and sold there. This speculation increased Marty's fortune, and it soon reached an almost fabulous extent. He now dabbled in government securities, and was several times enabled to help the government of Spain out of its momentary embarrassments. For this devotion, an equivalent had to be received, and it was offered him in the shape of knighthood and "letters of nobility" by the Spanish crown.

Thus he became not only powerful in Havana, but great also in Madrid, in which city he keeps his regular agents.

It has indeed been told me, that the Captain-general Concha had at one time determined upon depriving Marty of the privilege of exclusively dealing in fish. He had therefore obtained the revocation of the grant from the Spanish Ministry. The worthy Señor Francisco had, however, been informed of the proceedings with this view, by his agents, and had acted in accordance with the intelligence. When summoned by General Concha to the palace, and notified by him that his privilege had ceased, by command of the Queen, he very coolly asked the Captain-general the date of this order. The document was handed to him. Marty looked at it and drew another from his pocket, which was dated exactly one day later.

It revoked the former one and reinstated Don Francisco

Marty y Torrens in all his former rights and privileges. The General was for the moment thunderstruck, as Marty said to him—

"Your Excellency not appearing to have received the communication, believe me, I shall feel most happy in providing you with this copy of it."

But, in spite of his wealth, his power and his influence, Marty was not liked. The proud Castilian *noblesse* of the island absolutely refused to tolerate the slave-dealer and fish-seller in their society. He therefore determined upon forcing them to swallow the fish and digest the negro. To do this, he built a splendid Opera House, engaged first-rate Opera *troupes*, and became his own Manager.

At first, lovers of song as all Spaniards are, they refused to patronize him.

Enraged at this, Don Francisco committed an act, the egotism of which was so intense, that it almost amounts to genius.

He closed the doors of the Tacon theatre upon the public but retained the company.

The performances were continued for himself.

There he sat, but for a few friends, in solitary grandeur, listening to and enjoying the music, almost alone. Now he would applaud this, or hiss that artist—here, he would give a rapturous *encore*—there, he would throw a magnificent bracelet upon the stage, to a pretty *prima donna*—he himself, representing in his own person alike, the public, the management, the critics and the dead-heads. It strikes me, my good old friend, that the grand cynicism of this conduct has never been equalled. For this alone, do I confess, that I almost venerate the Señor Francisco Marty y Torrens.

However, the artists made acquaintances, and these acquaintances wished to hear them in Opera. Marty heard it, and, doubtless, chuckled inwardly. Externally, he was inexorable.

This strange, and, as it seemed to the majority of the public in Havana, unaccountable behavior, raised their curiosity to the highest pitch. After interposing many, and, as it appeared, insurmountable difficulties, Marty, perhaps wearied out of his solitary Sybaritism, consented to treat with the aristocracy of the Cuban capital. Provided a number of them would buy up the boxes of his house for a certain series of years, and provided they would make up a purse each season, for the management, he was willing to throw open the doors of the Tacon, and furnish first-class Operatic performances. As the Spanish Señoritas are exceedingly fond of music, and even more partial to display, the Spanish Señores were obliged, by the love of melody and the terror of their better halves, to comply with these terms. Don Francisco had won his first battle with the Havanese aristocracy.

Thanks, therefore, to the subscription and the compulsory *subvention*, which sometimes amounted to $30,000, Italian Opera flourished for a season in Havana.

In order to show you, my good Professor, how much Marty himself understood of those musical matters on which, for a time, he had chosen to sit as the sole judge, you will allow me to retail to you an anecdote, which has been given me as perfectly true.

Sitting once, during an operatic performance, in the first row of seats, near the Orchestra, he remarked a horn-player looking at his music without playing. For a time, the profoundly scientific Manager endured this, but, when some twenty bars had passed, without bringing any signs of life into the instrument, he at last lost his patience, and turned to the unlucky horn-player—

" Why the deuce don't you play, sir ?" he exclaimed.

" Señor—" queried the instrumentalist.

" Why don't you play ?"

Señor, I am counting my bars, now."

" Are you, you lazy scoundrel ? Counting your bars, indeed ! Why did you not count them before this ?"

" I am waiting before I begin, Señor !" said the unlucky musician, in a marked *tremolo*.

" Begin at once !" quoth Marty.

" Señor— ?" began the man imploringly.

" Begin !" repeated the *impressario*, " or, when pay-day comes, I shall count my dollars and wait before I pay you."

The threat was sufficient. The horn was raised to the musician's mouth, but no sooner was the first note blown, than the Conductor turned on the instrumentalist with a savage look. The brazen tube dropped from his mouth, and then only was Marty aware of the error which he had made. As the audience noted what had passed with the usual quickness of Southern musical intuition, they applauded the unlucky horn. Daggers were looked at Marty by the incensed Conductor, who ran round to the front of the house at the close of the act.

What he was about to say to Don Francisco Marty y Torrens, you and I, my dear Fischof, shall never know, for the Manager had departed that night from the theatre, earlier than usual, and, on the following morning, his season's salary dictated to him a wise forbearance.

As, however, it would have been difficult to procure available singers from Italy, and well nigh impossible to lure artists of decided merit to Havana for the few winter months, the Señor Marty was obliged to engage his company for a much longer period ; and, during the intervals that they could not remain in Cuba, in consequence of the great heat and their fears of the yellow fever, for two years he used to send them to New York. Here, they played in Castle Garden, once a

fort, afterwards an Opera house, and, now, the *dépôt* for emigrants from Europe. While his artists were no better than
those we had in New York, this *concurrence* was of no moment to the interests of the New York management. In
the summer of 1850, however, Marty sent to this city the
greatest *troupe* which had ever been heard in America. Indeed, in point of the integral talent, number and excellence of
the artists composing it, it must be admitted that it has seldom been excelled in any part of the Old World.

This party consisted of three *prime donne.* These were
the Signore Steffanone, Bosio and Tedesco. Its only *contralto*
was the Signora Vietti. There were three *tenors*, Salvi, Bettini and Lorini. Badiali and Corradi Setti were the two *barytones*, while the two *bassi* were Marini and Coletti. At the
head of this extraordinary company was the great *contra-bassist*
(I call him so, because he is best known by his wonderful skill
on that instrument) Bottesini, assisted by Arditi. It would
be useless, my old friend, to attempt to indicate to you the
excellence of this Company. You have long since known their
names, or been aware of their standing as artists, in the world
of Music. The greater portion of them enjoy a wide and well-
deserved European reputation, and their re-union, anywhere,
would form an almost incomparable Operatic *troupe.*

Bosio and Tedesco have since taken London, and Paris, and
St. Petersburgh by storm. Steffanone has recently returned to
Europe, and, in a short time, we shall, in all probability, hear
of her triumphs. Bettini has since that period been everywhere acknowledged in Italy, as its first *tenor.* Salvi, Marini,
and Badiali had established European reputations as artists of
the very first class, and these, too, long before their arrival in
America. Salvi, more especially, although inferior in voice to
Mario, equalled him in finish of style and method, while, as a
mere actor, he most undoubtedly at that time much surpassed

him : and Marini was known in London as the greatest
Italian *basso* who had ever sung there, with the solitary exception of Lablache.

This Company not only created a profound sensatión in
New York, but played at something less than half the usual
price.

The admission to Castle Garden, during their performances,
was no more than fifty cents.

In fact, it was purely a matter of the most perfect indifference to Marty, whether they made him money, or whether
they did not make him money, during their summer season.
Their salaries were provided for out of the receipts of their
winter performances in Havana, and their brief visit to a more
northern clime had no other object than that of increasing
their reputation, in order that such increase might react upon
Cuban society ; as well as the one of filling out the summer
without permitting them to be idle, or incurring the risk of
acclimating such valuable personal property as *soprani* and
tenori. Yellow fever is a very dangerous acquaintance, and
the second time it nods to you, if you are unfortunate enough
to incur the risk of a relapse, in nine cases out of ten, you are,
my good old friend, little better, to use an American expression, than "a gone coon."

At once, upon hearing them, I made up my mind, if it were
by any means possible, to secure them for this city.

My determination to do so was based upon two important
reasons.

First, it was evident enough to any one who was at all con-
versant with operatic matters in Europe, that neither New
York nor Havana would ever be able to bring so admirable a
company again together. While, secondly, I saw clearly
enough that such a company as this was, if left under the
management of Marty, would at their present prices become a

most dangerous and effective opposition to the New York management.

Therefore, I decided upon entering into immediate communication with the several artists composing the *troupe*.

This I accordingly did, and succeeded in securing all of them, with the single exception of Tedesco, for the United States, after the expiration of their present engagement with Marty.

With the acquisition of this company, I began firmly to believe that Italian Opera would be perpetually domiciled in my new country. " Man," however, "proposes, while Fate disposes." Just as difficult, as it would have been to find again, such a number of admirable artists collected under one management, would it have been to bring together such a capricious, conceited, egotistical, rapacious, intriguing, cheating, troublesome, mischievous and malicious set of vocalists. The perfect liberty which they enjoyed in New York, without the strict police regulations of either Italy or Havana, soon degenerated into impudence, insolence, and the most audacious contempt both for the public who came to listen to, and the management which paid them. But it would take up far too much time and space, my dear Professor, were my pen to attempt detailing to you all their quarrels, jealousies and intrigues amongst themselves, or their tricks, plots and conspiracies against their Manager. Not only had he (you must here understand myself) to contend with the unavoidable difficulties of his position, but he had also to suffer the consequences resulting from their private quarrels.

If one *prima donna* happened to be jealous of the applause which had been given another, she refused to sing, exactly when she was most wanted, in order to punish the Manager for the success which had attended her rival.

Should a pretty ballet-girl decline listening to the delicate propositions made her by the *primo tenore*, this last-named artist would become love-sick, and declare himself too indisposed to appear upon the stage.

Did the Opera in which the *barytone* had a prominent part create a *furore*, for that simple reason would the *basso* expressly contrive to kill the next work which the management placed upon the stage, that he might make me unmistakably appreciate his own importance.

In addition to this generic feature, each one of them had his particular whims and caprices.

One exception must, however, be made, and this is in favor of the Signora Steffanone. She was very generally sufficiently conscientious. This was perhaps more especially the case, while there was another *prima donna* in the company capable of treading in her buskins. She had nevertheless one decidedly physical drawback to her undoubted value, being subject to fits and convulsions, which materially prejudiced the management. These, I had remarked, never seized her while upon the stage. They generally chanced anterior to her advertised appearance before the public. Inquiring privately about these attacks, from her physician, I ascertained that they ordinarily returned at stated intervals, and could almost be predicted with a mathematical certainty. These days were therefore marked beforehand, in my Almanac, with a black line. Performances were set apart for them, in which Steffanone would have no necessity for appearing. In this manner and by these means, we managed to get along very well, and this continued for a long period. At length, Bosio quitted the company, and when she did so, it seemed to me that these convulsive attacks became exceedingly irregular. In consulting my Calendar, it appeared to me that they were at the very least twice as frequent as they had before been. Indeed, during the late operatic season, when the Chevalier Henry Wikoff was Acting Manager for the committee who conducted the Academy, their frequency had increased to a truly alarming extent. The clever Chevalier, who by his marvellous diplomatic skill had succeeded in engaging her at several hundred dollars larger salary than she had ever been paid by me, could neither find out the reason of nor prevent these repeated convulsions. Whispers indeed were in circulation respecting them, which it may be concluded never reached him. Otherwise, his diplomacy would certainly have been called upon to prevent their too frequent and continuous recurrence.

The Signora Angelina Bosio was a very talented and industrious lady, with only one great misfortune. She had a—husband.

No possible plague is there which can be greater for a luckless Manager than those which daily befall him, save the fact of his *prima donna*, or one of his two or three, being a married woman.

Sometimes, we find the husband of the vocalist is a green fish, recently caught in the army or navy, by the French paste and footlight glare upon the shrewd and experienced *cantatrice*. She has played her cards so ably, as to induce the hapless lover to offer marriage. These terms are the only ones upon which his suit for her heart can possibly be received. Here, it is a lucky and stalwart hotel-waiter, that enjoys the honor of being promoted by marriage to the bed of the popular favorite. Nor will you think, my amiable Fischof, that I am romancing in hinting at this possibility, for you, at least, can recall to your memory the case of one celebrated *prima donna*, whose *Fidelio* is renowned wherever music is known, that has picked up her husband in the aforesaid condition of life. Now and then, a sighing oboe or a sentimental violin, inspired by love or smitten with a desire not to pay out of his own pocket for his brandy-punches, has leapt over the foot-lights and the prompter's green umbrella into the arms of the enamored vocalist. Perhaps, a desperate *maestro di canto* may have accepted, as the last resort against suicide or starvation, the situation of husband to the inspired artist. Nay! I have even heard of one case, in which the *valet de chambre* of the lady's titled lover, who had filled the honorable post of Mercury to his master's *liaison*, was subsequently of necessity promoted to the nominal position of a husband, when a *marriage de convenance* became necessary to save her reputation, and to offer the public a formula to account for the figure which she was making in the world.

Be this as it may, the first object in the life of a *prima donna's* husband is to impress his wife with a vivid sense of his own importance to her.

Without him, she would be a comparatively lost reputation.

He detects and brings to light numberless hidden treasures (!) in his wife's school of vocalization, which have until now escaped the eyes both of the Managers and the public.

It is very possible that he may not have the slightest idea of what singing really should be. Yet to him, only, is it that she is indebted for any progress in her Art. When she is rehearsing with her *maestro*, he is occupied in industriously beating time. Assiduously does he turn over the leaves of the score of her part—most carefully does he wipe the dust from the notes of the piano—with what forethought does he either screw up or screw down the music-stool to suit her height, whether she be tall or short. Carrying the inevitable poodle in the right hand, and her clogs in the left, he bears with him the shawl over one arm and a roll of music squeezed under the other. No sooner is the rehearsal over, than he runs for the carriage. In nine cases out of ten, after carefully closing the door upon *his* spouse and *her cicisbeo*, he trots home rapidly, to see that the soup is hot and the champagne iced, and to look after the other ninety-nine affairs of the *ménage*. Ever on the watch to hermetically close the doors and windows, he never foregoes an opportunity of gently insinuating that the *maestro* owes far more to the musical knowledge of his wife than she owes to him, and slightly hints that both are under immeasurable obligations to himself for his untiring care of both their interests.

In addition to this, he quarrels with the Manager on the occasion of his wife's signing the contract. This is indeed an inevitable necessity for him. He makes a thousand new and unheard-of demands upon the exchequer of the management, amongst which are huge travelling expenses, benefits, extra-payments and costs for himself, servants, dogs, parrots, as well as the *cavaliere servente*.

To impress his wife with an adequate idea of his own importance, after the engagement has been signed he picks up a trifling difference with the Manager, which he has the skill to foster daily into the proportions of a grave quarrel. At last, this fearful affair is settled, and then does it appear that the exemplary husband has saved his most innocent wife from a horrible conspiracy which had been expressly formed for her ruin. Of this conspiracy, it would of course be utterly needless to add, that the miserable Manager had most indubitably been both part and parcel. While an infinitely more singular deduction may be drawn from the reports of everybody concerned in or with it. He was decidedly fool enough to be so, at the complete sacrifice of his own interests.

Such, be it observed, were the claims for her love and gratitude, which the Signor Panayotis di Xindavelonis possessed upon his spouse, the Signora Bosio.

Tedesco was the only one of the artists who formed the company, that quitted it instead of remaining with me.

Now, when she had arrived in this country from Havana, my much respected Professsor, the Signora Tedesco was possessed of *no* husband. She, however, enjoyed the care and affection of a near relative who was immeasurably worse than anything I have seen in the shape of a spouse of any *cantatrice.* This relative was *a* father. This father, I am compelled by my conscience to say, I have not the slightest doubt, descended in a direct and straightforward line from *Shylock* of Venice.

When he came to the theatre upon pay-day, for the purpose of receiving his daughter's salary, he was in the admirable and thoroughly delicate habit of subjecting each separate piece of gold to a peculiarly Jewish examination touching their Christian perfection. In a word, he was in the habit of carrying a small pair of scales in his breeches-pocket, with which he verified their respective weight.

His daughter, Fortunata, (so was she miscalled, for she was unfortunate enough in being compelled to own her descent from such a sire) bore, in her turn, a singular resemblance to the charming daughter of *Shylock*, Shakspeare's *Jessica.* As *Jessica* had done in the days upon which the great play-wright drew for plot and character, she fell in love with a Christian who had more or less of the white man in his blood, and like *Desdemona*, she married him in spite of all opposition, saying in all probability :—

> " I saw - - - - - 's visage in his mind,
> " And to his honors and his valiant parts
> " Did I my soul and fortune consecrate."

As for the principal *primo tenore*, this was the Signor Salvi. He believed himself in the Operatic world, a fixed star of the first magnitude, around whose twinkling lustre (but let me beg his pardon for that unlucky adjective : it should have been a broader and a larger one) all of the other and lesser planets had slowly and respectfully to revolve. He supposed himself to be the brilliant Sun from whom the nobodies who were his satellites had to obtain the whole of their light and warmth.

If, perchance, at times he descended from the height of self-appreciation upon which he dwelt, and for a moment admitted himself to be an ordinary mortal like you or myself, my dear Fischof, it was only that he might indulge in playing the *rôle* of a despotic sovereign. Then, I felt that he believed himself to be the Louis Quatorze of the lyric drama, and, at times, was under the impression that I should hear him exclaim, " *L'Opera, c'est moi.*"

As for the luckless Manager, Signor Salvi literally looked upon him in the light of his own dignity, as his bondsman. Providence had, with a kindly and liberal hand, consigned him to the *primo tenore*, to be plucked, squeezed and sucked out like a ripe and golden orange. When the juice had satisfied him, he was to be thrown away and kicked into the street like the rind of that luscious fruit. The public, however, was a necessary evil. He regarded them somewhat as a band of savages, whom he, however, like a second Orpheus, could appease with the wondrous melody of his voice.

Like every other despot by the grace of God, he was more alive to flattery than he was sensible of his duties. Unlike any other idol, he keenly enjoyed the worshipping of his private priests and the adoration of his private priestesses.

He recompensed their hymns in his favor, by forcing his Manager (?) to engage them. They must be provided for, whether they were wanted or not, and, indeed, whether they were good for anything or not.

A flattery to Signor Salvi was certain to cost the Manager a dozen season-tickets. The smallest service which had been rendered to this gentleman, was paid for, not out of his own purse, but by a place in the Orchestra or Chorus, or some office which was in the gift of the Manager. If, however, it should chance that some sacrifice had been made to the will or interest of the autocrat of the Opera, then he lanced an imperative Ukase at his aforesaid slave. He was ordered to engage the said person for a period of six, nine or twelve months, as the case might be, or the whim might seize his ruler, at so many hundred dollars, payable in advance. Such a document is a singular specimen of Salvi's imperative style of commanding obedience ; the menace of the penalty incurred, in the event of a non-compliance with his orders, being invariably contained in it. One specimen of the many in my possession I give you, my amiable friend, that you may see I am not exaggerating. Note how short and energetic, in fact how Napoleonic, Signor Salvi's style of issuing his orders was.

" *Caro Max*," *

Fa di tutto per iscritturare la Sidonia, altrimenti io non canto " *ne ' Don Giovanni', ne ' Norma', ne altri.*

" *A* 250 $ *il mese, e che la scrittura porti* 350 $. *Amen, e* " *cosi sia.*

" 19. 4. 53. *Il tuo Salvi.*"

Look at the date, my venerated Professor ! Examine the style. " *Amen ! e cosi sia.*" Does it not very strongly remind you of the style of the great Corsican ?

In fact, Fischof, man is reduplicated in every condition. The Borgias poisoned and committed adultery upon a large scale. How many smaller Borgias have been made most unfairly away with upon the scaffold ! Nero got rid of his mother, and how

* This letter, translated, verbally reads thus :

"My dear Max,

" Do everything to engage the Sidonia, otherwise, I shall neither sing " in the ' Don Giovanni,' in ' Norma,' or in other Operas.

" At 250 $ per month, but let the writing bear 350 $. Amen, and so " be it.

" 19. 4. 53. Yours, SALVI."

many mother-slayers have since that period been rope-throttled for a similar crime ! Therefore is it that I feel I have the right to parallel Signor Salvi's imperative despatches to me, with the equally imperative proclamations and despatches of a much greater man.

On other occasions, he would order that the Zaninis(husband and wife) the Signorina Ceriani, or the stage-tailor Locatelli and his spouse, (I might not be in need of a stage-tailor and tailoress) should be engaged. Occasionally, such a command for a round half-dozen of engagements, would come in at once. If not immediately complied with, the refusal, it was intimated, would cause him a bilious attack (!) which he positively knew beforehand (!!) would last *exactly* thirteen days.

This thirteen days' sickness was the highest penalty of *lèsè-majesté* in what it will scarcely be a jest to call the *Code Salvinien*.

You, my good old friend, ask me " wherefore ?"

Simply was it, that the great *tenore* never accepted an engagement from any Manager, unless, in the event of sickness, fourteen days of grace were given him. If therefore an unfortunately refractory Manager were condemned to suffer the penalty for high treason to his delicately voiced monarch, it was managed in this fashion. The domestic of Signor Salvi presented himself at the *bureau* of the management, with a medical certificate that the vocalist had an attack of bronchitis, yellow fever, or cholera morbus. Consequently, for thirteen days his name could not appear on the bills. On the fourteenth day, generally the morning of what Operatic Managers call an off-night, the *tenore* would announce his readiness to sing again, if required. On the fifteenth, he would make his appearance looking uncommonly well after thirteen days of the cholera, or singularly rosy after the same period of yellow fever, to draw his fortnights salary ; having only been too ill to sing for thirteen days of it. On the day following, he would have a relapse, and continue in this deplorable condition for another period of thirteen days, unless in the meantime the Manager should become a suppliant for peace, and submit himself humbly to each and every condition imposed upon him by the triumphant artist as a punishment for his rebellion against legitimate authority.

The other *tenore*, Signor Bettini, was a young man with a robust and vigorous voice, and a manly figure. He had but one fault. This, however, was a serious one.

He had a peculiar relish for amusing himself with select parties of those whom he considered his friends at "*petits soupées a la Régence.*" Here, he would drown his brains in a Champagne-flask and afterwards lose his money at the gambling-table during whole nights. The natural consequence of this would be, that he was unable to sing upon the following evening.

These moral if not actual breaches of his engagement became somewhat too frequent. Therefore, I concluded upon trying a remedy with this otherwise amiable gentleman.

Two watchmen were accordingly hired by me to keep him in constant *surveillance*. They were bidden to remain in sight of his residence; to let me know every person who entered his rooms, with the time of his arrival and departure; to follow Bettini whenever he went out, whether in the day or night-time, and to keep notes of the houses he might go to, his occupation there if they could discover it, the length of time he remained, the hour at which he returned, &c., &c., &c. It must be confessed that my two spies did their work admirably. Every morning I received from them, in my office, the most minute and authentic account of Signor Bettini's doings. I was as well posted up about them, as if I had never wandered an inch from his elbow. The secret police of Vienna or of Paris have never been better served. Nay, I feel convinced that my two purely impromptu officials might have risen to high distinction in the government-employment of this branch of police-duty, either in France or in Austria.

As I had expected, after a few days had elapsed, my dear Fischof, a letter was brought to me, about noon, from Bettini.

It profoundly regretted that a violent fever would prevent him from singing in the evening. He notified me in time, that I might change the bill or postpone the performance.

Neither of these was done; but, in answer to his note, he received from me an elaborate digest of all his proceedings for the last twenty-four hours. It stated, with admirable accuracy, the number of Champagne bottles which he had emptied at dinner and supper, on the preceding day, indicating also the round sum which he had flung away at the faro table on the evening succeeding, the hour at which he had returned home, together with sundry other interesting particulars, which it would be scarcely decorous to mention. This paper I requested him to read and to change any accidental misrepresentation which might occur in it, as it was my intention to have it *printed* and *distributed* amongst the public on that evening, who would, by this means, be fully possessed with the reasons for his " fever" and his consequent non-appearance.

In what manner the Signor Bettini received this missive has never been satisfactorily revealed to me.

Afterwards, he assured me that it was a capital joke.

My spies were unable to penetrate into his sitting-room; consequently, I am unable, my dear Professor, positively to asseverate that he did not do so, although it may appear to me rather dubious.

Certain is it, that he was visible upon the stage that same evening. Never, probably, in his whole life, had he sung better than he did upon this occasion. The *poignée du main* which

I received from him, was as gratefully affectionate, as that which an amiable young Parisian might, at the present moment, bestow upon a rival in an affair of the heart who was about proceeding to the Crimea. The means of knowing whether it were as genuine, have never been vouchsafed to me. However, the little lesson with which my espionage had enabled me to accommodate him, had a very salutary effect upon his subsequent career; and his talents have subsequently placed him in the acknowledged situation of the favorite *tenore* in Italy and Austria.

Badiali was an exception to the rest of this Company in many respects. As an artist he was singularly conscientious, and rarely, if ever, failed in doing his duty to the public. He, necessarily, speedily became a favorite. However, his extraordinary meanness and avarice, as well as a certain amount of trifling jealousy, have precluded him from winning the general regard of his professional brethren.

Undoubtedly, next to Lablache, Signor Marini must be considered the greatest Italian *basso* at present living. In the conception of some of his parts, such, for example, as *Sylva*, the *Duke* in "Lucretia Borgia," and *Marino Faliero*, he occasionally displayed histrionic talents worthy of a Talma or a Kean. His voice was nevertheless, occasionally, unreliable; while he was frequently ill-humored, as capricious in his affections as the most capricious of the fairer sex, strangely peevish and splenetic, and more in the habit of listening to, and following the advice of, a worthless set of Italian "suckers," (the word, my old friend, is a native one in my adopted country, and is eminently expressive, signifying humanity when it approximates to the parasitical feeders upon other and sturdier trees, or to the jelly-like and glutinous polypi,) than that of his friends, and, let me add it, whether you smile at the association or not, his Manager.

As for the secondary parts, they were, of course, filled by an inferior set of artists in every respect, but one. They had, were it possible, an even greater love for intrigue and trickery.

Yet, in spite of every fault which has been scored against them, and those which my sufferings in their management might tempt me, even yet, to add to these—in spite of their restless duplicity, their ungracious treatment of myself, and the want of wisdom shown in the conduct of their relations with the public, I am obliged to say, and this without the slightest possibility of gaining any advantage by flattering their self-love, for they have all quitted the United States save Coletti, who has married, and is, I believe, settled in New York, that this Company was, in every respect, the very best which has ever been got together upon this side of the Atlantic. Such " stars" may, subsequently to their appearance, have flashed upon us, as Sontag, Grisi and Mario, or Alboni. But, it must be remembered, that these, in every case, rose upon the public as merely isolated luminaries. They stood completely alone. The remainder of their separate *troupes* cannot for a single moment be weighed in the balance with the Havanese Company. This presented, in all its details, the nearest approach to perfection which has ever visited this hemisphere. You will necessarily understand, my dear Fischof, that I am simply referring to their qualification as artists.

This *troupe*, consisting, as it did, not only of the members who had actually sung in it, in Havana, but also of many of my previous Company, (Mesdames Steffanone, Bosio, Vietti, and Costini, with Mesdemoiselles Bertucca and Truffi, and the Signori Salvi, Bettini, Lorini, Marini, Badiali, Coletti, Beneventano, with others, forming it,) I arranged should give Operas in Castle Garden, at the low price of fifty cents for admission.

To this determination I was induced by several reasons.

In the first place, the major strength of my vocalists had already performed there at that price.   Next, I firmly believed that the low price of admission and the great excellence of the artists themselves, would tend to popularize Opera.   Should it do so, it would not only root Music into the nation, my darling desire, but would, from the capacity of Castle Garden, which could hold more than 5,000 persons comfortably seated, render it probable that I might be paid for the risk attendant upon it.   Dreaming a golden dream, I fancied that with such a Company as this actually was, with prices no higher than the regular theatrical ones, and a large house, the taste for Italian Opera might be established, not amongst the " Upper Ten," but in the public heart of New York.

My good and old friend, I had made one great mistake.   I am able to own it without shame, because many much greater and more talented men than myself have made a similar error.

This mistake was made in supposing that he who sows, invariably reaps the harvest.   Certainly, I scattered the seed then, but it will remain for another hand than mine, or another time than mine own, to gather in the crop.   A love for music is a thing that cannot bear fruit the same month in which its seeds have been scattered in the ground.   Suffice it, that very frequently did we play before an audience varying in number from 100 to 150 persons, scarcely enough to pay the mere printing bills of the evening.   When the first three months had ended, the result of my golden dream, my respected and respectable Fischof, was a clear and unmistakable deficit of $22,000.   The best operatic Company ever collected in the United States had failed, at the lowest prices ever asked for admission to such a class of entertainment as that provided for

the public, in drawing sufficient money to pay their own salaries.   Believe me that, had I then written to you, my signature would have been,

Your very miserable, &c., &c.,

Max Maretzek.

FIFTH LETTER.

TO M. W. BALFE, LONDON.

Musical Agents in New York—Catherine Hayes—Lola Montez—Niblo's Garden, as an Opera House, and William Niblo, as a Manager—Opposition—" Robert le Diable "—Meyerbeer's Operas—Origin of Opera—Rossini—Donetti's Troupe of Learned Dogs and Monkeys.

Paris 10 oc[t]

Mon cher ami

Je vous prie de me te[nir]
au courant de ce que vous a[vez]
fait pour rompre les engageme[nts]
de ces gens engagés à l'année
Il n'y a que M. Lumley seul au
monde qui pourrait bien faire ce[tte]
affaire je le crois au moins.
Je travaille comme un o[g]re
pour l'ouverture de Jullie[n]
écrivez moi le plus[t] possible
　　　　　Votre ami

28 Rue St Georges　　　M W Balf[e]

AUTOGRAPH LETTER OF M. W. BALFE.

LETTER V.

TO M. W. BALFE, ITALY.

NEW YORK, *September* 5, 1855.

DEAR FRIEND :—

IT is now some year and a half since the period at which
we last saw each other. This was, if you will take the
trouble of recalling it to your memory, at Milan, and in the
Hotel de la Belle Venise. A lapse of very nearly five years
had faded, day by day, over our heads, since the time at
which we had previously met. You were then rounder and
larger in every way. For myself, I was beginning to feel
the slight premonitory symptoms of an incipient double-chin.
Yet I was certainly as young as ever, while you had not lost
one jot of that springiness of temperament with which you
had, so abundantly, been blessed. Spiritually, at all events,
do I firmly believe that we were as, if not more, youthful
than we had formerly been. Want of success had not damped
my energies, as the converse had not rendered yours, supine.

As we were chatting together, one day, after dinner, over
a glass or two of that ruby juice which is forbidden to man
by the Sons of Temperance and the Maine Law, you manifested a strong desire to visit America, in company with your

talented daughter, whose charms, both of voice and person, will, I believe, soon place her in the rank of a leading *prima donna*.

I promised you, at that time, to write to you when a favorable moment for the realization of your wish should arrive, and volunteered to fill the post of your correspondent, for the purpose of keeping you posted up with regard to musical doings and musical matters upon my side of the Atlantic. In accordance with this promise, I was going to write to you, in last July, that stocks in the musical market were on the decline, when, one morning, I happened, while sipping my coffee, to turn over the pages of one of the New York journals.

There I read, that "M. W. Balfe had been engaged to come to America, for the purpose of taking the place of Max Maretzek during the next Operatic season."

Let me say, my dear friend, that I was more than pleased —I was *delighted* on reading this bit of musical intelligence.

You and my readers may smile, perchance, at this assertion. But let me conscientiously explain to you the reasons of my pleasure, and you, at least, may candidly admit that my self-valuation (all of us who are worth anything, have more or less of it) might be highly gratified by this announcement.

The idea of my dismissal could only have been originated by some of my personal enemies, and its realization could only have been effected by their influence with the Directors of the Academy of Music. As for the public at large, it could have had no desire of, and no interest in my removal from the position I had occupied. During seven years that I have been connected with Opera in the United States, I have never failed in doing my duty towards that public, to the best of my abilities. Moreover, I may frankly flatter myself, that at this moment, I still possess the positive sympathy and patronage of the impartial portion of it. It was, therefore, highly satisfactory to me that in carrying out their efforts to replace, or, rather, to displace me, my enemies should have publicly admitted that no reputation short of your own would suffice to cancel me in public estimation. And, indeed, I should hope that you also would feel some degree of self-appreciation in reflecting that I had been your assistant, and, in some sort, even your pupil, during the three years that you conducted the Orchestra of Her Majesty's Theatre in London; as these facts may prove to you that your then youthful assistant has done you and your high reputation no discredit.

But, not only would my personal pride have been satisfied in your engagement.

In you, I saw, instead of a powerful and dangerous rival, the very avenger whom I at this time needed.

The crimes, for which I had been indicted by the advisers of the last management of the Academy of Music, were a too great power over the members of my Orchestra and the Chorus; too much influence with the artists themselves; a disposition to protect the rights and interests (we all have our rights and interests, my good friend, whether in Republican America, Aristocratic England, or Imperial Russia) of the lower *employés* of the Academy; as well as an undisguised contempt for the Art-degrading braggadocio of a certain *Chevalier d'Industrie*, who was unfortunately engaged, during the last season, as the acting Manager. "Unfortunately," I say, and, what is more, "unfortunately for the management," as in other hands, "William Tell" and "Il Trovatore" with the success that they had, must have left a considerable balance in favor of the treasury of the establishment. Now, knowing well, by personal experience, your own temper, and your own feelings—knowing also your own position as a *maestro*—I foresaw that they were only making their way "out of the frying-pan" to fall "into the fire." As for the probable material loss which your presence in this country might have occasioned me, let me confess to you, that in thinking of it, I cast my eyes across the map of the United States. Curiously, as I had never before done, did I examine the relative proportions between the city of New York and the length and breadth of this Continent. After this careful scrutiny, I came to the conclusion that room and space for both of us might in all probability be found here. It appeared to me in some degree probable, that my reputation in America, as well as my American friends might possibly have been sufficient to enable me to enter upon some other musical speculation, and that your undertaking the musical direction of the Academy would have been no impervious obstacle to the continuance of our friendly intercourse of some ten years' standing.

Soon afterwards, however, I ascertained, much to my disappointment, that the whole of this story was a mere invention.

It had been framed in order to frighten me into greater pliancy, by one of those highwaymen upon the road of Art, who had the intention of laying hold of the management of the Academy for the present season with his own fingers, and putting it into his own pocket.

The knowledge of this fact was, of itself, amply sufficient to induce me to refuse any connection with the Academy of Music, in case this individual should hold any "official position" in it, and to raise, or determine upon raising a powerful opposition, the moment his notorious musical intrigues should obtain for himself an actual position in its management. This determination is it which, I flatter myself, has had a considerable influence in preventing his success. The management is again in most thoroughly respectable hands. His position in connection with it, is nameless, and I have been re-engaged as the Musical Director and Conductor attached to the establishment.

From the reasons which have been indicated to you, my dear Balfe, I regret that the announcement of your intended or projected arrival did not arise from a nobler motive, and had no more credible origin.

Believe me, when I say, that I should have hailed your arrival in this country with the most unbounded satisfaction.

Should you still retain the intention you expressed to me, when we last met, of visiting the United States, will you allow me to give you a few words of caution? These are, by all means, to have nothing to do with the class of men who denominate themselves musical agents or musical correspondents, in or for America. Expose yourself in no way to their meddling or interference with your concerns, but visit us yourself.

It may be presumed that you have seen enough, and had sufficient experience of the theatrical agents and correspondents in Italy, to measure them at their right value.

But, my friend, you cannot compare for one moment the Italian with the American branch of the same *genus*. It is true, that the Italian correspondent carries out a regular artistic slave-trade under the protection of the local authorities. The infamous extortions, abuses, impositions and degrading domination practised in Italy, by these *industriels*, upon artists, might furnish the rough material for a book which, if well wrought up, would surpass in interest the stirring scenes of the Romance (!) penned by that worthy dealer in fiction, Mrs. Beecher Stowe. Instead of "Uncle Tom's Cabin," let me advise some well-informed writer of fiction to trace the graphic outlines of a verbal picture, which may be denominated the "Boudoir of a Prima Donna."

Let him describe, and this too with a faithful and fearless pen, the life, the martyrdom, and the trials and sufferings of those vocalists who have unfortunately fallen into the hands of an Italian merchant in musical flesh. Let him explain to the public how they have been sold and resold, at so much *per* note, without the formality, at times, even of requiring their own consent. Let him narrate in what manner the cash for which their voices have been disposed of, has swollen other pockets than their own, while they have been left voiceless and moneyless, exposed to the bitter chances of this world.

But let him do this as he may—let talent, and wit, and shrewdness run from the point of his pen—let him evince the keenest of knowledges of human nature, yet would I, my dear friend, defy him, save by positive experience, to arrive at a due recognition of the various rascalities of the American musical agent.

In justice to my adopted country, allow me to tell you, my good Balfe, that he is almost invariably of foreign birth. German, English, French, or Irish he may be, but rarely is he a *bona-fide* out-and-out American.

The Italian, almost invariably, does his business openly and in the broad daylight. He speculates simply upon artistic poverty or folly. The miserable vocalist who sells himself or herself, knows beforehand what he or she has to expect. Knowing themselves to be the victims of their own necessities, chance may have given them a voice and a constitution strong enough to resist their slavery, and to outlive its term of labor. Then, they may be able to work upon their own account. That reputation which the musical slaveholder had created for his bondsman or bondswoman, may yet turn out of some advantage to them.

Afraid to act in an open and straightforward manner, the

musical agent in the United States lies in ambush for the unsuspecting stranger he has marked as his prey. Like the Vampyre, who plays such a prominent part in Hungarian legendary lore, he fans the artist to slumber with his flattery, and leaves him not, until the last drop of blood, *i. e.* of money, has been sucked out of him. As the Boa-Constrictor, when he has enveloped his victim in his coils, he licks his or her acuteness all over with his drivelling tongue, until it is at last unable to detect his dishonesty. Then he swallows the luckless vocalist's entire success, and retires for the summer months to sleep himself into renewed activity for the following autumn.

The Italian agent's own interest does not allow his victim's reputation to be starved into inanition. Here, the agent, after having ruined his client, is haunted with the dread of exposure. He, consequently, attempts to slay him or her with the poison of calumny. Not satisfied with the booty he has secured, he endeavors to cut the throat of the artist whose pockets he has plundered with the sharp edge of slander.

Beware, my beloved friend, then, how you suffer yourself to be inveigled within the coils of an operatic agent in America.

He will undertake to insure your success. But, believe me, it will be done with your own money, and very decidedly for his own interests. Firstly, he will cause a monster " serenade" to be given to you. It will be enacted under your windows, at nine or ten o'clock in the evening, and will be attended with prodigious enthusiasm. You will retire to your couch, and wrapped in pleasant slumbers, you will dream of that love for Art, and consequently for the artist, which has taken up its home bodily in the New World. As you are sitting in your room, the next morning, enveloped in your *robe de chambre* and soaking your slice of dry toast in your coffee, your pleasant convictions respecting the ovation of the preceding evening will be seriously disturbed. The bill for the serenade will be presented to you. You will find that each musician costs you about ten dollars, while the enthusiasm is collaterally valued at two dollars *per* pair of lungs. Thus, every piece of music to which you had listened with such a delighted and delightful patience, including "Yankee Doodle" (which you are bound to express your admiration of), costs you about twenty-five dollars, while each "Vivat" may be rated at some fifty cents.

As a mere matter of course, this money passes through the agent's hands, and, by a singular chance, one half at the least of it, is placed in his own pocket.

In the second place, he will have a brief sketch of your biography, (what does it matter to you, that it is filled with impossible and improbable lies?) anecdotes of your career (you need not trouble to detail them to him), as well as all kinds of puffs, prepared and published. These, be it observed, the press of New York will, with very few exceptions, most kindly insert, in the belief that they are forwarding your interests, for nothing. They know not that while they are doing it with the idea of assisting you, they are actually filling his purse. He will make you account to him for each line of your biography, in every paper it has appeared in, at the rate of some five or six cents.

Nay! not only will he expect you to pay him for that which he had procured without any payment, but will actually hint to you that he ought to receive a handsome present, as a mark of your esteem for his invaluable services, and your approbation of his integrity.

On the evening preceding your *début*, this conscientious individual will urge upon your attention the necessity (with him, it is a paramount one) of filling your house or concert-room with enthusiastic dead-heads. You believe him, and allow him to operate for you in this comparatively new branch of your musical career. On the morning following your appearance, you are astounded, in consequence, to hear that your crowded audience consisted of 1675 of these kindly supernumeraries, and 132 of the paying public; while, at the same time, instead of having your previously fancied receipts accounted for, you receive another bill from him for *claqueurs*, crowns, *bouquets*, and other ovations, you had conceived spontaneously offered to your own talent.

These, and manœuvres of a similar class, are repeated on each occasion when you arrive in a new city; for to you they are new cities, although by no means so to your agent.

At length, after a few months have expired, your patience gives way. You turn upon him, and ask for what you have been toiling, and sacrificing your money, your time and your labor. He will distend his eyes with a stare of injured innocence, and answer that he too has labored by day and night, simply, that he might have the undeniable glory of preparing your ultimate (!) success.

Necessarily, you are unwilling any longer to "foot" the losses incurred through his agency.

From that moment, your former agent becomes your open enemy. He declares that he has slaved, to insure your success, for nothing. In a word, he asserts that he has not been paid for his time, or for his unparalleled devotion to you and to your interests. He says, everywhere, that the reputation you enjoy, and have enjoyed, is owing entirely to the skill he has displayed in its manufacture. Your excellent houses would never have been filled, but for his management and his dead-heads. Perhaps he even goes still farther, and asserts that your execution, (should you be a vocal artist) or your manipulation (if you chance to be an instrumental one) is principally due to his advice and criticism. As a return for his sacrifices, his toil, and his losses, what have you repaid him with? He grieves to say it—he may possibly weep as he does so—you have repaid him with the basest ingratitude.

Therefore, my dear Balfe, let me entreat you, if ever you should come to America, to beware of suffering yourself to be trepanned by an Operatic Agent.

Possibly, their nuisance has latterly somewhat abated. But, at the period during which the reputation of Jenny Lind was in the ascendant, they actually swarmed upon us as mosquitoes do in the months of August and September.

The very call-boys in the theatres were ambitious of becoming Barnums. Not a hungry teacher of the piano, nor a theatrical check-taker, but had a longing to try his hand at the great game of sowing nothing and reaping dollars. There was not a dealer in concert-tickets but would have given the hair from his head to gather money by the speculation in operatic stars. Many really talented artists were induced, by the stories told them by embryo speculators of this stamp, to visit America, and necessarily fell into the trap laid for their attractions.

Amongst others, was your beautiful, spiritual, and genial countrywoman, Catherine Hayes.

She was engaged by an association of such would-be Barnums, who, as I believe, intentionally placed at their head an inexperienced and inoffensive *entrepreneur* of the name of Wardwell. I say, intentionally, for they kept sedulously in the background. It appears to me, now, when I reflect upon it, like a hungry set of wolves draping themselves in a sheepskin. They borrowed Mr. Wardwell's name, that they might the more readily and easily "humbug" the public, and take in Catherine Hayes.

However, in a pecuniary point of view, this enterprise utterly failed.

Remember, that I am not now speaking of the failure of the Irish *soprano*. Since she divorced her interests from theirs, it has been told me that she has succeeded, and I have every reason to believe this. In California, Australia, and India, she has alike gathered in a golden reward for her undoubted talent. But, with them, the speculative engagement of her voice came to an unlucky ending. For this, there were numerous reasons. In the first place, you will remember an old proverb, which exists in the language you were born to, as well as in mine own. It is this, Balfe, and is uncommonly expressive—"too many cooks spoil the broth." Now, if one agent is enough to ruin, in a general point of view, the chance for success of a single artist, only imagine how this must be quadrupled or quintupled when the number of them amounts to a round half-dozen, speculating under the thin mask of a single well-meaning and honest man. In the second place, they showed their want of a knowledge of their own country, or that to which they were at the time belonging, by the attempt to create an excitement in favor of the lady they had engaged, by appealing to the patriotism of the Irish portion of our population. This naturally produced a want of confidence in the abilities of the fair-haired Catherine, and, soon after, a decided reaction against her on the part of the American public. Finally, these speculators were purely without the slightest inventive genius. They attempted to follow in Barnum's course, by faithfully planting their feet in the foot-prints he had left behind him. His tactics were sedulously and most indiscreetly followed with scrupulous exactitude. They forgot that he had already worn them out.

Their effect had been already lost. Thus, one of their greatest errors was the attempt to proclaim the "holy immaculacy" of their *prima donna*. She may have, in truth, been everything which P. T. B. had proclaimed Jenny Lind to be, but this "puff" had succeeded for Jenny, on the score of its rich and unexampled novelty. The "Prince of Humbugs" had been accustomed to deal in all sorts of curiosities, and this time he had discovered a new one. In the repetition of this "puff," however, its attraction had been lost. The public, once entrapped, were not to be caught a second time. Once, they had admired in a vocalist those qualities, and estimated those virtues which might be found in almost every private family, among their own wives and daughters. Now, they felt that an artist had to depend simply upon his or her own artistic excellence, for artistic success. The fact was again recognized by them, that private goodness is not a quality which demands adulation. It is nothing more than a mere duty.

Not a doubt now exists upon my part, my good Balfe, but that Catherine Hayes could have stood the test of the severest criticism.

As a vocalist, she might, without losing a single laurel, have been named with almost any one of her contemporaries. No such blundering attempt was needed, to drape her excellencies with the mantle of morality, which, to tell the truth, had somewhat soiled in the hands of its original inventor, and frayed its edges upon the person of her for whom he had in the first place shapen it.

Besides these causes of her ill success, there was another. This was, I need scarcely say, perceptible enough to our public, who are by no means such ignoramuses in matters of Art as it has been the fashion to represent them in Europe.

The *troupe* which accompanied Miss Hayes to the United

States was by no means conspicuous for its first-rate talent. It consisted of Messrs. Mengis, Augustus Braham, and Lavenu. Mengis, you know, had been an unsuccessful *tenor*, and when his upper notes had failed him, had transmuted himself with the remainder into an incomplete *barytone*. As for Augustus Braham, he had been an officer in the English army, and had quitted it with a reliance on a fair *tenor* voice, and his patronymic, to endorse him as a vocalist. Lavenu was a good-fellow, with small claims to rank as a Conductor, for anything save quadrille-music. Now, when this company was compared with that which had assisted Jenny Lind —when Benedict and Lavenu were named together, when Mengis was measured with Beletti, and the Brahamling had his vocal inches counted off against those of Salvi, the result could scarcely remain doubtful. It was also very greatly inferior to the Havana Opera *troupe*, who were at this time playing under my direction in New York and Philadelphia. This fact, those who had the charge of Catherine Hayes and the artists who had accompanied her, soon found out, and it was thought necessary by them to add a portion of my attractions to the only attractive part of their company—Catherine Hayes herself.

Accordingly, one morning, a double-faced and double-tongued member of the fraternity of musical agents paid me a visit. His purpose was to propose an arrangement between myself and the Wardwell party, by which I should lend the services of some of my best artists to the Hayes Concerts. The terms to which we eventually came, when this had been discussed and agreed upon between us, were $5,000 *per* month.

The contract was duly drawn up and signed, and I allowed them to make use of the *tenors* Bettini and Lorini, the *barytone* Badiali, and the *basso* Marini, with Madame Bertucca-

Maretzek as a soloist on the harp. This they did, both at the Concerts in New York and Boston. Of course, with such an *entourage*, the indisputable talent of Miss Hayes, and her fresh voice, produced the required effect.

In the mean time, I had paid the salaries of these artists, and had advanced their necessary hotel expenses.

But when, at the termination of the first month of their services, I applied to Mr. Wardwell for the stipulated remuneration, I was not only paid (the only payment that I could induce him or his employers to make me, of their own accord) with abuse, but was actually accused of having intrigued against Catherine Hayes, and having done my best to ruin her reputation in this country. He, apparently, would not understand, or possibly was not allowed to do so by the agents in whose behalf he was ostensibly acting, that $5,000 *per* month, in aid of my expenses, was the best security he could have had to insure my support to his exertions. While it was unpaid me, should I not have been a fool, my dear friend, to have in any way attempted to injure her chance of filling his treasury?

This necessitated me to go to law with him. And here let me give you another word of advice, Balfe. The knowledge from which it comes has been rather expensively acquired, but believe me, it is none the less valuable, that Max Maretzek has paid to obtain it. Should you visit this country, never think of going to law in it.

After years of law-suits and their constant costs, I obtained from one of the employers of Mr. Wardwell the sum of $600.

This was all I ever got from them for the services of my artists. Yet I had actually disbursed some $3,800 in that month, for the salaries, hotel bills, and travelling expenses of those very artists. They had assisted Catherine Hayes in these concerts, given on behalf of Wardwell and the invisible Company behind him. But for their services I literally received something less than one-sixth of the sum, which I had paid with the view of assisting them, at the same time that I was insuring a portion of my own operatic season from actual loss.

At length, their *prima donna* herself got tired out with their constant inefficiency and ignorance of musical matters. She, consequently, broke her engagement with Cramer and Beale of London, through whom she had been re-leased to them, not, however, without being instigated to this breach of contract by some other musical agents, who meddled in the matter with the view of securing her for themselves. These, as it afterwards turned out, did not succeed in their purpose. She fell into the hands of Messrs. Kemp and Bushnell.

This loss of $5,000, added to those of my disastrous Opera season at Castle Garden, which have been detailed in a former letter to Professor Fischof (if I am right, an old acquaintance of yours), began very seriously to embarrass me.

However, I would not yet despair. You know, my good Balfe, that the musical element in the mental constitution of man is in all cases singularly hopeful.

Consequently, I divided my large and powerful company, and began for my third year with one portion of it at the Astor Place Opera House, while I sent another section of it to travel in the Southern States. My object was, at the close of my regular season in New York, to meet them, and unite both portions of my *troupe*, with the intention of making a trip to Mexico.

Before I, however, narrate the adventures of my venturous speculation, for a man who was at the time revolving round the yawning jaws of ruin, a task imposes itself upon my pen. This is the mention of another celebrity of world-wide reputation, who, attracted by the stories of the fabulous amount of profits attendant upon Jenny Lind's visit to these shores, had also decided upon honoring us with her presence. Need you be told that this was the Countess Von Lansfeldt-Head, *né* or self-christened (it would be impossible for you or myself either to say or to divine which) Lola Montez—the female Harry the Eighth, in all, at least, but the decapitation of her very numerous legitimate and illegitimate spouses.

Sickened out with Europe, disgusted with the *effête* and enervated human race of the Old World, she passed into the New one.

Her main object was necessarily the golden approbation which Barnum had so tangibly brought before the dazzled eyes of the children of the elder hemisphere. Her purely secondary one was to search for a new candidate for the matrimonial, though somewhat aged charms, which had been honored by the embraces of Royalty when in its dotage.

" She came, she saw," but, unlike him who passed the Rubicon, she did not conquer. On the contrary, she ingloriously failed.

Do not, however, for one instant imagine, that her failure was to be attributed to a too complete imitation of the Machiavelian tactics of the illustrious P. T. B. By no means was she likely to make too great a show of virtue and morality. On the contrary, she attempted to play the same game which was afterwards perfected in the singular success of Father Gavazzi. Yes, my good Balfe, she announced herself to the New World as a victim. She had been (so at least did she say) ruined by Jesuitical and Diplomatic intrigue. Had she been at all able, or had she possessed the

inclination to veil her previous character, she must undoubtedly have succeeded. Nay! had she but kept diplomacy in
the background, she might, in spite of that previous and notorious reputation, have done so. Unfortunately, diplomats
and dancers have been too often suspiciously linked together
in the eyes of the world. Sometimes one, and sometimes
the other, and not unfrequently both are victimized, although,
to tell the truth, the latter occurrence may be regarded as
somewhat of a rarity. Consequently, the public looked with
suspicion on all that was asseverated by her agents. They
valued the persecution she claimed as portion of her previous history at its right worth, and estimated her personal
excellency precisely at its true value.

When she first made her appearance upon the boards of
the Broadway Theatre, she attracted, as every novelty will
do when it has been sufficiently talked about, an immense
audience. Be it observed, however, that not a single lady
was present.

As for her style of dancing, that produced not the slightest
sensation. However, my dear friend, you must not attribute
to us a deadness to the attractions of the Terpsichorean Art,
upon this account.

You know, for you have seen Lola on the stage, (let me
not take the liberty of suggesting that you have ever spoken
to her off the arena of her saltatory exhibitions) that she
has her own peculiar mode of dancing. Need I remind you,
that this mode differs materially from that of any other of
the daughters of Terpsichore? Fanny Ellsler translates a
stanza of Tasso with an *entrechat*, or modulates a sonnet of
Petrarch into a *pirouette*. The lithe limbs and fawn-like
figure of Marie Taglioni embody, with their undulating movement, the tenderer emotions in Byron's "Don Juan." Plump
and round Cerito sings with her legs a voluptuous passage

from the heathen Ovid's "Art of Love;" while Carlotta Grisi and Rosati narrate, in their *pas seuls*, a fantastic tale from Hoffmann, or translate a legend from the "Thousand-and-one Nights," with a more witching grace than any which had before been infused into them by the pen of their transcribers.

However, the dancing of Lola Montez resembles another class of literature, and realizes a purely different style of verbal creation in its fleshly movement. In some degree, it approximates to a work which I have some indistinct remembrance of, called the "Memoirs of Casanova." Were I to fix on that, with the genius of which it is almost identical, my decision would unhesitatingly be given in favor of "Barnum's Autobiography."

This, alone, might suggest a sufficient reason for her failure.

Moreover, in America, she forbore to give those profuse exhibitions of her person, which, in her younger years in Europe, were added to her dancing. It may be that she had grown dubious of the propriety of exhibiting all the beauties which had once fascinated Liszt, and through his admiration of which, Ludwig Von Baiern had lost both his throne and his wits. Or was it, perchance, that European Diplomacy and Roman Catholic Jesuitism had worn away and destroyed their former grace? For I cannot believe that years had tamed her into modesty, or taught her to moralize in muslin and wear the pantalettes that redeem other weavers of *pirouettes* from the charge of want of modesty.

At any rate, she failed. Curiosity brought her a few fine houses, but curiosity created no admiration for her artistic talent.

Having done so, she departed for New Orleans. There, she kicked her Manager. Thence, she sailed for California. In that locality, she found another husband. You see, my dear Balfe, the beautiful appositeness of that terse old Latin saying—

> " Sic transit, gloria mundi."

Let me now return to my two Operatic companies, after having spun for your amusement the foregoing episode. If possibly not Homeric in the strictest sense of the term, believe me, when I say that no Επος of the events of the period connected with Operatic or Histrionic agency, could have been complete without it ; for this fact must be added to others, that Lola Montez was, to the full, as insatiable in her acquisition of agents as she might be of husbands, or of the temporary occupants of corresponding situations. To tell the truth, she had, at the least, a round dozen of either class during her peregrinations across this continent.

One of the sections of my original *troupe* I kept, as indeed you have earlier been told, in New York.

Here, Fortune once more smiled kindly upon my exertions. My efforts for success were amply and generously rewarded by the public. My promised season was fully carried out to a successful termination. This was, however, under my own direction.

But, woe to that Manager who suffers any portion of his company to pass from under his own *surveillance*.

The results of this folly I had already experienced, in allowing a portion of it to work under the directions of Mr. Wardwell. I was now doomed to make a second proof of this fact, and to make it by my own mismanagement.

The second section of my Operatic *troupe* went South, in the charge of an agent.

His name it will be unnecessary to mention. It does not merit the honor of having its ignorance and weakness exposed upon paper by my own pen.

You know, my dear friend, that all musicians, whether

they are instrumentalists, vocalists, or composers, are alike inflicted with a slight infirmity of temper. Indeed, they may very safely be classed as the most quarrelsome set of beings upon the face of God's round earth. Perhaps, even you and myself may not be altogether unfairly included in this category. There is an antique tradition, (it may be called antique in this New World, although scarcely entitled to such a name in Europe) that the Duke of Brunswick, some century since, (the presumed parent of George I. of England) who was called Frederick Augustus, was, at one time, confoundedly embarrassed by the resignation of his Musical Intendant. This officer, who was the Composer Steffani, had retired from his position in his Serene Highness's household, in consequence of the troubles and annoyances resulting from the quarrelsome habits of the Duke's Operatic singers, or, as he called them, "Operatic Savages."

Frederick Augustus reflected, and then determined upon trying to manage them himself.

He tried it for a week, after which, he sent for the ex-intendant.

"Steffani," he said, "at my request, you must withdraw your resignation."

"Your Highness must excuse me. I cannot."

The Duke walked abruptly across the chamber, and paused for a moment. Then he returned, and laid his hand on the composer's shoulder.

"You must, my old and faithful servant, return to your post."

"But—your Highness!"—

"*Donner und Teufel!*" burst out the great Prince. "But, I tell you, I need you."

"I am sorry"—commenced Steffani.

" Can you not see that I am even now on the Confessional ?"

" I do not understand what your Highness is saying," answered the composer.

" Why, I was about telling you, that I find it a far easier thing to command an army of fifty thousand men, than to manage half a dozen rascally Opera-singers."

Steffani bowed, and returned to his duties. He was satisfied with the Duke's avowal of incompetence. Frederick Augustus never again interfered with management.

Philosophically considered, it is a curious fact, my good Balfe, that the members of the most " harmonious" profession in the world should be, in almost every instance, the most " inharmonious" set of denizens upon its round surface. This, I confess myself unable to account for. Reflection has been spent upon it in vain, and it remains a riddle. Why melody should give the temper so keen an edge—why, after rehearsing the melting strains of the " Norma" or singing the laughter-moving music of the " Barbiere," the *soprano* should be in a temper to call her Manager " an idiot," while the *tenor* should attempt to pull the nose of the *basso*, and the *barytone* should manage to make a diabolical row because he has not been paid his salary some two days before it is due, has always puzzled me.

Did you ever know a Chorus who had not their daily grievances ? Certain is it, that I have yet to make an acquaintance with such a " *lusus naturæ*." Have you ever met with any Orchestra whose members could avoid differences among themselves, or had not to be ruled with an iron hand by their Conductor ? If you have done so, safely may it be said, that I never did.

Allow me to remind you of the witty epigram, made by a wag of the period, on the quarrels of the members of the

Conservatoire, at Paris, in the year 1802. These had taken such alarming proportions, as even to endanger the existence of that noble institution. It ran thus :*—

> "J'admire leurs talents, et même leur génie,
>   Mais au fond ils ont un grand tort ;
> C'est de s'intituler Professeurs d'Harmonie,
>   Et de n'être jamais d'accord."

However, it must fairly be owned, that in placing a portion of my company in the charge of an agent, I ought to have expected no better result. We all, my good friend, have to live and learn. This was one of the lessons I have been gathering as age grows upon me.

From Baltimore and Washington, my agent wrote two letters. In these, he informed me, that he was proceeding to New Orleans, where he was confident of having a profit of at the least $10,000, on the right side of his balance-sheet.

Imagine me, Balfe, as I walked down Broadway, with my pockets buttoned up and rejoicing in the conviction that this season would retrieve my previous losses. My spirit was Alnascharized. As the Utopian dreamer in the Arabian fable, I bore my basket of eggs.—No! unfortunately, I did not bear them upon my own head. Had I done so, greater care would very certainly have been taken of them. Scarcely

---

* Through the kindness of a friend, I am enabled to give the following rendering of the idea of this epigram. From the pun in the last line, it is impossible to translate it more nearly.

> Their talent and genius, I own, I admire,
>   And yet they commit a great wrong ;
> Though entitled Professors of Harmony,
>   No two e'er can sing the same song.

is it probable, that they would have been so thoroughly and completely smashed.

Shortly afterwards, the news came to me from Richmond, that my agent had managed to involve himself in a very prejudicial controversy with the press of that city.

This, I said to myself, was an accident. Had he not promised me a profit of $10,000?

While he was yet at Charleston, the intelligence reached me, that he had got into serious troubles with the vocalists placed under his charge.

It was to be expected, I muttered. When did a singer fail to quarrel with his or her Manager? The $10,000 still colored my thoughts.

One morning, when I had strolled down to the office of the Astor Place Opera House, what was my surprise to see him. My eyes opened, as do those of *Leporello*, when the statue of the *Commandante* first addresses *Don Juan*. The unlucky wretch had returned from Savannah, to detail me his misfortunes. He had quarrelled with his *troupe*, and, consequently, had been cowhided and beaten almost to a jelly by the refractory artists. In short, they had broken into open rebellion against his authority, and taken the opportunity of giving him a lesson. Not being able to face them, unblushingly, after this, and supposing that "discretion was the better part of valor," he had then run away. My company, or rather, the half of it, was therefore left alone. Like a blind worm, an oyster, or a polypus, it rejoiced in having neither head nor tail.

Now, although the artists who had placed themselves in this difficulty by an open act of rebellion, deserved no pity at my hands, there were many, in this instance, innocent subalterns (members of the Orchestra, Chorus, and other officials) connected with or engaged in the Southern division of my company, whom I could not conscientiously allow to remain in a strange city, without the means either of return or of subsistence.

It was true that I had made a good season in New York, but its profits had been swallowed up by the outstanding debts of my preceding musical campaign.

What, then, was I to do? The immediate necessity for action forced me to take the readiest means of assisting them which was in my power, and I was consequently obliged to sacrifice the greatest portion of my Operatic stock, consisting of music, dresses, and properties, to enable myself to bring back to New York the headless and tailless company who were amusing themselves as best they could in the city of Savannah.

Now, in making this sacrifice, it had been my intention to unite all my musical forces here, with the purpose of starting with the whole of them, by another *route*, under my own command.

This intention was unhappily doomed not to be put in execution. Some other of those musical agents who had lately so plentifully cropped out of the manure Barnum had spread upon the soil of American humanity, had recently become aware of my somewhat precarious position. Representing themselves, whether rightly or wrongly, it would be impossible to say, (the word of a musical agent can never be taken without doubt) as employed by Marty, the Havanese *impressario*, they began to disseminate discord in my company. These gentlemen (if I am not wrong in giving them such a name) intimated to the members of it, that Don Francisco had the intention of engaging them again for Havana, with the view of sending them, after the season for Opera in that city had terminated, to New Orleans, and thence to Mexico. If, however, they should determine upon accompanying me to New Orleans, Marty would certainly not engage them, as their novelty on one portion of the ground selected for his after musical campaign would clearly be destroyed. Therefore, in visiting that city with me, they would throw away the probability of obtaining an engagement of some eighteen or twenty-four months with him. These inventions were naturally listened to, and more foolishly believed. They thought it better to sacrifice their certain two or three months with me (they were still engaged for this period) than to risk the mere probability of a two years' engagement with Marty.

Having made up their minds, therefore, to this course, they not only refused to proceed with me to New Orleans, but announced their intention of definitely breaking their present engagement.

Knowing my reduced means, they leagued themselves with the view of performing on their own account, until—Marty should think proper to offer to re-engage them.

But the internal jealousies and dissensions which exist in every Opera *troupe* did not permit them fully and completely to carry out this plan. Mademoiselle Steffanone somehow did not altogether like Signora Bosio. It was a truly unfortunate circumstance, but the Signor Beneventano had one pet hatred. It happened that this was for Cesare Badiali. If there was any of the company whom Salvi specially disliked and mistrusted, it was Signor Bettini. But Madame Bosio had also her special *méfiance* of somebody else, while Badiali and Bettini could hate and distrust other members of the *troupe.* Suffice it to say, that I had not spent my time in management without learning some of its secrets. Taking advantage of these sentiments, whose existence had long been known to me, I succeeded in detaching Steffenone, Salvi, Beneventano and Marini from the league which had been formed against me, and was successful also in inducing the Signora Parodi once more to place herself under my direction. With these and other vocalists of less note, I was ready to start either for New Orleans, or to open a new season in this city.

The remainder of my company, consisting of Bosio, De Vries, Bettini, Lorini, Badiali, and Coletti, with some others, constituted themselves into an independent opposition.

They called themselves " The Artists' Union Italian Opera Company," and waited to receive a proposition from Don Francisco Marty y Torrens.

During the interval that they would have to linger, ere this hope would be fulfilled, they determined upon doing something. They, consequently, after some consultation, subscribed a portion of that money which they had earned under my management. Their object, evidently, was to cut my operatic throat with the expenditure of the cash which I had paid them. A truly benevolent idea, teeming with the most Christian gratitude, but it must candidly be said, a very musical example of Italian generosity. Well, Balfe, this " Artists' Union Italian Opera Company," with this money, purchased some music and hired or bought some dresses. They then engaged Niblo's Garden for their performances. This was naturally a comfort to Mr. Niblo, whose Garden was, at this time, unoccupied.

But believe not, my dear Balfe, that Niblo's Garden is *a* garden.

It resembles, in no ways, the Gardens at Cremorne or Vauxhall, to which your mind was already likening it.

You must know that in this moral country, in almost every city, one or two theatrical traps are set and baited with theatrical amusements, for the purpose of ensnaring the more religious portion of the community. To avoid naming them that which they are indubitably in fact, these theatrical traps cloak themselves under the name of Museums.

Such a garden, as Barnum's Museum is a Museum, is Niblo's Garden.

By this name, the scruples of conscience felt by a certain portion of the public, are appeased. To me, I must confess, it has always appeared a somewhat tight shave. But what matters it? The ear is satisfied, and the conscientious scruple may be considered unbroken.

Some twenty-five years ago, I must acknowledge, this theatre was simply a garden. In this garden, did the identical William Niblo sell his ice-creams, sherry-cobblers, and other liquors.

Now, however, it has completely changed. The Metropolitan Hotel, Niblo's Theatre, stores and other buildings occupy the locality. Of the former garden nothing remains, save the ice-cream and drinking-saloons attached to the theatre. These take up literally as much room in the building as its stage does, and prove that its proprietor has not altogether overlooked the earlier vocation which laid the foundation of his fortune. The name by which he calls it has never changed. It was Niblo's Garden, when loving couples ate their creams or drank their cobblers under the shadow of the trees. It is Niblo's Garden, now, when it is turned into a simple theatre, and hedged in with houses. Nay! in the very bills, which are circulated in the interior of the building during the performances, you may find, or might shortly since have found such an announcement as the following, appearing in large letters:—

" Between the second and third Acts"—or possibly, it may run thus, when Opera is not in the ascendant—" after the conclusion of the first piece, an intermission of twenty minutes takes place, for a promenade in the Garden."

You will, I feel certain, my good friend, admit that this is a marvellously delicate way of intimating to a gentleman who may feel "dry" (it is the right word, is it not?) that he will find the time to slake his thirst.

When he returns, and his lady inquires where he has been, he may reply if he wills it—

" Promenading in the garden."

Now, you and myself are not puritanical enough to condemn an honest man because he may chance to be the Manager of a theatre or the *impressario* of a bar-room. But were bad brandy, sold there, or if he placed, generally, upon the stage, the pantomimes which are given during a London Christmas at " Sadlers' Wells" and the " Surrey," or the mixture of mime and farce which are afforded the Parisian public, at the Funambules, we should decidedly not accord him the honor of an inner cabinet in our memories. Even more, while *Arlequins*, *Pierrots*, and *Columbines* are the " stars" of the establishment, much as we may laugh at their interchanges of blows and kicks and marvel at their footprints left in each other's backs, we can but regret that such things as these amuse the public, while we laugh with them.

About Opera, the Manager speaks in very contemptuous terms. Like the fox who has been unable to get at the grapes, he declares them " sour."

But in spite of this, one of the distinguishing characteristics of Mr. Niblo's tastes as a Manager is the desperate longing to make his Garden the New York Opera House. Could his opposition have effected it, he would have destroyed the Astor Place Theatre.*   Had he it in his power, he would ruin the Academy of Music.   He declares that he detests

* This he subsequently managed to do by an astuter mode than opposition.

Opera, but flirts around it every season, like a moth that is burning its wings in the too attractive flame of a candle.

Whenever any one has been willing to oppose the established operatic theatres, he had but to go to William Niblo. The taste of the Manager induced him to receive the individual who was willing to try his fortune, with open arms.

Thus, were his means mainly instrumental in enabling a musical agent, during the late season at the Academy, to bring out the La Grange *troupe* in order to oppose it. So, when the "Artists' Union Italian Opera Company" repaired to him, they found him delighted with the chance of opposition which it afforded his Garden.

Had I, at this time, allowed my former artists to amuse themselves with management, it is not to be doubted, but that I could have made money in New Orleans.

But this was not to be. Listening to the request of those vocalists, whom their likes and dislikes had induced to remain faithful to my fortunes, I ceded to the desires of the proprietors of the Astor Place Opera House. Frightened at the bare idea of opposition in another theatre, they also requested me not to leave New York. Moreover, there is a feeling amongst all mankind (at least all such as are worth anything) which prompts them to resist the appearance of doing that which they had determined upon putting in execution, should it seem to be done under compulsion.

This feeling I suffered, most unwisely, to operate upon my mind. In doing this, I committed a great error.

Complying with the wishes of my artists to annihilate their rivals, I yielded to the requests of those whose fears had alone impelled them to apply to me.

Therefore, my tour to New Orleans was postponed for the present, and I again opened the Opera House.

No sooner was this done by me, than the opposition company (acting, as has been said, under the advice of Mr. Niblo) lowered their prices of admission some fifty *per cent.* This was done on the presumed impossibility of my lowering mine, at all events in the same ratio, as I had already charged my subscribers at the full price. At first, this most materially injured me ; so much so, indeed, that for the first time in four years I asked the patrons and proprietors of the house to assist me. You, my dear friend, will believe me when I say that this was as much or more for the sake of their theatre, as or than it was for my own. But, although they had encouraged me in the attempt, and entreated me to save their house in this struggle, by and with my own means and talents, they themselves refused to risk a single cent for my doing so. From that moment, my determination was formed. Henceforth, theatrical proprietors, whoever they might be, might attend to and fight their own battles. My business, from that moment, has been simply to save or increase my artistic reputation, with as little pecuniary loss and as large a pecuniary gain, as is possible for that man who acts uprightly, and never evades the claims and calls of duty.

The remaining twelve subscription-nights were accordingly postponed, until further notice should be given. My prices of admission were lowered to fifty cents. The house was thrown open to the masses of the people, and for the first time, in New York, was the Italian version of Meyerbeer's "Robert le Diable" produced. No expense had been spared by me on the *mise en scène.* The dresses were superb. A grand *corps de ballet* had been engaged (I need not tell you that we had no Carlotta Grisi or Lucilla Grahn to place in it), and the cast was the following, which even you, accustomed as you have been to the London and Parisian casts, will admit was most excellent. Salvi, of course, took the part of *Robert,* while Marini sung and acted the *rôle* of *Bertram*, as I honestly believe, no vocalist who has ever trodden this earth has yet done. *Alice* was in the hands of Steffanone, and Bertucca appeared as the *Princess Isabella*. This Opera, thus supported and placed upon the stage, at once created a profound sensation. The doors of the house, or rather of its box office, on the days of performance, were literally besieged before their hour of opening. Tickets were, in innumerable instances, sold four and even six days ahead of the evening they were purchased for. Nightly, was the house crammed to suffocation. The public, very naturally, thought that I was making money. Never could there have been a greater mistake, although my entering upon this season was a far more expensive error.

In consequence of the limited size of the theatre, and the reduction of the price of admission, upon the one side, with the costly *mise en scène* and dresses, upon the other, the successful (!) production of "Roberto il Diavolo" was a dead loss. On every evening that the curtain was raised to a packed audience, and, as the journals phrased it, with "immense success," it fell upon a loss of some four hundred dollars.

You may imagine my feelings, my good Balfe, when I entered the house night after night, gazed round it, and took my seat, fully aware that four hundred dollars more than its contents would not pay my nightly expenses. Nevertheless, I was forced to continue. The opposition had to be driven from the battle-ground which I had so rashly entered upon. They were forced to quit it. Two weeks after the first performance of "Robert," they retired to Boston; and in two weeks more, the "Artists' Union Italian Opera Company" dispersed, amidst quarrels, blows, and mutual vituperation, having lost not only their time, but all the loose cash they had embarked in their untoward speculation.

As is the case, wherever Meyerbeer makes himself known, a new era in musical taste and discrimination commenced in New York. At the present time, his Operas, and some of the latter works of Rossini, are alone capable of interesting the American public.

Far be it from me, my dear friend, to intimate that I prefer Meyerbeer to Rossini, or Rossini to Meyerbeer.

The dissertations on their comparative merits are, in my opinion, to the full as absurd as the quarrels of the Gluckists and Piccinists at the close of the last century. My belief is neither in the Italian nor in the German, neither in the French nor in the Chinese school of melody. Indeed, I invariably feel unwell when I chance upon and read some very scientific and learned disquisition upon the various schools of music. For my own part, I recognize but two schools in music. Mozart, Rossini, Meyerbeer, Bellini, Weber, Beethoven, Piccini, Cimarosa, Gluck, Donizetti, and yourself, also, my good Balfe, belong to the one. This is the school of good music. Of the other, it will be perfectly unnecessary to speak.

But, let me return to Meyerbeer. His Operas have always appeared to me, in point of their conception, the wideness and truthfulness of his harmonic feeling, the adaptation of his melodies to their subjects, the light and shadow of his orchestration, his conscientiousness in the most difficult feature of all music—the positive discrimination of personal character, as well as his studious and exquisite variety, the nearest approach to perfection as Operatic writing, that has appeared up to the present day. Rossini, I admit, is an inexhaustible fountain of melody. Perhaps more of the genius, he is very certainly much less of the artist than is Meyerbeer. Or, rather, for I feel that this scarcely expresses what my fingers are striving to shape into written language, the first is the

Pope of Song, while the other is as decidedly its Martin Luther. Remember, that in speaking thus, or, as I ought to say, in writing thus, I allude strictly to Operatic song. Neither is it for Lutheranism of spirit that the Dramatic Muse is alone so strikingly and largely indebted to Meyerbeer. When an old score, wrought out by one of the earlier fathers of Opera, is compared with one of the scores of Meyerbeer, it reminds one of the measurement and mud-walls built and made by Romulus and Remus, when placed, in imagination, by the girdling marble and costly palaces and miles upon miles of circuit of Imperial Rome.

Many opinions have been broached touching the time when Opera had its first birth, but most of the more curious and learned gropers in the history of the past allow that this was at the close of the sixteenth century.

As for its earlier development, this is purely fabulous. The Greeks and Egyptians only dabbled in music, while Livy, who, at the commencement of his Seventh Book, speaks of the " *ludi scenici*," for which musicians from Etruria had been expressly engaged, leaves us in doubt as to whether the instruments were used to accompany the voice, or whether the melody was intended for secular amusement or religious purposes. But in whatever way music was originally used by the Romans, you and I may safely coincide with the details given by later scholiasts, who attribute the invention of Opera to a certain Rinuccini, *a poet*, (!) who wrote the *libretto* of a drama in verse, called " Eurydice," for which an early composer, named Jacopo Peri, composed the music. This work was, for the first time, represented in Florence in or about the year 1600, on the occasion of the festivities attending the marriage of Maria di Medicis with Henry the Fourth of France.

Seven years subsequently to this, was the first Opera sup·posed to have been printed.

This is called " L'Orfeo, una Favola in Musica." Its overture consisted only of eight bars, the repetition of which was enjoined upon the Orchestra, until the signal was given for drawing up the curtain. We have made, my dear Balfe, as it strikes me, a considerable advance in the two centuries and a half which have elapsed since this period. The whole Orchestra, indicated and required by this score, are a *quartette* of stringed instruments, consisting of two violins, a guitar (!) and a *contra-basso*, together with a single flute. It appears to me, that we have also made a stride forward in the constitution of our Orchestras. Instrumental music has certainly not slumbered. Yet, singular is it, that even at this epoch, criticism was, as it almost ever is, adverse to any tangible advance in Art. With a not uncommon pertinacity (even at the present day, similar examples are given us of it), the would-be connoisseurs of the time complained that the Orchestra, consisting of four stringed instruments and one flute, was somewhat too loud.

After Italy had made the first positive step forward, in adapting music to scenic representation, France followed; the first French Opera being performed at Issy, in 1659. It was called " Pomone," and had been composed by a musician named Cambert, who was the organist in the church of St. Honoré. The *libretto* was written by Perrin. This work was successful from its novelty, and the author was, shortly after, dignified with the title of Operatic Manager to the Court. Soon after he was, however, displaced by Louis Quatorze, who appointed Lully in his place. Under the *regime* of this great sovereign, Operatic Music made huge strides. Lully, who was a man of decided talent, was associated with the poet, Quinault, who advanced considerably upon the former writers of *libretti*.   At the present moment, Lully as you know, in all probability better than I do, is generally regarded as the father of modern Opera.   For him, the Academy of Music, then called the Royal Academy, although it has been baptized and re-baptized since that period with at the least a round score of names, was originally chartered. Under his direction, it was firmly established in national favor. He wrote nineteen Operas, and as many or more Ballets for the Court, in some of which we are told that Louis XIV. took part himself.   It may be marvelled, whether the music to which a great monarch condescended to execute his *entrechats*, was as good as that to which Lola Montez has been recently pirouetting.   Suffice it, Balfe, that I very considerably doubt it, and would lay a round wager that you agree with me.

It was about one hundred years after the establishment of the Royal Academy of Music in Paris, that the celebrated musical war between the Gluckists and Piccinists took place. In fury, it ceded to no civil strife, save that of the Guelfs and Ghibellines.   With less, or should I not say with no blood spilt in it, it far surpassed that in acerbity.

But to those with whom Music is as Religion, it may be said, that in spite of his judgment and his genius, Gluck is no more than the St. John in the Wilderness, sent before, to herald the advent of the musical Messiah, (do not believe that I speak it irreverently, my friend) for such is Mozart. Rossini and Meyerbeer only hold, when compared with him, the positions which I have already assigned them.   You must, however, allow me to say, in again speaking of Meyerbeer, that when I ranked him as the great innovator and Reformer in Music, I did not conceive that his intentions had been fully developed in the Opera to which I was then alluding.   Although it must ever be regarded as a remarkable work, in "Robert le Diable," Meyerbeer appears to have been wavering and unsettled in his musical convictions. As yet, he scarcely dared implicitly to confide in his own genius. He was fearful of opening the door of his will to his musical skepticism. Faint-hearted and timid, he was afraid to declare himself the antagonist of the recognized *maestro*, who had so long worn the Triple Crown in the realms of music—the Swan of Pesaro, Rossini. Previously to this, he had even crawled on his knees up the stony staircase (I am obliged to use the adjective, although it is inapplicable, for the purpose of identifying my simile) of Italian melody.

In his "Huguenots," he has, however, at length acquired courage. In this Opera, and more especially in the fourth Act of "Le Prophète," he gives a free rein to his imagination. He here expresses his musical convictions openly, and hurls his indignant protest against the abuses which had been tolerated and fostered by the Operatic genius of modern Italy. In the "Huguenots," he purifies the Lyric Drama from the sensuality which had been gradually debasing the character of Italian music. The evident frivolity which had so long been creeping upon the Italian composers, was fearlessly eschewed. No listener is there but must admire the novelty of the form, while he is impressed with the truth of expression, the melodic beauty, and the severe yet picturesque power exhibited by him, more especially in the fourth Act of either of these Operas. Indeed, the effect of the production of the "Huguenots," (which preceded that of the "Prophéte") was immense. Meyerbeer at once strode into his right position. He made proselytes and he gained partisans, on every side. Nearly every succeeding composer has trodden more or less in his foot-prints. Even in Italy, established *maestri* such as Donizetti and Verdi have bent to his teaching, and in their Operas of "La Favorita," "Don Sebastian," "Nabucco" and the "Vepres Siciliennes," have given in their adhesion to his dogmas. By this fact alone, the irresistible influence which his writings have had upon public opinion may be considered amply proven.

Rossini, although apparently indifferent, feels that he has lost a portion of that almost universal musical dominion which he once had. Occasionally, he shows his anger, by sarcastic remarks upon the leader of the reform movement in music, and his principal disciples.

Thus, one morning, when in Paris, a wandering organ-grinder accidentally played the tune of a romance from Halévy's " Guido and Ginevra," under his windows. Rossini summoned the luckless boy into his chamber, and catching hold of and shaking him, exclaimed—

" What do you mean by this, you little rascal?"

" Signor !" exclaims the unfortunately small malefactor, "don't beat me !"

" Have you not been paid, to play that infernal *charivari* under my windows? Answer, little whelp ! and at once."

The boy swore, by all his Italian gods, that this was not the case.

" You lie ! Confess, who sent you here to dose me with all this horrid music."

" No one, Signor !"

But the frantic Rossini was not to be persuaded that the infliction was not an intended foretaste of the pleasures of Purgatory. At length, he gave two napoleons to the street-musician, who opened his eyes when his fingers touched the gold.

" Here ! take these," he said. " Order for your organ a new barrel, with an *aria* from ' Tancredi.' Then, go and play it sixty times under the windows of M. Halevy. Do you understand me ? Sixty times !"

" Yes, Signor !" stammered the boy.

" It may be, that, afterwards, he will learn how to write music !"

Again, when he last year arrived in Paris, from Italy, an old friend inquired of him whether he had yet heard Meyerbeer's " Prophète."

" Yes !" he replied ; " in Florence."

" Indeed !" answered his interlocutor. " And how do you like it ?"

" Well !" said Rossini.

" I am delighted to hear our greatest composer say so."

" You know, they have ' cut ' the Opera confoundedly in Florence."

" Ah ! have they ?"

" Yes ! and it may be presumed, that by mistake they cut out the best portions of it. Consequently, I like it by a pure effort of faith."

Such remarks as these, although witty and spirited, in my opinion do little honor to such a giant, as all musicians must admit Rossini to have been.

But, my dear Balfe, I can imagine what has been passing through your mind, while you have been reading the last few pages of my letter. You naturally say—" What the deuce is Maretzek talking about ? Does the man think that I have never heard of Rossini, or that Meyerbeer is a complete novelty to me ? I want to hear about his own adventures in America. Facts respecting the American love of art would be worth more to me than a tome-full of critical disquisition, which I can manufacture myself a deuced deal better than he does."

All this is candidly granted by me, my good friend !

Simply have I wished to show you, that, in America, we appreciate the recent revolution in music as thoroughly as you do in Europe. If I have done this, I am contented. It will prove to you that, in visiting these shores, you will become acquainted with no tribe of savage Indians, but with a race as, or more generally polished, than any portion of the inhabitants of Europe—a race who will value you by your own merits, and unhesitatingly accord you that rank, as a composer, which you so worthily hold in the Old World.

Before, however, this letter can be closed, I have to inform you of the termination of the season at the Astor Place Opera House, after the success of " Roberto il Diavolo," and the defeat of the " Artists' Union Italian Opera Company."

After the losses which I had sustained previously in Castle Garden, (a misnomer, for which there was somewhat more justification than that to which I have earlier alluded,) the unfortunate surrender of a portion of my company temporarily to the Catherine Hayes management, and the money sunk upon, or in the " splendid triumph " achieved by me in the production of " Robert le Diable," it will scarcely be astonishing to you, to hear that my means and credit were alike utterly exhausted. The enemy had been beaten well and thoroughly, but the defeat had ruined the victor. Two weeks after they had ingloriously fled from New York, I was obliged to succumb. Bled to the last drop in my veins, (I, of course, allude to my purse and my pocket,) the doors of the Astor Place Opera House were closed upon the public. It was my determination to woo the fickle goddess, Fortune, elsewhere. Possibly, her blinded eyes might not recognize her old adorer, and she might even yet bestow upon me a few of her faithless smiles.

Again, however, after my departure, was the Opera House leased. But to whom, do you imagine, it was now abandoned by the exemplary wisdom of its proprietors?

To the identical William Niblo who had fostered and en-

couraged the opposition—the same William Niblo who had a
theatre (or let me give it his name, and call it—a Garden)
within the length of some three stone-throws from their own
House. It must be granted they did not foresee that which
was about to happen. But this will scarcely palliate the
folly of taking the head of a rival establishment for their
tenant.

This gentleman engaged the *troupe* of dogs and monkeys,
then in this country, under the charge of a certain Signor
Donetti.

Their dramatic performances were offered to the refined
and intelligent proprietors and patrons of this classic and
exclusive place of amusement. Naturally, they protested.
It was in vain. Then, they sued out an injunction against
this exhibition, on the ground that in Niblo's lease of the
premises, *only* respectable performances were permitted to
be given in the Opera House. On the "hearing to show
cause" for this injunction, Mr. Niblo called up Donetti,
or some of his friends, who testified that his aforesaid
dogs and monkeys had, in their younger days, appeared
before princes and princesses, and kings and queens. Moreover, witnesses were called, who declared, under oath, that
the previously mentioned dogs and monkeys behaved behind
the scenes more quietly and respectably than many Italian
singers. This fact I feel that I am not called upon to dispute ;
while you will naturally regard yourself, my good friend, as
not required to express any opinion upon such testimony. As
might be supposed, the injunction was dissolved.

As a matter of mere course, the House lost all its *prestige*
in the eyes of the community. Shortly afterwards, its contents were sold, and the shell of the Opera was turned into a
library. Its death-blow had been given it as a place for
theatrical amusement, by the astute Mr. William Niblo

To me, I may candidly confess that this was a matter of satisfaction.

It had been unable to sustain itself before I had become its lessee. During the three years of my lease, it had flourished and paid its proprietors an even large rental. It fell entirely and ingloriously, a few months after the period at which I had bidden it a final farewell.

Had the proprietors entertained any other view than that dictated to them by the meanest pecuniary interest, it might at present have been the most fashionable theatre in New York. As such a theatre, it could not but have paid them a handsome interest on its value.

Soon after the fall of this House from its position as the only operatic establishment in the city, another party of gentlemen took out a charter for the building of the Academy of Music. Having obtained it, they went to work and constructed the new Opera House. It was subsequent to my return from Mexico, where I had been absent nearly one year, that I, one morning, met William Niblo. His opinion respecting the future Academy of Music was asked by me.

"Why—" answered the cunning Manager, with his usual nasal voice—"I suppose, I shall have again to engage Donetti's dogs and monkeys."

Trusting that I have not wearied you, believe me, my dear Balfe,

As formerly, entirely yours.

M. M.

MME. FREZZOLINI.

SIXTH LETTER.

TO FREDERICK GYE, ESQ., LONDON.

Mexico—Opera and Bull-Fights—Mexican Notions—Mexican Law and
Justice—A Mexican Prima Donna—Mexican Revolutions—A Mexican Secretary of State in want of money—A Forced Loan—Mexican
Robbers—Puebla—Vera Cruz—Incidents, Accidents, and Adventures.

MARIETTA GAZZANIGA.

LETTER VI.

TO FREDERICK GYE,

(*Manager of the Royal Italian Opera, Covent Garden, London.*)

NEW YORK, *September* 18*th*, 1855.

DEAR SIR :—

ALLOW me to hope that, after a lapse of seven years, you may have forgotten my neglect to send you those compositions you had engaged from my pen, previous to my departure from London. Should you be inclined to read the first letter in the present volume, originally intended for Berlioz, although afterwards put through the mental mill for the general reader, you will see how it was that I failed to fulfil my engagement. Mixed up, during my first year in New York, with all the "miseries and mysteries" of Operatic management, you will comprehend that I had neither the time nor the inclination for composition.

You too have known what a life "behind the scenes" really is. Consequently, I feel assured of your sympathies.

In addition to this, my dear sir, I never really believed that you cared one straw about these compositions, or at all valued my talents as a composer, until we chanced to meet, once more, some two years ago. Then, to my astonishment, the reproaches which you addressed me showed that you had actually reckoned upon the fulfilment of my engagement.

However, you may easily console yourself for the non-reception of my insignificant labors. Since that period, you have dealt with greater *maestri* than I could pretend to be. You have produced far better and more profound compositions than any which I might perchance have sent you, and can enjoy the credit of having saved and restored by your energy, skill, and perseverance, Italian Opera in London. The smothering ashes of past failure which were about to crush that institution, you have swept away, and having located it in a new temple, have toiled at its perpetuation with, I trust, an ample reward for your labors in its present success.

You may remember that at my last visit to London, after having somewhat appeased your wrath touching my breach of promise, the question was put to you by me, whether you might not be inclined to send, during the winter months, (when the Royal Italian Opera is closed) your company across the Atlantic. In this way, you could have kept your artists employed the whole year, and might have made a personal experience of this continent.

At the time, you did not seem altogether indisposed to listen to this suggestion.

At length, you told me, that in the event of my getting up for you a subscription of £30,000 ($150,000), I might write to you, and that you would be willing to try the experiment. In the event of my being able to do so, you would see a reasonable chance of making a similar or even larger amount from the nightly receipts.

You must excuse me, my dear sir, for publishing the gist of our conversation. My reason for doing so is, that your (in my opinion, just) expectations and demands may tend to the edification of the operatic proprietors, stockholders, and subscribers in this city, who demand nothing less than such an operatic *troupe* as yours is in Covent Garden, yet refuse even the presumptive price of two dollars a seat, and would start back in utter horror at the idea of paying five dollars (something less than one guinea, the price of seats in your stalls) for the pleasure of hearing them.

It is, at the same time, my intention to give you in this letter a brief sketch of my operatic campaign in Mexico, the capital of which country is farther from New York, by the ordinary route, than it is from this city to London.

Through my doing so, you may possibly gain a more just idea of the manner in which musical speculations are managed in the New World.

In February, 1852, was it, that I had vanquished the Italian Operatic opposition at Niblo's Garden, and was left apparently defunct upon the battle-ground. Both companies were then unoccupied. Both were still actuated by a purely Italian jealousy of each other; while either party feared the engagement of the opposing one by Don Francisco Marty y Torrens, for the purpose of sending it to New Orleans, Mexico and Havana. Now, a precisely, or very nearly similar project, had been running for several months in my own brain—for I believe it is admitted that we all carry some portion of this article in the interior of our skulls. Although almost penniless, or let me say, centless, as it will be a much more expressive Americanism, I had been constantly working to outflank Marty or his agents. My object was to carry that portion of the company which had remained faithful to my fortunes, to Mexico, where I felt confident that it must make money. My confidence was based on the fact that the land of the *Caciques* was literally untrodden ground. In fact, Mexico was an almost purely virgin soil for Opera. Reflecting upon this, I came to the conclusion that it would be decidedly advisable to attempt visiting that country. The memories of Cortez rose upon me. With what means did he attempt his raid upon the temples and treasures of Montezuma? With a like abundance of the sinews of war, would I attempt to recruit my purse in Mexico. Accordingly, I proposed to the late artists of my company to take the risk of accompanying me there, pointing out to them that should we arrive the first, the "Artists' Union Italian Opera Company" would not dare to repeat the trial of an opposition to our attractions.

They at once accepted. Their acceptance was, however, clogged with the proviso that I should bear all the travelling expenses, and should increase their salaries some sixty *per cent*.

They had evidently, in spite of my recent failures, full confidence in my skill as a Manager. My pecuniary position was not unknown to them, yet they still had faith in my abilities to overbalance the weight which had recently ruined me. Nevertheless, they intended, in the event of a great success, to make the best they could out of me. On the other hand, I reasoned with myself thus: Once out of New Orleans and in Mexico, should my success not be so brilliant as to justify me in paying these increased salaries, they would become infinitely more tractable, and we should be enabled to make far easier and more liberal arrangements together. Therefore, I consented to this portion of their proposition. Moreover, I agreed to pay all their travelling expenses and hotel bills, provided they would sing a few times in New Orleans and Vera Cruz, to remunerate me. This they acceded to. Consequently, having settled these preliminaries, I went round to some of my friends, and borrowed sufficient money to send an agent in advance to Mexico. He had orders to engage a Chorus and Orchestra, to take the Opera House or theatre in that city, and to make all the preliminary arrangements which upon his arrival he might consider necessary.

After having done this, I then sold out, or mortgaged the remainder of my theatrical properties. By this means, I procured barely enough to send the entire company out of New York, on one fine spring morning, *en route* for New Orleans; none of the "Artists' Union Italian Opera Company," I may be permitted to observe, putting the slightest faith in what they had heard of my arrangements, or believing in the possibility of my "insanity." Such they chose to designate my attempt to carry to Mexico the *troupe* with which I had defeated their opposition.

The artists had been placed under the charge of my brother, Albert. They were to travel by the Ohio and Mississipi *route*, and he had instructions to give a concert, either in Cincinnati or Louisville, in case of necessity.

Myself and Madame Maretzek started some few days later. We took our line of travel through Charleston and Mobile.

After having thus provided for the travelling expenses of the members of the company, as far as New Orleans, and paying for the tickets of myself and my wife to the same destination, I found myself in the possession of the enormous capital of $54 on quitting New York.

It appears to me, my dear sir, that you must allow my faith in my "star" to be fully as great as that which Napoleon evinced in his.

This was the whole amount, with which in my possession, I undertook the task of carrying my artists from New Orleans to Mexico. With this prodigious capital, I was to open an Opera House, and carry on business in that city. To me, it was an entirely novel ground. Therefore, partially was it, that I relied on my capacity to do so. Confiding in the talents of my artists and my own luck, I travelled to the

" Crescent City," rejoicing in the idea of having once more completely outwitted the opposing coalition. I say "completely outwitted," for in this half of the world, the first attempt in any line of business is the only one that is certain to pay, and my determination to visit Mexico may be regarded as the first in which any good Operatic company really visited that capital. Therefore, to me, it appeared certain that I should gather the first-fruits of Mexican love for Operatic Music.

We all met at New Orleans, in good condition and good spirits. But Albert told me that he had been already obliged to give two concerts upon his road thither. The reason for this was, that the artists, feeling freed from the rivalry of their opponents, had again abandoned themselves to their old habits, whims and caprices. Having full faith in my ability to conduct their present campaign to a successful issue, they began again to live as if all the silver mines in Mexico had already been the property of their Manager. Instead of eighteen persons, moreover, the *troupe* had swollen to twenty-seven. Every *prima donna* having found the necessity of bringing with her, her aunt, sister, grandmamma, or her protector, without counting her lap-dogs or her parrots ; and each *tenor* carrying with him his *protégée* and his servant.

A similar style of living was continued in New Orleans. No representations on my part could induce them to abandon it. One complained about the rooms, and insisted upon having a private parlor. Another objected to the wine procured at the St. Louis Hotel, and requested me to perform the duties of his butler, or improvise him a wine-merchant. A third had the hiring of carriages and the furnishing of goods inserted in her bill, while a fourth astonished me with an exorbitant *item* for *soupés fins*, which I was expected to settle. In short, they all lived in a style which it is singularly unusual for an Italian artist to do, when he or she has any suspicion that it will have to be paid for, out of his or her own pocket. As a necessary consequence, the receipts at New Orleans were insufficient to carry us on to Vera Cruz. Nor only this, but they actually fell short, by several hundred dollars, of the sum necessary for hotel expenses.

Many persons would, on finding this agreeable result of a management which necessarily subjected them to such conduct, have backed out of their position. Mine was not at all enviable. You must observe, my dear sir, that not only did my sanguine nature paint to me a brilliant success in Mexico, but my ingrained modesty prevented me from being willing to return to New York, and affording my enemies a reasonable chance for laughing at me. Hence, whatever my difficulties might be, two chains linked me to the oar at which I was pulling, the one of which my natural obstinacy persisted in believing to be a silver fetter.

As I was sitting, one evening, ruminating upon my position and the posture which my affairs were gradually taking, a happy thought suggested itself to my mind. It was, as I must confess, a desperate chance which presented itself. But the beggars of Fortune's favors have no right to be choosers. At the present, let me own that I regard this idea, if I may say so without profanity, in the light of an inspiration. I had heard that the principal of a Mexican banking house was residing in New Orleans. This gentleman, I had never been introduced to. Nay! I had never even seen him. Nevertheless, it was to him that I determined upon applying. Accordingly, upon the next morning, I paid him a visit. Let me own that it was after spending an hour in screwing up my courage to the sticking point, that I was enabled to find enough to place my hat upon my head and draw on my gloves for the purpose of doing so.

After sending in my card, the Señor Martinez del Campo received me in his private office.

Here, he at once expressed his satisfaction with the *troupe*, which he had attended on every evening of performance in New Orleans. He did more. He predicted to me a glorious season in Mexico.

It was, I fear me, in very common-place terms that I acknowledged his compliments. All my courage seemed oozing out beneath my finger-nails. Not a word could I summon to my lips, to speak about the real object of my visit.

He at last hinted, that as I was going to visit Mexico, I, in all probability, wished for some letters of recommendation from him.

Somewhat encouraged by his apparent amiability, I, at length, managed to say, that—

"While I should be truly grateful for any letters of re-commendation he might give me, I had really come to ask him to accommodate me with"—my heart leapt into my mouth, as I said this—"money!"

"Money!" he exclaimed.

The word which had so humbly escaped my lips, was blurted out by him in that rough and hard tone which is so peculiar to bankers and brokers, and so very remarkably unpleasant to a poor devil of a threadbare musician.

A sensation marvellously like fainting came over me, as I noted the change in his voice. But as I involuntarily, for a second, closed my eyes, pictured upon their *retina* I saw the malicious laughter of Badiali, and a quiet smile stealing over the seraphic face of the gentle Bosio, who had been two of the leading members of the "Artists' Union Italian Opera Company." As these became visible, my courage again returned to me. Opening my eyes, I said to him—

"I had supposed, señor, that I should have made somewhat more money than I have actually done in New Orleans."

"Of course!" he muttered, in a contemptuous manner, that left me but little hope.

"I am consequently short of funds."

An ironical smile here curved his upper lip. It seemed to me as if he was about to say—"What the deuce have I to do with that?"

In my agony, I continued—"If I write to New York, the loss of time before I receive an answer will almost double the sum which I need, as my expenses will still be running on."

Here I paused, expecting some reply. This, however, only came in the shape of a piercing glance which he shot at me from beneath his half-closed eyelids.

"And as *you* yourself remarked to me, my company *is certain*"—this I remember emphasizing very strongly—"of a great success in Mexico, I would undertake to repay you, although I could never possibly repay your kindness, out of my first receipts."

As I reached this point I again gave way, when he brusquely exclaimed—

"I do not doubt you will."

Saying this, he arose and hurried out of the office.

This seemed to settle the business, and I had slowly arisen from my seat and was just taking my hat up to place it upon my head, when he again entered the room.

"Here! M. Maretzek!" he said to me, as he placed a paper in my hand—"is a check for $1,000, which you will have to return to my brother-in-law *the day after your opening the box-book* in Mexico; and here"—saying this, he tendered to me a sealed letter—" are a few lines to the postmaster at Vera Cruz."

I stammered as I attempted to thank him, but he would hear nothing, and telling me I had already taken up too much of his time (it was doubtless valuable, when a quarter of an hour had been worth so much to me), bowed me in a remarkably curt manner out of his office. If I do not here tell you how much I felt indebted to his liberal manner of doing me this favor, believe me, that it is simply because I have yet occasion to acknowledge his kindness.

On issuing from his office, I scarcely knew whether I was standing on my head or my feet. How I reached my hotel, it would be impossible for me to say. But for the passengers in the street, I should have executed a *pas seul* expressive of my intense delight. Fortunately, the memory of a gentleman of genius, whom I had once seen accommodated with a strait-waistcoat for gratifying himself in a similarly innocent manner, restrained me from indulging in this fancy, and I contrived to reach my temporary home without any gross violation of public decency. Here, I paid all the bills of my Company, and with the remaining $600 in my pocket, was fortunate enough to secure and charter a vessel for our passage—there being, at this period, no regular line of steamers or packets between New Orleans and Vera Cruz. This was the brig *America*, commanded by Captain Maloney. It was a small vessel, and could not have accommodated a greater number of passengers than ours was. He had agreed to charter it for $1,000, the half of which was payable in advance. Not caring, for the moment, how I might be able to pay the second half, I handed him $500—returned at once to my hotel, gave notice to my vocalists to prepare themselves for immediate embarkation, packed up the whole of my own traps, and was on the following morning floating down through one of the mouths of the Mississippi, on my way to Vera Cruz.

We were seven days in the Gulf of Mexico. Let me own to you, my dear sir, that there are periods in my life when I recognize in myself a sad deficiency in the more Christian virtues.

In a similarly un-Christianlike forgetfulness of the duties of my love for my fellow-man, did I find myself, on the second and third days of our voyage towards Mexico. Remembering the position in which the regardlessness of expense on my part, shown by my artists, had recently placed me, it was with a demon-like delight that I noted their sufferings. Every groan seemed an acknowledgment in the individual person of the sufferer, of their shameless conduct. Each qualm seemed a partial payment to me for their extravagance. The God of the Sea, old Neptune, seemed to have taken sides with me, and to pay himself with the contents of their stomachs for the bleeding they had inflicted upon my pocket. Woe is me! he was not contented with a legitimate vengeance. On the third night I retired to rest, and on the fourth morning I did not rise. Most profoundly careless did I feel whether we went at once to the bottom of the Gulf, or whether we arrived at last at Vera Cruz. For the time, Opera and Operatic singers, the "Artists' Union Italian Opera Company" and my own *troupe*, New York, New Orleans and Mexico were alike indifferent.

All this indifference vanished, however, when on the seventh day of our voyage we arrived at Vera Cruz.

Rushing on deck, I gazed longingly on the land of " Caballeros " and " Leperos," " Señoras" and " Niñas,"—on the land of Revolutions and Earthquakes, the flowering Cactus and the wondrously delicious (that is to say, provided you can accustom yourself to it) drink called " Pulque."

Feeling very much after the fashion of one of the Spaniards who sought it in the olden time, the white walls of the houses seemed glistening with gold and silver.

My hopes, however, were to arrive at the glittering possession of the precious metals in a more peaceful guise. Instead of swords and arquebuses, I had brought with me *tenori* and *soprani*. *Bassi* and *barytoni* were my cannon. For my glaive I carried a *baton*, and bore instead of a shield a music-book.

On our arrival, the boats of the captain of the port and the custom-house officers came out to meet us, filled with ladies and gentlemen. They boarded our brig and told us that my agent had announced our arrival, and that for the last week every vessel which had been signalled from New Orleans had been boarded in the same manner. This had been done, that they might have the satisfaction of hailing the arrival of the "great" Italian Opera Company, and also of inducing us to consent to give *one* concert in Vera Cruz, before we proceeded to Mexico. This was the very thing I actually needed, and had intended doing. Diplomacy, however, had occasionally been taught me. Here, it would decidedly benefit me. Therefore, I at once declined to comply with their wishes. They, of course, became only the more eager. After half an hour's warm entreaty, I appeared to be a little touched by their arguments in favor of my doing so, as well as flattered by the warmth of their reception, and told them that I would see them on the following day at my hotel, where we might discuss the matter more quietly, when I had partially recuperated myself from my fatigue. At any rate, I gave them to understand, that my sole dislike to perform in Vera Cruz arose from my intense wish, first, to win for my company the suffrages of their capital. This very evidently pleased them in one way, while it afflicted them in another. They were delighted to imagine that I did not consider success as a necessity amongst the *virtuosi* of Mexico, while they all but wept over the possibility of my leaving them without gratifying their wishes. No sooner had I settled this, than we went on shore.

When we arrived at the hotel (it was called the *Posada de las Diligencias*), I learned with great pleasure, that the proprietor was no other than Don Fernando Grinda, the very postmaster for whom the Señor Martinez del Campo had given me the letter of introduction. This letter I, consequently, lost no time in presenting to him.

Not an hour had I been comfortably installed in my room under his roof, when the worthy Captain Maloney, from the brig *America*, paid me a visit. Until that moment I had forgotten him, and what was of infinitely more importance, the remaining half of the fare. A shadow of regret swept over me that I had not burnt my vessel like Fernando Cortez. But it passed from me, when I reflected that it would have been necessary to have burnt Captain Maloney along with it. He was much too good a fellow to have been sacrificed as a bodily settlement of his claims upon me. However, I had scarcely forty dollars in my purse, and, at that moment, an exposure of the state of my finances would have been utter ruin to me. What was I to do? During the time that elapsed between the announcement of his visit and his entry into my chamber, I had space to reflect, but it was very brief. My determination was taken. Scarcely had he entered, than I broke forth into a torrent of compliments touching the gentlemanly manner and courtesy with which he had treated us on board of the brig, and taking my gold watch and chain from my own neck, begged him to accept them as a slight token of my esteem and satisfaction.

The fine-hearted Yankee skipper was struck with amazement, and while he was looking alternately at me and at " the slight token of my esteem and satisfaction," with his astonishment painted on his face, I explained to him, that I must request him to call upon me in three days' time for the remaining $500 due to him, as my only available means were letters of change drawn at three days after sight. Of course, to such a reason and such an expressive demonstration of gratitude, there could be no possible reply but one, from any man with such a large heart as that which Captain Maloney had seated in his bosom. He took the watch and chain, and left my room with a profusion of thanks.

Almost immediately afterwards, he had proclaimed my generosity in the parlor as well as in the office of the hotel.

This only contributed to increase the opinion entertained by the public of Vera Cruz, of my independence of them. Never was a watch and chain put out by any donor to better interest.

Consequently, the ambassadors from the leading society of Vera Cruz did not wait until the following morning to renew their applications. The very same evening did they wait upon me, and reiterated their entreaties that I would suffer myself to be persuaded to give a concert in that city. As the most natural excuse, I pleaded my want of time as well as the absence of my agent, through which I had no one with me to make the absolutely necessary arrangements for such an entertainment. In addition to this, my ignorance of the customs of the country, as well as the great expense consequent upon lingering in Vera Cruz several days longer, must very certainly render it almost an impossibility.

This " almost" was very skilfully introduced by me. They saw that I was far from being completely inexorable. Therefore they redoubled their entreaties, and, finally, I permitted myself to be persuaded to gratify them. It was agreed between us, that they should procure the house for the concert (it was to be given in the theatre); that the printing, advertising, and all other necessary expenses should be liquidated, and that the clear sum of $1,200 should be guaranteed me. The concert was also to take place upon the following day.

It did so, and although I chronicle the fact myself, it created an immense sensation. Every piece was encored, and at the close the stipulated sum was placed in my hands.

With this money, on the following morning, I paid to Captain Maloney the $500 which were still due to him. I then went to the postmaster to order twenty-seven places by the diligence to Mexico, and requested him to make out the bills both for our board and travelling. He went to his office and did so, after which he handed me the following account.

" Don Max Maretzek to Don Fernando Grinda,

27 persons. Board from three to four days, $10 each . .	$270
27 persons, *per* diligence to Mexico .	1,350
60 trunks, the luggage of the party .	300
	$1,920 "

As I looked upon this bill, I was speechless. You might have knocked me down with a feather.

The distance from Vera Cruz to Mexico is little more than the distance from New York to Boston. Reckoning the expense of travelling these few hundred miles at some $5 or $6 *per* head, and admitting *even* $10 board for each person, I had imagined that my $700 would have been amply sufficient. It was impossible for me to have supposed that this expense could by any means have been swollen to more than $60 *per* person and baggage. The non-existence of railroads in Mexico had been suffered to slip from my memory, and until this occurrence, I knew not that the whole of the stages or diligences in the Mexican Republic belong by privilege to a single person. Having no *concurrence*, in any form, to fear, this person is able to charge how and what he will. As a necessary consequence, the three hundred and fifty miles from Vera Cruz to Mexico cost nearly as much as the whole of the travelling from New York to Vera Cruz, which is by the ordinary route a distance of something more than 2,800 miles.

Gazing from the paper in my hand to the postmaster, and from the postmaster to the paper on which these figures were traced, my surprise rendered me literally incapable of uttering a single word.

At length, Don Fernando broke the silence, by saying—

" In the letter which you brought me from the Señor Martinez del Campo, he says, that as possibly it may be more convenient (!) to you to liquidate your travelling expenses after your arrival in Mexico, he will guarantee the fulfilment of your promise."

You, my dear sir, may imagine my astonishment better than I can by any chance describe it. Not only had the noble-hearted banker lent me the money to quit New Orleans, but had actually, foreseeing my present necessities, without a word extended his assistance to obviate them. This might have been accounted for, had he previously been acquainted with me. On the contrary, this assistance had been extended to one who was a perfect stranger to him; and must, very certainly, always demand from me the warmest and most thorough feeling of gratitude.

Turning to Don Fernando, I told him that I would take

advantage of his kindness and the Señor del Campo's letter, by paying him a portion of his bill at present, and settling the remainder of it in Mexico. Being perfectly satisfied with this arrangement, I gave him $600 on account, while for the remaining $1320 he drew up a promissory note and handed it to me to sign. The date at which it came due, was *on the day after the opening of the box-book.*

It was with a shudder that I attached my name to it, for the $1000 which had been lent me by the Señor Martinez had to be paid upon the same day.

With a vigorous effort of my will, however, all unpleasant reflections were for the moment discarded. At length, I was tolerably certain to arrive in Mexico.

It will be unnecessary for me to describe to you the beauties of the country through which we now travelled. This I leave for any Bayard Taylor who may come after me. My matter is business rather than loveliness, and it occurs to me that in reading this letter, you rather require the detail of events than the description of scenery. Therefore, I shall not dwell upon the forests of orange-trees, and the camps of gigantic aloes by which we passed. Neither shall I compare the snow-covered volcano of Orizaba, glistening in the morning sun, with an immense diamond of some 16,000 feet in height. I shall not terrify you with highly colored descriptions of Mexican banditti, nor endeavor to sketch for you a Mexican *hacienda*, but shall simply state that we arrived, after forty-eight hours of horrid travelling, in the town of Puebla. This is a stopping-place where travellers generally rest for the night, and is remarkable for containing a population of some 60,000 inhabitants, of which it appeared to me that nearly 10,000 were men, women and children, while the remaining 50,000 were very evidently monks.

Here, I found three letters from my agent in Mexico.

One of these requested me to give him due notice of my arrival in Puebla, *per* telegraph; to remain, then, the whole of one day in that city, and again telegraph him the hour at which I should leave it. By this means, he would not only have one clear day to prepare a public reception for us, but would be tolerably certain of the hour of our arrival. He also informed me, that the aforesaid reception would be a most imposing affair. A cavalcade of some two hundred horses and their riders, with military bands and flying banners, &c. &c., were to take part in it.

Now, foreseeing very clearly that I should have to pay all the expenses of the said reception, and counting over what these would probably be in a country where it costs a man some $50 or $60 to travel three hundred and fifty miles, I decided on not incurring them. Being also certain that my invaluable agent had arranged to pocket a very decent *per centage* on the gross amount of these expenses, and that there could only be one way of evading his saddling me with them, I determined upon adopting it. Therefore, I notified him, as he had desired, through telegraph, of my arrival in Puebla. As I said nothing about my departure, I reasonably concluded that he would imagine it was my intention to comply with his wishes, as regarded the period of it. At the same time, I ordered the horses to be attached to the diligence a few hours before daybreak on the following morning. By these means, I trusted, that in all probability we might steal a march upon his arrangements.

The second letter contained the cheering intelligence that he had already engaged an Orchestra, a Chorus, and a Ballet. In addition to these, painters, carpenters, and printers, had also been secured by his industry.

But, on examining the figures of these engagements, it became very evident to me that my agent had acted either for himself or for the persons engaged by him, or perchance for both. My interests would appear to have formed, in his mind, a purely secondary consideration. In short, to my horror and dismay, I discovered that his arrangements alone would run up my expenses, nightly, to considerably more than $1000 (!) in addition to the heavy salaries of the members of the company which I had brought on from New York with me, and, of course, wholly exclusive of the rent of the Opera House itself.

By the third letter, I was informed that he had taken the *Gran Teatro di Santa Anna.*

Its rent was $2400 *per* month, payable in advance. The first month's rent was to be paid on *the day after the opening of the box-book.*

This was the *coup de grace* for me. Hitherto, I had believed in Mexico. But I had learned, already, that Operatic or theatrical subscriptions were only taken for twelve nights in that city, and were then renewed for another twelve nights. Yet, out of the first subscription, were $1000 for the Señor Martinez del Campo in New Orleans—$1320 for Don Fernando Grinda at Vera Cruz, and $2400 for the rent of the *Gran Teatro di Santa Anna*—in all, amounting to $4720, to be taken.

Whence were the other necessary expenses attendant upon the opening of an Opera House to be drawn?

How, if the amount of the subscription for the first twelve nights should fall short of the sum absolutely requisite—$4720?

In New York, a twelve nights' proportion of the fifty nights' subscriptions never came near $4000.

What could I possibly do, should this be the case, in a strange country, without credit, name or friends?

These questions haunted me through the whole night,

which you may well believe was a sleepless one, in spite of my previous forty-eight hours of travel in a diligence over the most wretched roads you can imagine; for I defy you to have experienced any such in Europe. At any rate, it was no use shrinking, now we had to proceed. On the next morning, I accordingly rose, haggard and jaded by the weariness of dread; and on the evening of the same day we arrived in the city of Mexico, to the great annoyance of my agent, and the pecuniary loss of his hired circus-riders and street-musicians.

Once in the capital, I felt that regret was of no avail. Energy alone could save me, if salvation were possible for an Operatic Manager in such a situation as mine appeared to be.

Therefore, I at once sent a card to all of the newspapers, in which I thanked the citizens of Mexico for the intention they had expressed of giving me a public reception; declaring that I had managed to arrive a day anterior to that on which I had been expected, expressly, as neither myself, nor any of the artists who accompanied me, could think of accepting the slightest testimony of distinction from the public, until we had shown ourselves fully worthy of it.

This new style of advertising produced a more decided effect upon the Mexican public, than any number of street-parades could possibly have done. Advertising upon the principle of a Raree-Show, had been invented in the Old World. Upon this continent, it widened and developed itself into grandeur—*i. e.*, the grandeur of such a class of amusement. Under the inventive faculties of Fanny Ellsler's agent was it born. With the speculator in Singing-Birds and Fire-Annihilators, it had ripened into an acknowledged and openly avowed faculty for "humbug." An artist—Henry Herz, had himself carried it to Mexico. Judging merely from the arrangements made by my agent, it had ripened considerably since the period of his visit.

But, immediately below the above card, the following advertisement also appeared:—

" Any person engaged by the agent of Don Max Maretzek will have to present himself at the *Gran Teatro di Santa Anna*, within forty-eight hours, for examination, as well as for the ratification of his engagement."

The publication of this advertisement made my agent absolutely furious. He threatened, begged, blustered, implored and kicked up all kinds of rows. All this was of no use. My determination was taken. My prospects, my reputation as a Manager, and even my honor as a man of business, depended absolutely upon the manner in which I should commence my season.

At first, the Choristers presented themselves, and to do them justice, I must say, that a stranger looking set of individuals had never elsewhere placed themselves before me, with the view of getting an engagement for Operatic purposes.

All human races and colors were represented in this body of vocalists. Not a shade nor a mixture of complexion from white to ebony was there, which did not appear before me. Every tone of color from pepper and salt to orange-tawny could be discerned amongst them. As I gazed upon them with a marvelling appreciation of their variety of hue, I took the liberty of informing them, that their engagements had been made at much too high a figure to suit my pocket. What was my astonishment, when with a truly singular unanimity all of them declared their readiness to take fifteen *per cent.* less, provided I made a new contract, and the former one drawn up by my agent was declared void.

Nor was this the only abatement consented to by the local members of my new company.

Painters, printers, door-keepers, carpenters, tailors and copyists, also agreed to a similar diminution in their salaries, under the same conditions.

This unanimity was so extraordinary that I was unable to explain it to myself, until I at length saw the leader of the Orchestra. He gave me an explanation which unriddled the enigma. The name of this leader was Delgado. In spite of his color (for he was a mulatto), he was an excellent violinist, and a tolerably good leader. When he came into the room where I received him, he had a white handkerchief tied around his head and white kid gloves upon his hands. He complained of head-ache; and had powdered his face with flour or pearlash. It was at once evident that he had been attempting to whitewash himself, for this occasion.

Most ingenuously did I pity him for the head-ache with which he was afflicted, seeming not to remark in the slightest manner his voluntary transmutation of the tone of his complexion. Then, I asked him to reduce the price of the Orchestra.

In the most *naive* and innocent manner *possible* he told me that this would be *impossible*, unless, indeed, I should refuse to accept the old engagement, and myself draw up another.

"How is that?" I asked him. "I scarcely understand you."

"You see, Señor!" he replied, "as long as the engagement which has already been drawn up between myself and your agent exists, he takes fifteen *per cent.* from me and all the other musicians who are members of the Orchestra."

"Oh! upon my honor! he does that—does he?" I exclaimed.

The murder was, at last, out. Here was the secret of the readiness I had already experienced from the members of the local portion of my company, to abate this proportion of their stipulated salary.

However, seeing the class of individual with whom I had to do, I told him that the reduction of fifteen *per cent.* would by no means be enough. At the same time, I administered a small dose of flattery about his skill upon the violin, informing him that I had heard of it both in New York and Paris, and asked him why he had never yet visited the United States?

"There," I said, "I feel certain that you would do exceedingly well."

"Oh! I should be delighted to do so," was his reply; "but—" this he added in his usually *naive* style of conversation— "I feel frightened, lest they might take it into their heads to *sell* me."

As he said this, he seemed to recover his recollection, and his blood rushed into his face visibly beneath the pearl-powder. Almost unable to preserve my countenance, by a great effort I contrived to retain its immobility, and replied with an admirable simulation of the most intense surprise—

"Sell you, my dear Delgado! What nonsense! Sell a white (!) man in the United States! Who or what could have put that into your head?"

This was too much for him. The idea of being taken for a white man overpowered all resistance. The powder actually seemed to redden with his pleasure. He immediately lowered the figure of his demands several hundred dollars, and a new engagement was drawn up and signed between us.

In this manner, I had cut down somewhat more than $2000 of my expenses *per* month, the largest portion of which would have gone into the pockets of my invaluable agent.

However, with regard to the rent of the Opera House, I could do nothing. The lessees of the *Teatro di Santa Anna* had not been willing to sacrifice fifteen *per cent.* to my agent.

Therefore, they would abate me not one dollar. Neither was I able to procure any alteration in the stipulated time for payment. The first month's rent had to be paid *on the day following the opening of the box-book.*

The following Monday (May 11th, in 1852) was accordingly announced as the day upon which the office of the theatre would be opened, to receive subscriptions for the first period of twelve nights.

Feeling certain that the amount of these must fall far short of the demands upon my treasurer for the following day, you, my dear sir, may imagine how I felt. Looking towards it as a convicted criminal looks upon the proximate gallows or guilletine of his sentence, I longed intensely that the agony might be over. Every minute seemed no more than an addition to my anguish.

Not even was the satisfaction given me, of shaping any idea in my own mind respecting the taste of the Mexican public. All the theatres in the capital of Mexico were at this time closed. The Arena for Bull-fights alone contributed its material interests to popular amusement. This was flourishing. Having never before seen a bull-fight, and being even more anxious to take a view of that public before whom I was about to play the part of a musical *matador*, for one day I determined upon ridding myself of my doubt and dread; and upon the Sunday preceding the opening of the subscription-list for the Opera, I mustered sufficient resolution to make my appearance in the open amphitheatre where the bull-fights took place. From 10,000 to 12,000 persons must have been present. More than one-half of this immense gathering of spectators was packed together upon the sunny side of the arena (it is called "El Sol"), exposed to the scorching beams of a Mexican sun, with no protection for their heads save their *sombreros* and scarfs or mantles, waiting for the commencement. On the opposite or shady side of the arena, were boxes filled with elegantly dressed dames, and younger females attended by their cavaliers. This immense attendance at a place of amusement awoke some degree of hope in my own bosom. But when, as I subsequently turned, almost sickened out by the disgusting and barbarous spectacle exhibited in the arena, towards the spectators, and remarked the interest evinced by the better classes of society—both male and female—in the bloody and brutal drama enacting for their amusement; when I saw that the infuriated bull received far more encouragement than the *toreadores* or *matadores* who were endangering their lives to gratify that public; when I listened to the thunders of enthusiasm, and saw the waving of handkerchiefs bestowed upon the maddened beast whenever he killed a horse or wounded a man; and when I heard the groaning and hissing of that enormous multitude, when a *toreador* or *bandillero* missed his stroke at the bull, and thereby endangered his own life, let me own that I fled from the amphitheatre, disgusted and hopeless. Never could I have believed that in a city where such an exhibition could be sustained and patronized, sufficient taste could exist to support an Italian Opera.

On the next morning, therefore, I did not dare appear in the box-office myself. My brother was sent there, with the treasurer and his assistants, while I quitted the city and repaired to the Park surrounding the Castle of Chapultepec, that I might, were it at all possible to do so, for the time forget my miseries in the balmy air of the gorgeous Spring of Mexico, and deaden my anticipations of their completion by dreaming amid its beauties.

As I returned in the afternoon, by another road than that which the driver had taken to leave the city in the morning, he suddenly stopped the carriage.

Turning round, he exclaimed, "*Mira, V. Señor. Esto es el arbol del Cortez.*"

As he said this, he pointed out an immense cedar tree to me, and explained the story which was attached to its huge and giant bulk.

When Cortez was driven out of Mexico by the Indians with great slaughter, it is said that he paused in his retreat under this tree. Here, burying his face in his mantle, he wept long and bitterly. But, added the driver with a knowing look at my face, as if he partially divined the cause of my gloom—

" Cortez again returned, stronger than he had before been, and carried the City of the Islands by storm."

Alas! thought I to myself, as I descended from the carriage and walked around the aged cedar, such will not be my fate. I shall have no chance of running away from Mexico. On the contrary, to-morrow will settle that question. My creditors will detain me here for the non-payment of the various sums due to them. Nay! more—I swore internally, that in case I should by any chance get safe out of Mexico, there should be marvellously small chance of my imitating Cortez. Never again would I return to it upon a similar speculation.

When, at length, on re-entering my hotel, my first inquiry was about my brother, the domestics told me that he had not yet returned.

Now, had his nerves been constructed upon anything the same fashion as my own were, I might with much reason have concluded that he had been so dismayed by the result of the day, as to have made a slip-knot in his pocket-handkerchief, and attempted to secure an undisturbed exit from Mexico by means of strangulation. Knowing him, I however felt comparatively easy upon this head. Scarcely anything could possibly have disturbed the serene equanimity of his endurance.

Nevertheless, my dear sir, I can assure you that my pulse was jerking in an *Allegro vivacissimo*, while I felt the blood from my heart flooding my veins at the rate of one hundred and fifty beats *per* minute.

The waiter entered my chamber to inform me that dinner was on the table. Allow me to say that this was a perfectly useless attention upon his part. Very certainly was I unable, had I attempted it, to have swallowed a single morsel of food at this moment.

At length, steps were heard by me approaching the door of my apartment. My ear recognized them as those of my brother.

Swinging the door open to admit his remarkably leisurely approach, I gazed upon his face in the hope of reading the information of the day upon it. Imagination had painted to me that quiet physiognomy distorted by the sufferings of want of success. But you, my dear sir, may perchance remember that my excellent Albert possesses one of those peculiarly happy countenances which would appear to be totally unsusceptible of change in its expression. Nothing is there in the events of this life which could by any hazard derange its tranquillity. Whether he had your death-warrant carefully stowed away in his breeches' pocket, or bore you the intelligence of your having drawn a large prize in the lottery, my belief certainly is, that his face could appear equally indifferent to your sensations. As the door closed, therefore, I exclaimed—

" How was it, Albert?"

" Why! So! so!"

His tone was precisely that in which he might have replied to a question put to him touching the state of the weather.

"How much?" I impetuously required from him.

"What?" he demanded.

"Why! good Heavens! The amount of the subscriptions," I replied, stamping my foot impatiently.

"Oh! That is what you want to know?"

"To be sure it is!" I ejaculated, fast ripening into a rage. "Will you answer me, Albert, or will you not?"

"You may count it, yourself," was his phlegmatic reply.

As he said this, you may believe me, that his face betrayed not one jot more expression than the head of a Chinese Mandarin does that has been limned by a Chinese painter. But my wrath, which had begun to boil over, was suddenly checked by the appearance of a gigantic Indian bearing a moderately-sized bag upon his shoulders, at the half-open door through which my brother had entered the apartment.

Throwing it down upon the floor, I heard the agreeable and harmonious chink of silver as he retired from the room without uttering a word.

"One!" said my brother.

A second Indian entered, and repeated precisely the same operation.

"Two!"

Then came a third, who also deposited his sack of the precious metal upon the floor of the chamber, making it resound with the same musical voice.

"Three!" was counted with singular equanimity by my phlegmatic Albert.

"What does this mean?" I asked.

"Four!" said my brother, as a fourth bag chinked upon the boards.

I stared in literal astonishment as another Indian entered and deposited his contribution on the growing heap, while my brother tranquilly reckoned—

" Five !"

Still they followed on each other like the shadowy descendants of *Banquo*. Instead of a crown upon their heads, each bore a sack of Mexican dollars upon his shoulders, and my brother, unlike the "blood-boltered" progenitor of the shadowy race, did not

> " Smile on me
> And point at them for his,"

but quietly went on counting—" Six ! Seven ! Eight ! Nine ! Ten ! Eleven ! Twelve ! Thirteen ! Fourteen ! Fifteen ! Sixteen ! Seventeen !"

As the last of the Indians quitted the apartment, doubting the very evidence of my own eyes, I asked Albert—

" How much is there in each bag ?"

For the first time, the shadow of a smile seemed to flicker over his features, as he answered—

" Make a bargain with me, and I will give you one thousand dollars for the contents of each bag, without counting it."

Declining the bargain, I rung the bell, and at once ordered a capital dinner. It was a singular instance of the corporeal Philosophy of Life. No sooner was the weight of doubt removed from my mind, than my stomach reminded me of its share in my animal economy. It was very clear to me, that, as yet, I had neither dined nor broken my fast upon this day.

Such was the result of the *opening of the box-book* for subscriptions to the Opera.

From nine in the morning until five in the afternoon, the Mexican public had subscribed more than $18,000 for *only* twelve nights of Opera.

Allow me to say, my dear sir, that I respect, honor, and venerate the taste of the Mexican public for Operatic Music.

On the following morning, the immense amount of silver

we had received so far embrazened, or, it would probably be better to say, emboldened me, that I repaired to the box-office myself, and at 8 o'clock could hardly make my way through the crowd of would-be subscribers who were standing round it. At 9 o'clock, however, the Chief of Police inquired for me, and, on being admitted into the interior of the office, handed me a written order from the Governor of Mexico, not to receive any further subscriptions. This was based upon the fact that there was reason to believe the whole of the seats in the house might be taken by subscribers. In this case, the remainder of the public who could not afford a subscription for twelve nights, would be deprived of their share in the entertainment offered to them.

Naturally enough, my American feelings were offended by this order, and I asked what right the Governor had to intermeddle with my private affairs.

"Don Max Maretzek," replied the Chief of Police, very gravely, "you will find that in the city of Mexico you will *always* have to obey his orders." Saying this, he put himself in a dignified position, raised his hat, and with a sonorous voice, ejaculated—"*Dios e Libertad!*" Then he replaced it on his head, and continued—"Furthermore! you will not only have to obey his orders, but, even to anticipate them." His hat was again removed to allow him to utter once more —"*Dios e Libertad!* Moreover, let me inform you, that you must not publish even a bill of your performances without first forwarding it to his Excellency for inspection." Again did "*Dios e Libertad!*" ring on my ears. "You will also allow me to tell you, Don Max Maretzek, that you have neglected to send his Excellency the four boxes on the first tier, which are invariably retained for himself and the members of the *Ayuntamento. Dios e Libertad!*"

Therefore, as it appeared, that in the name of "God and

Liberty," I should not be allowed to dispose of any more subscription-tickets, I was obliged to communicate the order of his Excellency the Governor of Mexico to the assembled crowd.   Immediately, they volunteered to pay for a second subscription after the first twelve nights were terminated.   I was accordingly about to order my treasurer and his assistants to comply with their wishes, when the Chief of Police laid his hand upon my arm.

"Don Max Maretzek! by the laws of this country, the first subscriber has the right to retain his seats," he said, "for the second and third months, if he chooses to do so.   In addition to which, due notice must invariably be given him, three days before allowing any other persons to engage those seats."

As he concluded this, off came his hat and out rolled the inevitable "*Dios e Libertad!*"

This second order appeared to me, as I must frankly confess, somewhat inconsistent with the first injunction.   That protected the rights and amusements of the people, while this gave certain exclusive and undeniable privileges to the first-comers.

At all events, it gave me a tolerably sound notion of the contradictions of Mexican liberty.

The public, however, probably much better acquainted with their own freedom than I was, quietly dispersed; not, however, without having left their names, with many requests for the first chances, if any boxes should be left free during the next month. Amongst these was the French Ambassador, M. De Levasseur, who several times called upon me, and expressly begged me to keep the first box for the following month's subscription, which might not be retained by the present subscribers, for himself.

Nothing could have passed over better, than did our first

twelve nights. The artists were applauded—the subscribers
were delighted, and the public satisfied. After the tenth of
June, I accordingly announced a new subscription, giving
three days for reflection to the previous subscribers, and
stating in the papers and by posters, that those boxes which
were not retaken upon the third day subsequent to my advertisement, would be disposed of to those having the right
of pre-numeration in such a case.

The whole of the boxes, with one single exception, were
retaken upon the fourth day. This box had previously been
engaged by the banker, Rubio.

For one day more, I waited, and then, as the Senor Rubio
did not make his appearance, I offered it on the fifth day to
the French Ambassador, who immediately took it and paid
for it. The receipt for the cash was drawn up and handed
to him, together with the tickets and certificate for the box.

On the fifth day (the day previous to the commencement
of the second season) Senor Rubio sent his servant to me, to
inform me that he had decided upon retaining his box for
the following twelve nights. Even could I have given him
the box, this message was not accompanied with the amount
of the subscription. Most politely, therefore, did I send him
word, that I regretted not being able to comply with his
demand; as, after having waited for four days, I had conceived myself justified in allowing M. De Levasseur to
become my *locataire*.

With this, I had supposed the matter settled. But you
may judge of my astonishment, when some two hours later I
received a visit from a member of the *Ayuntamento*, who
also, with a singular regard for human economy, performed
the duties of a Sheriff.

" Senor *Empresario!*" he said, " you have been condemned
or fined to $100 penalty, or twenty-four hours prison, for

having let the box belonging to Senor Rubio to another person." He wound up this announcement with the usual satirical exclamation, accompanied by the raising of his hat, of—"*Dios e Libertad!*"

"What!" I exclaimed, "judged and condemned, on a simple accusation?"

"Yes, Senor!"

"Why, I have had no chance of defending myself. Convicted, before I had even received a summons! Is this the law in Mexico?"

"The law in Mexico *is* that you must pay," he replied, "or go to prison. Afterwards, you can make your appeal against the fine or imprisonment." He, of course, ended with the usual "*Dios e Libertad!*"

Not being inclined to resist this admirable judgment, I paid the $100. At any rate, said I to myself, I now know at what price I may let my boxes to whom I please. However, my conclusion was not based upon the *Codex* of the Mexican Republic. The first Sheriff had not quitted my apartment more than half an hour, when a second Sheriff entered. This one summoned me to appear next morning before the *Juez es Letteras*, to show cause why I should not deliver up the aforesaid box to the amiable Senor Rubio, or pay damages to him.

"Can a man be convicted twice in Mexico, Senor Sheriff, for the same offence?" I inquired.

"That is not my business, Senor *Empresario!*" was his reply.

"Nevertheless," I persisted, "I should like to know whether a murderer or assassin can be garroted twice?"

"All I have to tell you," he answered, "is, that you must appear before the *Juez es Letteras* to-morrow morning at nine o'clock" As usual, he concluded this information with the ordinary ejaculation, accompanied by a reverential lifting of his hat, of the abominable formula, " *Dios e Libertad !*" and then took himself out of my presence.

Necessarily, I was obliged to go to a lawyer, and went to one of the best in the Mexican capital. This was the Señor Olaguibel, who was also a Senator for the city, in the Mexican Congress. He, at once, declared that the complaint of Senor Rubio was not tenable. Accordingly, I accompanied him on the following morning, to plead our cause.

What was my astonishment, instead of going with him to the Courts, to find myself at the door of the Judge's private residence!

" It is customary, Señor Max !" he observed, when I commented on its singularity.

We were shown into the Judge's bed-room, where that functionary was sitting up in bed in his night-dress and with a silk night-cap on his bald head. It may be imagined that I opened my eyes. Soon after, the counsel for the plaintiff appeared. Coffee was handed round to us, after which the Judge removed his silk night-cap and tucked it under his pillow. Then offering us some *cigaritos,* he lit one himself, reclined his head upon his pillow, and closed his eyes with an appearance of the most profound resignation—saying—

" You can begin, Senores !"

But for the presence I was in, I must have laughed outright at that very presence.

The case then commenced.

Counsel for the plaintiff claimed the box, which had belonged for the last season of twelve nights to Senor Rubio, as his, by right and privilege.

Counsel for the defendant appealed to the law of advertising the new season for three days—proved that such had been done in the present case, and showed by my books, and the date when the money was received from M. De Levasseur for the rent of the box, that I had not only forborne letting it for three days, but for five. He also demonstrated, that having let that box to M. De Levasseur and received the money for it, I could have no right nor reason to require him now to give it up.

As for the Judge, he, without opening his eyes until the case was closed, made a gesture of assent to everything which my counsel advanced.

When Senor Olaguibel had ended, he sate bolt upright in bed, with his eyes wide open, offered me another *cigarito*, and then and there delivered his judgment.

This was, that the aforesaid box belonged (!) to the Senor Rubio, and must be delivered to him before the evening, or that the Manager of the *Gran Teatro di Santa Anna* must pay five hundred dollars damages.

Before I had a chance of giving any instructions to Senor Olaguibel, he appealed to a higher Court in order to stay judgment. On the same day, I was graciously informed that until the decision of the case (which might possibly come in six months or a year), the said higher Court had ordered that the aforesaid box should be closed and unoccupied either by its original owner, Senor Rubio, or its present owner, Senor De Levasseur, or any other living person. The rescript, which was handed to me, containing this order, terminated with the usual formula. Need I say that this was "*Dios e Libertad!*"

When I went to M. De Levasseur and told him what had happened, he informed me that he would force the door of the box which he had paid for.

"I should like to see," he said, "who here will dare attempt preventing the Minister of the French Republic from entering his box."

Entirely satisfied with his energetic determination, I returned to my hotel with the design of awaiting the result.

In the evening, the Minister of France came to the *Teatro di Santa Anna.* He found the door of his box nailed up, and four men and a Corporal in the Mexican uniform, with fixed bayonets, standing before it.

M. De Levasseur demanded that it should be opened, but the Mexican Secretary of State for Foreign Affairs happened most opportunely to pass through the corridor, at this very moment. With the most graceful *bonhommie,* he invited the French Minister into the President's box, and begged him by no means to interfere with the rights of Señor Rubio and the laws of Mexico. Not having heard this, I am unable to say whether he terminated his graceful little speech with the customary—" *Dios e Libertad !* " The informant who retailed to me this scene was, although a foreigner, a lengthy resident in the country. Probably he had grown so accustomed to the phrase, that he did not notice it.

On the following morning, M. De Levasseur, not being willing to involve the French and Mexican nations in a bloody war on account of an Opera-box, transferred all his right and title in it to Señor Rubio. Thus was this complicated affair settled.

Be not surprised, my dear sir, if, in recalling the incidents of my operatic campaign in Mexico, I also am often tempted to exclaim with the utmost enthusiasm—" *Dios e Libertad !* "

As another instance of Mexican law and Mexican justice, I may mention, that as often as a vocalist got really, or imaginarily, or wilfully sick, and necessitated a change in the performance which had been announced for the evening, it was the unfortunate Manager who was fined $100. In vain was it, that I represented to the Governor of the State, and even to the President of the Republic, His Excellency Señor

General Arista, that the guilty party was not the Manager. In vain did I endeavor to make them understand, that if the artist himself was the party who had to pay the fine, it was more than probable that the artist would manage to avoid getting sick, or at any rate so sick as to necessitate a change of performance after the bills of the evening had been published. The only answer which I received from them, was this—

"That the Representatives and the Senate of the Republic could alone modify or change the laws."

Nevertheless, I must exculpate the Republic of Mexico from the charge of treating the artists altogether with an unfair degree of leniency. As a proof of the fact that it does not, allow me, my dear sir, to relate an incident which happened towards the close of the second season's subscription.

Signor Salvi had indulged in some of the usual flirtations (which unindulged in, it would be impossible for an Italian *tenor* to exist) in Mexico. Anxious to display his equestrianism before the eyes of his fair Señora, he purchased a horse, and intended to exhibit himself in all his beauty and glory, astride of it, in the *Paseo*. Unfortunately for me, he had not displayed his equestrianism for more than two hundred yards, when his Bucephalus (a remarkably quiet one, by-the-bye), alarmed by the bright eyes and flirting fan of some passing Señorita, started and reared. Unable to keep his seat, Salvi fell from his steed and managed to break his arm. He was immediately carried home, where the physician who was called in to him declared, that although there was not the slightest danger, it would very certainly be six weeks at the least before he could again appear upon the stage. With this announcement, all my reasonable prospects of continuing my campaign successfully, vanished; for it cannot be denied that Salvi was one of my leading attractions. At all events, I

endeavored, as far as was in my power, to remedy this unforeseen misfortune for the time being. The Opera announced for the same evening was Donizetti's "La Favorita."
As I knew that Forti had repeatedly sung this part before,
and had even requested it from me, as a favor, I went to him
and asked him to be kind enough to undertake it.

Knowing that it would be utterly impossible for Salvi to
appear for several weeks, he believed that his time was arrived. At any rate, he showed his inclination to vault into
the throne which had heretofore been occupied by that
tenor.

Point-blank, he refused to sing upon this evening. His
excuse was sickness.

But, as if determined to show me that this was not the
actual reason, and, at the same time, to demonstrate that if
not a better vocalist, he was at any rate a better rider than his
rival (if, indeed, Salvi could be called the rival of any *tenor*
who has been in this country, with the solitary exception of
Mario), he went on the very same evening, on horseback, to
the neighboring village of Tacubaya.

Going immediately to the Governor, I informed him of
what had happened. He chanced to be in a good-humor,
and permitted me to give a miscellaneous Concert on that
evening, instead of the Opera which had been announced,
without paying the customary fine of $100. In the mean
time, four soldiers with a Corporal, the usual Operatic *quota*,
were posted at the Gate of Mexico on the road to Tacubaya.
Instructions were given them to wait for the return of the
willing absentee from his Operatic duties, and to bring him as
soon as he entered the city before the Governor.

The concert took place during his absence, and I am
obliged to say that the audience, having heard of Salvi's

accident, bore Forti's absence with the most exemplary equanimity.

During the whole night, the non-commissioned officer, with his four men, waited for the refractory *tenor*. At about nine o'clock on the following morning, he returned. He was in high spirits touching the trick which he had played me, and was humming, as I was afterwards told, one of the very airs from "La Favorita" which he had so decidedly declined singing. As he entered the city, the Corporal strode before him.

" You are the Señor Forti?" was the soldier's address to the vocalist, as he laid his hand upon the bridle of his horse.

" Yes! my good fellow, I am."

" Dismount, then."

" But—"

" Dismount!"

" My dear sir, what on earth does this mean?"

" Dismount!"

" Allow me to ask—" commenced the trembling *tenor*.

" Dismount!" repeated the Corporal, " or I shall be obliged to make you."

The miserable Forti was compelled to obey the imperative order addressed to him, by a man to whom, twelve hours before, he would not have spoken a single word.

Then, he was placed between two of the soldiers, while the two others led his horse between them.

" *Dios e Libertad!*" said the corporal reverently, but without removing his *shako*, as, in obedience to his orders, they began to march through the streets of Mexico towards the *Deputacion*, as the City Hall is there called.

When arrived there, the *tenor* was immediately carried before the Governor.

What was my astonishment, on learning that without a

trial, and even without a hearing, he was condemned to a fortnight's imprisonment.

This order was at once carried into execution. Without giving him time even to change his clothes, permitting him to get clean linen, or to remove the spurs from his boots, he was hurried off to the common jail. Here he was thrust into the society of all the robbers, thieves, *leperos*, and other scoundrels, who had incurred the notice of the Mexican law. Delighted with his company, these respectable gentlemen disburdened him in the first fifteen minutes that he spent amongst them, of his watch and chain, money, rings, spurs, cigar-box, pocket-handkerchief, riding-whip, gloves, and other supernumerary articles as they conceived in such an establishment.

Now this was a just visitation, I will not deny, my dear sir, upon Forti.

But you must observe that his punishment fell with double weight upon my shoulders. Salvi, with his broken arm and confined to his bed-room, might reasonably grumble. While Forti in prison, and thrown among such company, was certainly to the full as much to be pitied. But the miserable Manager appeared to me to stand in the least enviable situation. He had by far the worst in the matter. They could not sing, while he was unable to give Opera. Their only answer was required by him, personally. His excuse must be given to, as it was demanded by his subscribers.

Of course, we all visited the unfortunate Forti, bearing with us tokens of affection as well as of our pity and condolence.

One bore him a box of fragrant Havanas. Another contributed a cold roast turkey to his creature comforts. This one carried him a bottle of brandy, and that one sent him half a dozen of Champagne. But, ere our interview with him had terminated, these had all vanished. His associates in the interior of the prison laughed at the sympathy of his friends without the walls. They held the doctrine of a community of property amongst the compulsory inhabitants of that enforced Republic (let me here exclaim " *Dios e Libertad!* ") and appropriated to themselves the larger proportion of these gifts, as soon as he had received them. Some devoured the turkey, and others drank the Champagne. These emptied his bottle of brandy, and those made free with the cigars. Nothing was left of them save the bones, the bottle, and the box. It was in vain that a *Pate de Foie gras* was contributed to the list of his imprisoned enjoyments. They had cleaned it out while his back was turned and he was talking to his benefactor. Uselessly was a cold haunch of mutton sent him. In ten minutes he could only contemplate the dish upon which it had erewhile stood.

Meanwhile, pitying him and myself too, I, the miserable Manager, had besieged the Governor with supplications for his release.

With great exertion, the permission for the release of Forti was obtained by me, on such evenings as his performance might be required. On these occasions, he was accompanied by four soldiers, who brought him to the theatre and delivered him into my hands, half an hour or an hour before the Opera commenced. At its conclusion, they marched him again off to the jail. Pity for Forti, after this, gained fast upon my feelings. Rehearsals were arranged, which necessitated his presence, and he was kept out of his enforced residence for the whole of the day. However, he had still to sleep under lock and key. At length, upon the fifth day, by dint of the most unremitting exertions, I obtained from the President himself the remission of the remainder of his term of imprisonment, or, rather, its commutation into a fine of $100.

After this, Forti never afterwards missed a performance in Mexico for sickness (!) or any other cause.

The second subscription was now drawing quickly to a close, and Salvi was not expected to recover sufficiently to appear before the scenes for some four weeks. Under such circumstances, there was very little chance of getting up a third subscription, as Forti was not relished as a *primo tenore* by the public.

As I was meditating upon what means I could adopt, or what I might invent for the purpose of raising a new excitement or keeping up the old one, a friend and acquaintance in Mexico, who was no other than the youngest son of the unfortunate Liberator and Emperor, Iturbide; entered my apartment. He requested me to accompany him to hear a young lady sing, and give him my candid opinion respecting her talents. Now Don Augustino Iturbide had in several instances shown himself a sincerely attached friend to me, and, although pre-occupied with my own affairs, I could not refuse him. Therefore, I took my hat and accompanied him. On our road, he informed me that this lady was the daughter of a General who had fallen in the war of Liberation. The pension of his widow being by no means regularly paid by the government, herself and her daughters were occasionally reduced to extreme poverty. It was consequently in the hope that my recommendation and testimony as to her abilities might procure for the daughter some situation as a church-vocalist, that he principally wished me to hear her.

We arrived at the house of her mother, and I was introduced by Señor Iturbide to his *protégée*. She was both young and good-looking; but, although her voice was a tolerable *contralto,* let me own that I was by no means satisfied with her singing.

Nevertheless, the kindness which Iturbide had invariably shown to myself, as well as the poverty of the family which he had made known to me, induced me to promise to write her a complimentary letter. This letter, when written, she might use as she pleased.

But while occupied the next day in writing this epistle, the idea struck me that it might be possible to turn her vocalism to far better account for *her* necessities, while it might prove of no small advantage to *myself.* You may call it a stratagem, my dear sir, if you like; but remember that all stratagems are fair either in love, war, politics, or theatrical management. Has not Barnum speculated upon the Feejée Mermaid, and did not your own Lumley bring out a native *contralto* baptized as the Signora Favanti? Reflecting upon these two instances of keen management, I jumped up and paid another visit to the lady. She was at home, and I was admitted to her room, where she was seated with her mother, speculating on the probable advantages of my letter.

" Señorita," I said, " upon reflection, I have determined not to write you that letter."

" Señor !" screeched out the mother.

" Señor !" ejaculated the daughter, in her two highest *contralto* notes. " You cannot be so cruel !"

" But, Señorita ——"

" Why did you promise it to me ?"

" Will you allow me to speak ——"

" It is unkind and ungentlemanly, Señor, in the extreme," almost sobbed out the daughter.

" Let us hear what he has to say, to excuse such barbarous conduct," said the mamma.

" Excuse it ! He never can."

"To be sure he can't. But I should like to hear him try to do so."

"Very well! Senoras, I will."

"Just listen to him. He will actually try to do so!" moaned the young lady.

Then, for a moment, both of them were silent. Like a skilful general, I seized on the opportunity to open my batteries.

"Senora," I said, with an air of the most profound respect, turning to the parent, "on thinking this matter over, I have come to the conclusion that your daughter's great talents and profound musical taste would be completely sacrificed, were she condemned to execute nothing but church-music."

The daughter was partially mollified, and recovered her self-possession as she listened to this delicately put bit of flattery; but the unappeased mother was by no means so easily satisfied.

"That may be all very well, Senor; but what on earth is she to do with them?"

"Go upon the stage, Senora!"

Had a bomb-shell fallen through the window, between the three of us, it could scarcely have produced a more astounding effect than this piece of advice did.

"The stage!" screamed the younger lady, springing to her feet. "Never! Senor."

"The stage!" groaned the elder dame, sinking back in her chair. "What would her deceased and much-respected parent, my lamented and never-enough-to-be-wept-for husband say, if he only heard this?"

"I am willing to offer her an engagement for two months."

"For two months!" repeated the mother. But I remarked

that the younger lady remained perfectly silent. This gave me some hope.

"At $400 *per* month."

"$400!" ejaculated the mother, looking at her daughter in astonishment.

"To be paid in advance!" I said, taking out my pocket-book.

The last shot told.

"Señor," modestly uttered the daughter, "I am totally unable to resist such astonishing liberality."

The treaty was, therefore, speedily concluded. Pen, ink and paper being brought me, I drew up the duplicate contracts, and handed them to the younger Senora to sign. Then I signed them, myself. Handing her one of them, I drew a blank order on the treasurer of the company out of my *porte-feuille*, and filled it up for the sum which was stipulated. This I passed to her. The crisp paper crackled in her white little fingers, as she received the legibly filled draft.

"And now, Senorita, you must begin to work, and at once."

"I am ready, Senor!"

"You yesterday sung to me some of the music belonging to the *rôle* of *Arsace*, in the 'Semiramide.' We will begin with that."

"Senor, I am perfectly willing."

"When can you be ready?" I inquired.

"In one week."

With a profound bow I took my leave, being convinced that I had saved my next month's season from the danger which had been threatening it.

Necessarily, Don Augustino Iturbide was informed of this engagement. He was, however, requested to keep it secret for a few days. In the meantime, the last evening of the second subscription had arrived, but no *programme* for a third

had been issued, and the indifference of the public was sufficiently evidenced, in the fact, that no inquiries of any kind
had been made respecting it.   It was, therefore, clear enough,
that this engagement had been the only chance left me, in
consequence of Salvi's unlucky mishap, for prolonging the
excitement which had previously existed with regard to the
Italian Opera.

My plan for the opening of the next month's campaign had
been silently and very carefully prepared.

Independently of Salvi, I had determined that the company
should make a pecuniary success.

Therefore, between the first and second Acts of the performance on this evening, I caused the intelligence to be
circulated in the lobbies of the house, by a few of my Mexican
friends, that after two or three more " farewell" nights, it was
my intention with my whole company to quit Mexico.

This intelligence, at once, kindled something like regret in
the minds of those who had patronized the Opera.   They felt
that with my quitting them, they would possibly lose for a
long period the chance of having any Operatic entertainment
in the Mexican capital.   In consequence of this feeling,
several of the more distinguished subscribers came to me at
the close of the second Act, to inquire whether it would be
impossible for me to remain, could another month's subscription be arranged for me.   Naturally, I, by no means, told
them that it was my intention to do so, in any case.   A circular had already been printed by my orders, which was distributed throughout the boxes and every part of the theatre,
during the interval which passed between the third and fourth
Acts of the Opera.   This circular contained an invitation to
the subscribers to come upon the next evening, and "attend
an Extraordinary Grand Performance, gratuitously given to
them, as, after their great liberality, the Manager was un-

willing to reckon the Miscellaneous Concert given on the occasion when Signor Forti had declined appearing, as one of the regular subscription nights." It was further said " that the Manager trusted the subscribers would accept the invitation, as an evidence of his grateful feelings towards them."

This was so perfectly new, that it completely took·them by surprise. So rarely does any Manager give those who support him more performances than the number agreed on (the contrary, indeed, being generally the case), that they were unable to restrain their expressions of astonishment. Moreover, the concluding lines appeared to intimate that we were about to bid them a speedy farewell. Little else was now wanting to kindle their enthusiasm.

On the following day numerous communications and inquiries, touching another subscription, proved to me that the dose given under my treatment had operated beneficially.

In the evening, upon my entrance in the Orchestra, I was loudly and vehemently cheered. This proved to me that their enthusiasm had recovered from its sickliness, and was again warming to a respectable blood-heat.

Accordingly, after the first Act, circulars were again distributed through the house. These announced, that, on the following day, a third subscription for twelve nights would be opened, during which " The Mexican *prima donna*, Senorita Eufrasia Amat, would make her first appearance upon any stage, as *Arsace*, in Rossini's Grand Opera of "Semiramide." This was followed by a biography of the Senorita Eufrasia, drawn up in the regular fashion of such biographies. Her father's services and his distinguished gallantry as shown in the war for the liberation of his country from the Spanish yoke, were recalled in a manner sufficient to make every Mexican heart beat with pride and patriotism. And, finally, I declared " myself most happy to have discovered in the daughter of this hero" (who, unfortunately, had been previously forgotten by his countrymen) " such transcendent vocal qualifications" (I was very careful not to call them such *transcendent vocal excellencies*) as to justify me in entertaining the belief that Mexico's native *prima donna* would, at some *future*" (this adjective, my dear sir, was very carefully inserted) " day, shine as a star of the first magnitude among the Operatic celebrities of the world."

It would be needless to say that the public was in raptures, at this announcement.

In the moment of their excitement, no one remembered that Signor Salvi would be unable to sing during the period of the third subscription. He was, for the time, totally forgotten.

Nay, I believe that nobody thought of anything else than rushing to the box-office, for the purpose of prolonging their subscription.

No sooner had this announcement gone forth, than Don Augustino Iturbide and his friends took it upon themselves to see that a purely patriotic encouragement was not wanting the Mexican *contralto*. On the evening of her *début*, military bands, playing the national hymn and other Mexican airs, were stationed outside of the *Teatro di Santa Anna*. The exterior of the building was brilliantly illuminated; while the audience-portion of the house was decorated with garlands of flowers, and a plentiful supply of *bouquets* and poetry was provided. Need I tell you, that none of this, my good sir, was done by the management. The whole of it came out of the pockets of the patriots of Mexico.

But, I see that you are about to inquire of me, how she succeeded?

You perhaps imagine that, having exhausted Europe in

the search for novelties, you may at last find one in the New World.

If so, believe me, you are in error. It may be naturally supposed that, in the excitement of the performance, the public occupied with reading the sonnets addressed to the Senorita Eufrasia, and placed (printed, I should observe, in gold letters, upon tissue-paper) in all of the boxes, had no time to appreciate the miraculously discovered qualifications (remember, I do not say *excellencies*) of the daughter of their previously unappreciated hero. At any rate, so it was. Yet, we both realized our object. My third subscription was as good as either of my two first, in spite of Signor Salvi's having broken his arm. Donna Eufrasia Amat, although she may not shine at the present moment as a vocal star, was indubitably paid $800 for her first appearance before the Mexican public, and in all probability obtained her desired situation, as a church vocalist, in the Capital of Mexico.

After the twelve nights had terminated, the broken-armed *tenor* recovered his capability of appearing on the stage.

We therefore remained for several months in the city, with somewhat varying luck.

At length, the Revolution which was fomented in Guadalaxara against the President, spread into the State of Mexico. From that moment, the business became not only bad, but disastrous. After some reflection, I determined upon returning to New York, instead of proceeding into the interior of the Republic, as we had at first proposed doing. Indeed, the day of our departure had been already fixed, when on one morning, a communication was received by me from the *Ministro di Hacienda* (an official, holding a position equivalent to our Secretary of State for the Treasury) which invited me to wait upon him. What on earth this invitation could have reference to, it was utterly impossible for me to imagine. With this Minister my affairs, up to the present moment, had not the slightest possible connection. Attendance however to such an invitation in Mexico was decidedly compulsory, and I therefore obeyed it. Receiving me with the most gracious politeness, and after having requested me to be seated and tendered me the almost inevitable *cigarito*, he thus addressed me:

" Do you know, Senor Maretzek, that for several months you have neglected to pay the requisite contributions to the State ?"

When he said this, I stared at him.

" Indeed! you have neglected them altogether."

" Excuse me, Excellency ! I have paid $100 every month, and have sent four private purses to the Governor of the State, not reckoning the fines and penalties which the Governor has been pleased to demand from the management."

" I see you do not understand me."

" I do not, your Excellency."

" The $100 each month are required for your license," he continued.

" So I was told."

" I am alluding to your contributions."

" What contributions ?"

" By the laws of Mexico," he replied, " every artist is obliged to pay ten *per cent.* from his salary, as a contribution to the Treasury."

Let me confess, my dear sir, that I was not altogether sorry to find that my artists were likely to have some of their wool shorn from them. In forcing me to raise their salaries some sixty *per cent.* more than they had been in New York, they had certainly seized upon not only the lion's share of the profits, but had, latterly, even compelled me to settle with them some of the outstanding scores from the last season at the Astor Place Opera House, where we had been working together against the opposition company.

Therefore, I smilingly replied to the Minister, " All your Excellency will have to do, in that case, will be to ask the artists themselves for their contributions."

" Oh ! no. By no means !" he replied. " That would take up by far too much time and trouble. We are in a hurry (at the moment, I scarcely understood what this meant) on account of the troubled state of affairs in this country. Now, the law is very explicit. It says, most clearly, that the *Empresario* is compelled to deduct the ten *per cent.* demanded by the State, and to retain it in his own hands. Consequently, we know but one responsible person invariably, and in the present instance this person is, of course, yourself."

" But, your Excellency, I have paid them their salary, not having been notified that there was such a law in existence."

" That does not matter."

" Supposing that they should refuse—Italians are very capable of refusing the payment of money—to return it to me."

" You can take it from their future salary," was his quiet and curt reply.

" Should they refuse to sing, in consequence of my having done so ?"

" They shall be compelled to sing," he responded with a knowing smile.

" But, your Excellency ! how am I to procure the money, supposing their engagement is at an end ?"

" Then you must pay it from your own treasury."

" That may be empty."

" Then I shall simply have the whole of your personal property seized."

" But, if I should have no property here, which you could lay your hands upon ?"

"In such a case," he responded with a provoking smile, "I shall secure your person."

Meanwhile, this conversation had excited me. It appeared such a wanton exercise of power to fine me (you will remember that I had smiled internally, when I had imagined the fine was to fall only upon the artists) simply for having brought into Mexico an Italian Operatic Company, that I could not restrain myself. With the natural interest of a stranger and an American, I had read all the details which were published of the Rebellion, and knew almost as much as any private individual in Mexico at that period could have known, of the situation of the government. Consequently, I replied—

"In a few days, your Excellency, I may be liberated."

"How so?" he coolly inquired.

"Forsooth! it appears to me pretty clear. A new President and a new Secretary of State may possibly interfere in the matter."

He, however, did not lose his temper. But smiling on me with a serene look of the most gracious benevolence, he replied—

"That is very true. But in the mean time we are in a state of siege. Remember this, if you please to do so, Senor *Empresario!* I—" he laid an ugly emphasis on the "*I*'— "can do what I please with you."

This last remark which he had made, had sufficient truth in it to tone down my excitement considerably. Accordingly, I remained silent for two or three minutes. While I did not speak, I was revolving in my own mind what was to be done. At last, I decided on resuming the conversation.

"And how much, your Excellency, is it that I am required to contribute?"

"Upon my word," he replied, "that is a difficult matter to say. However, in order not to lose any time" (he was evidently in a great hurry) "let us say $5000. Provided you pay me this at once, I shall be contented to give you a receipt in full for the seven months."

" Your Excellency," I replied, rising from my seat, " will have the kindness to send me a written order (!) to this ef‑ fect. I shall consult my lawyer, and if I find that I am compelled to liquidate it, I presume that I must do so."

" Don Max," he replied, " you shall receive the order." When he had said this I quietly bowed to him, and retired without saying another word.

Returning home (or rather returning to my temporary apartments in the city), I determined not yet to apply to a lawyer. Knowing sufficient of the Mexican internal politics, to see that every hour saved would be so much gained in the attempt to evade the settlement of this most unjust demand, I determined at present upon the observation of a masterly neutrality. However, the Secretary of State was by no means inclined to let such a valuable pecuniary case as mine was, slumber. In less than two hours, therefore, I received from him the " written order." It was remarked by me, that the individual who bore it was not an official servant of the Ministry. He appeared more like a humble personal dependant attached to the person of the Secretary, himself. Indeed, I was confirmed in this idea, by seeing him look carefully round the room to see that no one (my wife alone was present) was in it, but himself and your " highly-respected and many-talented" servant, the Senor Max Maretzek. Then, bowing very profoundly, he intimated to me that the *Ministro di Hacienda* wished me immediately to return to him, as he thought that this matter might be arranged without the assistance or interference of a lawyer.

In obedience to this hint, I accordingly returned with this person to the Ministry. On being shown into the same apartment I had previously seen the minister in, I found, instead of the Secretary of State, another high functionary of the government, who after asking me to be seated, also tendered me another of the inevitable *cigaritos*. This, naturally enough, I did not dare to refuse. As I took and lit it, the following conversation ensued between us.

"This matter, Senor Maretzek—" he commenced.

"The matter of the contribution, your Excellency?" I inquired.

"Precisely! It has been reconsidered. If the State did not in its present position actually require money, it would not be so pressing. But the present rebellion has completely drained the Treasury, and forces us to make the present demand. Therefore, we are unable to help you."

Here he stopped speaking, as if he expected an answer. But I was silent, and he continued after a momentary pause—

"If you will immediately pay $3000 instead of $5000, you may consider the matter settled."

"I have to inform your Excellency, that I shall do nothing of the sort."

"Now, pray do not get excited, Senor *Empresario!*" he replied, as he noticed my anger. "Let us talk like men of the world."

Saying this, he looked round him to see that the doors of the apartment were closed, and, then drawing his chair nearer to mine, he gazed into my face. Laying his hand upon my knee, he said in a remarkably confidential tone of voice—indeed I am not aware that I should be doing wrong, in calling it a whisper—

"If you give us $3000, we—why, *we* will give you a receipt for $5000! Eh! Senor Max! What do you think of this arrangement?"

"Simply," I replied, "that I do not understand what it means."

"It means this, Senor!" he answered. "You can, should you wish to do so, retain $5000 from the salaries of your artists, having only paid the government $3000 out of your receipts."

"Well, then, supposing I decline this offer?"

"But you will not do so."

"I am by no means so certain of that fact, your Excellency!"

He looked at me, as though he could not believe in the possibility of this.

"Or, supposing that my artists positively decline permitting me to retain even the first *claquo* from their salary."

"In either case, Senor Maretzek, I shall be obliged to put the following rescript in execution."

As he said this, he took a paper from his pocket, unfolded it, and displayed it to me. It was a signed and sealed order for the seizure of the receipts at the door of, as well as any other property in the *Teatro di Santa Anna*, upon the same evening. When I saw this, the blood rushed into my face, and I felt myself trembling with passion. What was to be done? A thousand thoughts passed through my mind, and one of them appeared to me to present a possible solution to my difficulties. I accordingly rose from my seat.

"Knowing the existence of this order," I said, "I shall give no performance on this evening."

His face showed me that he had not reckoned upon this probability.

"Moreover, I shall state to the public my reasons for not doing so."

"You shall not be allowed to speak!"

"Then I *will* write or print."

It was now his turn to become excited, and let me do him the justice to say, my good sir, that his excitement was far more demonstrative than mine had been. He stamped, gesticulated and threw his arms about, as only a Spaniard, an Italian, a Portuguese or a Mexican can do. Something like the names of half a dozen of the more respectable Mexican Saints escaped from his lips, the while he was thus amusing himself. At length, he partially calmed down and resumed the conversation, although his lips were white and his fingers quivering, the while he did so.

" For the sake of the Holy Virgin! Senor Maretzek!" he said, " if you will not pay $3000, let us make some arrangement together."

I shook my head, in reply to this adjuration.

" Let us say $2500!"

" I cannot, your Excellency."

" Make me some offer!"

Again I shook my head.

" What will you pay?" he asked.

" If it is possible—*nothing!*"

" Let me assure you, Senor, that you will cause yourself serious—very serious annoyance, if you decline settling this matter."

While he uttered this, he had been pacing the chamber, but on its conclusion again approached me, and in a confidential, imploring, good-fellow-like style of tone, thus appealed to me:

" Now, my dear Senor Max! do be reasonable. Give us $2000—only $2000! If possible, we will pay it back to you when we have settled the present disturbances. Now, be a good friend to us, and give us $2000."

Willingly would I, at the moment, have paid him this sum for the chance of daring to laugh in his face, when I saw the turn which matters were taking. However, foreseeing that it would be somewhat difficult to evade complying in some fashion with a portion of his demands, I jestingly said to him—

"I will give your Excellency no more than $1000—believe me."

"That is not enough."

"I can't help it."

"Now do not be quite so hard-hearted, my dear friend. In the name of San José, give us at least $1800.

"Not one *claquo* over $1000!" was my brief and sharp reply.

"By the Holy Virgin and the Twelve Apostles! you are too hard upon us," he uttered imploringly. "Let us finish. We will take $1500."

"Not a single *claquo* above $1000."

"Well! say $1200?"

"No!"

"By Santa Guadaloupa! you are the most difficult man to deal with, I ever met. Suppose we say $1100, my very good Senor?"

"I have named the amount, your Excellency!"

"Well! What must be, must be, I suppose," was his reply. "Hand me over the $1000."

It was all I could do to stifle my laughter. Not a single word more could I have spoken in his presence, without abandoning myself to its paroxysms. So I seated myself at his table, and wrote out an order upon my banker, for $1000. When I arose from my seat and handed it to him, he gave me a receipt in full for my seven months' contributions to the expenses of the State. This receipt, my dear sir, I still have. It is preserved as a slight memorial of my having contributed my share, to give the Mexican *Ministro di Hacienda* the means of retiring into private life. You ask me what I mean by the last phrase. Simply this. On the following morning, the news throughout the city was that the President Arista had abdicated, having quitted Mexico in a clandestine manner on the preceding night. As a new Ministry was immediately formed, it was easy enough to divine why the old Secretary had been in such a hurry to obtain my contribution to the expenses of the State, the day before the new incumbent came into office.

Under the circumstances arising from the disturbed condition of Mexico, it was evident to me that in another week, another Ministry of State might require another contribution towards the expenses of another government. Not being a Mexican, it may be supposed that I had not another $1000's worth of patriotism, which I should particularly relish investing in it. Moreover, on mentioning this fact to my artists, singular to relate, they were all of my opinion. Such a strange unanimity has rarely been before evinced (at any rate, under my management it never has) by any Italian Operatic Company. Therefore, upon a brief consultation, we decided that it would be expedient to pack up our trunks, and to return by Puebla, to Vera Cruz. Anarchy had not, as yet, spread to these two cities, and we all divined the possibility of making some advantage of the time yet remaining to us, as we fled before her very visible and rapid approach.

Upon the same day, consequently, I engaged two entire stages or diligences, without experiencing any of the same difficulty which had attended my arrangements with the Postmaster of Vera Cruz.

Also, I may here state, that the appearance of the whole company was strangely different on the morning of our departure, to what it had been some eight months before.

When they arrived at the post-house, they looked rather like a horde of Mexican banditti than a peaceful company of Italian vocalists. You might almost have smelt blood amongst them, as they passed under your nose. All were armed to the teeth. Each one of them carried a double-barrelled gun, two revolvers, and a huge Bowie knife. Even the very ladies looked like the Amazonian warriors of a former age, dressed and armed in the fashion of the present day. Not one of them was there, who did not carry her pistol. Indeed, one of the male members of the company (Herr Kreutzer) had provided himself with a small brass cannon, which he had very scientifically loaded with thirty pistol bullets, and I am unable to say how many pounds of powder. Suffice it, that I prayed with a most earnest and exemplary fervor that we might fall among no banditti. This would preclude his having any chance of discharging the formidable weapon, which, it was feared by me, might very possibly have done much more damage to his allies than to his enemies.

In fact, each of the stages resembled a moving fortress. As either of them contained nine seats, three of which were in the centre, these last were exclusively occupied by ladies.

On either side of them, sat three gentlemen, each with his bellicose double-barrel leaning out of the windows of the diligence.

Upon the top of either stage, immediately behind the driver, sate two well-armed servants, for the purpose of keeping a sharp look-out, and giving the alarm in case of any suspicious-looking characters appearing upon the road.

Indeed, we had taken the trouble of warning the two drivers, that if, in case of an attack upon the party, they should either stop or upset the diligence (a somewhat common case, in Mexico, being their collusion with the wholesale plunderers on the highways) at that instant, the two first bullets of each of his companions would be destined for his head. On the other hand, if matters went on smoothly, a round *bonus* was promised both of them on our arrival at our destination.   I feel that you ask me, wherefore we had taken these precautions.   If I tell you, my good sir, that we were laden with the precious metals, you must not impute to me the folly of carrying my money with me.   That which I had made in Mexico had already been forwarded, through a banking-house, to New York.   The members of my company, however, had, with the customary avarice of Italian operatic or musical artists, preferred bringing theirs with them, for the sake of saving the ten *per cent.* discount on taking bills of exchange drawn upon the United States.

Plenty of suspicious-looking and armed riders were met by us on the road.   But, either our formidable appearance or some secret warning conveyed to them by our drivers, caused them to abandon the idea of making any hostile demonstration.

Nor must you think, my dear sir, that I am at all romancing about the dangers attendant upon travelling in Mexico.

The Mexican robber is generally both cunning and daring. Some of their bands are even admirably organized, and keep their agents in the Capital and others of the principal cities, through whose activity regular notice is transmitted them of any occasion which may chance for seizing upon a rich booty. Passports are occasionally sold by these agents, at a high price, which the traveller has only to show when attacked. He is then permitted to continue his way unmolested, or may, if he wishes it, partake the hospitality of these ordinarily unscrupulous gentlemen.   Neither is a Mexican bandit always a bandit, unless the love of excitement should happen to preclude his abandoning his professional avocations.   Once, when in Tacubaya, I remarked a beautiful villa, with a splendid view from its windows across the lakes of the city of Mexico.   Being somewhat curious as to the ownership of

this lovely dwelling, I asked a *ranchero* who was passing—
"to whom it belonged?"

"It is Don——'s, who, some fifteen years since, was Captain of a band of robbers."

"Indeed!"

"Yes," he *naively* continued. "He has now retired from business."

As the *ranchero* gave me this piece of information, his countenance was as calm as that of the driver of a New York omnibus might have been, in replying to a question touching the residence of a retired ship-builder, or some Alderman who had quitted office.

There are many stories afloat about these Mexican banditti, of more or less veracity. One of these, I am unable to refrain from mentioning to you, although it has little connection with the main object of this letter.

The proceedings in the criminal courts prove its truth. A heavy penalty was paid for its daring by the principal offender.

One of the leading bankers in Mexico was a particular friend of General Santa Anna, when he was many years since the President of that Republic. While this friendship was in full flower, he visited the General for the purpose of taking leave of him for a few days. The reason of this was, that he was going to a neighboring city to marry his son or one of his sons with a wealthy heiress, whose place of residence lay in that neighborhood.

"I congratulate you, my dear friend," said Santa Anna. "I presume that you will astonish the bride with the *trousseau* you have provided."

"Why, yes, your Highness, I rather flatter myself that I shall. $30,000 are a tolerably high figure for jewelry, and silks and satins."

"They are, indeed."

"Yet such is the amount," said the banker, with a considerable degree of pride.

"And do you intend carrying that amount with you?" asked Santa Anna.

"Why not?"

"Are you not afraid of the robbers which infest the roads to the Capital?"

"Not at all, your Highness! I have this time outwitted them."

"How so?" inquired Santa Anna, with some degree of curiosity.

"I will tell your Highness, confidentially, of course. But it must go no farther."

"Certainly not."

"Last week I received a carriage from Paris, made expressly for me. With this carriage, I shall certainly puzzle the rascals if they attack me."

"Indeed!"

"It, simply, has a double bottom. But, in order to come at it, and open it, it is necessary to remove the hind-wheels and dismount the axletree. Just above the centre of this, is an invisible spring. Touch this, and the false bottom opens, inside the carriage. It is very ingenious. Is it not?"

"Admirably so, my friend!"

"There shall I stow away the jewelry, and there they will certainly not find it."

"It is unlikely."

"Say, rather, that it is impossible," said the banker, with a triumphant smile, as, amid congratulations and witty remarks, the two friends separated.

Next morning, the banker, with the intended bridegroom, left Mexico. They were scarcely four leagues out of the city, when the carriage was stopped by a dozen or more of masked banditti.

The banker did not attempt any defence, but said to the robbers—

" *Caballeros!* I have only ten ' ounces' with me. You are welcome to nine of them."

The chief took the nine " ounces" which were offered him, and then, with great courtesy, requested the banker and his son to quit the carriage. Naturally, they obeyed him, as he and his companions were well armed. An ironical smile curled the banker's lip as he foresaw that they were going to search the vehicle. But who can picture his intense amazement, when he saw that no sooner had he placed his foot upon the ground, than two of the robbers, without even searching the interior of it, removed the hind-wheels and dismounted the axletree. Then, they touched the invisible spring. No sooner had they done so, than the false bottom opened inside the carriage, and, bringing a sack forward, the others began to fill its yawning mouth with the contents of that which he had fancied a secure hiding-place. When this work had been completed, the Captain of the band, who had been engaged in watching them, advanced towards the banker, and, with exemplary politeness, raised his hat.

" Senor !" he said, " if the ' ounce' which is left in your pocket should not be enough to carry you to the place of your destination, I shall be happy to advance you any amount you may require, upon your note. Your banking-house is well enough known, to warrant my cashing anything which bears your name."

The banker declined the offer, and after being relieved of his unpleasant companions, abandoning his carriage to the care of the driver, returned with his son, on horseback, to Mexico.

His first visit was to Santa Anna.

" I thought," said the President, " that you had already quitted the city."

" I did so, your Highness! But I have been robbed," was the answer.

" Robbed!" ejaculated Santa Anna.

" Yes! your Highness."

" But the double-bottomed carriage!"

" That is it," said the banker. " By the Holy Virgin! I tell you that they removed the hind-wheels, dismounted the axletree, touched the spring, and carried off *my* property."

" That is strange."

" Yes! your Highness, it is strange—very strange; and so much the more strange, as no one save *you* and myself knew the secret of it."

" But you must have shown it to somebody else, or, how should they have discovered it?"

" To no one!" replied the banker.

" But this is impossible."

" It was not. I, myself, concealed the goods without help or attendance," persisted the angry banker.

" Why! you do not suppose that I could have so far forgotten *myself* as to rob *you*?"

" No! your Highness, I do not."

" What do you mean, then?"

" You may have played rather too brilliant a jest upon your humble servant," angrily continued the banker,

" Senor!" said Santa Anna haughtily, pointing to the door, " you are impertinent."

" Within the week, the banker's son was married. His bride was furnished with a *trousseau* procured in the city where she resided. The manner in which the secret had been discovered remained an apparently impenetrable mystery. His dear friend no longer visited the President, and Santa Anna frowned whenever that dear friend's name was mentioned in his presence. At length, on a morning some few months later, an individual offered to sell a jeweller an object which that jeweller recognized as having been bought from himself. It had been purchased by the banker, and was one of the very articles of which he had been robbed. This individual was immediately arrested, and after many examinations the confession was wrung from him, that he belonged to a band of robbers, of which one of the aides-de-camp of Santa Anna was the chief.

He had been in the ante-chamber when the banker had made his disclosure to the President, and through the partially open door, had heard the whole of it. In consequence of this chance information, he had planned the robbery and accomplished it.

Justice was once done in Mexico. Santa Anna had him publicly "garroted."

Let me, my dear sir, again return to the chronicles of my professional trip through Mexico. We paused upon our route to Puebla. It will doubtless gratify you to hear that we arrived there, safe and unplundered.

As I had neither Orchestra nor Chorus with me, I was obliged to search for both before we could think of performing in that city. A dozen tolerable musicians were easily found in Puebla. It was, as I have earlier indicated, a place where churches abounded. These were necessarily all Catholic ones, and the principal attractions of Catholic churches are good music and good musicians. My Orchestra was consequently safe. A Chorus, however, was somewhat more difficult to find. This was not that the voices were lacking, or the capacity to use them. But the will was wanting. They would sing Rossini's music in a church. Rossini upon the stage was a perfectly different thing. This settled in my mind the question as regarded the production of Opera, and I determined to try a Concert. So poor was the attendance at this Concert, that I at once ordered all the luggage containing the Operatic music, dresses and other properties, to be forwarded to Vera Cruz.

However, as, upon inquiry respecting our own departure, I found that we could not leave immediately, the music of " Don Pasquale" was alone kept back.

My reason for doing this was, simply, that " Don Pasquale" can be played in citizen's dress, as well as without a Chorus. I accordingly announced our last appearance in Puebla, in this Opera, without any very great expectation of an audience. But I had reckoned " without mine host" in this instance. Whether it was that the priestly inhabitants of Puebla were sound critics, and valued the musical talents of the artists engaged in my *troupe* more after hearing them than they had done in hearing about them through the journals of Mexico, which, truth to say, would have been no great wonder ; or, whether it was the word " Opera" instead of " Concert" which galvanized their monkish intelligence into an unwonted activity, it would be absolutely impossible for me to say. But, on the evening of the performance, the theatre was crammed to its fullest extent within ten minutes after the doors were opened. Not even standing room could be obtained in it. In short, like *Petrillo* in the Spanish " Jack the Giant-Killer," who sliced his doublet and let out the chopped sausages (this was for the purpose of terrifying his gigantic enemy), I thought it necessary to keep the doors of the boxes open, to prevent their bursting with repletion.

About this large audience, there was also one singularity which confirmed me in that opinion anteriorly laid down by me, respecting the population of Puebla. Two-thirds of it were distinguished by the clerical tonsure, and wore the dun and black gowns of the Roman Catholic priesthood.

Nothing could have exceeded the enthusiasm displayed by this audience, whether in its lay or clerical sections. In the interval between the second and third Acts, the public—priests, and monks—dames and cavaliers, alike stood up, and with shrill screams and yells demanded that we should give them one or two performances more. Nothing, my good sir, could have exceeded that Babel. To any individual possessed of the greatest requisite of poetry—a fertile imagination—it might have given a faint, although a tolerably perfect idea of Pandemonium. Marini, who entered the stage when the curtain drew up, attempted to proceed with his part in vain. He was literally screeched into silence, and obliged to abandon the effort to make play with his ponderous voice against the tumult. At my request, he then came forward, announcing to the excitable and excited public, that—

"Our music and dresses had already been forwarded to Vera Cruz, and that, consequently, we had nothing which we could perform."

"Except 'Don Pasquale,'" vociferated one fat little monk, with a prodigiously full *bass* roar.

"Then give us 'Don Pasquale!'"

As this was shouted out by the whole house, men, women, and priests, it was obvious that we should be forced to obey. The formal promise that this Opera should be repeated upon the morrow, was therefore given, after a modest moment's appearance of doubt and hesitation, simply imposed upon us by the paramount necessity (in all cases this is paramount) of appearing totally independent of the will of the public.

On the following day, an even greater crowd and a larger number of priestly dresses (if either of these things were possible) made their appearance in the theatre. Scarcely had the second Act terminated, than a precisely similar scene to that which had taken place upon the preceding evening was repeated. The public, with yells and screams, rose, and demanded another performance. I was just going to request Marini to announce the third repetition of "Don Pasquale," when the very same fat little wretch who had specified this Opera on the preceding evening, stood up on his seat, and with his shorn and shaven head glistening in the oil-light of the theatre, roared out—

"Give us 'Norma!'"

No sooner had the public heard his abominable *basso*, than they also shouted out—

"Yes, yes! Give us 'Norma!'"

"'Norma!' 'Norma!'"

"We want 'Norma!'"

Here was a position to be placed in. Without either music or dresses for the "Norma," we were required to give it. With a heroism unusual in an Italian, when he is obliged to decline taking the contents of the public purse, Marini, at my request, again stepped forward. The voice of the audience calmed into silence, and he began a delicate explanation of our unfortunate situation.

"Ladies and gentlemen," he said, neglecting to add monks to his specification of the sexes of his audience," I am truly sorry to tell you, that the music of 'Norma' is by this time nearly at Vera Cruz!"

"Never mind!" roared the squab little priest, who was still standing on his seat, "we have it."

"*E viva, el Padre* Juanito!" shouted the whole house, like one man."

"We sing it in our church at High Mass! You shall use our score."

Marini, being beaten upon this point, like a clever general, attempted another.

"But, ladies and gentlemen, we have no Chorus!" he remonstrated.

"*Al C———— los Coros!*" was the polite answer made by the musical audience, in which, conscience, my dear sir, forces me to say that my ears very accurately detected the roar of the round little priestly *basso*. Be it remembered, also, to the eternal shame of Puebla, that more than one half of the audience in the first tier were ladies. Deeply do I regret that their presence did not tame the tongues of the male half of creation. But truth is truth. The pen is in my hand, and I am obliged to record this ungentlemanly effervescence of feeling. At the same time, my dear sir, my conscience is unable to repudiate the fact, that a similar destination has not, unoften, appeared to me a fitting one for many of the Choruses upon this side of the broad Atlantic.

"I am sorry to say," continued Marini, in a remarkably timid voice, toned down, by his increasing nervousness, into a truly remarkable affinity with a cracked *soprano*, "that we have no dresses."

"Can't you play it in your own?" bellowed out his tormentor, in a tone that might have claimed relationship with the accents of a Chinese gong.

"Yes! yes! 'Norma' in citizens' dress!"

"We want 'Norma!'"

"You must give us 'Norma' in some shape or other!"

"We will have it!" screamed out the public.

Seeing there was no way of appeasing them but one, and that this was the promising a compliance with their wishes, Marini was obliged to announce that "Norma" should be performed upon the following evening. After this understood pledge to obey their will, the performance of "Don Pasquale" was graciously permitted to proceed.

But no sooner had it terminated, than remonstrances of every kind were addressed to me, upon the subject of that promise which Marini had given.

"Only reflect upon *Pollio* in a blue frock-coat and drab pantaloons," said Salvi.

Steffanone, in a gracious tone of remonstrance, asked me, "What I thought of *Norma*, dressed in black silk, cut after the fashion of the day?"

Adalgisa was furious. She had, unfortunately, sent on her private baggage with the boxes containing the stage-ward-robe, to Vera Cruz.

Nobody was pleasant but Marini, who was lost in medita-tion. He, in all probability, was considering the possibility of converting a couple of sheets taken from his Mexican bed into something resembling the white robes of a Gaulish Druid. Mind me, my dear sir, I do not by any means posi-tively affirm that this was the case. But, when you consider the resources of genius taken at a *nonplus*, you, I feel, will join me in the conclusion that this was very likely.

Against this general dissatisfaction, which, to do justice to them, was not altogether unreasonable, as places had been secured by the diligences upon the following day, I found myself unable to do battle. Ingloriously, therefore, was I compelled to make up my mind to run away and leave the priestly public of Puebla in undisturbed possession of the battle-ground. Therefore, everybody was notified to be in readiness to start at 3 o'clock, A. M. Perhaps—but, mind me, that I by no means assert this—my own brain enter-tained some doubts as to the propriety of tampering too much with the enthusiasm of such a remarkably excitable public. Bellini is doubtless an admirably popular writer, and "Norma" is probably one of his finest Operas; but without a Chorus, it would, very likely, scarcely answer to the ideas of the dead *maestro*. Without dresses or scenery, it would as certainly not coincide with the expectations of a New York, London, or Parisian audience. While played from the music which we might reasonably suppose had been scored by our rotund little friend, the small monk with the prodigious *bass* voice, and played too by a local Orchestra with only one rehearsal, it might not unnaturally be imagined that it would scarcely suit the taste of the Pueblan public.

Under the influence of all these ideas, which floated through my brain at the tail of the reproaches which had been addressed to me by my company, did I seat myself on the following morning in the diligence, in the midst of Italian *tenors* and double-barrelled guns, delicate *soprani* and Colt's revolvers, Herr Kreutzer and his field-piece, Bowie-knives, *bassi*, and *barytones*.

Let me inform you, that we arrived in the afternoon of the second day following, at Vera Cruz, unplundered.

Now, the bad success of our concert at Puebla had imposed upon me the belief, that, save in extraordinary circumstances—such, for example, as those which had attended our first performance in Vera Cruz—concerts were by no means adapted to the musical taste of the Mexicans. For this, there are many reasons, but the principal one is, that they are Roman Catholic. Their cathedrals and their churches supply them with vocal music, which is, in very many instances, far from contemptible, and render them able to dispense with better professional vocalism when unassisted by dresses and scenery. Opera localizes music in the theatre, and appeals to their eyes as well as their ears. While to the latter, alone, it presents an almost distinct combination of the resources of melody. Necessarily, on arriving at these conclusions respecting the taste for music in the Mexican Republic, I determined upon, if possible, giving Opera in Vera Cruz.

However, there were two great difficulties which presented themselves to me in the accomplishment of this. These were, the providing myself both with a Chorus and an Orchestra.

It was not, that I might not probably have found some who were willing to enact the part of members of the first of these two bodies. But I had not the necessary time to teach them, granting, even, that they were willing to be taught their duties.

What was I to do? After a little thought, my dear sir, I hit upon the following scheme.

This was, that the whole of my company, whether rejoicing in the title of *primo* or *secondo tenore*, whether *basso* or *barytone*, whether *prima* or *secunda donna* or *contralto*, in fact, that every vocalist who was not required in the Opera as it was cast, should sing in the Chorus. Furthermore, I imagined that the chambermaids or servants to the different artists, being connected with vocalists and constantly hearing them at rehearsal, (whether in the theatre or in their private apartments,) most certainly could or would, and therefore *should* sing for their masters' and mistresses' as well as my own benefit. By this means, a tolerably numerous Chorus would be constituted. The only difficulty, as it appeared to me, would lie in the inducing such artists as Steffanone, Salvi, Marini and others to consent to it. Here, contrary to my expectations, I met with not the slightest. It may have been that they saw the impossibility of our gaining anything at Vera Cruz, unless they consented to it. But I prefer thinking, that it was for the sake of the novelty of the experiment (it was, if I am right, then tried for the first time), as well as to gratify me after having led them through such a successful season in Mexico, that they agreed to do so. With the other and purely secondary members of such a Chorus, I had, as I had divined, but little trouble. Their previously involuntary acquirement of musical knowledge now stood both them and myself in good stead, and rendered their teaching a work of comparatively little labor.

Suffice it, that though far from numerous, this Chorus was very decidedly the best which I have ever had under my management. Indeed, such a Chorus has very rarely been listened to in any part of this world, if it ever has.

Sometimes, let me own that it was strange to me to see, when Forti and Rosi, or Beneventano and Costini sung the principal parts, such singers as Steffanone, Bertucca, Salvi, Marini and others, standing amongst the Chorus. The manner of Salvi's singing would perhaps be the most bitter criticism which could be addressed in a quiet manner to the other *tenors*, while Steffanone's would offer a lively lesson to the *soprani*. Even the ladies' maids, men-servants, and theatrical tailors knew the old Operas by heart, and were inspirited by the contact of their voices with those of these artists. The last-named had also plenty of fun out of it, and occasionally gratified their intense appreciation of applause in a somewhat singular manner. When the public had sometimes been sufficiently bored by the vocalism of Beneventano or Forti, they would call the Choristers by name before them. The gentlemen would be cheered. *Bouquets* would be thrown to the ladies, and possibly between the Acts a few dozen of sparkling Champagne would be sent round to all of them, to cheer them in their novel labors.

With the formation of the Orchestra I had, however, far more difficulty. Musicians were very evidently, a considerable rarity in Vera Cruz.

As for white musicians, such objects were not discoverable in the market. All that I could find were twelve jetty-black ones, who formed the band attached to the city.

The population being much scantier than that of Puebla, this paucity may naturally be accounted for.

After a long search for something of a mulatto tone—a human whity brown in the shape of a violinist, I was at length obliged to make an arrangement with these twelve sable-colored musicians. After having done this, the day for our first Rehearsal was appointed. Punctual to the moment, they arrived at the theatre. Evidently vain of their new position, each darkie was got up to the best of his ability. Trifling incongruities of attire might be visible. Some tendency to glaring colors they might display in their vests and neckcloths, while their linen might have been whiter and finer, yet I must own (am I not, my dear sir, upon the confessional stool?) that their appearance agreeably surprised me.

" Come. All is not gold that glitters," I said to myself. " Neither is the devil so black as" (should I not have said the negro? however, let Satan pass for once) " he is invariably painted."

We went into the Orchestra. The music-books were opened. I looked round me, tapped my desk with my *baton* and the Overture began.

Ye Heavens! what was I listening to? Jumping up from my desk, I threw my arms up in despair. Immediately they all stopped playing. Rubbing my eyes, I almost fancied that I had been sleeping. But, no! I could not doubt but that I was then, at least, wide awake.

" Let us try it once more," I muttered to myself, as I again tapped the desk and once more commenced the task of conducting my jetty musicians.

Holy Cecilia! It was far worse even than it had before been.

Could I have imagined a dozen tom-cats giving vent to their amorous feelings on the roof of my dwelling, at one o'clock in the morning, it would scarcely have been worse. The antique Orchestra devoted to scolding wives, and composed of those singularly harmonious instruments, marrow-bones and cleavers, could by no means have rivalled their execution. King Philip of Pergamus could not have kept his prisoners from the balmy blessings of sleep, with a more frightfully horrid and unmusical din. Wagner's want of melodic feeling could by no possibility have imagined such an absence of all music. A dozen saw-mills, all arranged in contrary keys, could not have emulated it. Had a hyena, a bear, two jackasses, four monkeys and a rattle-snake been shut up together, and compelled to dance on a red-hot iron plate, their yelling, growling, braying, chattering, hissing and rattling, could certainly not have surpassed it. Leaping up from my seat, I rushed into my dressing-room, threw myself into a chair, and should undoubtedly have fainted, had not Salvi, who had also been present, followed me.

" What is the matter ?" he asked.

" Champagne !" was all that I could utter, as I held out my hand.

Luckily, he understood me and ran to his room, whence he returned in some two minutes with a pint-flask of that, to musical conductors and vocalists, most precious stimulant.

There was no glass, but with praiseworthy benevolence, he cut the wires and tendered me the bottle. Scarcely knowing what I did, I lifted it to my mouth. But in doing this the cork exploded. With, I am ashamed to say, an oath, I dropped the bottle upon the ground and laid my hand upon my nose.   At the moment, I thought that the end of it was lost, forever.

" The wine is gone !" said Salvi in despair.

" And the top of my nose !" I moaned out in agony.

As bodily pain is good in many cases of mental suffering to relieve the mind of man, so, it may be concluded that in the present instance, this contusion of my nose saved me from incipient madness.   Agony—the agony of a mind keenly alive to music—gave way to wrath.   Roaring out to Havercorn, (my musical librarian on this *tour*) I bade him summon that " black scoundrel !"

He looked at me as if astonished.

" The leader !" I reiterated.   " He ought to be hung !"

For the moment, Havercorn imagined that I was insane.

" Or grilled over a slow fire."

With a look of dread he vanished from the apartment. Evidently, he thought it by far the wisest thing he could do to give me as wide a berth as possible, at this moment.

The leader came.

" Listen to me, you black rascal !" I said in the best Spanish I could muster.   " If you, or any of your companions, ever dare to play another note in my Orchestra, I dismiss you."

" But—Senor !—" he began.

" Listen to me and be silent," I interjected, cutting him short, "If you wish to be paid, it is best for you to obey my orders.   Otherwise you can leave me, and this at once."

Seeing that I was most thoroughly in earnest, he thought it advisable to remain perfectly silent the while I continued addressing him.

" Remember, black individual," I said, "that I only consent to retain you in my Orchestra, upon the simple condition of your not having the impudence to play, save when I bid you.   You must, however, pretend to do so.   You must put

your horns and flutes to your mouths and appear to blow—
you must scrape away at your violins and seem to fiddle—
but, woe to the whole of you, if my ear catches a single note
escaping from any of your instruments. Do you understand
me?"

" Yes, Señor!"

" Now go and practice the last eight bars—only the last
eight of the first Act of the Opera (in Italian Operas, these
are invariably alike in all the Acts) under Herr Kreutzer.
These I allow you to play, as a great favor, provided you
practice them continually, the whole of to-day and to-morrow."

He looked at me, as a thoroughly humbled negro only can
look.

Suffice it, that I was contented with the impression I had
made upon him. After furthermore imprinting upon his
mind the necessity of preserving a scrupulous silence with
regard to my instructions, if his band at all wished to retain
their posts and salaries in my Orchestra (!) I allowed him
to leave me.

My next necessity was to procure a decently good piano-
forte. This was done, although with some little difficulty.

With this instrument, Herr Kreutzer's violin (an excellent one for orchestral purposes) and Signor Beletti's clarionet, I actually played and rendered the whole of every Opera
which was given under my management, in the city of Vera
Cruz, only permitting the negro Orchestra to play the last
eight bars in each Act. This, I am happy to say, they at
last learned to do tolerably well. But I am also happy to
say, that they never played anything nearly as well as they
acted playing. Nothing could well have been more glorious
than to see the French horn's cheeks distended with his imaginary efforts, or to note the way in which the bows simu-
lated the scraping of the strings of the violins. Nothing

could have more admirably shammed the reality. By this means, we at all events kept up the semblance of an Orchestra, and ended all our Acts with the regular noise and uproar of an Orchestra of fifteen members, although I feel conscientiously bound to affirm that my piano, Kreutzer's violin, and Beletti's clarionet, were even then by far its most prominent members.

You will observe, my dear sir, that pain and pleasure in the musical world, as well as elsewhere, are pretty fairly and evenly balanced.

My pleasure in Vera Cruz, let me candidly own it, was my Chorus, while my Orchestra was my pain.

When Forti perchance saw Salvi, who was singing in the Chorus, called for and more applauded than he himself was, he would meet my glance of triumph boldly, and cast a look at my Orchestra. He saw me working with my two assistants for the whole of it, and at once recovered his equanimity. Did I feel inclined to curse my stars for having condemned me to the piano, as I thumped away on it night after night, I would gaze on Beneventano's sufferings at feeling that the artists in the Chorus gathered more applause than he did, and feel, for the moment, completely reconciled to my labors. As for the public, they taught me one great lesson. This is, that the adaptation of your means to your end is the great and, indeed, the only secret of success. That which might succeed in Vera Cruz, would not be fitted for Mexico. Did you produce anything which paid in New York, that very thing would succeed, with half the means, in Natchez or in Pittsburg. A section of the talent requisite for success in London or Paris, will ensure it in Bordeaux or Liverpool. This, if I had known before, I had never had it so clearly and so indisputably thrust upon me, as it was in the performances which I made money by, in Vera Cruz.

But, during our stay in this city, I received important intelligence (at least so it was to a musical man) from New York. Two new Operatic companies were performing in that city.

The one of these was under the management of Madame Sontag. The other was under the direction of Marshall of the Broadway Theatre. In this company, Madame Alboni was the *prima donna*. But Sontag, as well as Alboni herself, had committed the fatal mistake which had marked the advent of Catherine Hayes under the *régime* of Mr. Wardwell. Saving and excepting the two *prima donnas* themselves, neither of the companies contained the slightest point of any attraction.

Thinking over this, I foresaw that good vocalists, and by a necessary *ratio*, far more great artists would be in demand in New York.

This would be more necessarily the case with Salvi and Marini.

On the other hand, it would be far from advisable for me to embark in an opposition to these two companies. They had, in fact, completely occupied the ground which I had vacated. But if I myself, with Salvi and Marini, were to join either of these parties, it was evident to me that the other must be crushed by the additional weight thrown into the opposite scale. These reflections determined me, therefore, to start for New York a few days in advance of my *troupe*, for the purpose of coming to an understanding with the management of either the Sontag or Alboni party, previous to the arrival of my artists. Accordingly, a conditional arrangement was entered into between Salvi and Marini and myself, for the proximate six months; and it was agreed that I should leave for the commercial and intellectual capital of the United States, immediately.

In accordance with this arrangement, I took twenty-seven passages in the steamer *Albatross*, for New York, and provided each person with his ticket. Then, after liquidating their hotel-bills up to the time of my departure, I requested them to divide the receipts on their last performances among themselves, in the proportion of their respective salaries.

Having settled these matters, I prepared myself to take my departure in the English steamer for Havana. Thence, I could easily reach the city in which I am, at the present moment, residing.

But no sooner had this been settled, than with the natural mistrust all Italians evince for those with whom they have any business, a visible feeling of *méfiance* towards each other rooted itself in almost the whole of that company which had agreed so well together, under my management. Had you then seen them, my good sir, you would have imagined that each felt himself amongst a party of robbers. Even Signor Beletti and Herr Kreutzer buttoned up their pockets, and walked about with the settled conviction that they were about to be plundered. Indeed, on the day previous to my leaving, almost every member of the *troupe* came to ask for a few moments of private conversation with me. Naturally, I was forced to accord it to them. What was my surprise, to find that each of them had visited me on that morning, to reveal to my ears their opinions of their brother artists, and to disclose to me the deplorable state in which the affairs of the Company would be left upon my departure. Every one of them told me that unavoidable anarchy would reign amongst them. Each of them told me that everybody would wish, and, what was more, would attempt to make himself the master. They all agreed that not one of the whole party would be inclined to obey any of the others. Then, each one pointed out to me, those bad qualities in every one of the others, which

would positively unfit him for having the management confided to him. This one was much too quarrelsome. That
one was a fool. One was too timid, and another was too
easy. Here was one who would swindle, and there was another who would be swindled by everybody. Having settled
this to their own satisfaction, all of them requested me to
name my representative, and to give this said representative
a power of attorney to take the receipts and make a fair division of them.

Need I tell you, that each one of them represented himself
as the best man to carry on the business, and to care for the
money.

These asseverations and insinuations convinced me that
anarchy was indeed likely to reign amongst them. But, on
the other side, I knew if I gave a power of attorney to any
one of them, that a musical revolution would break out in the
company in less than twenty-four hours, and the said attorney
would most inevitably be deposed. The choice for me, as
their Manager, lay between two evils; when, it suddenly
struck me that as every one of them was interested in their
joint success, it might be possible, by a little trick, to force
them, not only by their pecuniary interests, but by a certain
feeling of shame, to agree as well as Italian vocalists could
agree, together.

Therefore, I gave to every person who asked it, a power
of attorney to represent me, and to carry on the Opera
"*together with the other members of the company*" during my
absence, until the period of their own departure in the
Albatross.

At the same time, I strictly enjoined on each of them the
necessity of keeping the fact a secret until my departure,
which was to take place on the following day, as I believe I
have earlier observed.

Had I been present when they all met at Rehearsal, some two hours subsequent to my steaming out of the harbor of Vera Cruz, candidly is it my belief, that the Epitaph on Max Maretzek would contain the assertion that he "quitted this life, in consequence of a paroxysm of laughter." It must have been delicious to see the first of them take his authorization, to act as my representative, out of his pocket. Could you then have noticed his oblique stare of utter horror, when a second thrust his own, under his nose? Salvi would have been worth painting, as an epitome of vocal dignity, when he quietly moved up the stage with his power of attorney buried in the depths of his own pocket, from which by the merest chance he had not been the first to draw it; while Herr Kreutzer's intense disgust at finding himself only sharing that power, the whole of which he had craved, would have been an example of outraged feeling of the most admirable kind.

At any rate, the lesson had a decidedly good result. Some complaints were made me, when I saw them. But these were not urged against me; they were directed against each other. Shame was too powerful with them to permit them to remonstrate. They knew that I had exhibited no unjustifiable mistrust of them. Feeling·that I had been right, they did not dare make my action with regard to them a cause for quarrel with me, when they afterwards arrived in this city. Consequently, their momentary annoyance did not prove a future bone of contention between us.

But I greatly fear that this letter may have already proved too lengthy for you. Let me, therefore, further only mention that I arrived here in capital health, and one week sooner than the rest of my company. It was with a comparatively unspeakable joy that I shook hands and took the customary "drink" with the first friend whom I met on Broadway, on the first day of my return. However, as to the number of hands offered me, and the number of "drinks" taken by me, the deponent sayeth nothing.

Believe me, my dear sir, yours,

&c., &c., &c., &c.,

MAX MARETZEK.

HENRIETTA SONTAG.

SEVENTH LETTER.

TO CARL ECKERT,

(*Conductor at the Imperial Opera, Vienna.*)

Madame Henrietta Sontag, Comtesse de Rossi—Her Career in the
United States—Her Death in Mexico.

PEPPITA GASSIER.

LETTER VII.

TO CARL ECKERT,

(Conductor of the Imperial Opera, Vienna.)

New York, *September 27th,* 1855.

Good and Dear Friend :—

You will be, in all probability, astonished that I should address the letter on which my pen is about to be employed, to you. You wonder that I should prefix your name to the pages in the present work, which refer to the career of Henrietta Sontag in this country. Nor is it very singular that you should do so. In your younger years having been her *protégé*, and in subsequent ones, her faithful friend and adviser—nay! having accompanied her through the earlier portion of her *tour* in this half of the globe, you will naturally ask me what I can have to say about her, with which you are not acquainted.

You will tell me, that you know more of Madame Sontag's private as well as public career, than any other of her musical friends can possibly do. This, dear Eckert, I candidly and willingly confess to you and my readers.

For this very reason is it, that to you, my present letter is addressed.

You know all the great qualities of an artist, who, in her own line, was well nigh unapproachable. You know all the excellencies of that noble-minded and heroic woman. It is because you know that her return to the lyric stage was dictated neither by ambition nor by cupidity, but by the simple feelings of a wife faithful to the fortunes of her husband, and a true-hearted and loving parent, that I have determined upon addressing you in the present pages of my work. In addition to this, the fact that you had quitted Madame Sontag in New York, for the purpose of returning to Europe and taking that situation or post which you now fill so worthily, and had neither accompanied her to New Orleans or Mexico, induces me to believe that you are not positively informed, respecting that which took place during the last months of her life. This, the more especially, from the many partially absurd and conflicting rumors which have been placed in circulation respecting her, whose Countess-ship of Rossi may be considered as swallowed up by the reputation acquired by Madame Sontag, from Mexico even to St. Petersburg.

The object, therefore, which now places the pen in my hand, is not so much to detail to you the events of her career in this country as they are publicly and generally known.

It is rather to trace back these rumors to their original source, and to enlighten you on some of the actual facts respecting them, which have come to my knowledge. In doing so, it may be feared that I dare not say all which I might tell you, fearless as my nature naturally is. Suffice it, if, from what I say, you can sufficiently gather the truth. When I again meet you, believe me, that a candid answer shall be given to every question which you may feel called upon to address me.

The subject is a grave one. If, therefore, I abstain from coquetting with my pen as I have done in some of my previous correspondence, let me express my conviction that you will not blame me.

It is no longer a Comedy of Human Life which I have to describe, but a Drama with which I have to deal—a Drama full of mournful interest, and with whose course of action you are specially interested. In this letter, I shall not wish to invite a smile upon your lips, by painting the vanity or jealousy of the artists, or drawing with, I trust, no malicious pen the innocent follies of their and mine would-be patrons. On the contrary, it is a tear which I ask from you and my other readers, over the grave of one of the greatest artists and most accomplished women of her day. Be not astonished, therefore, my dear Eckert, that I am serious, for I am about to tell you some of the facts which are known by myself and others, without fearing the consequences. The menaces which have already found their way to my ears, since it was known that I had determined to write upon this subject, will not have the slightest influence upon me.

For you may rest assured that nothing shall be either disturbed or distorted in my present letter.

On my return to Vera Cruz from Mexico, I found as I have already told Mr. Gye, that two operatic companies had been formed in New York. These were the companies in which Madames Sontag and Alboni were the *prime donne.* At the same time, I learned that Madame Sontag had taken Mr. Bernard Ullmann, into her service as one of her musical agents. I was, let me own, considerably surprised at this. It was extraordinary, and has always appeared so to me, that such a noble and excellent woman, as Henrietta Sontag had ever been, could consent to associate herself in any way with the agent whom Henry Herz had dismissed from his service in Mexico, whose ears had been boxed by another of his employers (this was Maurice Strakosch, whom it may be presumed you are acquainted with) in Havana, whose back had been scored by a cow-hide in the hands of Benedetti when in Baltimore, and who had been condignly kicked out of the Astor Place Opera House, by Mr. R. Martin, then the treasurer of that establishment, for an offence which not being at all necessitated to allude to, I shall here refrain from naming.

Remember, my dear Eckert, that I by no means enter an apology for the man who would so far forget himself, as to lay his hand on such a defenceless person as the aforesaid Bernard Ullmann. This fact is only adduced to show that each of the persons who had punished him for his conduct, in this violent and personal manner, has been either his employer or superior (as much as any one can be the superior of another, in the only free country in the world) in position or talent. *Par consequence*, it is evident that such a person could neither be a valuable nor a peaceful agent.

Since this time, it has been told me that Mr. Ullmann in anticipation of the announced arrival of Sontag on a professional visit to this country, had implored a letter of introduction and recommendation to her, from the Editor of the *Herald*. Mr. Bennett, in pure commiseration of Ullmann's then somewhat precarious situation, had furnished him with one. Madame Sontag on receiving this letter, with the view, in all probability, of obliging such a powerful protector of her interests as Mr. Bennett afterwards proved himself in more instances than one, consented to engage him as her agent. But had Mr. Bennett known the consequences of that letter, he would never have given it. Nor, had Madame Sontag then imagined what was to be the result of her engaging him, would she have thought of obliging Mr. Bennett.

At all events, let me confess to you, my beloved friend, that the fact of this person having been taken by Madame Sontag as her agent, had occupied my mind during the whole of my brief passage from Vera Cruz to Havana.

When I at length arrived there, letters were awaiting me from my correspondents in New York.

Amongst these were some of the circulars, as well as Journals containing the Bills and advertised *programme* of the Sontag *troupe*.

In these, I at once recognized her agent's style of thought and peculiarities of expression. Indeed, upon perusing the circulars, was I the more especially and painfully struck by the over-drawn and cringing style of flattery with which he appealed to the taste of the New York public, as well as the excessive servility with which he spoke of their well-known liberality.

Experience had, long since, very clearly taught me that a short and straight-forward course, the more particularly on bringing before it such undeniable and indisputable talent as that of Henrietta Sontag was, would have a much more profound effect with the general population both of New York and the United States. Therefore, I not unnaturally regretted the unmistakable error which had been made by her in permitting such a class of appeal to be put forth, under her name, for the universal dollar.

As, in the afternoon, I was walking through the streets of Havana, my thoughts were still upon the same subject, when in passing by a book-store my eyes involuntarily fell upon a pamphlet.

Upon its title-page, I saw a name. This name was no other than Bernard Ullmann.

Let me honestly confess to you, that for the moment my

mind could scarcely credit mine own eyes.   Never before had my brain suspected him to be anything of an author.   In doubt, I turned away my head, supposing it to be some species of mental jugglery or an optical delusion.   A second time did I turn towards the windows of the store, and look at the pamphlet.   The name was still there.   For a third time did I gaze upon it but, each time, I read the following inscription palpably set forth upon the title-page :

"Diez Anos de Musica *

en

Los Estados Unidos

Por Bernardo Ullmann

Habana

Imprenta de Antonio Davila

1852"

Rushing into the store, I bought half a dozen copies of it, and casting my eyes over its contents ere I again emerged into the street, I saw sufficient touching Henry Herz, Sivori, Max Maretzek, Parodi and others, to confirm me in the belief that this pamphlet was written by no other than the

* I subjoin the translation for those who cannot read Spanish,

Ten Years of Music

in

The United States

By Bernard Ullmann

Havana

Printed by Antonio Davila

1852

very individual upon whom my thoughts had recently been running.

In order, however, to be perfectly sure, before quitting the store I inquired of its owner—

" Who is the author of this *brochure* ?"

" Señor," said the man, " you see his name upon the title-page."

" But what Bernard Ullmann is it?"

" The agent of Señor Strakosch and the Senorita Parodi who visited Havana during the last Spring," was his very clear reply.

Having thus ascertained, beyond the possibility of any doubt, who this Bernardo Ullmann, whose name stood upon its title-page, really was, I began to read the pamphlet after my return to my Hotel, whither I immediately hurried back as fast as my legs would carry me.

The first Chapter bears this title—

" LOS AMERICANOS *
Y SU GUSTO POR LA MUSICA."

On the table beside me, were still lying the circulars which I had previously mentioned as containing such over-drawn flatteries of the New York public and their musical taste. In my hands, I held a pamphlet written by him in Spanish, or published at all events by his authority and with his name appended to it. This last abounded with abuse and slander levelled against and written of the public of New York, especially, and the American people, generally. For your edification and their judgment, I design giving a few extracts from this publication, specifying the fact that I still retain a

* The Americans and their musical taste.

copy of it in my hands, for the benefit of any Spanish scholar among my friends in this country who may wish to peruse it.

On the second page may be found the following sentences :—

** " La grande estrella literaria de la Inglaterra, el illustro Shakespeare, escribió hace doscientos años estas graves y verídicas palabras : " El hombre que no posee musica en su alma, es apto para la traicion." Se esta frase del gran génio Inglés encerase una completa verdad, podría llegarse à creer que los Americanos son aptos para toda clase de traiciones, porche: tiene algo de musica el alma del Anglo-Americano."

Now, Don Bernardo Ullmann, the Spanish author, or at all events the gentleman who has prefixed his name to this very remarkable *brochure*, hereby declares that *the American people are fitted for any kind of treason*, or, at any rate, he rather more than implies it.

But Mr. Bernard Ullmann, previously to her death, Madame Sontag's principal agent, *was a naturalized American.*

Would he, therefore, have the world (or, should I not say, his readers, for that the world and his readers are entirely different classes of the community, is sufficiently evident by the fact that he can yet remain in New York) believe that he had willingly and wantonly affiliated himself upon a nation of traitors ?

** " The great literary star of England, the illustrious Shakespeare, some two hundred years since wrote these serious and true words—

" The man that hath not music in his soul
    Is fit for treason."

If this phrase of the great English genius contains a complete truth, it may lead us to believe that the Americans are fitted for every class of treason, for the reason that the soul of the Anglo-American contains no taste for music.

Remember, my dear Eckert, that this very American people whom this Hungarian speaks of in the foregoing ungrateful terms, have given him a, by no means, grudging hospitality—a hospitality which has been demonstrated towards myself and thousands upon thousands of Europeans who have settled upon their shores—a hospitality, which I am proud to say, the larger portion of us most thankfully and gratefully acknowledge. For ten years previous to that publication, they had received (!) and fed (!) and clothed (!) this identical individual from Hungary. Who is there, allow me to ask you, in reading these lines, that will not remember the tale of the peasant, who, having picked up a half-frozen snake, restored it to life by the warmth of his own fire. No sooner was it recovered, than it began to hiss and protrude its fangs at its benefactor.

" Oh, ho! you brute!" quoth the peasant, "if it is thus you repay my benefits, the sooner I put you out of the way the better."

But again, on the third page of Don Bernardo Ullmann's grateful lucubration, you can read the following :—

" Añàdase á esto, que la inmensa inmigracion Europea trae consigo el amor y la comprension de la música, pero, no obstante esto, los Americanos están colocados, respecto á gusto musical algunos escalones mas bajòs que sus padres los Ingleses."*

But, allow me to ask you, how you can imagine that the aforesaid Don Bernardo Ullmann can reconcile it to his own musical soul to remain in such a barbarously unmusical country, as he seems to consider the United States? Why

* " In addition to this, the immense European emigration bears with it the love and comprehension of music, yet, in spite of it, the Americans stand, with respect to musical taste, a few degrees lower than their parents the English."

does he so perseveringly try to become a Manager amongst such a tasteless and barbarous nation as that people, of which I am proud to own myself an adopted son, are, according to his views of them? Why is it that he has not betaken himself to England, where, according to his opinion, they stand a few steps higher upon the ladder of musical taste? Or why, my dear Eckert, is it, that he has not taken up his abode in Havana, among the Cuban Creoles whom un-musical Marty was compelled to force into Operatic patronage? From his pamphlet, it may be presumed, that he, Don Bernardo Ullmann, attributes to them the highest degree of musical taste.

Almost immediately after, may be found the following wholesale slander upon the American public:—

"Non hay effecto sin causa. Quál es la causa de esta imperfeccion en la organizacion musical de los Anglo-Americanos? La primera y principal consiste en el desenfrenado amor que profesan a su venerado dollard, *adorado sobre todas las cosas de este mundo y del otro! Dinero!* La existencia del Anglo-Americano está toda consagrada, *desde antes que nace, hasta despues que se muere, á la adquisicion de su Unico Dios.*"*

By this quotation, you will see what estimation the Spanish writer, Don Bernardo Ullmann, places on the mental and moral nature of the American nation. Who, after reading this, will fancy that an American can venerate and love his parents, wife, children, or friends? Give him a dollar. He adores that alone. Who will, after reading this, on your side

* "There is no effect without a cause. What is the cause of this imperfection in the musical organization of the Anglo-Americans? The first and principal consists in the unbridled love that they profess to their venerated dollar, *adored beyond all things in this world and the other. Money!* The existence of the Americans is consecrated, *from before his birth until after his death, to the acquisition of his only God.*"

of the world (if indeed, any one has read or will read it) will believe that the American can adore his country, and the patriots who with their blood and brain stamped out its Constitution ? Give him a dollar. He worships that alone. Who will, for a moment, imagine that any American can believe in a Creator or trust in the immortality of his own soul ? Does not Don Bernardo Ullmann declare, that the whole existence of the American is consecrated from *before* his birth until *after* his death, to the acquisition of his only God—money ?

It may be considered a curious metaphysical fact, my dear friend, that this man should thus judge of the nature of the Americans.

The first person which a new-born baby ordinarily recognizes, is the one which nourishes and cares for it, whether that person be the wet-nurse or its mother. From this fact, it has naturally been deduced, that gratitude is the first sentiment or instinctive feeling which is enkindled in the soul of man. Gratitude is imbibed with the milk which nourishes the infant and animates the human heart, long ere the sense of religion is awakened, which is neither more nor less than a simply more holy and reverential form of gratitude towards Him to whose Will we owe our existence.

How then is it, that a man who owes his very means of living to the American nation—who has again and again returned to these shores to speculate upon their tastes and good-will, both towards himself and those artists for whom he has been acting, can be so utterly lost to that feeling which may almost be regarded as universal amongst mankind, as malignantly and unnecessarily to debase their character in the eyes of the Cuban Creole ? Was it, perchance, that he was then speculating upon the feelings which he must have known to exist amongst the Spanish officials of the island of

Havana with regard to the American nation? No gentleman is there, either in this or in the other half of the world, who would willingly suppose this. Was it that he did not really think what he was then writing, but simply displayed his own diseased appetite for the dollar (!) in his own person? No gentleman is there who would wish to conceive that this might be the case.

Be it sufficient, Eckert, for ourselves, that I will not pretend to determine.

You know as well, or perchance far better than I do, that in the kingdom of Hungary, that land which has the honor of claiming him as one of its children, every offence committed, whether in speech, print, or act, against its sovereign, your own Emperor, is condignly punished with the dungeon or with the rope. But I would have you, my good Eckert (provided, that you dare do so) proclaim in Vienna as a proof of the magnanimity of the American people, that the very man who has thus slandered 25,000,000 of the American rulers of their own soil, walks about upon it, amongst them, and draws money out of their pockets, unnoticed, unmolested, and literally uncared for.

Be patient, my good friend, and excuse me if I once more trespass upon your time with another quotation. Here it is:

" Cómo pedir, que lloren ante un tierno adagio, los ojos y el corazon que solo saben llorar quando un negocio sale mal, y cuando se escapa el dollard que pensaban adquirir? Qué es para un Americano una partitura de Bellini, de Auber, de Mayerbeer, en comparacion con el armónico libro mayor, que canta en su última página una ganancia de miles de pesos. Es Verdi comerciante, ó siquicera director de una compañia de seguros? Ha sido Mayerbeer, alguna vez, director de un Banco, ó de una sociedad anonima? No! Pues, cómo tienen la insolencia de aspirar á que el ciudadino Anglo-Americano se detenga á pensar en ellos un solo momente?"*

It may reasonably be presumed from the singularly accurate mode in which the worthy and most scrupulous Don Bernardo Ullman here guages American feeling, that no citizen of this country, whether a Yankee or a Southerner, could weep, supposing the Cuban Spaniards to attempt the annexation of the States to their own island, provided that they left him the "harmonic" account jotted down at the bottom of his balance sheet. Neither, my beloved Eckert, do I candidly, all things considere'd, think that they would be inclined to do so. Tears would, very certainly, not be shed upon this occasion. On the contrary, my supposition is that some long-legged Kentuckian, or a swift-footed hunter from the upper end of Lake Superior, would step down for a moment to inquire into the matter. Should he, by any chance, find that the Spaniards were at all disposed to be troublesome, why, without giving them any time to annoy us, he would simply "squat" the life out of Havana with the butt-end of his rifle. Having done so, he would once more return to his forest-home, and forget in the course of the following month the mission which he had taken upon himself, and so easily accomplished.

But, my good friend, you will also see that the Spanish

* "How can you ask for tears from those eyes to a tender adagio which only know how to shed them when a speculation turns out badly, or when the dollar they had expected to acquire, escapes them? Let an American be shown a production by Bellini, by Auber, or by Meyerbeer, side by side with that book which shows on its balance-sheet the harmonious sum total of thousands on thousands! Is Verdi a merchant or director of a company? Has Meyerbeer at any time been the President of a Bank, or the head of some society of brokers? No! Then how can you have the insolence to imagine that the beforesaid Anglo-American can waste his time in thinking upon them a single moment?"

Don Bernardo also thinks proper to inquire of the Cuban how he can have the insolence to believe that an Anglo-American (with what a consummate insolence does he bestow this name upon the nation of which he has become a part; might not the Englishman as well be called the Norman-Angle, or the Frenchman the Gascon-Breton?) can waste his time in thinking upon the works of such *maestri* or Bellini, Verdi, or Meyerbeer, even for a single moment.

Permit me, my dear Eckert, to grant him that this may be the case.

But let me tell him, and you also, that the men who are building up the power of a greater nation than the world has yet seen—a nation which, as yet, has by no means stridden into its full manhood—may be very fairly excused, if they cannot find time to abandon to the cultivation of the mere graces of life.

Yet you have been amongst us, and know that these graces *are* cultivated; and this with neither a niggard nor grudging hand.

Our Spanish preceptor, Don Bernardo Ullmann, would seem to forget that the artistic thought of the United States is at the present moment engaged in developing itself through the female half of the population.   Nor am I by any means suggesting a new idea in stating that it is so.   The ladies in this country are the real amateurs and patrons of our own Art.   In the hands of woman is it, that more than one-half of the literary talent of the United States develops itself.   Do not, for one moment, imagine that I am drawing upon my imagination for these facts.   While such women as Mrs. Sigourney, Mrs. Beecher Stowe, Alice Carey, Mrs. Anne Stephens, and scores of others almost as great, may be found scattered on every side around you—while there is scarcely a single Journal, whether in the North or South, which has not counted or does not count a female pen amongst its contributors, it may be felt that I am putting forward no startling truth, and advancing no unknown fact.

It may be possible (mind, I simply state that it may be possible, for I by no means undertake to reason philosophically upon it) that the genius of production does not so fully and completely develop itself in the female intellect, as it does in the male.

Yet the genius of appreciation does so, even more thoroughly and readily. This works with a two-fold influence upon the development of the national intellect.

Thus, by a singularly wise and admirable compensation of nature, while the male portion of the stamina of this country has been almost solely engaged upon the task of maturing and increasing that colossal strength and earnest vigor which have more than quintupled themselves, at the least, within the last twenty years, its female section has been performing a labor to the full as valuable, although its results are at present scarcely as fully evident as they will be in the course of another score of years. It has done its share of the work of national progress in maturing and encouraging the growth of its more refined tastes.

The fact is, my good friend, that Bellini's "Norma" has never yet failed to attract a large audience, whenever it has been given in America. Yet this, and the knowledge that Meyerbeer's Operas, and even Verdi's, have been hailed with enthusiasm in New York whenever produced, proves nothing to Don Bernardo Ullmann. In his belief the American is, as he implies in this pamphlet, a barbarian, a traitor, and also an atheist.

But, where was it that the grateful Don Bernardo took it upon himself to write thus?

In the Island of Cuba.

For whom was it that he thought proper to write thus?

For the Spaniards! Mind me, I do not say for the Cuban Creoles.

Against whom did he write thus?

Against the very nation of whom he had, himself, long since become an adopted citizen.

Allow me to say, my good Eckert, that it appears to me Don Bernardo Ullmann himself would seem to have been a far more intense and baser devotee of the "dollar" than any American I have yet had the chance of encountering. The man who could, in his hunger, sell his birthright to his brother for a mess of potage (it was Esau, if I remember rightly, was it not?) scarcely seems, at least in my eyes, to have even approximated to his degree of fleshly and creature-worship.

But I feel that I have been wandering from the intents and purposes of this letter.

You, unlike myself, are not a citizen of this country, and consequently, cannot feel the same interest in these matters which they excite in my mind.

Let me, therefore, return to that subject which I have told you it was my intention to write upon.

After my arrival in New York from Havana, it was with infinite regret that the conviction was more completely forced upon me than it had before been, that my apprehensions respecting the management of Madame Sontag's Operatic concerns, and the part which she would be made to play in them, had been unfortunately correct.

It will be scarcely necessary for me to recall to your recollection the manner in which that unfortunate lady was one evening intruded upon, between the Acts of one of those Operas with which she was gratifying the public, by an officer of the law. This officer handed her a summons to appear and answer the claim of a Chorus-singer, against one of her agents for the paltry sum of $15, which was owing to him.   Justly indignant that she should have been subjected to this, Madame Sontag immediately sent for the individual.   You will understand that I allude to the agent and not to the Chorus-singer.

"Why do you not pay this man?" was the inquiry of Madame Sontag.

"Because the affair will do no harm to our business, Madame *la Comtesse!*"

"How?"

"If Madame *la Comtesse* were to appear a few times in the courts—"

"But I have no desire to do so."

"It would decidedly increase the curiosity of the public respecting her vocal abilities."

"That man must be paid."

"I am quite aware, Madame *la Comtesse*, that you must pay him, because the money is due to him."

"Then, why not pay him at once?"

"If Madame *la Comtesse* were to appear in court, it would make the affair a town-talk!"

"I have no desire to do so."

"Jenny Lind appeared in court, Madame *la Comtesse*. This was one of the secrets of Mr. Barnum's mode of management.   He was a singularly talented man."

"But I tell you that I do not wish to appear there, sir."

"But, Madame—"

"I believe that I may succeed in America, without the public scandal of refusing to pay one of my Chorus-singers $15 which are due to him, as you state yourself."

"You are mistaken, Madame *la Comtesse!*   Scandal

is the system and secret of all management in the United States."

It was, therefore, of no earthly use to her, that Madame Sontag's own sense of honor and ladylike uprightness revolted at her agent's dictation. She was obliged to consent to be led from one District Court-room to another, to endure the curious stares and listen to all that was said respecting her, by the crowd, whom the rumor of this case had drawn together. The miserable Chorus-singer who was, as it happened, the father of a large family, had to wait several months for his small one week's salary. This he only received through my mediation, when, several months subsequently, Henrietta Sontag sung with me in the then summer Opera House of New York—Castle Garden, which has recently been converted into a *dépôt* for the poorer class of emigrants.

You will also remember, my dear friend, how one of her agents used her name upon all and every occasion. How he would drag her into all manner of newspaper disputes, simply that he might seize upon the occasion of associating his own name in the public eye with hers, as the agent of Madame *la Comtesse*. An admirable association was it, indeed. Such might it have been, if the blind bard of Greece had linked Euterpe together with his own invention, the mal-formed buffoon Thersites.

In all probability, you have not yet lost the recollection of a certain agent's bitter animosity against yourself and Pozzolini, simply, because you could not and would not debase yourselves so far as to appear to be on friendly terms with him.

The contemptible intrigues may recur to your memory which he excited and constantly fomented around you, because Henrietta Sontag, with the strong sense of justice which was so marked a feature in her character, and a true and intuitive feeling of artistic fraternity, preferred both yourself and Pozzolini to him. You may remember how continually she was obliged to interpose and defend you against the machinations of this agent. The fact will also present itself to you, when I recall it, that Madame Sontag, worn out by her imposed submission to the trickery and manœuvering of one of her agents, and weary of lending her name to him in his constant quarrels with everything and everybody, had at length determined upon his dismissal. When she had finally and completely decided upon this, her husband, the Count Rossi, was requested by her to call upon him and inform him that his services were no longer necessary to her. In other words, he was requested to give him his dismissal.

All this, my dear Eckert, you doubtless know as well or far better than I am able to tell you. But there is one part of the tale which you are unacquainted with. This I intend to impart to you. It will afford you some information respecting the interview between the Count Rossi and the individual in question, which it is improbable—or may I not say, impossible—that you should have yet received.

At first, their conversation was conducted with considerable quietude. It may be presumed, that during this time, the Count stated to this person that Madame Sontag had determined upon dismissing him. However, after having retained a fair regard for the proprieties until this point in their interview, the agent got warmer and finally fell into a passion. In this, he was imitated by the Count. They got warmer and warmer, until they at last screamed and vituperated so loudly, that four individuals who chanced to be in the next room, only separated from them by a closet, were enabled to hear every word which passed between them.

Towards you, my good friend, this agent thought proper to use the most bitter and abusive terms.

As a gentleman, the Count Rossi actually and absolutely refused to listen to him.

Finding himself foiled in this attempt to injure you, in his anxiety to keep his situation, or, at all events if he failed to do so, to achieve all the mischief which lay within his power, he uttered a gross and infamous slander against one of the purest and most noble of women. Need I further explain what was the slander uttered by this man, in the very face of Henrietta Sontag's husband? I feel that it is unnecessary to do so. It would merely be to soil the name of a great and noble artist, by repeating that which none who knew her could believe. While the Count remained mute and horror-stricken at hearing this atrocious falsehood, the agent in question had the further audacity to tell him, that either Pozzolini and yourself must be at once discharged, or that *he*, the agent aforesaid, *would take it upon himself to make known and circulate this slander*—a slander which in all probability was his own invention, as he was, very certainly, the first person who had given it utterance.

Without having known this, you, my dear Eckert, will remember what followed upon this skilful invention (so he, doubtless, considered it) of his genius.

The Count Rossi returned home, of course not believing him ; but felt himself weak enough to take those measures which had been imposed upon him.

You, yourself, shortly after this left for Germany, while Pozzolini accepted an engagement in Arditi's *troupe*, then about starting in a Southern direction.

Neither was this person (not knowing that the major portion of his conversation with Count Rossi had been overheard) able to refrain from boasting of that act which he had effected by so base a slander. Some few days afterwards, he was heard valuing himself in the presence of several gentlemen, upon that which he had done. He did not, however, dare to tell his hearers of the means by which it had been effected. He said, simply, that he had driven you out of America, and had forced Pozzolini to retire from the Company which *he* managed for Henrietta Sontag. Furthermore, he announced to all who chose to listen to him, that Madame *la Comtesse* was absolutely forced to retain him as her agent against her own wishes, as both she and the Count—her husband—dreaded the power of *his* pen, and *his* influence with the Press.

When, at length, unable any longer to support his presence, Madame Sontag found herself at New Orleans, she, with her husband's concurrence, gave him a large sum of money and sent him to Europe. His mission was, ostensibly, to engage some new artists. Her design was purely to get rid of him. Henrietta Sontag, whose feelings had been so deeply wounded by his slanderous imputations, declined visibly in health previous to the time at which she, meanwhile, having accepted an engagement to visit Mexico and sing there, departed for that country.

While there—but, No!—

There is not the slightest need that I should inform you of that which subsequently took place.

You know, and so does everybody who takes any interest in the career of such a great vocalist as Henrietta Sontag had been, and then was, that she died while in Mexico. She died of Cholera. Rossi, Beretta, and three others of the Company also died of Cholera. Poor Pozzolini, who had also got an engagement given him by M. Masson, who carried the company to Mexico, also died there. He died of Cholera.

Do you wish to know, Eckert, to whom in my own soul, I, Max Maretzek, conscientiously and unhesitatingly attribute this termination of her great and singularly brilliant career—

a career which blossomed two-fold—once, when she had just entered life, by the retiring figure of Pasta and at the side of Malibran, and again, when Grisi was on the wane and Jenny Lind had retired from the Operatic stage?

Then—let me tell you.

When on the final day of Earthly life and Earthly struggle—when the World no longer possesses any attractions for our Souls, and wakened from our long sleep we stand before the Judgment Seat, to be valued by Him who weighs the virtues and the misdeeds of Man, you will, I trust, be placed on the right side of His Throne, along with those who have an upright heart and a clear conscience. Then look around, and let your eyes fall for a moment upon those who are standing upon its left. When you remark amongst them, a pale and abject being trembling at the chidings of his then awakened Soul, and quivering with his fears—when you look upon a shape which you may safely pronounce the most wretched in that wretched group of wretched ones, then, Eckert, you may safely exclaim—

" That is the man, whose cowardly tongue calumniated one of the best and purest beings who had moved upon the earth—Henrietta Sontag, the Countess of Rossi!"

Requiescat in pace.

MAX MARETZEK.

MY POSTSCRIPT.

TO THE PUBLIC.

The Academy of Music—Five Chapters in its History—Its Management—The Stockholder—A Word or Two respecting Myself.

MARIETTA PICCOLOMINI.

MY POSTSCRIPT.

NEW YORK, *October 5th*, 1855.

MY VERY DEAR PUBLIC,

Whom, some three or four hundred pages since, my fingers addressed with fear and trembling, in consideration of the task which had been imposed upon them, allow me candidly to state to you that if you have read thus much of my correspondence, my natural terrors have all long since departed. That man is neither more nor less than a fool, who finishes a bottle of wine because he has paid for it, should it chance either to be flat or corky. When he is seen emptying the last glass, it may be concluded that he finds it of a fair flavor. He who indues his upper man in an ill-fitting vest, or badly-made pair of pantaloons, simply upon the score that he has liquidated his tailor's bill, suffers his regard for economy to trench pretty closely upon his personal comfort. Therefore is it, that being enabled to talk with you on the present page, I congratulate myself to discover that you have, without halting, travelled so far with me. In my conviction that it is so, I lose much of my modesty—at the moment I am invisible to you, and you cannot see my blushes.

With this introduction, you of course perceive, that I am about to excuse myself.

My original intention was to have written in detail, upon the subject of the Academy of Music, to the gentleman or Chevalier who performed the duties of Acting Manager during the last season. Unfortunately, more than three hundred and twenty of the pages of the present volume have been engrossed by the material of my preceding letters. Consequently, about twenty pages are all of it which remain to me. Now, although the Academy of Music has scarcely as yet stepped out of its nonage (having barely entered upon the second year of its *bona fide* existence), its true and faithful history would supply me with more than enough of the most interesting material to fill, at least, another three hundred pages.

The very history of its origin and the curiously conducted negotiations respecting its first lease for its present purpose, would be sufficient for an entire letter.

Madame Grisi's and Signor Mario's advent to this establishment, would yield me the matter for a second epistle. The collateral advertisement of the personal charms of the latter vocalist through the curious medium of Miss Coutts (?) and the mis-management of that very excellent *Falstaff*, but singularly bad Operatic Manager—Mr. Hackett—would form some of its most interesting details.

Neither would the determined folly of Ole Bull in becoming its lessee, with the view of making his *début* as the savior of Opera in this country, nor the manner in which his lawyer so grandly mismanaged its affairs during the two weeks that his principal continued at the head of them, fail to form a less amusing chapter. Indeed, it may very safely be affirmed by me, that it would constitute the most ludicrous of the three which I have already mentioned.

Next, in order, would come the enterprise undertaken by some of the principal stockholders. In this, the Chevalier,

Henry Wikoff himself, was the Acting Manager of the House as well as of the Press. This would be to the full as crowded with amusing incidents, as I trust that my *tour* through Mexico has already proved itself.

Moreover, the arrival of the La Grange *troupe*, with their provincial flight as far as Cincinnati and back again, would constitute a fifth and capital letter.

But besides, that there is no room for me to do more than merely glance at all of these, there are other reasons which induce me to refrain at present from speaking, at length, upon all of them. No man can conscientiously become the historian of the time he is actually moving in. For instance, supposing that I were to speak well and kindly of those gentlemen who have been recently engaged in Operatic management, what would you say to me? Not altogether unreasonably might you look one at the other, and exclaim—

"Ah! Mr. Max Maretzek, you very certainly have a tolerably clear idea, as to which side your bread has recently been buttered."

Were I, on the other hand, to choose to expose their mismanagement, you would undoubtedly say—

"Only see what an ungrateful and graceless varlet is Max Maretzek. It is a pity he is not in California. There he would be 'lynched' quickly enough."

Consequently, my respected Public, feeling tolerably certain that this would be your mode of viewing the matter, I shall, for the present, most certainly refrain from giving you any description of the detailed events of either of those letters which have been indicated above. If you demand them, after my frank *exposé* of the motives which induce me to hesitate upon giving them to you, why *that* is quite another thing. *My* fault would then become *yours*. A servant of the Public, however good friends he and his many-headed master may be, has no choice but implicit obedience. Only, do I beg you to remember that I, by no means, come forward to volunteer them.

However, some few facts are there, upon which I may speak without laying myself open to either the above sarcasm or the latter charge.

One of these is the building of the Academy of Music. Immediately after the closing of the Astor Place Opera House through Donetti, his canine actors, and the astute managerial agency of Mr. William Niblo, the growing musical taste of New York suggested the formation and building of a new Opera House. A party of gentlemen, therefore, unactuated by the desire of pecuniary gain, although they had undoubtedly no desire to throw away their loose cash, determined upon rearing a splendid edifice for the performance of Operatic entertainments. Hence sprung the Academy of Music.

Undoubtedly the musical profession to which I belong, as well as yourself, my very good friend and patron the public, are, in this respect, much indebted to the go-ahead and business activity, as well as the love for Music displayed in this instance by Messrs. Phalen and Coit—the latter of which gentlemen has been a consistent friend of the Opera in this country, from the time at which I first knew him.

Furthermore, it may be considered as a good sign of the times with regard to the increased feeling for Art in the United States, that the first appeal made by these gentlemen to yourselves, brought them in applications for more than two hundred subscriptions for stock. This alone might show, were there no other evidence of it, that musical feeling has made a prodigious stride in advance, since I first arrived in my present country. Each subscription was accordingly made $1000, in amount, and they were limited to two hundred in number. By these means $200,000 were at once raised, without either calling upon the aid of the Government or taxing the people, as is generally done in Europe, when a nation wishes to rear a Temple to the Muse of Song.

In addition to this, it is also worthy of remark, that where a want of Managers, or, at all events, of such Managers whose pecuniary responsibility was fitted for dealing with the interests of such an establishment, was felt by the stockholders, one of them,* and subsequently, two others,† carried on the business of the Academy during almost the whole period of its existence, and this in the one instance, entirely, and in the other pretty nearly so, at their own personal risk and inconvenience.

However, with the best of possible wills upon my part, here is the commendation, that I have felt rejoiced to bestow, obliged to terminate.

No doubt can exist but that the intentions of all the originators of, and stockholders in this scheme of rearing an Academy of Music or Opera House in the city of New York, which might be worthy of a great and wealthy Capital, were disinterested. Yet, it would seem that in some way or other, mistakes had crept into the conditions of the Charter of the Academy, as well as in the construction of the building itself.

At the Astor Place Opera House, as probably many of you know, the one hundred and fifty-two first subscriptions paid the rent of the building for the Manager. These subscriptions went at once to the proprietors. He, therefore, had literally to pay the whole of his year's rent in advance, before he began his business. At any rate, he had to

---

* This was Mr. Payne, the present Manager, who carried it on, during the second month of Mario and Grisi's engagement, after its first instalment by Mr. Hackett had terminated.

† Messrs. Phalen and Coit.

pay the rent of the whole year out of his first subscription for four months, as in four months, his season would be finished. The mere fact of retaining about $12,000 from the Managers' hands at the period of his season in which he requires the most capital, and which necessitates the larger proportion of his outlay and expenditure, was, in every case, both onerous and disastrous.

But in the Academy of Music, a rent of $24,000 (the double of that demanded for the Astor Place Opera House, is asked), while two hundred choice seats for every performance, during the whole year, are required for the stockholders. These, the best seats in the House, can neither be let to, nor occupied by paying persons, upon any occasion.

This, it is obvious, is a glaring error on the part of the proprietors.

As reasonably might a man who builds and lets a dwelling at a fair rental, require that its occupant or lessee should invariably keep a seat for him at his table. As reasonably might a man who sells a painter a canvass, at its value, ask that four inches of the painting should be cut from the principal object in it, and handed to him when the aforesaid painting should be completed. As reasonably might the dealer who furnishes a merchant with his Day-books and Ledgers, demand the right of inspecting them whenever he might think proper. Perhaps, however, this right might be conceded to them as a courtesy by the Management, supposing that after the first Act of the Opera was terminated, these seats should be free to any of those who were in the House. But—No! These seats must be retained for the stockholders, subject to the chance of their visiting the Academy at any time during the evening.

This error, it will fortunately be an easy thing to remedy, when the necessity of attending to it is forced upon them.

Let us now examine the construction of the building. When built, it was intended to contain 4,500 persons, comfortably. This was in order that you, my good friends, might be accommodated *en masse*, and also at prices which should be acceptable to your ideas and your pockets. It was not the original intention to have built a theatre, whose prices of admission should establish the fact that it was an institution, destined only for the patronage of the "Upper Ten." You, as well as I, know how this has been carried out. By some fault or other in carrying out the designs of the architect, or, very possibly by some error upon his part, the Academy of Music, by the manner in which its seats are at present arranged, cannot comfortably accommodate and seat one-half of the proposed number. That is, more than one-half of 4,500 persons cannot sit in it, and see as well as hear, without personal discomfort, that which passes upon the stage. By this means it is at once rendered impossible for any Manager to employ a first-rate Company and open the House at reasonable prices of admission, while he places new Operas before them. But in addition to this, the heavy expenses in scenery, dresses, &c. &c., attendant upon the first managements in any and every new theatre, cripple the means of the early Managers, and necessitate either a failure, or the sinking of a large amount of capital.

Now, when the stockholders originally subscribed their names to the contract and paid their money, it may be fairly concluded that they did so, simply and honestly, in the belief that they were thereby helping and protecting the interests of Art in this country.

Let us, therefore, see in what manner they have been paid for doing so.

If we examine the seats which they have claimed and received during the first year of the existence of the Academy of Music, without for a moment looking at the rent which has more than paid the interest upon the amount of capital invested in its building and decoration, we may form a tolerably fair idea of this. Suffice it that the interest paid by the seats which have been placed at their disposal constitutes alone, a reasonably fair *ratio* of proceeds even in the past year's tightness of the money market.

The Mario and Grisi *troupe* played in this theatre some forty nights. The seats, therefore, retained invariably for each stockholder at the regular rate of admission—$2— amount in the forty nights of the season, to $80.

Ole Bull gave them seven nights with a new Opera expensively brought out, at the price of $1.50 *per* seat. This amounts to $10.50.

The Committee of Management, consisting of Messrs. Phalen and Coit, gave them thirty-two performances. These at the same price, amounted to $48.

And finally, the La Grange *troupe*, under at that time a mixed *régime*, gave them fourteen nights of performance, at no advance upon the preceding prices. This brings the amount of the admissions which the stockholders did not pay for, to $21.

The total amounts to $159.50, paid to each stockholder of $1000's worth of stock, in ninety-three seats for the different performances.

Without, therefore, counting the Balls, Concerts, and Lectures, or the day performances, to which their holding a share in the stock of the Academy also entitles them to admission, you will find that these ninety-three performances, alone, have paid them at the rate of sixteen *per cent.* (or within a mere fraction of it) for their invested stock of $1000. When to this the rent of $24,000, which has to be paid by the lessee, is added, it strikes me, my dear Public, that you will see Virtue may sometimes very thoroughly verify the old adage, and be its own reward. The stockholders of the Academy intended in the first instance to benefit the taste for Art. It must be admitted, that up to the present time, they have done this in the most profitable manner possible to themselves personally.

But, in addition to this, be it remembered that the seats given to the stockholders are transferable.

Consequently, should the Manager make a hit, with a new Opera, which renders it advisable for him to run it for a reasonably long period, the stockholder may, after having seen the new Opera some two or three times, transfer his ticket to a friend, or on successive nights to half a dozen of his friends, who would, otherwise, be well able and willing to pay for his or their admission. The loss which falls upon the treasury of the Academy (or rather should I say, the treasury of its Manager) during a year's performances of ninety-three nights, cannot well be less than $10,000, for it will be not simply during the run of new Operas that this is constantly done. Need I point out to you, my dear Public, that this is a gross error in the constitution of the Academy as a paying Opera House. It requires a large amount of reform, ere a Manager can get up new Operas in it, and place them upon the stage at reasonable prices, which may bring them fairly within the reach of every musically disposed person.

These facts, in deference to the feelings of many of the stockholders with whom I chance to be acquainted, would, let me own, scarcely have been stated by me, were it not that I am compelled to do so. This has been enforced, as it were, by the meddling of some of those indefatigable busy-bodies who contrive to make themselves far better acquainted with the secret intentions of your and my souls, than we profess to be, ourselves.

Indeed, I have been obliged to write on this subject purely in self-defence against their tattling impertinence.

No sooner was it generally known that I was engaged upon arranging and writing this present series of letters, than they chose to know considerably more, about my purpose in so doing, than I did myself. One of them, in the coolest manner possible, affirmed that the book was being written to avenge myself on the proprietors and stockholders of the Academy—that, in fact, it was neither more nor less than a sheer production of spite, because they had not thought proper to make me their lessee. Another, no less boldly and unhesitatingly, volunteered the proposition that it was simply intended as a *bolus* of flattery. Indeed, he stated, although not quite in such coarse terms, that it was intended to wheedle them into the idea of ultimately confiding its management into my hands. What was I to do between the two stools which were so graciously volunteered me, save by sitting upon neither of them, and giving a clear statement of the facts, which rendered it very unlikely, certainly, that I should wish to do so, to prove most conclusively that no such idea as either of these, could have originated my idea of writing this volume.

But there are also others, whose attacks upon my system of Opera management, induce me to go somewhat further.

These, seeing that I am at present simply engaged as a musical Director and Conductor in the Academy, have imagined that there is nothing more to hope from me. Or, perhaps, having forgotten that all their knowledge of Operatic affairs has been acquired (you must pardon me, my dear Public, if that modesty which I have already declared to be one of the prominent features in my character, seems, in the present instance, to be forgotten) under my tuition, they believe that they may pull to pieces my system of conducting Operatic business.

To these, I can oppose no other defence than that of making you acquainted with the real results of the management of the first nine months of the Academy of Music.

In spite of the invariable declarations of success and prosperity, which were issued during the last season from the *bureaux* of this establishment, the losses sustained by those gentlemen who had so nobly (yet I must say, so ignorantly) rushed into management, were singularly heavy. In truth, they were so enormous, that all the other previously bad results of Operatic management in this country, fade into the merest trifles in comparison with them. If previous Managers as well as myself, had no millions of dollars (!) at their back, to enable them to withstand the actual as well as moral shock of their losses, this was no fault of ours. We can but say, that we are pleased to find men of large capital, who might be disposed to prove that the management of Opera was by no means that inexpensive amusement which they had previously imagined.

If, however, the luckless Managers with small means at their command (naturally, my beloved Public, I myself must be included among these) have done as much or more, and lost less, it must candidly be admitted that the mode of management which they adopted was by no means a bad one. Neither will you withhold from them your esteem, even should they not have been able to convince you that their management was attended with the most complete success. Nor, indeed, do I feel myself unentitled to ask you for it. Such Operas as I was then enabled, by the personal superintendence which was exercised by me over every division of my company, both in Castle

Garden and at the Astor Place Opera House, to place upon
the stage, at fifty cents admission, supported by such artists
as Bosio, Henrietta Sontag, Steffanone, Salvi, Bettini, Pozzolini, Badiali, Marini, and others whom it would be needless
for me to enumerate, have not as yet been surpassed anywhere upon this continent.   For this, I may undoubtedly appeal to the opinion of any real and impartial lover of Operatic music.

The " star" system of management, as it is called, I have
most certainly always repudiated; but allow me to ask you,
whether any one of those artists whom I have named was
not fitted to have shone alone, had my rules of conducting
Operatic affairs permitted me to deal in this line of business.   Bosio was as great an artist then, as she is now,
when she has achieved her rank as one of the European " gal-
axy" of well-known names in modern vocalism.   Sontag was
as much a " star" under my management, as she was when
she first appeared in this country.   If with me, her beams
were not permitted to engross the whole of popular admiration, it was simply that I neither could, nor would aid in per-
petrating such an injustice upon the other artists who, with
her, formed my company.   Steffenone is too well understood
and valued in this section of the world, to render it necessary
for me to dilate upon her planetary proportions.   Salvi, *if*
second to any other living *tenor*, could only have been considered second to Mario.   Badiali was and is one of the three
best *barytones* to be met with, on this or on the other side of
the Atlantic; while Marini, as I have elsewhere stated, stands
alone with Lablache at the head of all the *bassi* of their period.
Better ones may have been.   At all events, neither yourself,
my beloved Public, nor myself, have heard any such.   Better
ones may, at some future period, be.   Very possibly, neither
you nor I shall live to hear them.   If, then, in no more than

one instance, I have resorted to (and this was compulsorily, in the case of Parodi) the "starring" system, it has not been for the want of planets, had I chosen to employ them.

There is such a thing as an *embarras des richesses*. The man, who has his pockets full of gold eagles, would be the least likely person in the world to have a hole bored through one of them, and suspend it round his neck.

Such an act of vanity could only be perpetrated by a Caffre-Hottentot or a Mosquito-Indian.

In order, however, to justify myself in that which I have advanced, and to protect myself against the imputation of undervaluing the success of recent managements, I shall take it upon myself to name the sums which in my belief and estimation, and indeed to my tolerably certain knowledge, have been sunk during the last year at the Academy of Music in the production of Italian Opera. And it may be trusted, that the various lessees will excuse that which is very assuredly no breach of confidence upon my part, as their losses have been common topics of conversation with all who were or are connected with the establishment.

Mr. Hackett opened this theatre with the Operatic *troupe* that he brought out to this country accompanying Mario and Grisi. After the first month of Opera, he threatened to quit it, whether by reason of his too heavy losses, or from the immense trouble of counting his receipts, let me confess myself, without inquiry, unable to determine—not having been at this period in New York. Perhaps a shrewd guess might be made by me, but it would be useless. Let me, therefore, admit that at the end of this month Mr. Hackett's balance-sheet came out perfectly fair, and that, if on examining it, he found he had made nothing, he was at any rate equally convinced that his treasury exhibited no very visible deficiency. Be this as it may, in the second month of the Grisi and Mario engagement, these artists were under the management of a party of the stockholders of the Academy.

This month's losses were, at least	$8,000
Mr. W. H. Payne, together with Mr. Hackett, carried it on for the third month. Their losses were, at least	4,000
Ole Bull, (although I confess I had believed him to have made $4 in his speculative attempt on management,) considering that he has sold his property under its value, and neglected to accept the engagements made by Strakosch, will find himself the sufferer (not, certainly, to the tune of $13,000, as he has stated) to the amount of, at least	4,000
The Committee of Management, with the Chevalier Henry Wikoff as Acting Manager, lost, with " crowded houses," the sum of, at least	28,000
The La Grange Operatic Company, or their proprietors and Managers, could not have lost during their short season, less than, at the least . ; . .	12,000
Total loss from November, 1854, to July, 1855, at the least	$56,000

Considering, that in reckoning this as nearly as a person is able to do who has not access to the books of either management, I have neither counted Mr. Hackett's first and opening month, nor the loss consequent upon the house having been closed during the month of last January and the half of last February to the stockholders, it may be seen that the various managements lost, in scarcely more than seven months, the immense sum of $56,000.

This sum which was sunk in seven months, is, at the least, three times as much as the whole of my losses in six years of management. While the fourth part of this sum would be more than sufficient to settle all the liabilities which have been contracted by me in this period, for the sake of carrying out the establishment of regular Operatic entertainments in this city.

With such losses in prospect (because they have invariably occurred), it is at once evident that Managers will by no means present themselves with great plenty, for the Academy of Music, in Fourteenth Street.

It is true that Mr. W. H. Payne has undertaken, once more, the risks and probable losses attendant upon this singularly seductive business. His means and his position may be considered an ample guarantee for the termination of the season. Nay! He possesses qualities, that with the experience of some few years in the business, might ripen him into an admirable Manager. But, my kind Public, my belief is that, when the present season has drawn to a close, he will be satisfied with the experiment. Should this be the case, it is, I must be allowed to say, high time that the stockholders should revolve the future prospects of their magnificent Operatic establishment. Indeed, they must do so, sooner or later, if they would place it upon a sure basis, and prevent it at last experiencing the fate of the Astor Place Opera House.

They have the means in their hands to establish an Operatic theatre. They certainly, at one time, had the will to do so.

Why is it that they should be unable to carry out their intentions?

If they really wish to benefit the musical taste of this country, they are necessitated to reduce the rent to the lowest possible figure, which may return them a fair *per centage* upon their original outlay. On the present terms, two or three more attempts may be made to carry on an Operatic business in the establishment. But such a gallant love for Music, my dear Public, must soon be extinguished by its inevitable losses.   The best of us cannot, for your gratification, continue management at a certain and dead loss.   In addition to this I must be permitted to state, that they ought to be contented with a certain number of admissions for a certain number of nights in each season.   On these nights, each of these admissions might be valued at one dollar.   But should they choose to have secured seats, for each seat so secured, they ought to pay that additional fifty cents *per* night, *which the stockholders in the new Theatre at Boston have consented to pay*.   By these means, and by these alone, is it possible that the Academy of Music might flourish and honestly pay not only the stockholders, but its management.

With sixty admissions each year, on these terms, they would make six *per cent.* on their capital, and for securing their seats, if they thought proper to do so, it would only cost them the trifling sum of $30 additional, upon a season of sixty nights.

If, however, the stockholders are determined to change nothing in the statutes and by-laws of their constitution, then let them join, and jointly carry on the Academy of Music.   Let them select a good and clever man of some business tact from their own body (there are many such amongst them), and constitute him their Acting Manager. Let them give him their joint authority for all their business and monetary transactions.   Then, let them engage some able musical man for the management of musical matters and the stage.   In all, the number of stockholders is 200, and in such a case this number might be increased. Should a bad season result, which it is impossible for any amount of foresight at all times to obviate, each of them might lose the comparative trifle of $40 to $50, which multiplied by 200 (supposing that they have not increased their number), would amount to—from $8,000 to $10,000 for the year. But there is the chance that in choosing their Manager well, they might come out tolerably clear, or even make a reasonable profit upon the experiment. This might either go into their individual pockets, or should they possess a taste for a more elevated and abstract kind of pleasure than that of a mere pecuniary profit, it might be devoted to the institution and formation of a school—an American school—for either vocalism or composition, or possibly, for both of these branches of musical taste and musical education.

And now, my kind friends, I have completed the book which you asked me for. That it is by no means a wonderful example of the choicest and most elegant English, you need not tell me.

My knowledge of style and manner, even in your language, convinces me that its faults are many. Let me hope that these may be overbalanced, by the interest your love for Music may induce you to take in the events recorded. If my continental education has induced me to deal sharply with many of whom I have written, remember, that I have earned the right *to speak* by my submission *to having been spoken of.* Those who play at bowls must expect rubs, at some time or other. At present, the ball has been in my hands, and I will not deny that it was used with a tolerably willing arm. If it has ever rolled contrary to its true bias, it has been from a want of training in the muscle that was sending it towards its mark. The error has been not so much in the will as in the manner of my action. In a word, it is because my shoulders have not felt at ease in the garb of another language than mine own. Find fault with me, if you will, for my errors in this respect, and I will bear it patiently. To your discipline I have always bowed.

But, believe me, when I tell you that purely personal criticism will be utterly thrown away upon me.

Those who feel aggrieved, may, should they wish to do so, retaliate upon me. Too long have I been connected with the Press, both in France and Germany, not to know what I have to expect.

Thus, having eased and cleared out my soul, I throw down my pen and confide myself to your judgment. Your support has invariably been the only reward which I have sought for my exertions, since the lesson which was given me by my first season's management at the Astor Place Opera House. My care has, since that period, been only for your decision. My appeals have ever been made simply to your liking. Show me that you relish my " crotchets and quavers," and my modesty (!) will be amply satisfied. Grant that I have fairly used my present language, and the sneers at my ignorance of its forms will by no means worry me. Permit me, therefore, to assure you, that I remain as I have always done—

Yours, most gratefully for past kindness,

and, hopefully for future favors,

MAX MARETZEK.

Sharps and Flats

PREFACE.

TO THE READER:

If you expect to find learned critical dissertations of music in general and of opera in particular in these pages, you will be disappointed.

I know there are plenty of those musical surgeons who delight in analyzing and dissecting the musical works of great composers, and are able to discover in the construction of a full score, intentions, which the author himself probably never dreamed of, and who try with high-sounding technical terms to explain its mathematical combinations, without caring for the inspiration which caused the production of a masterwork.

I, however, and I suppose many others, prefer to judge a musical composition by the effect and the emotions it produces on the mind. Heinrich Heine, the great German poet, says that a handsome woman is a poem, which the Creator has written in the album of nature, and we all (I mean the male portion of the world) agree with Heinrich Heine, that God has produced a wonderful poem in creating woman, but while at the sight of a beautiful woman any one may feel inclined to admire and adore her, nobody would think of thrusting a scalpel into her body to find out its structure and organism.

Music is a universal language; comprehensible to any intelligence, and accessible to the feeling of every heart. Of all the arts music has the great advantage of being the same universal language, from the days of Orpheus to the time of Richard Wagner, expressing in different forms our feelings of joy or distress, our passions and ecstacies. Considering that passions have never changed in human nature, and that feelings of joy, love, mourning, patriotism, etc., have been the same for thousands of years as they are now, it may be hard to understand how one kind of music should express the human sentiments of the past, and another kind of music do the same thing for the future. The forms of such expression may change, the means and resources of its production may be varying and augmenting, but in reality there is no music of the past, none of the present, and none of the future; there is only one music, as only one truth.

Still, the art of music, like any philosophical system or social study, is bound to undergo certain evolutions in the course of time, and many champions in their flight to catch their ideals, instead of creating a revolution in music are, perhaps, nothing but the chosen instruments for the evolution of the same matter known as the seven notes of the musical scale. If, however, you think that you will find only biographical sketches of operatic divinities, and records of their marvelous accomplishments and social virtues, you will also be mistaken.

Operatic divinities are exclusively of the feminine sex, and therefore are usually called "divas," and like the ancient Grecian goddesses are divided into divas and demi-divas, according to their positions in the legitimate opera, or the bouffe-opera. The biographies of most divas are nearly alike, the only slight differences between them being that some, when small babies, could repeat and hum the gems of an opera at a single hearing, while others could do the same without ever having heard them, and still others could sing them before they were composed. But one undisputed fact remains in all their biographies—the graces surrounded their cradles from the moment of their birth; Venus bathed them in the bloom of youth and Cupid fanned the flies away from their little dimpled faces. The next important step in the life of many divas when arrived at the age of discretion, is to give to their mothers a suitable and becoming education, so as to make them fit for the high position they are destined to occupy as mothers of divas behind the scenes, and to make them presentable to the future worshipers at the shrine of the coming operatic divinity.

The demi-divas, as the opera-bouffe prima donnas are called, are usually distinguished from the legitimate divas by an entire absence of voice. They sing with their feet, make shakes with their heads, *arpeggios* and chromatic scales with their hands, *gruppettos* with their eyes, cadenzas with an undulating movement of their body, and their talent and strength lays just there where the vulnerable spot of *Siegfried* in the Nibelungen is located. All divas and demi-divas with a few exceptions are enchanting at a distance, when viewed through an opera glass, but if you would know them as near as I do, you would soon realize that they are no more real stars than those painted on any theatrical scenery; that the crowns those queens of song wear are only pasteboard or gilded tin, and that they are only divas or "Goddesses" of an Ingersollian type, *id est:* as long as their impresarios find it to their interest to pay for advertising them as such.

You will ask me, then, what to expect to find in this book? Well! A serio-comic history of opera in America for the last forty years, with reminiscences and anecdotes, of artists, maestros, impresarios, journalists, patrons, stockholders and other deadheads, together with theatrical and social gossip, and some spicy recollections, the perusal of which I hope may give you some information, and perhaps cause you some amusement.

You are not obliged to endorse my opinion as expressed here, nor requested to swallow those of others, when quoted in these pages, and should any one of you find himself portrayed in this book, and not like the picture on account of not being flattered, then, I beg you not to mind it, and to remember that I don't spare even myself when there is an occasion to poke some harmless fun; still, I continue to live on the best terms with myself, and I desire to sustain the same relations with you.

Yours sincerely,

MAX MARETZEK.

INTRODUCTION.

" No public of any city, where once opera flourished for a season, will ever be fully satisfied with any other kind of musical entertainments, however meritorious. They will crave for opera again, and await restlessly its return."

These remarks, pronounced with a certain emphasis of conviction, woke me up from a soft slumber in a railroad car one morning in France. I had entered the previous evening alone, and found myself now in company with five other passengers in the same compartment. They were placed there during the night at different stations. I looked at the person who had so earnestly expressed his opinion about opera, and he appeared to be a jovial, easy-going young Frenchman, who addressed his remarks to a strawberry blond German who sat opposite to him. The other occupants of the compartment were a slender, tall, elderly gentleman, whom, by the cut of his hair and moustache and his facial expression, I judged to be a Hungarian or Austrian officer—further, a well-fed Catholic priest, moving his fingers on a rosary and his lips mechanically, as if in prayer, and, lastly, an American from New York, whom I recognized as one of Tweed-ring politicians, probably abroad for the benefit of his health by the advice of his lawyers—the atmosphere in New York not being invigorating enough for politicians of his denomination.

"I repeat once more, sir," said the Frenchman, raising the pitch of his voice, to the German, "where opera has once planted its seed, it will bear fruit, and cannot be routed out by any concerts or any musical amateur societies—just as wherever the public has once enjoyed a season of a dramatic company, with tragedies of Shakespeare, they will never be contented afterward with recitals or spelling matches."

"For heaven's sake," retorted the American abruptly, "there, you have been singing to yourself the whole night, and early in the morning you already begin an animated discussion about music! Have you no feelings for your fellow passengers, who may be in want of rest and sleep?"

"Oh, you want sleep," answered the voluble Frenchman, "then I will sing you the slumber song of 'Masaniello;' it will cradle you into heavenly regions; or I will hum you the slumber song from 'Zampa;' a delicious bit of melody, or do you prefer *Selika's* song from the 'Africaine,' when she fans and sings *Vasco di Gama* to sleep? And when you have had a good rest I could wake you up with the serenade from the ' Barber of Seville ' or from ' Don Giovanni,' which shall be, sir ?"

"Can't you talk anything else than music?" hissed the impatient American.

"What can a sensible fellow talk but music or love?"

"Well, if you must talk, discuss politics with me."

" Politics! Ha, ha! Prudhome once said ' Property is theft.' (*La Propriete c'est le vol.*) I think Prudhome's axiom is absurd, because I have some property myself, but politics! Bah! Politics is usurpation—nothing else. Either usurpation of influential positions from a throne down to a place of jail-keeper, or spoliation of the monies of tax-payers. Politics are hazardous games! you may win a prize, or you may catch disgrace or exile." suddenly, as if stung by a wasp, the American turned round, coiled himself in his corner seat, and pretended to sleep.

Then followed a slight lull in the conversation, the German perusing a pamphlet he had taken out his carpet-bag, the Hungarian studying the landscape, perhaps making stragetic calculations, and the priest counting the beads of his rosary and murmuring inaudible prayers. The Frenchman, however, soon took advantage of the opportunity and resumed his vocalizations. First came a strain from " William Tell " ("Oh, Mathilda "), then the ballad from " Favorita " (" tant d'amour "), then the tenor aria from the " Jewess " (" Oh, Rachel "), and several others, when at once he broke out in the melody of " di quella pira," from the " Trovatore." That was too much for the ears of the German. He could stand all the others, but Verdi he held in horror generally, and the " Trovatore " particularly.

" I suppose you are a singer by profession ? " he asked the warbler.

" No Sir! I am Mr. de P——; my grandfather was Secretary of State under Charles X., I am going to the chateau of my future mother-in-law, Mme. F——, in Bretagne, where I am going to be married to the loveliest girl in France and Navarre, who besides her beauty and many other accomplishments has a fortune of 10,000,000 francs, which, together with my hereditary possessions, dispenses me from following any profession. I live only for music and love ; all other functions are in my opinion only necessities to sustain health and life, and all other passions only foamy illusions."

" But don't you like any other kind of music but operatic music ?"

" I like them *all*, but it is with music just as it is with love. You see, a simple ballad or song is only a flirtation with the eyes ; chamber music of string quartets is good for a country seat in rainy weather—a small family affair, with the schoolmaster and the parson of the village as invited guests to a cup of tea and cold cuts, in return for which they must play second fiddle or viola, and where the family tries to cure the loneliness of the evening by a dose of sonatas for string instruments on the principle of the homeopathic system. About orchestral symphonies, however, I have a better opinion. A symphony by a great master is like passionate courtships. The first movement represents the first meeting of lovers, the electric spark of love at first sight, the magnetic attraction of two souls, etc.

The second movement, usually the *andante*, means the sentimental cooing and wooing of lovers. The *scherzo* portrays the poutings, the insignificant quarrels incidental to lovemaking ; also, small disappointments, such as the unexpected intrusion of the younger brother into the room, the breaking of a chair in the parlor, the disagreeable striking of the too fast advancing clock in the hall, etc. And the last movement, the *allegro*, is the picture of the stormy passions of love.

" Oratorios have the effect on my mind of conventional engagements for marriage, by previous arrangement between parents ; obtained from the bride by persuasion, and from the groom by calculation and convenience, where the question of real love is left in suspense, until after the accomplished fact, to bloom and blossom ; or to fade away ; or to be nipped in the bud, according to circumstances ; therefore, oratorios, in my opinion, are very quiet, agreeable, palatable and soothing affairs, but seldom exhilirating and never intoxicating ? But give me opera! Opera is *the* thing for me! Opera is not an innocent flirtation, nor a remedy against weariness, nor a simple courtship, nor a matrimonial convenience. Opera is the *honeymoon* of a passionately loving couple, such as I intend to have soon."

" Hold on," roared the German, " if songs are trifles, if chamber music is indifferent, if symphonies only cooings and wooings, oratorios second rate concerns, and if the opera is the *honeymoon*, pray what is then, in your opinion, the latest evolution in music, what, then, is the music-drama ?"

" I never heard myself any music drama," answered Monsieur de P——, "but as a possible consequence of the honeymoon, it may be the divorce."

At this unexpected joke, which only a prejudiced Frenchman could have perpetrated, everybody started with a roar of laughter. The German seemed nonplussed for a moment; the priest stopped his murmurings; the officer twisted his mustache; addressing the Frenchman by asking him what he thinks of military music. For an answer Mons. de P—— stood up, took a deep respiration, and with all the power of a strong voice struck up the " Marseillaise," which brought down the compartment with applause, re-echoed by the passengers in the other cars.

" Now my dear Mons. de P——," humbly suggested the priest, " having given your highly intelligent opinion about all styles and species of music, what do you think of sacred music and its reference to religion?"

" A prayer, such as Stradella wrote and sung, or a choral and anthem sung by well trained voices, a sacred song like ' I Know that my Redeemer Liveth,' and others by Handel, Bach, etc., will never fail to impress the hearer with pious feeling, but such so-called sacred music with ornamental vocalization, requiring florid execution of ascending and descending chromatic passages, *arpeggio* written for the purpose of giving ample scope to the church singer to captivate and attract the public to the church, I consider meretricious music, but worse still if I hear in a church, music arranged expressly from operas of Flotow and Offenbach, with the words of the holy rite, adapted to a gallopade or a cancan taken from the last favorite opera, I believe it an infringement on the rights of opera managers and composers, and a mean trick of rivalry to coax the people from the theatres to the church."

Here the priest collapsed and assumed his prayers, but the German had recovered enough by this time for a new attack on the French champion of "music and love," and he ventured to say, " So you have never heard Wagner's music dramas ? "

" No, sir. They are so far not played in France. I have never had occasion to appreciate them, but on my wedding tour I intend to go to Germany, and I am curious to learn how they will impress me."

" Then I advise you before going to Germany to read carefully all the commentaries on Wagner's music dramas. You can never fully understand and appreciate the grandeur of Wagner's conceptions unless you read the explanatory books on his masterpieces. If you like I will write you down a number of them, which you may procure."

" No, thank you, sir. I prefer to hear the music first, and then explain it myself.

" Oh, you will not like it at first, but you must hear it often, and read about it, and then hear it again, till you get used to it."

" I think and I hope I will get used to it by hearing it often, and will ultimately finish by liking it without the help of commentarists," said the polite Frenchman.

The Austrian officer, who had kept quiet since the singing of the " Marseillaise," now interrupted the speaker.

" Indeed, there is nothing like getting used to a thing. By continued use you finish by desiring and cherishing something that may not have impressed you favorably at the beginning. I have had a curious experience in that line. I am colonel in retreat of a Croatian regiment. In olden time we yet used corporal punishment on the common soldiers for any breach of discipline or misdemeanors. There was a soldier in my regiment, an uncouth, rough fellow, who usually every Friday received his " Schlag," as it is termed in Austria. After a time he got quite subdued and even civilized, and behaved splendidly the entire week till Thursday evening. But the nearer it came to Friday morning, which was the fixed day for corrections, the more restless he became, and before the morning he was sure to commit some slight offense which resulted in his receiving the usual punishment. Once I reprimanded him, and asked whether he could not let pass *one single Friday* without being beaten?"

"Excuse me, Colonel," answered the poor soldier, "I cannot help it; I got used to it, and I finished by liking it. In fact it has at last so taken hold of me, that when it is Thursday evening, I feel such a tickling on a certain part of my body, that I must commit some offense, in order to be relieved of that tickling sensation by the application of the Corporal's baton."

During all this conversation I remained silent, without uttering one word. At last the American gentleman, who latterly had been looking at me several times, turned toward me and addressed me as follows:

"Ain't you Mr. Maretzek from New York?" "Yes, sir," I answered, without pronouncing, however, his name, believing that he might prefer remaining incognito; "Going to New York? home?" "Yes, sir." "If you meet Governor Hoffman or Oakey Hall, give them my regards."

"I shall not fail to do so."

"Well why did you not join the conversation this morning?"

"*I never discuss politics*, RELIGION or WAGNER. It always makes bad blood and originates quarrels."

"Brest! All out for Brest!" cried the conductor, and I was the first out of the cars.

CHAPTER I.

MARIETTA ALBONI AND HENRIETTA SONTAG.

After a hearty breakfast I drove down to the steamer *Pereire* to resume my trip home to New York. The Frenchman's words that " where opera has once flourished no other kind of musical entertainment would satisfy," lingered in my mind, and I remembered how often I heard it said and how often I read in the papers that " opera is dead " and how quickly it reappeared. The fact is, managers may be sacrificed, opera houses may be consumed by fire, or may change their location, but opera itself, contrary to Monsieur Cambronne, may surrender, but never die! When, in 1852, the Astor Place Opera was occupied by Donnelly's monkeys and learned dogs, and shortly afterward sold to the Mercantile Library Association, and I had left with my company for Mexico, there was a general opinion expressed that opera was dead, but after a very short lapse of time, toward the end of the same year, suddenly appeared in New York two of the greatest operatic stars of that time and, perhaps of their century, both accompanied by some artists, who could form a nucleus for an opera company. Those two stars were no other than Marietta Alboni and Henrietta Sontag. Alboni brought with her Sig. San Giovanni, a light tenor with a small voice but an excellent method, who now is professor of vocal culture at the Conservatory in Milan, and Sig. Rovere, the great buffo ; Mme. Sontag was accompanied by Sig. Pozzolini, a sweet tenor, also associated with her the baritone Badiali, who was staying in New York during my first trip to Mexico. The agent for Mme. Alboni was Le Grand Smith, formerly connected with P. T. Barnum during the Jenny Lind tour in America, and the musical conductor, Sig. Arditi. Mme. Sontag was managed by her husband, the Count Rossi, and by Mr. Bernard Ullmann, and Mr. Eckert was her musical director.

Marietta Alboni unquestionably possessed the most beautiful contralto voice known to present time, with an even extension from F below to C sharp, which enabled her also to sing soprano parts, as in "Daughter of the Regiment," "Don Pasquale," and even "Sonnambula" by slightly transposing the key of the first cavatina and of the last rondo. Alboni was born in 1822, in Cesena, Italy; made her first appearance in 1842, in Bologna, and after in Milan, Vienna, Berlin and St. Petersburg. She made her debut in London at Covent Garden, on the 6th of April, 1847, as *Arsace* in " Semiramis." I remember the occasion, and the prodigious success she obtained. Her name was hardly known, except by a few professional musicians in London, the day before her debut, but the next morning she was the conversation of the day, the principal topic in the newspapers, the envy of all singers of both opera houses in London, and the terror of Mr. Lumley, the manager of the rival opera house, Her Majesty's Theatre, whose only hope was in the approaching appearance and success of Jenny Lind, which took place a few weeks later, on the 4th of May, and saved Mr. Lumley and his opera company from utter ruin; not, however, without a hard struggle against the increasing popularity of Alboni. The war carried on between Covent Garden and Her Majesty's was fierce and for a time undecided, until Mr. Lumley advanced his reserve corps in the shape of the four most celebrated dancers of that time, Mlle. Marie Taglioni (the elder), Mlle. Carlotta Grisi, Fanny Cerito, and Lucille Grahn, making them appear all four together in a *pas de quatre*. This strategical move on the part of Mr. Lumley, together with the choreographic accomplishments of the four dancers, overbalanced the forces of the Covent Garden Opera. The idea of a joint dance by these four artists was certainly a happy one, but to carry out such a plan was more difficult than to form it, and its execution proved the genius of Lumley as a manager. Each of these four celebrities considered themselves stars, and had been engaged by the terms of their contracts, as *prima ballerina assoluta*, which gave them the right to the principal part in any play or dance they would have to appear in, and so they danced alternating in one or the other ballet, but never two of them together in the same piece. Which of these four shall have the first part? Who will condescend to take the second, third, or fourth part? Which of them will agree to dance her variations or bit of solo before or after the other? The question of Danubian principalities could be easier solved than this terpsichorean knot of etiquette and precedence among dancers. Therefore when the plan of dancing all four together was broached to those demi-goddesses, a Homeric laughter broke out among them, and they rushed off the stage, leaving Mr. Lumley and Mr. Perrot, the ballet master, to their own reflections about the difference between conception and execution. Mr. Lumley, however, was not the man to give it up so easily. After twenty-four hours of seclusion, he summoned to a private consultation Mr. Balfe, musical director, Mr. Perrot, ballet master, Mr. de la Ballinay, the diplomatic secretary, Mr. Barnett, musical editor of the London *Morning Post*, and myself, as assistant conductor. He said that that contemplated *pas de quatre* must take place or the house be soon closed, in spite of Jenny Lind and all the rest of the operatic and choreographic stars. "But how?" we inquired. "Easy enough," he answered; "listen to my plan. You, Mr. Barnett, will please work the *Morning Post*, and insist that the aristocratic subscribers have put their heart upon the realization of that *pas de quatre*, and repeat every day the same theme with different variations. Mr. de la Ballinay will take care of Mlle. Taglioni, Mr. Perrot shall renew his old friendship with his pupil Mlle. Carlotta Grisi, Mr. Balfe will advise Mlle. Cerito, and Mr. Maretzek play the amiable to Mlle. Grahn. Each of you will make your assigned *diva* understand that the subscribers and the public desire the *pas de quatre*, and that the first one who will notify that she is willing to dance with the others will be the idol of the public, the press and the manager; that in doing so, there is not the slightest danger; the thing will never really take place, as the other three will never consent." This Macchiavelian plan succeeded fully, and the next day Mr. Lumley received four notes, each of the ladies declaring her willingness to dance with the others and take any part Mr. Perrot would assign to them. Imagine the surprise of the four dancers, when, a few days after, all the papers announced that all of them had given their consent to the *pas de quatre*. The same game had to be continued, however, at rehearsals until the very evening of the first performance, making each one believe that the others would back out at the last moment.

But to return to Mlle. Alboni and to Mme. Sontag. Both of them had tried a few concerts, and in January, 1853, the former opened the Broadway Theatre, and the latter Niblo's Garden with the "Daughter of the Regiment," and continued at intervals with the "Barber of Seville," "Sonnambula" and other operas which did not require a strong cast, nor a great array of talent. Two opera companies at the same time, and both playing the same repertoire could not prove to either of them a pecuniary success, and my arrival early in March with the Mexican Opera Company, consisting of Salvi, Marini,

Beneventano, Steffanone, Bertucca, and with a great and varied repertory ready at a moment's notice, convinced both the managers of Alboni and of Sontag, that if we performed all three separately, we all must fail financially, but if two of us should combine, the third one would be obliged to beat a hasty retreat. I understood the situation just as well, and had before my arrival already decided to arrange with both of them, at least one after the other. Knowing that Alboni desired to return for the summer to London, and that Sontag intended to make a long stay in America, I closed at once with Alboni for a short season in the spring at Niblo's, and secured Castle Garden for the summer months; thus preventing Mr. Ullmann from playing an opposition during the spring, to this formidable amalgamation of my own troupe with that of Alboni, and forcing him to accept either an arrangement with me, during the summer at Castle Garden, or to remain idle with Mme. Sontag, as at that time Castle Garden was the only available place for a summer season of opera. We opened on March 27, 1853, in "Don Pasquale" with Alboni, Salvi, Marini and Beneventaro, and producing in rapid succession "Favorita," "Norma," "Lucrezia," "Cenerentola" "Gazza Ladra," etc., closed the spring season on May 6, with "Don Giovanni," Mme. Alboni singing *Zerlina*, Rose Devries *Donna Anna*, Mme. Amalia Patti *Elvira*, Salvi *Don Ottavio*, Beneventano *Don Giovanni*, Marini *Leporello*, and Rovere *Massetto*, at the price of admission of $1 !

On July 11, the summer season at Castle Garden was inaugurated with the performance of "Lucia" by Mme. Sontag, Salvi, Badiali and Rosi, at the uniform price of $1 admission to all parts of the house. It may be gratifying to the reader to learn the terms on which Mme. Sontag, the greatest operatic prima donna at that time (Jenny Lind having retired from the stage), sang at Castle Garden. I, as manager, took the first $1,100 of the nightly receipts when Sontag appeared, for a part payment of artists and house, and the remainder was divided equally between Mme. Sontag and myself. Therefore, if the receipts should not reach $1,100, (which, however, never happened), Mme. Sontag would have had to sing for nothing—ye prima donnas of the present day, think of that! Mme. Sontag during her career had only one rival, and that was Mme. Malibran. In 1828 they both sang in the same opera house in Paris and in London, and the public in both cities were divided into partisans for Malibran or for Sontag. But although the *dilettanti* were divided about the superiority of these prima donnas, and were ever ready to defend their opinion at the point of the sword, the two artists were friends, and made no objection to appear together in the same operas. Malibran sang *Arsace* to Sontag's *Semiramis*, and Sontag sang *Donna Anna* to Malibran's *Zerlina*, and in "Nozze di Figaro" Malibran was the *Susanna* and Sontag the *Countess* in London. Even here during the Castle Garden season, I once requested Mme. Sontag on the occasion of a visit to the opera by President Pierce to take the secondary part of the *Princess* in "Robert le Diable," while Mme. Steffanone was cast for the first part of *Alice*, she most gracefully condescended and sang it, against the wish of her husband, the Count Rossi. Which of the present operatic stars would do the same? Mme. Sontag was also the most conscientious artist I ever met with, holding the duties of an artist toward the public as sacred. During the Castle Garden season on August 17, 1855, the opera of "Puritani" had been announced with Mme. Steffanone, Salvi, Badiali and Marini. About noon on the same day I received a note from Steffanone, informing me of her inability to appear that evening on account of an attack of chills and fever. I rushed to her house, I begged, I implored, I promised to apologize to the public for any shortcomings; I advised to cut out the heaviest pieces of the opera, but of no avail. Steffanone would not sing. What could be done? Appeal to the kindness of Mme. Sontag. The Countess was living on Staten Island, in a cottage near the Narrows; it was nearly three o'clock before I arrived at her house, where I found her in conversation with her husband and with Mr. Ullmann. I had hardly stated my embarrassing position when the two above named gentlemen jumped up simultaneously, and asked whether I would have the impudence to propose to the Countess (they never addressed her otherwise), to act and sing as a substitute or an understudy to Mme. Steffanone.

"Madame Sontag is too well known in the whole world, and only fools would take her for an understudy to any one," I answered.

"Your expressions are not exactly according to the usages of diplomatic language," retorted the husband, with a glance at the door.

My blood began to boil, and I said "you are not a diplomat here, but the husband of my prima donna, to whom I came for help, and I see no impudence in asking it, leaving it to her to decide for herself. But my duty toward the public and the other artists compels me to take this step anyhow."

"You will not sing," said the Count to Mme. Sontag in an abrupt manner.

"Mme. La Countess," meekly stepping forward, Mr. Ullmann remarked, "it would be useless for you to sing; as you are not announced to sing there will be a poor house, and a storm is also coming up from the South; there will not be $1,100 in the house, and you will have " to sing *for nothing*."

Mme. Sontag, who had listened quietly till now, stopped the conversation. "That is enough, gentlemen," she said; "this is not a question of dignity nor of money—it is to prevent *a disappointment to the public*." Take an example, you so-called *divas* of the present day!

"I will sing," she proceeded, "only, please, Mr. Maretzek, inform Mme. Steffanone for politeness' sake that I will sing her part, if she has no objections. Further, please ask Mr. Salvi, who lives also on Staten Island, a short distance from here, to pass a moment before going to the theatre, and rehearse with me the duo in the third act."

"Thank you, madame," and in a moment I was out in the street on my way to Salvi, who was staying in the candle factory of Meucci, now Bachmann's brewery. Mrs. Meucci informed me that I would find Mr. Salvi in the factory, the building next door. On entering there a great surprise, a Homeric spectacle, struck my astonished eyes. There I beheld in front of a large trough, with their arms bare up to the elbows, the perspiration on their brows, kneading hot, melted, and smelling tallow, Signor Lopenzo Salvi, the great tenor, Giuseppe Garibaldi, the great general, and our friend Meucci, the great inventor. The illustrious trio greeted me by extending their wet and greasy hands for a cordial shake, which on this occasion I politely declined. I made a hasty retreat, after begging the favorite tenor, the pet of the New York ladies, to immediately see Mme. Sontag, recommending him, however, to take first a sponge bath, to don clean linen, and to put some eau de Cologne on his handkerchief.

The house on Staten Island where Garibaldi, Salvi, and Meucci then lived, once belonged to Mr. Townsend, one of the former proprietors of the *Evening Express*. In 1850 I had that cottage rented for my summer residence, and not using it the following winter, I offered it to Garibaldi, who occupied it with Captain Franchi, his *aide de camp*, and a few of his young followers. There they were living, sustaining themselves by fishing and hunting and baking their own bread. Garibaldi would never accept anything from any one, and would not touch even any of the many chickens which I had left on the place, and used to send or bring the eggs himself to my house in New York. The following summer, when Salvi and Meucci arrived with Marty's Opera Company in New York, they bought the house and grounds from Mr. Townsend and established a candle factory. The very same house exists still, only it has been transferred from the right to the left of the road by Mr. Bachmann, who bought the land and built his brewery there. Among the followers of Garibaldi was a young boy, then only known as "Giovanni," whom Salvi took into his service. Giovanni was a very bright fellow for his age, and good humoredly carried the bundles for Signor Salvi to the theatre, carried messages, brushed his clothes, and shined his boots. Giovanni often came to ask for boxes or seats for Salvi, and usually begged for a pass to the gallery for himself. After the departure of Salvi for Europe, I remember having seen young Giovanni working on the railroad on Staten Island. Several years after I met him in James Fisk's office counting railroad tickets. Still later he was heard to be the body guard of Jay Gould, and now is the five times millionaire, Giovanni B. Morosini, whose daughter Victoria made such a commotion in fashionable circles a few years ago by her elopement with her father's coachman, Mr. Hulskamp. The rich banker Morosini was not only disconsolate, but raving mad, and all the papers of the country for months commented on this *mesalliance*. Mrs. Victoria Morosini-Hulskamp, however, seemed to enjoy the notoriety, and in order to keep it up decided to become a singer, being possessed of a fair voice, very strong in the upper notes and weak in the middle register. She appeared first in concert under Mr. Amberg's management, and afterward applied to Max Strakosch to bring her out as an opera singer; he agreed, and brought her to me with the request to coach her in the part of *Norina*, in "Don Pasquale." During the conversation I told her that I knew her father before she was born, and narrated all the above stated facts. Her husband, who was present, suddenly exclaimed, "What do I hear, Victoria? Your father when young was a servant to an opera singer, carried bundles, brushed clothes, etc., eh? I really don't see why they kick up such a row and talk about your *mesalliance*. If your mother married an Italian bootblack, I don't see why you could not marry a German coachman."

But to return to the Castle Garden season and to Mme. Sontag. She did sing that evening and the season closed about the 26th of August with a double performance of "Lucrezia" in the afternoon, Steffanone, Pozzolini and Marini in the cast, and with "Lucia" in the evening with Mme. Sontag, Salvi, and Badiali. Mme. Sontag after this season went to Mexico under an engagement with Mr. Masson, formerly the editor of the *Trait d'Union*, who had rented the Teatro Naçional; her triumphs in both hemispheres were ended by her untimely death on the 17th of June, 1854, at the early age of forty-nine years. She was born in 1805, made her debut at the age of six years in a comic opera, "Das Donau Weibchen" (The Fairy of the Danube), in Darmstadt, where her father, an actor, was a member of the Court Theatre. She retired from the stage in 1829, after her marriage with the Count Rossi, ambassador from Turin to Berlin and resumed her career again in 1849 in London under the direction of Mr. Lumley. She was a great artist, a noble woman, and a devoted wife and mother. Her remains were transported to Germany, and buried in the Abbey of Marienstein, in Saxony.

CHAPTER II.

THE ACADEMY OF MUSIC.

" For the permanent establishment of Italian Opera," has been for the last fifty years the favorite phrase whenever a new project to build an opera house has been started in New York.

Projectors are usually diplomats, who use a certain phrase which conceals their real meaning. Their object when desiring to establish Italian opera in New York on a permanent basis has been to dispose of some vacant lot and its surroundings on the most advantageous terms ; and the *modus operandi* has usually been to appeal, ostensibly to the love of music in this enlightened community, but in reality to the ever-growing taste for exclusiveness, and the imitation of the aristocratic manners of European society. Until recently, the promises to buyers of stock, of free choice seats or boxes, and of a dividend in the shape of rent (requested from guileless lessees and managers), were sufficient to obtain the necessary subscriptions, but the result was invariably the same. The stockholders saved themselves by the increase in the value of the real estate, and the manager usually failed.

The Richmond Hill Italian Opera House, in 1832, under the management of Montressor, with Mrs. Wood and Signora Pedrotti as prime donne, had a very short existence, and the next year another new opera house, at the corner of Leonard and Church streets, leased by Rafinolli, and managed by Da Ponte, who wrote the libretto to Mozart's "Don Giovanni," opened on the 18th of November, 1833, with Rossini's "La Gazza Ladra," and soon closed after a brief and disastrous season.

Everybody of the last generation remembers the fate of poor Palmo, who afterward, in 1844, managed the Palmo Opera House in Chambers street, and lost a fortune in less than two years.

The Astor Place Opera House was erected and opened in 1847, under the direction of Sanquirico and Patti, the father of Adelina Patti. The first season lasted a few months, and resulted in the utter failure and bankruptcy of the two managers.

The following year Mr. Edward Fry embarked in the enterprise of Italian opera at the Astor Place, but was stranded and completely wrecked after a six months' season.

In the first volume of my " Crotchets and Quavers," I described how from 1849 to 1852, I galvanized the Astor Place Opera House into an artificial life, but after three years had to give it up as a bad job, and seek in Mexico other fields and pastures new. After the advent of Alboni and Sontag, the necessity of another new opera house being again felt by some real estate brokers, Mr. James Phalen was pursuaded to sacrifice a vacant lot in Fourteenth street for the sum of $60,000, and to issue stock for several hundred thousand for the purpose of erecting the Academy of Music. The condition imposed upon the luckless lessees were more than sufficient to crush any enterprising manager. At the old Astor Place Opera House, the money taken for the first 150 seats from subscribers for the season was kept by the proprietors for rent; the poor manager thus being compelled to pay his landlords a whole year's rent in advance; but at the Academy of Music, besides a rental from $20,000 to $30,000, according to the length of the operatic season, the stockholders retained for themselves 200 free and transferable choice seats for any performance, even if the house was underlet for balls, concerts, or dramatic representations.

A long run of a new opera under these circumstances was an impossibility, as the stockholders after having heard an opera twice, either sold their seats or gave them to their friends, who otherwise would have paid for their admission. The subletting of the house, which otherwise would have been a source of revenue to the lessee, was wrought with difficulties for the same reason.

How the Academy of Music, under the old stockholders' system, could have been kept open for twenty years, can only be accounted for by the rivalry then existing between Ullmann, Strakosch, and myself, each striving to keep the lead in operatic matters here, and their foolhardiness in risking a swim over the operatic whirlpool at the Academy of Music.

After the departure of Mme. Sontag, another season of Italian opera under my management was inaugurated at Niblo's Garden, on September 29, 1853, which lasted till December 18 of the same year. In default of an operatic star, the principal feature of that season was the production for the first time in America of Meyerbeer's " Prophete," on November 25, 1853, with a splendid *mise en scene* of entirely new scenery, new dresses, machinery after exact models brought from Paris, and a cast comprising Steffanone, Bertucca, Salvi, Marini, Beneventano, Vietti, Rosi, and a complete *corps de ballet*, military bands and 200 auxiliaries in the coronation scene. On this occasion roller skating and the electric light were introduced in America. The last two named novelties seemed to make a greater impression on the public than the music of Meyerbeer, but the receipts, although with crowded houses, could not cover the preliminary outlays for the production and the expenses for the run of the piece owing to the low price of admission, which was only $1.

Mr. William Niblo, after witnessing the opera, called me in his office, and told me, that in his opinion, it was foolish to waste such an amount of money, and advised me to dispense with all the artists, orchestra, and choruses, etc., etc., and to lay simply a floor over the parquet, and to give only the *roller skating scene*, lighted by the *electric apparatus ;* to charge admission of fifty cents, and furnish skates for the evening to any gentleman or lady who would like to try the new amusement of roller skating.

Of course I laughed at his advice, and pitied his taste, but thirty years after, when skating rinks were erected in every town and hamlet in America, I remembered William Niblo, and admired his foresight and his business tact.

The artistic success, however, of the " Prophete," hastened the completion of the projected new Academy of Music, and the *vox populi* pointed me out as the only competent future manager of it. After some preliminary negotiations I went to Europe to look for new artists, and there I received the following letter:

47 WALL STREET, NEW YORK, March 21, 1854.

MAX MARETZEK, Esq.

Dear Sir : I am authorized by the directors to offer to lease you the New York Academy of Music for one year from the first of September next, for $30,000; $6,000 to be deposited by you as security, and the rent payable semi-monthly in advance, or forfeiture of the lease and the deposit.

The insurance, taxes, assessments and external repairs to be paid by the directors. You to pay the license, Croton water tax, fuel, gas bills, etc.

The stockholders, not to exceed 250 in number, to have the right of admission on all occasions, with secured seats. The maximum price of admission, and the character of entertainments to be given, other than Italian opera, the same as assented to in your letter proposing to lease the house before you left New York.

The directors would caution you against acting on this offer, or engaging performers, as they will not consider this proposal as binding on their part until the $6,000 is deposited, and the conditions of the lease subscribed to on your part.   Yours very respectfully,

JAMES PHALEN,
President of the New York Academy of Music.

P. S.—A reply by return of mail is expected.   J. P.

I answered this offer on the 10th of April from Mr. Phalen, by accepting, and adding a few immaterial conditions about the time of opening, and asking a few questions about the seats to the stockholders, in case of underletting the house.   In due time Mr. Phalen's answer came as follows:

NEW YORK, May 6, 1854.

My Dear Sir: Your letter of the 10th of April was duly received, but in consequence of your having added conditions to the offer I had the honor to make you for leasing the New York Academy of Music, it became necessary to call a meeting of the directors, to whom was submitted the correspondence between us.   At this meeting it was

Resolved, That the president be authorized to enter into an arrangement with Isaac V. Fowler, Esq., to lease to Max Maretzek the Academy of Music for one year from the first day of September, 1854, on the terms and conditions contained in the president's letter to Mr. Maretzek, under date of the 21st of March, 1854, on receiving from Mr. Fowler his guarantee of obligation for the payment of $6,000, liquidated damages, provided the said lease is not executed and the preliminary conditions complied with by Mr. Maretzek on or before the first day of July, 1854.

I sent a copy of the above resolution to Mr. Fowler, and received from him a letter in reply, stating that he would give to our Board of Directors his obligation for $6,000, liquidated damages, provided you do not execute a lease of the opera house on the terms proposed in my letter of March 21.

There being other and very pressing applications to lease the Academy of Music, you would have lost it if your friend Mr. Fowler had not accepted *unconditionally* the terms of my letter of 21st of March, as the directors felt themselves at perfect liberty to negotiate with Mr. Hackett, or any other person, by reason of your neglect to comply with the terms of my letter.

As you have been so fortunate as to secure the promise of a lease of the Academy of Music, I sincerely hope you may be equally fortunate in securing the requisite talent to make it attractive and to ensure success.

I think you told me before leaving New York that you thought the 15th of September early enough to begin the opera season.   If in making your engagements should you prefer to open on the 15th instead of the 1st of September, the directors will doubtless consent to have the year commence on the 15th, if you will advise me that you so desire.   Be pleased to acknowledge the receipt of this letter by return mail.

Yours respectfully,   JAMES PHALEN,
President of the New York Academy of Music.

MR. MAX MARETZEK.

From the foregoing it will be easily understood that the stockholders did not change anything from their first offer of the date of March 21, made no concessions whatever, but on the contrary, received, to them, a satisfactory guaranty for the stipulated advance payment or forfeiture of $6,000, and congratulated me on having secured the promise of the lease!

On the strength of this agreement I made conditional arrangements in Italy with an array of artists for the opening of the Academy, but learning that Mr. Hackett had been negotiating with Grisi and Mario, and mistrusting the mention of his name in Mr. Phalen's letter, I hastened back to New York only to learn that my suspicions were not imaginary. Mr. Hackett had concluded his engagements with Grisi and Mario, and the directors of the Academy were anxious that their new opera house should be opened by Grisi and Mario. . Their only hope was centred in my failure to pay in cash the $6,000 stipulated, and they hinted kindly that they would release Mr. Fowler of his responsibility to pay the forfeiture; but when I offered a certified check of the required sum, I was informed that, according to the letters sent to me to Europe, I had secured only a *promise* of the lease, but not the lease itself! But if I would quietly submit to let Mr. Hackett have the opening and a few weeks for a short season, they would faithfully again promise to make all reasonable concessions if I wanted the house afterward, and would help and do all in their power to make me at last a successful opera manager, even to advance money for the engagement of great artists. Knowing that it would be foolish and costly to go to law with millionaires, and in fact not thinking it advisable to have an opposition of Mario and Grisi in any other house, I yielded, and the Academy of Music was opened October 2, 1854, with Mario and Grisi in " Norma." From the day of its opening by Hackett until its final close as an opera house under Mapleson, the inside history of the Academy is nothing but a succession of merry wars between the opera managers and the stockholders or their Board of Directors. The more Ullmann, or Strackosh, or I tried to outbid each other by the importation of great artists or the production of new operas, the more valuable the stock of the Academy became, and good bargains were made by some of the stockholders by selling their seats to speculators outside when they had heard an opera once or twice. The payment of rent was scrupulously enforced, and if not forthcoming the music, dresses and properties were seized and kept for half or one-third their value, and afterward rented out to the new lessee or manager. A side-door was opened as a special private entrance for stockholders, as any contamination by entering at the same door with such low persons as pay for their admission would be degrading. Still they were kind enough to pay themselves the door-keeper of their private entrance the sum of $1.50 per night out of their own funds, to alleviate the expenses of the manager, but the door-keeper, of course, grateful to his employers, was not over punctilious about letting eight persons go in on a ticket of four stocks, if required, and in return their secretary did not discharge him if the manager complained that besides the regular stockholders and their freinds, aunts and cousins and even some strangers found ingress by that door. I learned since that one of the door-keepers bought a house from his savings of $1.50 salary per night, or $6 per week. At certain times the lease of the Academy could not be obtained at all unless a certain prima donna was engaged, whether you needed her or not, to please the president; at other times to oblige the secretary, the manager had to take all the stage hands, doorkeepers and ticket sellers he recommended. This state of affairs lasted for over twenty years, with its ever recurring quarrels, until the contending managers either left for Europe, like Ullmann and Maurice Strackosh, or others gave it up in disgust, leaving the Academy to its fate and the stockholders to the contemplation of the bare walls of their temple of music. The ultimate fate of the Academy and its stockholders appeared at last under the guise of Mr. Mapleson, who on his arrival here, recognized at once the deplorable situation, and taking advantage of the position of the stockholders, and in no immediate danger of any formidable rival at that time, succeeded first in obtaining a lease free of rent and afterward forced them to give a subvention in hard cash for their choice seats. They, however, soon got tired of paying for their boxes, and of the exactions of Mr. Mapleson, and the Academy of Music was sold, and shared the fate of the Astor Place Opera House, with the only difference that instead of Donnelly's learned dogs and monkeys of the Astor Place Opera House, trained horses were introduced at the Academy of Music after its musical occupation was gone. This proves the progress and the higher evolution of musical art, as developed by the aid and encouragement of the projectors and stockholders of the New York Academy of Music.

The Grisi and Mario season closed with the performance of "Favorita" on the 29th of December, 1859. Mr. Hackett, the manager, and his partners, who hoped to renew the excitement of the Jenny Lind engagement, and to reap a harvest of dollars like Barnum, were disappointed so far, as they hardly made more than their expenses. The new house itself was considered a failure in its construction, as nearly one-third of the audience could not see the stage and hardly hear the singers. The surroundings of Grisi and Mario were second rate, the orchestra and chorus not sufficiently strong for the large building. Grisi herself was immensely great as *Norma, Semiramis,* and even *Elvira,* although at that time she had passed the period of youthful freshness, but she was never fitted for such parts as *Lucia, Amina* and *Rosina.* Giulietta Grisi was born in 1812, in Milan, and made her debut in 1828, at the theatre in Bologna, in a small part in Rossini's "Zelmira." From there she went to Venice, and sang the part of *Juliet,* in Vaccai's Opera of "Romeo." After her engagement in Venice, she was transferred by her manager, Sig. Lanari, to the manager of the Scala, in Milan, Sig. Crivelli, where she created the parts of *Jane Seymour* in Donizetti's "Anna Bolena" and *Adalgisa* in Bellini's "Norma," playing second parts to Mme. Pasta in both these operas. Bellini, the composer, recognized the talent of Grisi and wrote for her the principal part in "I Puritani," which for the first time was produced in Paris on the 24th of January, 1835, with Rubini, Tamburini and Lablache in the cast.

What a quartet of singers! In 1836, Giulietta Grisi was married to Mr. Auguste de Melcy, with whom she lived only a short time, and had to leave on account of his uncontrollable temper. A few years after her professional career brought her in contact with the tenor Mario, whose real name was Count di Candia; love at sight was the result of their first meeting and a few lovely daughters the further consequence. Grisi used to call them jokingly "Grisettes," and Mario "Marionettes." They had agreed to join their fortunes with the understanding that he should provide for the entertainment of their household with his earnings, which he did in too lavish manner, and she should save and deposit all her earnings for her daughters. They both calculated without their host. Mr. de Melcy after the death of Mme. Grisi-Melcy, as the legitimate husband, took—according to French law at that time, where no divorce was possible—possession of all her fortune, and left her daughters and Sig. Mario penniless.

Mr. Hackett did not seem anxious to renew his lease of the Academy of Music after the Mario and Grisi season, and the Board of Directors were offering their house to every available manager, including myself, Mr. Maurice Strakosch, Mr. Ullmann, and others. Each of us were willing to take the lease for a spring season after Lent, or for a winter season from October, 1855, but not immediately in the middle of winter, when it would have been hard to procure new artists, and the new Academy of Music went begging for a tenant, when at once a would-be savior of the opera appeared in the person of Mr. Ole Bull, who at first proposed a partnership with myself and Maurice Strakosch, but upon second thought, after Strakosch had promptly started for Europe in search of new artists, obtained from Mr. Phalen a lease for himself alone, giving me an engagement as conductor, and forgetting to provide for Strakosch. He promised to manage the opera on a new departure, offered a prize of a thousand dollars for the best American opera, by an American composer, drafted a plan for a National Conservatory according to the charter of the Legislature, as an attachment to the Opera House; surrounded himself with secretaries who listened to the demands of any person who called for him, employed expressly a lawyer with an office in the Academy, to cross-examine any one at length who dared to present a bill; established a red-tape aristocratic administration, to the delight of Mr. Phalen, who, in expectation of the great things that Mr. Ole Bull would accomplish, advanced him $4,000; and really succeeded in being admired by the astonished public as a nine-days' wonder. After great flourishing of trumpets and beating of big drums, Ole Bull at last opened on February 15, 1854, with "Rigoletto," and after four performances of that opera, and one of "Favorita," for the debut of Mme. Vestvali he collapsed. The nine-days' wonder only lasted six nights.

The day just after Ole Bull's collapse, Sig. Brignoli and Sig. Amodio, who had been sent by Maurice Strakosch from Europe, arrived in New York. Mr. Phalen, for his money advanced, seized upon the scenes and dresses, etc., of "Rigoletto," "Trovatore," and "William Tell," which had been prepared, and on the contracts of Brignoli and Amodio; and himself, with Mr. Coit as partner, myself as musical director, and Mr. Wikoff as business manager, continued the season. Brignoli made his first debut in New York on the 15th of March, 1855, in "Lucia di Lammermoor." This short season ought to be remembered as the debuts of Brignoli and Amodio, who became immense favorites, and remained in America until their deaths, and by the first production of Verdi's "Trovatore," which since has been repeated many hundred times to crowded houses, and the first production of Rossini's "William Tell" in its entirety, and strictly according to the original score. The first cast of "Trovatore" in New York, was the following: *Lenora*, Mme. Steffanone; *Azucena*, Mme. Vestvali; *Manrico*, Sig. Brignoli; *Count de Luna*, Sig. Amodio, and *Fernando*, Sig. Coletti. From an artistic point of view this season was a brilliant one, but Messrs. Phalen and Coit claimed a loss of over $20,000, and being fully satisfied with their experiment, again offered the lease of the Academy to the highest bidder.

They did not wait a long time for the fly to walk into the spider's parlor. One morning in 1855, Mr. William H. Paine, himself a stockholder, a wealthy man in his own right, and son of a millionaire, sent for me, and asked me whether I would accept the position of musical director, for a salary and a percentage in the profits, if he would take the lease of the Academy of Music for next season of 1855-56, and procure an entirely new and complete opera company, dispensing with all the artists now in New York, with the exception of Brignoli and Amodio. I at once agreed, putting my salary a little higher, and the percentage of the profits a little lower than he offered. Mr. Paine had already before been a silent partner of Mr. Hackett, and having tasted only the little enjoyment of life behind the scenes, and taking a liking to the excitement of an impresario, without having yet experienced the anxieties and troubles of that calling, and in anticipation of plenty of fun (as he called it), he took the Opera House, from September, 1855, to May, 1856. Good luck seemed to favor him in the beginning, for Mme. Anna de La Grange had just arrived, under contract with Mr. B. Ullmann, which however (the lease of the Academy having again escaped him), might prove too heavy for him to carry out. Mr. Paine offered to take the contract off his hands, and Mr. Ullmann for a consideration transferred Mme. La Grange to Mr. Paine. Thus as the Italians used to say, "The cheese fell from heaven on the maccaroni." Mr. Paine secured unexpectedly and by chance, one of the greatest prima donnas that ever visited the United States, and the only one who could replace Bosio, Alboni and Mme. Sontag. Mme. de La Grange also, to satisfy the scrutinous investigation of high society in Fifth avenue, could claim the titles of nobility like Mme. Countess Sontag-Rossi, or the Marchioness of Alboni-Peppoli, being to the manor born herself and married to the Baron de Stankowitch, of Montenegro. With the aid of theatrical agents in Paris and Milan, whom I had recommended, Mr. Paine succeeded in engaging a really formidable company, comprising Mme. Anna de La Grange, Mme. Nantier Didier as contralto—another excellent acquisition—Brignoli and Salviani (alias Alberic Second, the well-known French novelist) as tenors, Amodio and Morelli as baritones, and Marini as basso.

Mr. Paine, like all new-fledged managers, desired to encourage native talent in the shape of good looking young ladies, and in order to rejuvenate the body of the choruses, advertised for and listened to applicants for small parts and for situations in the chorus; among others a young, poorly clad girl introduced herself, with the request to have her voice tried. She sang sweetly and displayed a good soprano voice and good taste. She could not be called handsome, but with a well-shaped figure and large brown eyes, she made a favorable impression on Mr. Paine. He engaged her at once, made her study the parts of *Adalgisa* in "Norma," and of *Bertha* in the "Prophete," which she sang afterward successfully. Her name was Eliza Hensler. Her father was a poor tailor in Boston, who kept a small shop in a basement in West street, in that city. This young girl made the most remarkable career of any woman who ever entered the theatrical profession. After a season in New York, Mr. Paine sent her to Paris to continue her studies, and recommended her to his theatrical agent, Mr. Carini, who in course of time procured her an engagement at the Opera in Lisbon. Dom Fernando, the consort of Queen Maria della Gloria of Portugal, took her there under his protection. Soon after the death of the Queen he created Eliza Countess of Edla, and after paying due respect to the Queen's memory, Dom Fernando married the Countess Edla, *nee* Eliza Hensler.

Her husband being originally a prince of the house of Coburg, the Boston tailor's daughter thus became the sister-in-law to Queen Victoria, and aunt to the Prince of Wales and to the present King of the Belgians, and mother-in-law of the reigning King of Portugal.

When Queen Isabella of Spain was sent into exile, Prince Bismarck tried to put a Hohenzollern on the Spanish throne, and Louis Napoleon III. opposed such pretensions, with an eye of a Bonaparte for that position. At the same time a strong coalition of grandees of Spain favored the candidacy of Dom Fernando of Portugal to the throne of Spain, with all the chances in his favor. If the grandees were satisfied with Dom Fernando their wives most decidedly declared that they would never appear at Court, should ever the plebian Boston girl Eliza be allowed to do the honors of the Court. A compromise was proposed in secret caucus to obtain a divorce from the Pope, Pius IX., but Dom Fernando, sooner than give up Eliza, refused the throne of Spain. The indirect consequences of this heroic royal attachment were the Franco-German war, the downfall of Napoleon III., the loss of two provinces to France, and the still uncertain future of Spain.

Without the Boston tailor's girl Eliza, the Bonaparte dynasty might still be reigning in France, and Bismarck might not have become the arbiter of Europe. What remarkable events! "And all on account of Eliza!"—to quote the classical verse in the opera of "Billee Taylor."

Mr. Paine opened the fall season of 1855 on the first of October, and wonderful to relate, there were no quarrels among the artists, no disappointments to the public and no newspaper controversies. The salaries were regularly paid, nobody interfered with the dispositions of the musical director, and everything went on as merrily as marriage bells. Mr. Paine, on his part, although he lost money good humoredly, got all the fun he had bargained for, read his papers and smoked his cigars in the office in the morning, invited Mme. La Grange and Mme. Didier, with their husbands, to dinner, initiated these two lucky husbands into the mysteries of the national game of poker during the afternoon, attended the opera in his box in the evening, took supper with Eliza Hensler after the performance; and was considered a benefactor to society in Fifth avenue circles.

He closed his first season in January, 1856, to be followed by a few representations in Philadelphia, Baltimore and Washington, previous to the reopening of the Academy for the spring season of 1856.

On the 5th day of January, Mme. La Grange, Mme. Nantier Didier, Miss Eliza Hensler, Mr. Paine, Mr. Stankowitch and myself started for Philadelphia on the ten o'clock morning train, to join there the rest of the company, who had left on a previous train to be ready for a performance in the evening. Our party was attended by my servant, to look after the baggage, bundles and carpet-bags. A snow storm was raging when we left New York, and a few miles after New Brunswick we came to a sudden halt, the engine being buried in a snow drift. At first the ladies laughed at the accident, but the hours dragged along and no advance could be made; the storm increased in fury, and soon we were snowed in from all sides. The ladies of our party began to suffer from cold and from hunger, and they presented a pitiful sight of misery and despair, and suffered agonies of hunger. "Is there nobody who has had the sense and forethought of bringing a roll of bread with him? We will starve here, will be sick, unable to sing for at least a week." "Who would think of taking provisions for a journey of two hours," muttered Mr. Paine. "A kingdom for a piece of bread and cheese," roared Mr. Stankowitch. During all this time my German servant, Heferkorn, moved up and down the car in a nervous, excited manner, tried to speak to me, and did not dare, and behaved in a strange way, as if a deep secret was oppressing him heavily. At last he braced up, and calling me in the other car, he addressed me in a woeful tone:

"Mr. Maretzek, if you only forgive me this time, I will never do it again."

"What do you mean, you fool, what have you done?"

"Oh, I can't say, until you promise to forgive me."

"How can I forgive until you say what you have done?"

"Well, I cannot see those poor ladies suffer any longer, it chokes me; but for their sake I must tell you. Well, then, you see, I went yesterday to your house on Staten Island to fetch some things you needed for your travel, and there—well there I stole a big turkey and two bottles of wine. The turkey is well roasted in that carpet bag and the two bottles in this satchel. I have brought for myself also a loaf of bread. There now, kill me if you like, but give this to the poor ladies."

"You are forgiven, and bring the turkey and the wine immediately in the next car, and serve it to our party."

I rushed to Mme. La Grange, and said that I had discovered a restaurant and dinner would be served immediately. " How can you make fun of us at this sad moment," said Mme. Didier. " This is a poor joke, and cruel too," said the Miss Hensler. " I see no fun and no joke," said Mme. La Grange,. and changing at once the expression in her face and opening wide her eyes, when Heferkorn entered, she continued, " I see a turkey ! And I see two bottles of wine !" and in a moment the gloom was changed into general hilarity. They did not lose time in carving the turkey ; they tore it with their delicate hands to pieces, and devoured it with a vengeance; they drank the wine out of the bottle, and did not seem to care for the absence of napkin forks, knives or glasses, and they all eulogized my servant for—his honesty !

We arrived at last in Philadelphia at 8 P. M., having made the trip from New York in ten hours, and came just in time for a good supper, but too late for an opera performance.

The company returned to New York after a successful trip to Washington,. Baltimore, etc., and reopened the spring season on the 12th of March, 1856. The principal feature was the production of Arditi's opera " La Spia," the libretto taken from Cooper's "Spy." The music was beautiful and well per-formed by Mme. Le Grange, Miss Hensler, and Sig. Brignoli as the *Spy*, and the *mise en scene* was splendid, but the American public seems not to believe in American subjects for opera, otherwise the four best American operas ever written, viz., " Rip Van Winkle," the " Spy," " Sleepy Hollow," and " Uncle Tom's Cabin," would have been added to the standard operatic repertory. If either of these four operas had been first brought out in Paris or London, they would have become popular there, and would have been imported to this country with a flourish of trumpets. Mr. William H. Paine closed his season in April, 1856, and at that time thought he had had all the fun he wanted, and his wife, Mrs. Paine, thought that he had had more of it than was good for him and for her. Mr. Paine had already sold one of his houses during the season to meet the losses, and when at the close he had to sell another one, Mrs. Paine, according to rumor, only gave her consent, which was necessary to make the sale legal, on condition that he should give up that funny business of managing opera.

Mme. Anna de la Grange was one of the most extraordinary artists ever known. She was able to sing any contralto or soprano part with equal skill. She could sing equally well the leading roles of " Norma," or " Sonnam-bula," and the " Prophete," or the " Barber of Seville." Her repertory was the most extensive that any artist ever had. Her endurance was wonderful. She remained with me many years, singing in Northern and Southern cities, passing from the extreme North to Havana in the same wintry season, and in all that time never once disappointed the public or missed an engage-ment. She is still living, but long since retired from the stage, giving lessons to talented pupils in Paris, and preparing them for the operatic career.

CHAPTER III.

THE MERRY THIRTY DAYS' WAR.

Hardly had Mr. Paine notified the committee of stockholders that he would not renew the lease of the Academy for next year, nor intended to give the usual supplementary spring season, than I was actually waited upon by Messrs. Phalen, Coit and W. H. Wolfe, with the request to continue the present season for some time longer, and the inquiry whether I would take the lease for the next theatrical year. Mr. Maurice Strakosch then was traveling on a concert tour with Adelina Patti as a wonder child, and Mr. Ullmann was in Europe trying to induce the great pianist Thalberg to visit America under his (Ullmann's) guidance. I was, therefore, for the moment the only available manager, and the only hope to keep the Academy open and supply the public and shareholders with opera. I agreed to continue the season for a few weeks longer on my own risk and responsibility, provided Mr. Paine had no objections, but declined to take the lease for the next year, unless the stockholders would agree, first, not to transfer their free admissions and seats to outsiders on opera nights, and to waive entirely their rights of admission, whenever the Academy was sublet for other entertainments than opera. The negotiations lasted nearly all summer without any result, until I yielded on the first point, and insisted only on the second condition. They solemnly agreed to this condition, and requested me to go on with my preparations for the next season. Trusting to their good faith, I completed my arrangements, but the promised lease with the stipulated clause was not forthcoming. Upon my pressing demands for the document they begged me to sign the following circular to the stockholders, and promised that they would carry it around and obtain the necessary signatures :

TO THE STOCKHOLDERS OF THE NEW YORK ACADEMY OF MUSIC:

"Mr. Max Maretzek proposes to lease the Academy of Music for one year at $22,000, and agrees to give at least fifty nights of Italian opera during the season.

"Said Maretzek requests that the stockholders should waive their right of admission to all performances that may take place on the off-nights, when the Academy is let for concerts, lectures, balls, etc., etc., except when *Italian Opera* is given.

"The Executive and Finance Committee, though personally willing as stockholders to accede to the above conditions, do not feel authorized to bind the other stockholders to this arrangement—they, therefore, submit the matter to every stockholder for his approval.

"New York, August, 1856."

Weeks passed again, but neither the lease nor the circular with the needed signatures were forthcoming, but the opening night was already announced.

Upon my assuming a menacing tone in my demands, Mr. Phalen pacified me, giving as an excuse, that most of the stockholders were out of town and could not be reached; advised me to open the season, and if the opera company were satisfactory they certainly would gladly sign on their return to town. Consequently, I did arrange to open the season on the 14th of September, 1856, with "Trovatore," and in quick succession produced for the first time in America "La Traviata," by Verdi, and the "Star of the North," by Meyerbeer. Both operas were highly successful, and the second one created a sensation for its dazzling *mise en scène,* and the strength of its cast, comprising Mme. La Grange, Mme. Bertrucca-Maretzek, Miss Susan Pyne, Miss Seidenburg, Sig. Brignoli, Amodio, Arnoldi and Coletti.

On the first night of the "Star of the North," September 24, 1856, the house was crowded, and I noticed all the boxes and seats of the stockholders occupied. I, therefore, next morning peremptorily requested Mr. Phalen to send at once either the lease, with the signatured clause in, or to return my circular addressed to the stockholders. Instead of the lease he dispatched Mr. Henry Wickoff, who, with a diplomatic smile, first congratulated me on the stupendous success of the new opera and prognosticated a run of at least a hundred crowded houses, and afterward handed me my circular, remarking in a cavalier manner, that "this circular is really of no importance, as the triumphs of 'Traviata' and the 'Star of the North,' etc., are the best guarantees of a profitable season." I opened the circular and found that only the following gentlemen had signed:

JAMES PHALEN, ⎫
HENRY A. COIT, ⎬ *Executive Commitee.*
N. H. WOLFE, ⎭

MOSES GRINNELL,   WILLIAM H. PAINE,
CH. A. HECKSHEN,   MOSES TAYLOR,

JAMES PENNEMAN.

Eight gentlemen, representing thirty-five shares out of 200!

I folded the paper, and coldly said to Mr. Wickoff: "Please tell Mr. Phalen to send the lease *as agreed* upon within three days or to dispose of the Academy by the end of this week."

"Oh, you will not cut your own throat, now that you at last have your fortune within your grasp," retorted Mr. Wickoff, and bowed himself out with an ironical expression in his face.

I immediately telegraphed to Messrs. Tompkins and Thayer whether I could have the Boston Theatre within a week, and received an affirmative reply, and then drove down to Mr. Negretti, agent of Don Francisco Marti in Havana, who had invited me to come to the Tacon Theatre, and requested him to negotiate for a season in Havana. On the 30th of September, 1856, on the second performance of the "Star of the North" not having received any further communication from Mr. Phalen, between the acts I stepped before the curtain, and in a somewhat caustic speech stated my grievances against the board of directors, condemned the exclusive system of their arrangement, did not spare the shareholders, and announced that to my great sorrow and regret, under these circumstances I should stop operations that very night. At first the audience listened with astonishment, but soon recovered, and at every allusion to the directors or shareholders broke out in such vehement demonstrations of approbation that most of the stockholders prudently left their seats and hastened out of the house. Next day hostilities broke out, and caused a very ludicrous operatic row, which contributed for a few weeks to the general hilarity of the community, and was for some time afterward known as "The Merry Thirty Days' War."

The revengeful board of directors met in solmen conclave, and in order to punish me for my audacity unanimously resolved: "That the Academy of Music should never be leased again to me," and covered themselves with ridicule, by refusing to me the very same thing, which I did not want. Some of the newspapers asked them whether they obtained the consent of all the stockholders for that decision, or whether they felt on this occasion authorized to act without their approbation, and commented harshly upon their faithless and illiberal conduct toward me. The matrons and desolate maidens of upper tendom were in a state of languishment over the lack of opera, the milliners roundly denounced the board of directors for ruining their business for the fall season; even politics were forgotten, and the unpleasantness between myself and the stockholders was the topic of the day.

Under these circumstances something had to be done to render me and my name harmless, and the wily diplomat, Henry Wickoff, was instructed by Messrs. Phalen, Coit and Wolfe, to write and continually send anonymous communications to the papers to make me in my turn appear ridiculous in the eyes of the public. One day he wrote my obituary after my suicide induced by having delivered that famous speech. The next day he advised me to buy with the remnant of my fortune a barrel organ and a monkey, and grind my way in the streets of New York as a last resort to make a living.

At another time, ironically alluding to my home at Princes Bay, on Staten Island, he guessed that I would soon turn up as an impresario of native oysters, or that I should retire to the Salt River, where was reported to own a large planation, and mourn in solitude the mistake of insulting the directors of the Academy.

Having fully ascertained through Mr. Paine, who still remained friendly toward me, the source of these attacks, I resolved to answer, and sent a communication to the New York *Herald*, the substance of which as far as I remember, was that the public at large cared no more whether I "had plantations, oyster-beds, or other properties, than it would care whether any of the directors of the Academy of Music had made their fortunes in lottery speculations, in investments in the African trade, or in trying to monopolize the grain market; the only question between me and the public was whether I gave to them and to the stockholders the value for the money they paid for admission to the opera."

The New York *Herald*, which at that time never missed an occasion to tackle the parvenus of Japonicaville, published a half dozen editorials, requesting me to name the persons who had made their money in lottery speculations and other not strictly legitimate ways. The committee of directors felt themselves seriously hurt, and decided to resent this new outrage by a bull of excommunication against me, and without again asking the signature of all the shareholders resolved, "That no lessee of the Academy of Music should ever be allowed to engage Max Maretzek in any capacity whatsoever, nor should I be permitted to enter the house, unless as a paying auditor." No sooner had I learned of this awful decree, than I constituted myself a standing committee of one, and on my part resolved: "That immediately after my Boston season and previous to my going to Havana, I shall in the intervening time, instead of going to Philadelphia and other cities, enter the Academy of Music in New York, and then and there conduct an opera season, notwithstanding any previous or future resolutions of Messrs. Phalen, Coit and Wolfe."

I therefore sent immediately for Mr. Stankowitch, the husband of Mme. La Grange, begged him to take the next train to New York and ask for himself the Academy of Music for a season of four weeks at least, and to say that he had taken the company off my hands and intended to risk opera management. I further instructed him in case the directors of the Academy should try to enforce their last resolution regarding myself, to make at first a decent show of a fight in my favor, so as not to make them suspicious, but to yield reluctantly this point, to pity my fate, and to promise that Mr. Kreutzer, the leader of the orchestra, should conduct the opera.

Everything went as straight as a bullet from an Armstrong gun. The committee of directors fell into the trap. Mr. Stankowitch leased the house, and announced under his management the La Grange troupe to open with "Trovatore," on Monday, December 10, 1856. The performance took place with the artists as advertised, but with many other features not in the bill. My modesty, or perhaps, my partiality, does not allow me to report that memorable performance, therefore I reproduce hereby a few extracts from the newspaper accounts of that time.

"II TROVATORE" BY THE LA GRANGE OPERA TROUPE.

A Curious Scene at the Academy of Music.

"Behold the opening night! La Grange in the 'Trovatore;' Mme. Maretzek in her old position in the opera, and Herr Kreutzer, Maretzek's right hand man, in the conductor's seat. What cry is that? Max! Maretzek! Maretzek! Check! Retchek! Maxmerechek! the handsome ex-con-ductor's name in every possible mode of pronouncing and mispronouncing it; Maretzek, or no play! The play and Maretzek! Kreutzer, the sly dog, turns round on his stool, and smilingly bows to the audience! No use! We must have Maretzek and nothing else! And the upshot was that Max was ushered into the orchestra, amidst reverberating thunders of applause, and shaking hands (Pickwickianly) with the superseded Kreutzer, took his seat and his baton tinkled the tin, and led off the overture. Max had conquered by the aid of his old stand-bys, the masses, with whom he has always been exceedingly popular.

"At the end of the opera he was called out, and in a few modest words thanked his friends for their kindness, but declined making a speech, the last he had made on those boards, he pleasantly hinted, having such a prodigious effect. Witty Max!"

From the Times, December 13, 1856.

SECOND NIGHT OF THE LA GRANGE OPERA.

"The Star of the North"—The Last of the Executive Committee— Opening of the Opera Season.

"There was an uninterrupted performance last evening at the Academy of Music, and a magnificent house expressed its satisfaction at the commence-ment of the opera by loudly applauding Max Maretzek. Mr. Maretzek wears his honors meekly and pretends, the rogue, not to know that he has gained a great and important victory, of which the many-mouthed public were his large and valorous champions. Max is like a certain domestic animal famil-iar to our hearths, and proverbial for its happy faculty of coming down safely on its feet; he is also like a lobster and shows brightest after having been in hot water; he also resembles the Chevalier Bayard, an admirable man, excel-lent alike in letters and in war. Indeed, the more we survey the excellent proportions of the redoubtable *chef*, the more we are struck with his general resemblance to the human family. We cannot fail to detect that he is more or less like all men of genius.

"Popular sovereignty has never triumphed in a more thorough and com-plete style. After the demonstration of Monday, when it will be remembered the people insisted on having Max back in his old place, despite the mandate and hisses of the shareholders, Baron de Stankowitch felt it necessary for his own protection to address a letter to Mr. Paine begging him to intercede with his brother stockholders and assuring him that Max Maretzek was the only person in New York at the moment capable of conducting Italian opera.

All sorts of attempts were made to extract an apology from Max, but the blood of all the Maretzeks revolted at the idea. He desired to be led away in chains; to have his little ones butchered before his paternal eyes; to be torn from the embraces of his fond wife; to have his humble cot a pile of smoldering ruins; his corn fields ravished, and his vineyards trodden beneath the feet of the oppressor. He was ready for anything in the world, even to die, Roman-like, on the point of his own baton, but apologize? Never!

"The directors gave up the point in despair, and seeing, most likely, how completely they were in the wrong, 'hitched on' to M. Stankowitch's letter. On motion of Mr. Wolfe, a resolution was passed conceding all that the public ever demanded, and leaving everything in a satisfactory state. Next to avoiding a blunder, the best thing is to acknowledge it. In doing so the directors of the Academy have behaved like straightforward, sensible men. There will now, we hope, be a prosperous season of Italian opera. We publish elsewhere Mr. de Stankowitch's letter and the resolution of the executive committee."

On Wednesday, December 12, Mr. Phalen tendered his resignation as president of the board of directors; on the following Saturday, the 15th, he sailed into voluntary exile to Europe, and on Sunday, the 16th, the young ladies of Fifth avenue and dressmakers of Broadway sang a "Te Deum."

CHAPTER IV.

NEW SERIES.—No. IV.—OPERA IN HAVANA.

Senor Don Francisco Marti, the proprietor of the Tacon Theatre, had been pouting with the public of Havana, and from 1853 to 1856 the capital of the ever-faithful island of Cuba had been deprived three years of Italian opera. For a year or so the Habaneros consoled themselves with bull-fights and with some Spanish Zarzuellas, but in the natural course of events, having learned to appreciate what they had lost, the senoritas began to grow tired of toreadors and were longing for sweet tenors, and the caballeros, satiated with the blood of bulls and horses, were clamoring for prima donnas and ballerinas.

Don Francisco Marti at first remained inexorable, but having received some hints from the authorities and the Captain General Concha himself, finally agreed to let the Tacon Theatre, on very reasonable terms, to any one who would bring an Italian opera, but refused to take the risk or responsibility himself.

Several influential persons and mercantile houses in Havana wrote to their commercial agents, Messrs. Negretti & Leoni, in New York, who, in their turn, applied to me just at a moment when the last row between myself and the directors of the Academy of Music in New York had taken place.

About the end of December, 1856, I started for Havana with a company, consisting of Mme. Anna de La Grange, Miss Adelaide Phillips, Mme. Bertucca-Maretzek, Miss Siedenberg, Brignoli, Ceresa, Amodio, Taffanelli, Coletti, and others, and a ready repertoire of all the old standard operas, and half-a-dozen new ones in that place; and after a pleasant trip of five days, arrived safely at our destination.

We were all young, light-hearted and careless, confident in our abilities and good luck. But owing to the suddenness of my resolution to go to Havana, and the haste of our departure from New York, there was hardly any time left for preliminary advertising, programs, pamphlets and other publications usual under similar circumstances, previous to our arrival in the capital of Cuba.

However, a ludicrous occurrence, on coming ashore, did all the necessary advertising for us, and saved the trouble and expense of extensive publicity.

Signor Amodio, whom many will yet remember as a man weighing about 300 pounds, with a body like a Heidelberg wine cask surmounted by the head of a young boy, had hardly made his appearance on the dock when a crowd of boys, fishermen and negroes surrounded him, jostled and cheered him and poked fun at him. Negretti and two *gens d'armes* had the greatest difficulty to move him along among the ever increasing crowd to the next stand of public conveyances, and when Amodio beheld for the first time in his life a Cuban *volante*, with the black driver on horseback, his legs encased in tops of gigantic cavalry boots reaching to his ears, with spurs strapped to his bare feet—his naked toes and heels protruding under the tops—a fit of laughter seized him, and he commenced to jeer at the driver in good Neapolitan lazzaroni style, who in his turn so chuckled at the sight of Amodio, as to nearly lose his equilibrium on his horse. The scene resembled the first meeting of *Papageno* and *Monostatos* in Mozart's " Magic Flute." At last Amodio was pushed from behind, or rather thrown inside the *volante*, but the light and fragile vehicle could not support the weight of Amodio. The bottom of the *volante*, consisting of a few tiny boards, caved in immediately.

and our baritone landed with his feet through the hole on the pavement. The horse, frightened by the shock, started, and Amodio, with his head above and his feet below the *volante*, had to run under a scorching sun about six blocks in the Calle Obispo, among repeated cheers and screams of the following crowd, until at last rescued by the police, who escorted and landed him safely at Legrand Hotel.

From that day until the end of the season, whenever Amodio approached a stand of *volantes*, there was a general stampede among the black drivers, who stoutly refused to carry and to have their *volantes* broken by that monster.

The incident of the morning, however, went like a wildfire through all classes of society in Havana, and without further advertising, before the evening of that day, every seat was taken for the first performance, as everybody was anxious to hear " E nino gordo " (the fat baby), as he was called thereafter in Havana.

The first evening, Mme. La Grange, Miss Anna Phillips, Brignoli and Amodio sang " Il Trovatore." The first three above-named were received by a cold audience, without the slightest token of welcome or encouragement at their several entrees, but before the end of the opera they had firmly established themselves in the favor and good graces of the public of Havana. Amodio, at his first appearance, was greeted by an outburst of Homeric laughter, several times renewed, before he was allowed to open his mouth. He stood it quietly without losing his temper, and seemed to enjoy beforehand the revenge he intended to take upon the audience with his singing; and hardly had he finished his first recitative, when the house again rang from pit to dome, but this time with prolonged applause. After his aria in the second act, " Il balen," the audience grew wild with enthusiasm, and Amodio became the spoiled fat baby of the Havanese.

The second evening, "Lucia di Lammermoor " did not fare so well as the " Trovatore." Sig. Ceresa, the *tenore robusto*, insisted, against the advice of friendly patrons of the opera, making his debut as *Edgardo*. The rendering of that part by Signor Salvi was yet too fresh in the memory of the public, and Ceresa, although displaying a powerful and clear tenor voice, was received and listened to in dead silence, in his duo with *Lucia*; and when toward the end of the first act he might have obtained some recognition by singing well the " Addio," with his beautiful high-chest notes, an unfortunate circumstance spoiled the finale. In entering to meet *Lucia*, he threw his hat, adorned with a curled feather, on the floor; and before taking leave, grasped for his hat, and without proper care put it on his head the wrong side. The feather, instead of curving gracefully behind his ear, covered his face, tickled his nose, crept into his mouth, choked his breath, obstructed the emission of the high B, and instead of himself singing the " Addio," the parquet rose like one man and screamed at the top of their voices, " Addio, Addio, Señor Ceresa!"

The parquet in the Tacon Theatre holds about 500 seats, exclusively occupied by gentlemen, and in the second act, when *Edgardo* had to sing the malediction, the gentlemen of the parquet kindly volunteered to help poor Ceresa, by shouting in unison each time the high A or B occurred. When the curtain went down, after the second act, the boys in the upper gallery applauded the gentlemen in the parquet, and screamed : " Bravo muy bien los tenores di abajo," and the parquet bowed to the gallery in mock acknowledgment of the compliment.

In Havana and in every Spanish theatre, one member of the *ayuntamento* (municipality) presides in the middle box facing the stage, as judge, to see that the performance be given as announced, without curtailments and without change of cast, unless previously agreed and approved by him, but also to keep order in the house and to prevent or subdue any disturbance on the part of the audience. Between the second and third acts on that evening, the presiding magistrate sent a few officers down in the parquet to forbid any further demonstration, and with the order to abstain from hissing, shouting and singing, and to give the poor tenor at least some chance to redeem himself.

The *caballeros* held a short consultation under the porch of the theatre, disappeared in different directions for a short time, but soon returned, after having ransacked a couple of toy-shops and having bought a hundred of crying-dolls. With solemn faces, like hired mourners at a funeral, they took their seats, but quietly placed a doll between their seats and themselves, and as soon as Sig. Ceresa began to sing his duet with *Ashton* (usually omitted in New York), there arose a sound of a hundred crying and weeping babies. Everybody in the boxes and galleries roared, and the officers looked around to find out where the crying came from, but no change of a muscle in any face in the parquet could be discovered. The following mad-scene was quietly listened to and applauded. But when *Edgardo* came out to sing his death scene, the audience rose and crept out of the house on tip-toe, avoiding the slightest noise; and before the recitative had ended, the luckless tenor was left alone with the orchestra in the vast house.

At the conclusion of that memorable performance of "Lucia," which I had conducted myself, on arriving on the stage from the orchestra, two young officers in full uniform approached me, and introducing themselves as *aids-de-camp* to Captain-General Concha, informed me that His Excellency desired me to call at the palace very early, between six and seven o'clock next morning.

"What does the General want of me?" I asked, rather gruffly, being out of humor in consequence of the proceedings during the performance.

"Perhaps he wishes to make your personal acquaintance," said one of them, the Marquis de Villanueva.

"Or to talk about operas and singing birds," interrupted the other, the Conde d'Oreilly.

"Operas and singing birds will soon take a homeward flight, if treated like cattle, and if there is no distinction here between an opera and a bull fight," I frankly answered.

"Be calm," retorted Villanueva. "The Captain-General does not receive at all bull-fighters, but considers an opera manager an official person, who, as such, should be in communication with him. Perhaps you can already perceive the distinction." Considering myself beaten by his remark, I bowed and promised to avail myself of the honor.

Shortly after six the next day, I went to the palace and found in the ante-room the same two *aides-de-camp*, who ushered me into the presence of General Concha.

He received me in the most affable manner, and invited me to walk with him up and down the hall, as he did not like to be seated so early in the morning.

"Do you speak the Castilian language?" he asked.

"Yes, but not so fluently as French or Italian."

"Well, let us speak French. How did you like the performance yesterday?"

"Which one do you mean, General; the one on the stage or off the stage?"

"Both," he answered.

"Well, the one on the stage cannot be judged, as there was no fair trial; but the one in the parquet seemed to me disgraceful."

"You hinted to my young men yesterday evening that you would return to New York if things continued that way."

"I did, my General, and, in fact, I don't think I could control the services of the singers if the authorities don't stop the coarse treatment to which they seem to be exposed."

"The authorities cannot well create a disturbance themselves by ejecting forcibly from the theatre 500 young men who have paid their subscription, and deprive them of the liberty of expressing their opinion; at least, at places of amusement. Neither you nor your artists should take it seriously."

"But, General, how can it be expected that artists will sing and act with a vim, knowing beforehand that they are exposed to insult; and please consider the position of an erratic impresario who left New York because he did not wish to give free boxes to the stockholders, and who is now expected, in Havana, to give the young men liberty to let off their overflowing spirits at his expense.

At the word "liberty," which I had emphasized a little, General Concha threw up his head and looked sternly at me, but when he heard the end of the sentence he resumed his affability and continued:

"I understand you and your position, and believe you ought to have a subvention like the Opera in Madrid, but the *ayuntamento* is too poor, and the Government has had, so far, to deal with Don Francisco Marti, who needs no subvention. However, I can give you some advice to abate the nuisance of interrupting the singers and help you indirectly to fill your treasury better than a paltry subvention could do."

"I would feel under the greatest obligation."

"Listen and don't interrupt me. First of all, put Sig. Ceresa on the bills again without fear, and in another opera than ' Lucia,' but have it circulated well in town that you and your company will leave the Island at the end of your first series of twelve nights, if the demonstrations of yesterday are repeated. I will have editorials written about your threats to withdraw in the *Official Gazette*, and you will see the result."

I thanked his Excellency and moved to retire, when he called me back and continued:

"I see that you have announced ' I Puritani' for next week."

"Yes, sir; and Mme. La Grange is immense as *Elvira*."

"I do not doubt it; she is really a great artist, but I suppose your Sig. Amodio must be very powerful in the so-called ' Liberty Duet' in the second act?"

This time it was his turn to emphasize the word "liberty" very ironically.

"Indeed, he electrifies the audience," I answered. "But I know we must not sing *liberta* here, but *lealta* instead, and I will instruct Amodio and Coletti on that point."

"How do you know that we substitute *lealta* for *liberta*?"

"Because Marini told me in New York that he once risked singing the word *liberta* in Havana, and was sent to the calaboose and fined $50."

"Oh, well! would Amodio risk to sing *liberta*?"

"He would risk it, certainly, if I asked it as a favor; and he would not mind a night in the calaboose, provided I promise to pay the fine and advance him a little more money on his salary."

"Then by all means make him sing *liberta* in the ' Puritani,' but it must be kept a secret, and the public must be taken by surprise."

"But, General, I really don't understand"—

"You will understand, when, by following my advice, your houses will be crowded and your pockets filled with ounces. We want the opera here, and in default of a subvention, you come, every week once to see me, and I will help you to manage the public of Havana, but will leave you to manage your artists alone."

I left with a light heart and in better spirits, and had no difficulty in inveigling Amodio into agreeing to sing, as requested, in "Puritani," and to surprise the public with it, which he considered capital fun.

On the evening of the performance of "Puritani," Mme. La Grange had renewed her former triumphs by the brilliancy of her execution, and had incited the audience to a demonstrative mood; but when Amodio, true to his promise, in the duo, poured out with his glorious voice, for the first time, the words "Gridando libertà," the public seemed struck with a terrific awe. Every head and eye turned with dreadful apprehension toward the box of the Captain-General, and not one of the usually noisy occupants of the parquet dared to give the slightest sign of approbation.

In ending the musical phrase Amodio had to repeat the same words, and did it most emphatically. General Concha, at the last note and word, leaned forward from his box so as to be seen from all points, and began to applaud furiously and to scream "Bravo! Amodio, Bis! Encore!" Such a storm of applause from every part of the house as then burst forth, such cheering addressed to Concha and Amodio has probably never before or since been witnessed inside any theatre, and it lasted several minutes before Amodio could comply with the request for repetition. At the conclusion of the opera the two *aides-de-camp* brought the message that I should announce in the morning papers the repetition of "Puritani" for three nights, by "special request." Of course, the house was crammed every night, and when I paid my respects again and expressed my thanks, General Concha said : "Don't you think that I know how to carry an opera without a subvention ?"

Emboldened by his kindness, I asked him to allow me to produce the opera of "Masaniello," which was prohibited and never before played in Havana.

"Masaniello ?" he said. "The Neapolitan rebel against Spanish rule. This is more serious than ' Puritani.' But who will sing *Masaniello ?*"

"Brignoli," I answered.

"Oh, he will do well for the slumber aria in the fourth act, but he won't create a revolution in Cuba! And who will be cast for *Pietro*, the conspirator ?

"Your Excellency seems to be very well acquainted with the opera of ' Masaniello.' Of course. Amodio will be *Pietro*."

"He is a jolly figure for a villain," he remarked laughingly. "Well, as it is a new opera here, send the libretto to the censor; I will see that he gives his permission; but if you wish to make money with such a cast in ' Masaniello,' I advise you to make Amodio dance a tarantella with *Fenella* in the market scene before the outbreak of the revolt."

I took the hint, and Amodio did dance a tarantella, and the public of Havana thought and pronounced "Masaniello" a capital opera bouffe.

The rest of the first season went off smoothly and successfully. The public appreciated and welcomed the artists even in their private houses, while the artists indulged in all the pleasures and temptations which the city and its beautiful surroundings offered.

One of the many temptations in Havana is the prevailing fashion of gambling among all classes, and the members of the opera company could not resist the contagion. Some of them played cards, but all, with the exception of the father of Miss Adelaide Phillips, invested heavily in lottery tickets, with the firm belief of drawing the capital prize and returning to New

York with a draft for a hundred thousand dollars in their pockets. Only Papa Phillips scorned and ridiculed the idea of buying a lottery ticket, and preferred to spend his loose cash in Spanish wines and French cognacs. He used to pass his leisure hours at the Café Escavorizza, next door to Legrand Hotel, tasting and discussing with the guests the merits of the different brands of Xeres and Manzanilla, listening to the encomiums bestowed upon his daughter Adelaide, and allowing himself to be treated to copious libations by her admirers.

One day a gentlemanly-looking fellow invited him to a drink, and, after repeating the dose half a dozen times, put his hands in his pockets and turned them inside out to find, to his real or assumed astonishment, that he had no money within. He excused himself and begged Papa Phillips to foot the bill, amounting to about $1, which Phillips stoutly refused, saying, in a loud voice, that he would sooner see the imposter in a warmer place than Havana than pay for drinks that he had not ordered himself. An altercation ensued which would have finished in blows had not the barkeeper and the bystanders interfered. The stranger again upturned all his pockets, and at last found, in a small watch pocket of his vest, a sixteenth of a lottery ticket, which he offered to Mr. Phillips, provided he paid the bill.

" I don't want to buy any of your deuced tickets and shall not pay a cent ! " vociferated Mr. Phillips; but when the barkeeper hinted that he might be obliged to send for the police, he indignantly threw down a silver dollar on the counter, snatched up the lottery ticket and left the place.

Three days after, the number of Mr. Phillips' ticket drew the first prize, and he pocketed for his sixteenth the sum of $6,250 in Spanish gold doubloons.

The extraordinary good luck of Papa Phillips excited the operatic artists to more gambling, but Dame Fortune is fickle, and like many other ladies, flirts often with one who treats her with indifference, and does not consent to notice the most assiduous followers. Many of the singers left the greater part of their earnings in the treasury of the " Real Lotteria," or deposited it with the cashiers of " faro banks." Amodio, the good-hearted and light-headed, even fell a prey to professional gamblers, who, probably with pin-marked cards, not only won all the salary of the guileless baritone, but contrived to make themselves his creditors for several thousand dollars. The day previous to our departure from Havana for Charleston and Philadelphia, where we were engaged to open the new Academy of Music, Amodio came with tears in his eyes and confessed to me that he owed gambling debts to a large amount to two well-known gamblers, and would be arrested if he should try to leave Havana with the company.

Apprehending some serious trouble for him and for me, my first thought was to remove him from the clutches of the gamblers, and my first consideration to secure his person for the opening of the new house in Philadelphia.

I promised to settle the matter, privately, if possible, provided he would go with me at once on board the steamer and remain there until we landed in Charleston. This proposition he at first refused, as, although frequently unscrupulous about paying his tailor or hotel bills, he believed his honor to be at stake in paying fraudulent gambling debts; but, upon arguing that a settlement would be easier if he was out of the way, and promising faithfully to accomplish a satisfactory arrangement with his creditors, he consented to be driven down to the steamer. Once there, I took Captain Adams (from Baltimore), a good, old and trusty friend, into my confidence, and begged him to treat Amodio in princely style, but to keep him a prisoner on board and not to allow any one to see him till next morning, all of which he promised and faithfully carried out.

From the boat I went straight to the Captain-General to tell him the story and ask his kind advice how to settle the matter on the easiest terms.

"What you have done with Amodio," he said, "is not strictly according to our laws, but these two gamblers are well known to the police, and are bad characters, who may play some unpleasant trick on Amodio if he does not pay; nor do I advise you to see them personally in negotiating a settlement, or be known as interfering at all. How much would you or Amodio pay for their claim?"

"Anything under $500," I answered.

"Well, say ten cents on the dollar. Go home, and if the Chief of Police calls on you and hands you a release from these worthy gentlemen, hand him over the amount."

Three hours after everything was done and settled as General Concha had proposed. Still, I did not think it advisable to let Amodio come on shore; and, obliged to explain his absence to the hotel keeper and answer anxious inquiries from the artists, I had to reveal his hiding place and the reasons of his concealment. Some members of the company, ever ready for a practical joke at the expense of the credulous Amodio, went early next morning on board and told him that the sheriffs and the police were after him, and would search the steamer, with warrants for his arrest. They succeeded in gaining the co-operation of the purser and engineer, and Amodio, trembling with apprehension of a prison in the Castle Moro, begged to be saved, and consented to be locked up in a dark coal-hole.

Every five or ten minutes they frightened him by sending some person down calling for Amodio, and insisting that they must find the man dead or alive, and would stop the departure of the steamer until he was found or delivered up. When I arrived on board later, I inquired for Amodio, and just when the steamer started I learned his whereabouts, and had him liberated. He appeared on deck with a black face, black hands, and black drops of perspiration running down his light-colored garments, amid shouts of laughter from the company, the passengers and crew; and when he was informed that everything was satisfactorily settled, he swore off gambling for the rest of his life.

The following year, returning to Havana, I introduced Mme. Frezzolini and Mme. Gazzaniga, who both were at that time at the zenith of their careers, and for the first time the great baritone, Giorgio Ronconi.

In dramatic intensity Mme. Gazzaniga had few rivals, and in the art of singing Mme. Frezzolini was superior to any of her predecessors in Havana. Mme. Gazzaniga made a hit in operas like "Sapho," "Medea," "Favorita," "Norma," and in the fourth act of "Traviata;" she surpassed any other Violetta on the stage, while Mme. Frezzolini in such operas as "Sonnambula," "Lucia," "Rigoletto" and others, could compare favorably with Jenny Lind and the present Adelina Patti. As a matter of course, a rivalry sprang up between the two prima donnas, and as each of them represented a different specialty each of them had their partisans and their admirers, and, in the same ratio as the two prima donnas tried to get the ascendancy, partly by their endeavors on the stage, partly by their intrigues off the stage, so their partisans developed into two antagonistic parties, culminating in a state of bitter hatred between the two singers and their followers.

The entire city seemed divided into two hostile camps, and even the ladies took part in the demonstrations; whichever of the two prima donnas sang in the evening was sure to be hissed by the opposite party and overwhelmed with applause and flowers by her friends. Politics was forgotten to the delight of the administration, and business neglected for the sake of arguing and discussing at home, in the streets, on the exchange, and in the hotels and cafés, the merits or the shortcomings of the prima donnas.

The treasury of the manager was the principal gainer by this war of prima donnas, and whenever one party gained an advantage over the opposition I immediately came to the rescue of the weaker, or beaten, party by pulling the wires in her favor, by giving her a better chance in the distribution of the repertoire and the casting of their operas, and did everything in my power not to let the raging fire die out for want of a gentle breeze in the right direction.

But in spite of all my diplomatic skill to sustain the balance of power between the belligerents, the " Gazzanigas " gained ground on the " Frezzolinis." The first husband of Mme. Gazzaniga, Marquis de Malaspina, having access to the aristocratic society of Havana, made easy proselytes for his wife among the nobility, while Frezzolini's energetic style pleased the gallery boys just as well. Frezzolini's party consisted of the *tiers-etat*, composed of artists, poets, musicians, students and foreigners, who could fully appreciate the poetry in Mme. Frezzolini's singing. The " Gazzanigas," more powerful and more bold, would not shrink from any stratagem, however Machiavellic, to insure success to their party and beat the opposition.

One evening, at a performance of " Traviata," Mme. Gazzaniga, at her entrance, received a shower of bouquets, but without acknowledging the compliments by the usual smiles and condescending bows, went off at once toward a cunning little white wreath, took it up, looked at it, threw it indignantly on the floor, and pushed it with contempt away with her feet. Her friends looked in astonishment, and the opposition began to hiss her for such disrespectful behavior, when she once more took up the same weed, stepped to the footlights and held the wreath at arm's length before the audience for their contemplation. It looked like a splendid crown of white little roses, and not even myself, sitting in the conductor's chair, could believe it to be otherwise. Having signified her intention to speak, the uproar ceased for a moment, and she burst out : " Es una corona de ajos " (it is a crown of garlic), at the same time glancing furiously at some of the well-known leaders of the opposition party.

From that moment the Frezzolini party was not only split but completely crushed, as everybody thought it his duty to revenge the insult offered to Marietta Gazzaniga. I, on my part, wondered how she could have singled out among so many flowers and crowns the particular one which needed an explanation as to its composing material, and a close inspection to distinguish it from real white roses.

Toward the end of the season I overheard a conversation of the French cook at Legrand's with his scullions, about the opera and the singers, and among other things I heard him say : " That was a fine and paying job—that crown of garlic which the Marquis of Malaspina had ordered."

Mme. Frezzolini did not care to contract any of these intrigues herself; nor did she allow her adorers to retaliate against Gazzaniga. She liked to employ her spare time in a more agreeable way, and to make a better use of her lovers, than to waste their time in plots and conspiracies against rival singers ; for while she sang like a syren on the stage, and enchanted the public at large, she acted also the part of a syren in private life, and drowned her adorers in a whirlpool of excitement. In her younger days she allowed many to fight for the glory of ruining themselves for her, and in her latter days she ruined herself for others, to enable her to continue a life of pleasure and extravagance. She died in poverty, after having earned more money than any singer, with the exception of Adelina Patti. She had sang only for about two decades, but had loved enough for two centuries.

Mme. Frezzolini, after the episode of the crown of garlic, refused any renewal of engagement for the next season in Havana. Her determination was a source of regret to the management, and a great loss to the lovers of the good, true, broad and genuine school of singing, which, with a few exceptions, is now passing away.

It cannot be denied that some great opera composers have engendered a characteristic speciality in the use of the voice, in order to give to their works a proper expression by which they are distinguished from all others; but there is and can be only one real and true method of singing, and whoever had fully acquired that only good manner of vocalization as in the sentimental strains of Bellini, in the dramatic expression required by Verdi, or in the declamatory recitations of Wagner, was an artist. Mme. Frezzolini belonged to that class of versatile artists who were equally good in rendering any composition from Mozart to Donizetti, and from Rossini to Verdi.

Whoever had the good fortune of seeing and hearing Frezzolini and Ronconi in the last act of " Maria di Rohan," as they appeared in Havana, will cherish the impression for the rest of their lives ; and whoever missed that opportunity will never understand how it is possible that the artistic merit and individual greatness of the performer can carry the listener so far as to make one admire an otherwise indifferent musical composition like Donizetti's " Maria di Rohan," and to cause a lasting emotion, such as the so-called intellectual music of the present composers would hardly be able to produce.

Having leased the Tacon Theatre for a third season, the determination of Mme. Frezzolini not to return placed the manager in an awkward position, as it was not only difficult to replace such a prima donna, but also necessary to find one who could counterbalance the power Mme. Gazzaniga exercised in Havana. At last my choice fell upon Mme. Gassier, whom I succeeded in engaging together with her husband, the famous baritone, M. Gassier, and the tenors Musiani and Errani. All of these engagements proved successful, and Mme. Gassier, being by birth a Spanish lady from Madrid, soon became the idol of the party of powerful Castilians, Catalonians and other proud scions of old Spain, while Mme. Gazzaniga retained the homage and support of the Cubans and American residents.

The war between the prima donnas and their adherents was renewed, but this season with an inkling of mixing politics with their quarrels about their merits and attractions, to the displeasure of the government but to the full satisfaction of the impresario and his treasurer. Considering that the greatest troubles and vexations that befall an operatic impresario consist of the disappointments caused to the public and himself by real or pretended hoarseness and colds of the singers, Havana is the promised land of managers —the Atlantis of managerial desire. If any singer notifies the manager of his or her inability to appear when announced, all the manager has to do, and is even obliged to do, is to send the communication to the presiding judge appointed for the current week, who, on his part, will take matters in hand, and first dispatch a doctor from the next police station or from the city hospital, and if said doctor reports that neither fever nor inflammation of the throat has been discovered, and the singer still refuses to appear, then a corporal and four soldiers will be intrusted with the delicate mission of seizing and delivering the reluctant artist safe and sound at the theatre, and there leave him the choice of advancing toward the stage before him, or retreating with four bayonets behind him.

Under these circumstances the singers were never backward in appreciating the points and moved eagerly forward to fulfill their duty. In fact it is seldom that the authorities or the artists carry matters further, and usually the visit of the official doctor, or a warning note on stamped paper, has the desired effect.

Once our esteemed Sig. Brignoli concluded that it would be desirable to be sick. The Marquis de Aguas Cearas, president of the *Ayuntamento*, sent a doctor to visit the distinguished tenor, and to report the result of his investigations. Unable to discover any alarming symptoms, except an insatiable appetite for macaroni and a sentimental longing for a *dolce far niente*, the gentlemanly young doctor ordered Brignoli to take a substantial dinner, and in the evening a drive to the opera, and to sing his part in the usual manner, and predicted to him a full restoration of health by following the advice.

The silver-voiced tenor shared the doctor's opinion as far as to the prescription of a good dinner, but demurred from the order of singing in the evening. The judge, upon hearing the doctor's report, sent a gentle warning to Brignoli, who, however, answered that the doctor who had visited him seemed, like *Crispino*, to be more a cobbler than a doctor, and did not understand his illness, whereupon the magistrate dispatched another doctor from the military hospital with two attendants.

After having felt Brignoli's pulse, looked into his throat and examined his eyes, the new doctor most solemnly declared, with a serious shake of his head, " really some precursory symptoms " of yellow fever, but that by employing 200 leeches immediately on the shoulders of the patient the great evil may be averted.

" Mama mia ! " screamed Brignoli, with his clear, beautiful, tenor voice, reaching with ease on that occasion the high B, " 200 leeches. You are a fool, but not a doctor ! I am perfectly well."

"No, hijo mio," replied the doctor, " you are sick and cannot sing to-night," giving at the same time instructions to his attendants for the operation.

" Clear out," vociferated Brignoli, " I will show you whether and how I can sing this evening."

And he did sing better than ever.

Any one can imagine the supreme relief a manager would feel by knowing that the paternal watchfulness of the government will not allow a disappointment to occur, and by carrying on the operatic business in a country where hoarseness and colds of singers are banished by law, and a refusal to sing for such reasons ignored.

But, alas ! there is a homely proverb which says: " You can drive a horse to the water, but cannot make him drink," and so you may take a hoarse singer to the stage, but cannot make him sing.

One fine day, when the weather was cool, and the *volantes* presented inviting charms, Mme. and M. Gassier thought a drive in the " Cerro " more pleasant than to sing in a concert announced for that evening. So she sent a short note to the manager " to change or omit their two pieces for this evening, as they were suffering from cold and sore throats."

Knowing that in the faithful island of Cuba the law denies to throats the privilege of catching colds, I laughed at the information, sent quietly the note to the judge for the week, took my afternoon nap, and dreamed never to be unhappy on account of other peoples' throats and lungs.

The doctor and the messenger found the residence of the Gassiers empty, and were informed that the pair had taken a drive to Marianao.

It may have been despotic, and certainly ungallant, but Mme. and M. Gassier were arrested on the road by mounted soldiers, their *volante* driven to the theatre, where they were delivered to the police, who actually brought them on the stage.

In his box, facing the stage, was the dignitary who had ordered their arrest directing savage glances on the couple when they made their entry. The orchestra struck up the *ritornello* for their duet, and the audience listened.

But they may be listening yet, for the resolute culprits (she crying, he laughing) refused to open their mouths. They were fined $100 each, but did not sing one note.

The stream was there, but the team would not drink !

Mme. Gassier had a voice as clear, flexible, and extensive as Frezzolini, but did not sing with the same grace and feeling. She had also the same instincts as Frezzolini, but added intemperance and a quick Spanish temper to the other foibles of her charming predecessor.

Frezzolini, who had married Sig. Poggi, a famous tenor, left him immediately after having discovered his *liaison* with the Russian Princess Samoileff.

Mme. Gassier, on a similiar occasion, did nothing of the kind, but taught her husband to understand that the sauce which is good for a gander like him may also be tried for a turtle dove like her. And M. Gassier was a docile scholar, made great progress in the profession of henpecked and accommodating husbands, and succeeded so far as to consider those his best friends who paid homage to his wife, and to hate any one who seemed indifferent to her charms and talents. Mme. Gassier exerted herself to the utmost of her powers and consequently M. Gassier had plenty of friends in Havana and hardly any enemies.

Mme. Gassier, too, died too soon for having lived too much.

CHAPTER V.

THE NEW YORK ACADEMY OF MUSIC UNDER THE REGIME OF BERNARD ULLMANN AND MAURICE STRAKOSCH.

The time for the realization of the loftiest aspirations and the highest ambitions of Mr. Ullmann had at last arrived after my departure for Havana, and the conclusion of the thirty days' merry war between myself and the board of directors of the Academy of Music.

On the twenty-fourth day of February, 1857, Mr. Bernard Ullmann and Sigismund Thalberg became the lessees of the Academy, but before the expiration of one week Mr. Thalberg, for the sum of $1 paid in hand, "did sell, assign and transfer all his rights, titles, etc.," of said lease to Mr. Ullmann. The fact is that Mr. Thalberg, perceiving that all the monetary burdens of the enterprise would fall upon him alone, did not "sell for $1 his rights, etc.," but bought his release from Ullmann by advancing to his penniless partner a few thousand dollars, to enable him to begin operations. But in Thalberg's place, Mr. Maurice Strakosch—till then a confirmed enemy of Ullmann—stepped in and formed a partnership with the very man whom for years he had abused publicly and privately. Common instinct makes strange bedfellows. Both of these gentlemen, however, were men of great talent as managers, although their tactics ran in opposite directions; which, however, for that very reason made them more dangerous to any concurrent manager. Mr. Ullmann had a decided talent for advertising, a clever way of putting himself in communication with the public, and shaping his announcements like confidential communications of his business affairs; and he possessed an extraordinary capacity for combinations, schemes and intrigues without being overscrupulous concerning truth and good faith. Still he was honest in his intentions to pay any of his obligations, very sober in his habits and modest in his expenses for his own wants; but he would not shrink from wasting any money of his own or of his friends to do some harm to his opponent. As an administrator he was not better than an innocent child. He would lay in bed till two o'clock in the afternoon scheming which artists he would try to engage next season, or which opera he would play on a certain day twelve months hence, but would not inquire what was going on that very same day at the Academy, or where the money was to come from for the payment of the artists next day. It was, therefore, a stroke of good luck for him to have found a partner in Maurice Strakosch, who was a matter-of-fact business man, a believer in the star system, with one great artist at a high salary, and all the rest as economical as possible; a man remarkable for the sauvity of his manners; a kind of everybody's friend, on and off the stage. His system of managing was to invent the most extravagant and exaggerated puffs for his star, and thus to centre the attention, or rather the curiosity, of the public on one particular artist, and by ignoring the rest of his company, not to raise great expectations for his other artists. He used to say that out of a thousand persons ten might laugh at his puffs and biographies, but 990 were fools enough to bite at the hook, and he added that those ten who laughed would procure for him as much publicity by their jokes as the 990 by their credulity. He opened a preliminary short season early in 1857 with Parodi, Cora de Wilhorst, and the tenor Tiberini, whom he announced as a lineal descendant of the Emperor Tiberius of ancient Rome. Cora de Wilhorst, a charming little American society lady, with a charming little voice, and a charming little temper, made her debut, under his management, on the 28th of January, 1857, as *Lucia* to the noble Roman's *Edgardo*.

After maturing well their plans of action, the new managers concluded to pursue a different course to the one adopted by me, and instead of fighting the stockholders, to worm their way into their good graces. They proposed to make alterations in the auditorium, to build front boxes in the first tier instead of the seats until then in use, and to let the stockholders occupy said boxes. Formerly the stockholders were scattered through the house, and could hardly be distinguished from the rest of the audience; now they spread themselves out in the front boxes, free of any charge, and could look with contempt on those common people who for their money had to take back seats! The ladies of railroad kings and financial nabobs, of course, could never consent to sit behind the wives of lawyers, grain merchants and hoop-skirt manufacturers; and as only a limited number of front boxes, and only a certain number of stocks could be sold, the shares of the Academy of Music naturally rose in value, but the popularity of the house as a place of amusement suffered greatly in consequence of the hostility of the paying middle classes to the exclusiveness and mannerisms of the non-paying stockholders. To counteract the bad impression caused in public opinion by the occupation of the front boxes by stockholders, and to cover the gaps in the benches of the parquet, Mr. Ullmann resorted to the expediency of filling the house with so-called deadheads. Three young employees, Mr. Henry Palmer, Mr. Jacob Grau, Mr. J. Gosche (all three afterward managers themselves), were daily occupied in selecting names from the city directory, and three boys in mailing free tickets to doctors, clergymen, politicians, and journalists, etc., in order to give the house an appearance of increasing popularity and a thriving business. In order to prove that I am not exaggerating. I hereby republish one of the circulars usually enclosed in the envelopes with the free tickets:

NEW YORK ACADEMY OF MUSIC, September 7, 1857.

DEAR SIR: By and with the consent of Mr. Maurice Strakosch, my partner, I have the pleasure of informing you that we have determined to continue during the present opera season the system introduced, with regard to the free list, at Mr. Thalberg's concerts.

We shall be pleased if you will honor us with your attendance at the opera, and accept the admission ticket that will reach you in the same way as for last winter.

We seize the present opportunity to recommend to your notice the great number of stars who will appear at the opera next season, and respectfully request you to lend us your valuable assistance in enabling us to successfully carry out a grand undertaking, requiring so much risk and labor.

I am, dear sir, your obedient servant,

B. ULLMANN.

Mr. Ullmann then had not yet learned that deadheads are the most severe critics, and that any person who once goes to the theatre on a free ticket will sooner agree to pay for a $10 supper at Delmonico's after the opera than ever again give the entrance fee of $1.

As if the introduction of the star, and the dead head system, and the yielding of more privileges to the stockholders were not enough to ruin any management, Messrs. Ullmann and Strakosch undertook to regulate also the press, that powerful *tiers etat* between the public and the artists in the realm of an opera manager, and while Mr. Strakosch determined only to advertise in the *Herald, Times* and *Tribune*, to the exclusion of all other daily and weekly papers, Mr. Ullmann indulged in a quarrel with the editors of the *Courier des*

Etats Unis stigmatizing Messieurs Lassalle, Arpin and De Trobriand as the "Three hungry Frenchmen," and insulting personally Mr. George Wilkes, of the *Spirit of the Times*. The gentlemen from the *Courier des Etats Unis* retorted in the truly French fashion by throwing ridicule and sarcasm upon Mr. Ullmann, but Mr. Wilkes had a "big pull" on political gangs in New York, who one evening invaded the Academy of Music and prevented the peaceable performance until Mr. Ullmann had made an apology from the stage through a proxy, his lawyer, Mr. Moultrie.

That under these circumstances, and under many other difficulties, as will be hereafter narrated, Messrs. Ullmann and Maurice Strakosch still held out at the Academy for three years can only be accounted for by their otherwise clever management on the stage, and by the excellence of some of the artists whom they succeeded in engaging from time to time.

The principal features of their *regime* were the introduction of the conductor Karl Anshutz and the basso Formes in 1857, the engagement of Marie Piccolomini in 1858, and the debut on the operatic stage of Adelina Patti in 1859.

The name of Karl Formes is known in every household in Germany, England, and the United States, and if anything could be stronger than his voice it was his own good opinion of himself.

Once there were at the same time Lablache, Marini, Staudigl, and Formes in London during the summer season. Opinions were divided which of them ought to be considered the greatest basso, and a party of gentlemen at the Parthenon Club determined to have the four gentlemen interviewed and to ask each of them the question, whom they considered the greatest basso in London. Modest Staudigl immediately answered: "Without any doubt Lablache is the best." Lablache replied: "If Staudigl were not here I would believe myself the best, but I cannot decide whether it is me or him." Marini, after thinking the matter over, said: "I cannot say who is the *first* basso in London, but I am sure Lablache is the *second*." Formes, without any hesitation, at once exclaimed: "The greatest basso, sir? *That's me!*" And I admit that in "Robert le Diable," in the "Huguenots," in the "Jewess," Formes was the best I ever heard in any country; but in Italian operas I preferred Lablache and Marini, and in all kinds of operas Staudigl could rival any of them.

I will now follow the example of modesty and good nature set by Staudigl, and declare that Karl Auschutz, whom Ullmann brought over in opposition to me, was the best operatic conductor and one of the most versatile and learned musicians we ever have had in this country. I wish it well understood that I say the best *operatic* conductor, and do not intend to infringe upon the claims of others as conductors of symphonies, oratorios, etc. Mr. Theodore Thomas is the prince of symphony conductors, but too rigid for operas. Herr Seidl has specialty for Wagner's music-dramas, but is a great deal too careless for the operas of other composers. While Sig. Arditi is superior in pure Italian opera, he cannot compare with Anschutz in classical operas and even those of the French school. The late Dr. Damrosch was the best oratorio conductor here, but, with the exception of "Die Walkure" and others of Wagner's, a poor opera conductor. His directing operas like "Masaniello" and "Jewess" were, the least said, more the work of an amateur than a maestro. Muzio knew only the operas of Verdi well, and Bergmann was too timid for opera. In versatility, at least, I believe Adolf Neuendorf to come nearest to Karl Anshutz. As regards myself, who for many years have been called the Napoleon of opera conductors—I am—in St. Helena! But I only wish to express my individual opinion about the different conductors, knowing too well how fallacious criticisms of musicians are concerning their fellow-musicians. It is known that doctors disagree, but they observe certain rules of etiquette and usually polite intercourse between themselves. Politicians disagree and quarrel, but submit nowadays to the vote of the majority. Religious creeds disagree and hate each other heartily, but modern civilization has compelled them to keep the peace. But none more than musicians disagree in their opinions, tastes and theories. Mendelssohn wrote about Berlioz to his mother, in 1831, from Rome : " Berlioz is a real caricature, without talent, groping in the dark and writing detestable music!"

Richard Wagner, in the Paris *Menestrel*, October 4, 1854, is accused of saying about Berlioz generally, and about his Symphonie Fantastique : " It contains many faults and offenses against good taste and artistic economy, without any beauty of form. It is extremely audacious, but also extremely disagreeable."

Blaze de Bury, a distinguished French critic, published, in 1838, in the *Revue des Deux Mondes :* " Mr. Berlioz enters the arena of art with the ferocious instincts of a Jacobin of 1793. I defy any one to record that Mr. Berlioz has respected any glorious tradition, whether of melody, rhythm or human voice. Melody usually escapes from him, and if, perchance, he catches one, he would torture it with a barbarous glee, just as a bad boy would pluck the feathers of a live bird."

And Berlioz ! Did he not in his letters call the composer of " Norma " and " Puritani " a " petit polisson " (a little blackguard) "by the name of Bellini?" and the composer of " Saffo " (Pacini) " miserable eunuch ?" and did he not say that the music of Donizetti's opera, " The Elixir of Love," made him " shiver as if insects were crawling over his body ?" Even Haydn said of Beethoven, that " he is a great pianist and nothing more." Handel said that " his cook was just as good a musician as Gluck." And Rossini remarked that " Wagner had some fine moments but ugly quarter-hours " (" Quelques beaux moments, mais de fichus quatre d'heures.") And everybody remembers the opinion of Richard Wagner about Meyerbeer, Mendelssohn, and Halévy, and about " Judaism " in music. The matter has been sufficiently discussed, but why does not some illustrious critic take up the theme, spin it out, or make variations by just as well accusing Rubinstein, Glinka, and Dvořák of " Panslavism," Rossini and Verdi of fervent " Catholicism," Robert Schumann of frigid " Calvinism," Berlioz and Massenet of " Chauvinism," Offenbach and Lecocq of " Mormonism," and Wagner of " Teutonic Mysticism ?"

The theories of the so-called Wagnerites about the union of poetry, music, painting, and stage effects are nothing new, and in substance can be found already advocated and expounded in Jean Jacques Rousseau's " Dictionary of Music." (See article on Opera, " Edition Veuve Duchesne," Paris, 1762.) Nor are the fiery polemics of the adherents of Wagner and their opponents anything new. Over a hundred years ago exactly the same bitter partisanship existed between the Gluckists and the Piccinists, which often degenerated into personalities during the performances between the different parties. It happened once that in Gluck's " Alceste," at the Academy Royale in Paris, Mlle. Levasseur had to sing in the finale of the second act the words " Il me dechire et m'arrache le coeur" (He is breaking and tearing my heart). A confirmed adherent of Piccini screamed from one of the boxes, " and you are tearing my ears out with such music." . . Immediately a Gluckist rose from the parquet and roared at the fellow in the box : " Lucky for you if she did. Now go and procure a new pair of ears and get them a little shorter." All this proves that however honest musical criticisms, whether approving or condemning, they are in general unreliable; and as I am neither a Berlioz nor a Haydn, my opinion about Mr. Karl Anshutz need not offend the musical conductors in New York of the present day. It is, however, an undeniable fact that to Karl Anshutz and to Karl Formes belong the honor of the first season of 1857–58 under Ullmann's management. The principal artists, besides Formes, were the soprano Mme. Caradori, the contralto D'Angri, the tenors Bignardi and Labocetta, and the baritone Gassier. Mme. La Grange and Mme. Frezzolini also appeared for a few nights. The only novelties produced during the season were Beethoven's "Fidelio," in Italian, and Wm. H. Fry's opera of "Leonora"—the libretto founded on Bulwer's "Lady of Lyons." Fry's opera was produced on January 20, 1858, and made a very favorable impression.

Artistically the first season of B. Ullmann and Maurice Strakosch was a success, but financially it had the same fate as the usual operatic enterprises at the Academy of Music. And to make things worse, Messrs. Ullmann and Strakosch were hemmed in and bottled up in New York and could not profitably make the usual excursions to Philadelphia and other places, as I had a special agreement with Mr. E. A. Marshall, lessee of the new Philadelphia Academy of Music, to produce my Havana Companies exclusively in that house, and usually stole a march on the New York managers by getting before the end of their New York season to Boston and to take off the cream of the Boston patronage. Boston has always been considered the best city for a short season of three weeks, the Mecca of believers in operatic ventures, the surest resort to recuperate for damaged managers to replenish the empty cash-box, and the progress which Boston has made in musical matters since 1850 is wonderful. Yes, I remember well the time when Boston glorified in the possession of a Philharmonic society and all the accessories pertaining to it, with the exception, however, of an orchestra, a chorus, and good singers; and how, in order to remedy such small inconveniences, I was induced by Mr. Marsh, the vice-president of that society, to come every Saturday during the winter season, with the orchestra and the artists of the New York Astor Place Opera House, to act as auxiliary supernumeraries in the concerts of the Philharmonic Society of Boston. Fridays being the fashionable opera nights, we had to leave New York early in the morning each Saturday, and after a tedious journey, perform in the evening at the Tremont Temple; and as the trains did not run with such speed as nowadays, and were sometimes detained on the road by snowbanks, it often happened that, to be in time for the concert, we had to change our dress in the cars and hasten without a meal from the depot to the concert-room. But such a rush as Truffi, Benedetti, Beneventano and Rossi used to make after the performance to the hospitable supper rooms at the Tremont House, where mountains of macaronies awaited them, and the bee-line which the German fiddlers and blowers made for Pfaff's Hotel to moisten their quivering lips and parched tongues!

You may think that the orchestra, after the fatigue of travel and the exertions at the concert and the revels at Pfaff's, retired, as well-behaved provisory members of the Boston Philharmonic Society ought to do. Not at all. Mr. Marsh, the vice-president of the honorable society, gave them a bad example, and being kind of a *Lovelace* in Boston, induced them, by the promise of more beer, to start out again in the middle of the night to serenade his lady acquaintances, and thus to disturb the slumbers of the solid men of Boston during the first hours of the Sabbath. The night watchmen, also influenced by Mr. Marsh, usually retired in good order at the approach of the flying band of musicians, and adjourned to enjoy a quiet nap somewhere far enough from the scenes of disturbance. Sunday mornings the orchestra performed in the parlors of Pfaff's Hotel sacred operas (?) until, one fine Sunday morning, the whole orchestra and all the guests were bagged by the police, and I had great trouble to bail them out and liberate them in time for the Monday morning train for New York.

Boston at that time was called the "Athens" of America; and, in fact, there were there many wise men, philosophers, legislators, etc.

And I remember, some years after, the several opera companies that could be heard in Boston at the old Howard and at the Federal Street Theatre. There were Steffanone, Bosio, Tedesco, Salvi, Bettini, Badiali, Marini in one and the same company; and not one of these singers pretended to be a "star,' nor did the managers present them as such or charge exorbitant prices of admission Still, the Boston public knew how to appreciate, already, at that time, a good opera, and the rush was such an unprecedented one that the seats had to be put at auction, and brought on some occasions $18 each! No city in America can show such a record of musical enthusiasm and liberality.

And I remember once at the Howard Athenæum, when Mme. Barili-Patti, the mother of the Patti sisters, sang the part of *Norma*, with Amalia Patti as *Adalgisa*, and Adelina Patti figured as one of the children of *Norma*. Adelina, then a little child, insisted at rehearsal singing also the music with her mother and sister during the duo of " Mira, Norma," and when, after several admonitions she would still continue to sing, her irascible mother took her up and gave her a regular spanking before the eyes of the assembled orchestra and the members of the company. Now Adelina Patti receives $4,000 a night for singing instead of a spanking.

And I remember at another occasion of a performance of " Norma," sung by Theresa Parodi and Amalia Patti at the Federal Street Theatre, when the two children of *Norma* in the same scene acted " so naturally " that Parodi ran off the stage, Amalia Patti fainted, and the curtain had to be dropped amidst the shouting and roaring of the audience.

And I remember well old miser Paine, who was then considered the best musical critic in Boston, and who for many years used to beg for free tickets and free meals, which, in my belief of his extreme poverty, I never refused. His leaving half a million dollars after his death is too well known to be discussed over again. After my first season in Havana I opened the new Academy of Music in Philadelphia in February, 1857, and returned again the following year.

These excursions to Philadephia and Boston proved detrimental to the interest of Mr. Ullmann, and his only resource to partly balance the deficits of the opera were concert tours with Mr. Thalberg and with some of his singers, principally with Mme. Elena D'Angri, who before the advent of Alboni, was recognized as one of the best contraltos, and had been singing in all the capitals of Europe before her arrival in America. Mme. D'Angri in her many travels had learned all that is worth knowing, and, among other things, how to entangle a gentleman who had no other occupation except playing occasionally two of his own compositions on the piano, and who consequently must have felt lonesome all the rest of his time. Mme. D'Angri, who in manners and character greatly resembled *Mme. d'Angot*, had a young and handsome daughter not unlike *la Fille de Madame d'Angot*

The mother invited Mr. Thalberg to pass his leisure hours in her parlor ; and there and then they managed to cobweb Mr. Thalberg and amuse him by teaching him to play the part of *Ange Pitou*.

This paraphrase of Lecocq's opera bouffe had two conseqences. The first was the sudden arrival of Mrs. Thalberg (a daughter of the great basso

Lablache), in Boston, which caused the sudden departure of Thalberg from New York without waiting for the fond embraces of his wife, and the second consequence was the debut of a granddaughter of Mme. D'Angri, under the name of Mlle. Thalberg, about twenty years later, as *Zerlina* in "Don Giovanni" at London.

For their second year, beginning October, 1858, Ullmann and Maurice Strakosch succeeded in making arrangements with Mr. Lumley by which Mlle. Marietta Piccolomini was transferred to the New York managers for the consideration of a certain share of the receipts for her services. The rest of their company included as principal artists Mme. Laborde, Mme. Poinsot; the tenors Tamaro and Perring; the baritones Gassier and Ardavani; and the bassos Formes and Susini. The only novelty produced was Donizetti's "Poliuto."

Marietta Piccolomini was born in Sienna in 1834, and claims to be a descendant of the ancient noble family of the Piccolominis, who counted in their genealogy some members who filled the posts of generals, cardinals, and even one pope—Pius II.

Mr. Maurice Strakosch, not satisfied with even such a distinguished relationship of his prima donna, announced her as a lineal descendant of Charlemagne, and a great-grand daughter of Max Piccolomini, the hero of Schiller's tragedy of "Wallenstein."

Marietta Piccolomini was a sprightly, graceful, bewitching young lady, with an everlasting smile on her face, and a clear, light, flexible soprano voice. Her pronunciation was distinct and her manners fascinating. These qualities lent a certain charm to her impersonations in "Traviata," "Daughter of the Regiment," "Don Pasquale," *Zerlina* in "Don Giovanni," and in others capable of expressing coquetry varying with a certain amount of tender feeling; but her petite figure and her vivacity in acting did not fit her for tragic roles. After having sung in various theatres in Italy, she obtained an engagement from Mr. Lumley, of Her Majesty's Theatre in London, where she made her successful debut in "Traviata" on May 24, 1856; and repeated her triumph in the same opera in Paris on December 6 of the same year. After her season in America she returned to London in 1859, and the following year retired from the stage on fulfilling a matrimonial engagement with the Marquis Gaetani.

Owing to the heavy expenses of so large a company, and to the lion's share—which Mr. Lumley took out—of the receipts, the financial affairs of Ullmann and Maurice Strakosch were not in a prosperous condition, and salaries could not be paid regularly

Maurice Strakosch, as a business man, proposed to pay only seventy-five per cent. of the salaries, and to remain indebted for the rest. Mr. Ullmann, as a visionary dreamer, objected, and asked: "Supposing the artists should accept three-fourths of their appointments this week, how will we do the following week to pay the full amount and the shortcomings of this week?"

"Well, next week, if we cannot pay all, we will offer them instead of seventy-five per cent. only sixty per cent. What can they do? They will take it and wait for the rest."

"Oh, my dear Maurice, I see! You wish to try the same experiment as the peasant did with his donkey—by giving every day a little less oats to see whether, with time and patience, he may get accustomed not to eat at all."

"Exactly so," replied Maurice; "but I hope we may be able not to let the donkeys starve."

"I have not the courage to propose it."

' Well, then, you will go into the office and pay out, and I will remain outside and speak to each one before he or she enters to get their money."

With his suave and insinuating manners, the honey-tongued Maurice persuaded his artists to accept that week a reduction, and little Ullmann, in closing the office, said to Strakosch : " You are a great farmer. The donkey was satisfied."

" Oh, he will get accustomed to it, if necessary," said Maurice.

For several weeks the artists patiently took what they could get ; but one day Sig. Susini listened with bad grace to the sweet words of Maurice, and entered Mr. Ullmann's office. Unfortunately the moneys for all the artists were laying on the table, and when Ullmann offered to big Susini half salary, the discontented basso grasped with one hand at the pile before him, and half seriously and half jesting, with a tremendous knock of his other hand on the table, he said · " You have here the money; either you pay me all or I kill you."

" Help ! help ! murder ! thieves ! help !" screamed the easily frightened Ullmann, at the top of his falsetto voice, and Maurice rushed in. " What's the matter? What's happened ? What's the difficulty ?"

" What's the matter ?" sneered the trembling little Ullmann. " There ! the donkey kicks; your donkey, Mr. Strakosch, declines to be accustomed; this donkey wants all the oats he sees before him."

Mr. Susini himself could not help laughing at the scene, and good humoredly relaxed his grasp on the money and took what was intended for him.

Previous to the arrival of Piccolomini, Messrs. Ullmann and Maurice Strakosch, fearing again my flank movements to Philadelphia and Boston, after my return from Havana, had come to the conclusion to arrange a *modus vivendi* between ourselves, and at the first convention between us Mr. Ullmann in an off-hand manner proposed that " he should remain alone in peaceable possession of New York, Philadelphia, Boston and all the Atlantic cities; that Maurice Strakosch should take the west and south of the United States, and that I might keep Havana, the West Indian Islands, and add to it, if I chose, Mexico." Maurice Strakosch objected, because, not that he cared for the lease of the Academy of Music, but he wanted his headquarters in New York for his concert tours, and I objected, because I doubted that Spain, Mexico and the United States would sanction Ullmann's proposed partition of their territory.

It was, however, agreed that for a small sum of money I should give up playing in Philadelphia and Boston during the following spring and summer, that I might have a preliminary fall season to rehearse and prepare my company for Havana, and that sometimes we should exchange artists. This agreement was kept on both sides for more than a year, but the restless mind of Mr. Ullmann did not allow him to control his disposition for mischief, and if by his agreement he felt restrained from scheming against my business he delighted to play practical jokes on me, with the intention of having a laugh at me, or to expose me to some ridicule, or to cause me some inconvenience.

Every business man has some moments when he may be short of money and obliged to ask credit, and opera managers are not the exceptions to this rule; on the contrary, they have seldom moments where they are out of debt. It therefore happened that a certain tenor had a claim of several hundred dollars against me, which I promised him to pay on my next return to Havana, and as he intended to leave for Europe and assign his claim to a friend, I agreed to confess a judgment to quiet him and his assignee and guarantee them against any possible litigation. On my return I had sent with the previous steamer an invoice of 10,000 fine Partagas cigars, partly ordered by some friends, which I had promised to buy for them, and partly for presents and for my own use. Ullmann had seen in the list in the

Journal of Commerce the arrival of a case of 10,000 cigars for Maretzek. He could not resist the temptation to cause me some disappointment and to have some fun at my expense, and persuaded my judgment creditor to seize on the cases of cigars, and thus insure my immediate payment or to sell those goods. The sheriff seized, but could not remove the goods without the payment of duties, which amounted to about $200. My creditor had no money. Ullmann then advanced the funds to pay the duties, and the case was removed by the sheriff.

On my arrival I was informed by Deputy Sheriff Mr. Bensel of the mean trick that had been played on me, and that unless I paid the judgment, the costs and the duties, he had to sell the cigars at public auction, adding at the same time that it was no business of his for how much they must be sold as long as the sheriff's fees of about $60 were covered. I told him to sell, but requested him to sell soon, and to kindly, as a favor, to notify me when they were to be sold.

"Of course I will notify you, and the other parties too," Mr. Bensel answered.

On the day of the sale I and my friends, Negretti and Leoni, commission merchants from William street, were at the sheriff's sale before ten o'clock; nobody else being yet present, Mr. Negretti alleging that he had a great deal of business to attend to during the day, asked whether Mr. Bensel would not at once put up at auction that certain case of cigars, as there were three buyers for it present. Mr. Bensel, with a slight twinkle in his eye, said: "All right, the sooner we sell it the better." Mr. Leoni bid $20 for the case, I went $20 better, Negretti $20 more; I offered $70 all, Negretti $80. "Going, going, going—nobody more? Eighty dollars, eighty dollars, I am offered —nobody more? One, two, three; nobody more? Sold!" Ten minutes later the case of 10,000 Paratgas Napoleons were in Negretti's office, and about eleven o'clock Mr. Ullmann, my judgment creditor and their lawyer leisurely walked in and for an hour waited in anticipation of the sale of cigars. At last the lawyer asked when that case of cigars would be sold.

"What cigars?" asked Mr. Bensel indifferently.

"Don't you know? Those 10,000 Partagas cigars sent by Maretzek to his own order, which you have seized and announced for sale to-day."

"Oh, yes; I remember now," said the sheriff, as if awaking from a dream. "Those cigars? Yes, yes, they are sold."

"What, sold! When sold? For how much sold?" vociferated the lawyer.

"Sold two hours ago for $80; there remains after paying my fees about $17 for you," replied the sheriff, at the same time offering for sale a lot of grappling irons with five claws.

"Heavens!" ejaculated the creditor. "My judgment!" "H——l!" interrupted the lawyer. "My costs and fees!" "Alas!" cried Ullmann, "my $200 duties paid."

The same evening I went to dinner at Buhler's restaurant, corner of Eighth street and Broadway, where Ullmann used to take his meals, and after dinner I offered him a half dozen Partagas cigars, which I told him I bought that very morning at auction. "I owe you one," said Ullmann, but accepted the cigars.

The judgment, however, I settled, and the satisfaction-piece is still in my hands.

After the second year of their management, Ullmann & Strakosch, with hat in hand, begged for a loan to enable them to engage new artists for the ensuing year, and obtained from twenty-four patrons, some of them stockholders, at the rate of $500 from each, the sum of $12,000, on condition that all moneys received for subscription or from the daily receipts should be taken by their representative, Mr. Kingsland, and by him paid out to artists and employees, and the remainder, if any, to be divided among these twenty-four liberal patrons.

By this transaction the two managers became merely unpaid agents of Mr. Kingsland and servants of twenty-four masters, who, instead of helping them, only accelerated their speed in reaching the end of their managerial career at the New York Academy of Music.

Strakosch engaged in Europe for the season 1859-60 the tenor Beaucardè, the baritone Ferri and Mme. Albertini, three very good artists in their prime, but rather played out when they came to America, and two young prima donnas, Signora Crescimano and Signora Speranza. The last two were dismal failures. After the debut of Mlle. Speranza, Strakosch asked my opinion and I answered with Dante's " Ogni speranza lasciate."

Muzio was the conductor, and brought out for the first time Verdi's "Sicilian Vespers," which so far only drew a few paying houses. In this emergency Mr. Maurice Strakosch proposed to his partner Ullmann, to produce as an opera singer little Adelina Patti, who until then had only been singing in different concert tours with Gottschalk, Ole Bull and Strakosch. Adelina Patti made her first appearance in public under my own direction in a concert at Trippler Hall seven years before, in February, 1852. She was then a child of about nine years, and at that early age not only gave evidence of her precocity in vocalizing, but also in making bargains. The conditions on which she agreed to sing then were a hatful of candies, and she insisted upon receiving it before she went out to appear before the public.

The story in Mr. Mortier's " Biography," that she came out before the audience with her doll in her arms, and that she had to be lifted on a table to be seen, is like many other items narrated by Mons. Mortier—all bosh! Adelina at that time already knew better than playing with dolls. Adelina made her operatic debut November 24, as *Lucia di Lammermoor*, and at once created a furore. The season was saved so far as to enable the managers to carry it to its end without interruption; but as Patti could not sing every night, and her repertoire was yet very limited, the performances without Adelina were sung to empty benches and the treasury was at the end of the season in a lamentable condition. The successful debut of Adelina Patti and the ovations she received every time she appeared stirred up the ambition of every young girl in New York who had any voice, to become a great prima donna. Only few, however, succeeded; among them Miss Kellogg, Miss Minnie Hauk, Laura Harris, Mme. Durand, Morensi, Anna Louise Cary, Mrs. and Miss Van Zandt, and nearly all of these were introduced by me to the public and entered through me on a career of prosperity and renown. But among the aspirants to fame and glory were many cranks, as is usually the case, and it is incredible to believe the craziness of many letters I used to receive during my administration of the opera. I cannot refrain from publishing one as a sample of human folly.

" February 7, 1864.

" Mr. Maretzek:

" *Sir :* I desire to see you in relation to my voice, I am a young widow lady from the South, and about six months ago, at a spiritual circle, *Malibran* appeared and said she would throw her voice into me, and advised me go upon the stage as a singer, I was a skeptic, but latterly my voice has astonished myself and friends. I can range a note as high as Jenny Lind in F, and can warble and trill naturally. I never had any instruction in music; as you will perceive, I am a natural singer, if such can be. I desire to see you

ADELINA PATTI.

Mon cher Maretzek

Voulez vous remercier de ma part
M. M^{rs} et Mesdames les choristes du
Th. de sa majesté, et les prévenir
que nous répèterons le chœur des
Sylphes avec l'orchestre Mardi
prochain 27 à midi à Hanover
Square Room. Je compte sur votre
obligeante amitié pour venir mettre
en ordre le chœur et le disposer
comme il devra être disposé pour
le jour du concert. Cela ne vous
prendra que peu de temps.
J'espère que Bouché sera remis.
Je le verrai d'ici là.

Tout à vous
mille amitiés dévouées
H. Berlioz

P. S. n'oubliez pas
la partition, ni les
parties du chœur.

AUTOGRAPH LETTER OF H. BERLIOZ.

at my residence at your earliest opportunity and hear my voice, as I should be *less intimidated* there, than anywhere else, and *free from intrusion.* I wish to see if I can make an arrangement with you to study opera music. I hope you will not think me vain. I am only stating facts, and my friends think my voice a most wonderful mezzo-soprano, I think they call it.

"Be so kind as to call upon me at your earliest convenience and state by note, if you please, what day you will favor me with a visit, that I may be at home. It is proper to add my social standing is most unexceptional, being connected with the best blood of the South.

"Excuse this scrawl, I write in haste.

"Yours respectfully,   MRS. M. A. SWELT,
"361 Pacific street, Brooklyn."

The original of this letter is still in my possession.

Mr. Ullmann, elated by the success of Adelina Patti's debut, had forgotten all about his agreement with me, and not only neglected to send me certain artists to Havana, but wrote frequently to Don Francisco Marti and other influential persons in Havana that he would like to take the Tacon Theatre and bring Mlle. Adelina Patti there, who, in fact, had a private separate arrangement with Maurice Strakosch, in which Mr. Ullmann had no interest at all.

This proceeding was identical to a declaration of war, and knowing that Ullmann was preparing for a spring season of 1860 to produce Halevy's "Jewess," I hired the Winter Garden Theatre, engaged his unpaid tenor Stighelli, and his dissatisfied conductor, Carl Anshutz, added to my Havana company Mme. Fabbri, in addition to Frezzolini and Mme. Gassier, opened Winter Garden in April, 1860, producing "La Juive" before Ullmann had time to finish his rehearsals, and followed in rapid succession with the operas of "Masnadieri," "The Robbers," by Verdi, from Schiller's tragedy, and forced Ullmann to shut the Academy of Music. The following autumn, Ullmann and Strakosch tried to make up a company with the floating remnant of their former artists and with Adelina Patti, but they were crippled by previous debts and embarrassed in their action by Mr. Kingsland, who still acted as trustee for the advanced money of some of the stockholders, and were unable to make both ends meet. Their only hope of salvation was the arrival of the Prince of Wales in this country and the expectations of some gala nights in Philadelphia and New York to replenish the empty treasury. But they were counting without Mr. Kingsland. On October 6, 1860, the entire company was sent to Philadelphia for a performance in honor of Lord Renfrew (the Prince of Wales), and I also was engaged to conduct a portion of the performance, the program of which I deem interesting enough to reprint herewith.

PHILADELPHIA AMERICAN ACADEMY OF MUSIC.

GRAND GALA NIGHT !

IN HONOR OF LORD RENFREW,

by the

ULLMANN & STRAKOSCH CELEBRATED ITALIAN OPÈRA COMPANY,

Wednesday, October 10, 1860,

Under the supervision of the committee of arrangements,

When the following operatic entertainment will be presented, in accordance with the wishes of Lord Renfrew, to whom the repertoire was submitted for selection, viz., Flotow's grand opera of

"MARTHA,"

and the first act of Verdi's opera of

"LA TRAVIATA."

The performance will commence precisely at eight o'clock, with
the English national anthem,
"GOD SAVE THE QUEEN;"
Followed by Flotow's *chef d'œuvre*,
"MARTHA."
Characters :

Lady Henrietta..Miss Adelina Patti
Nancy ....Signorina Fanny Natali
Lionel.. ....Signor Brignoli
Tristan...Signor N. Barilli
Plunket (his great original role)........................Herr Karl Formes
His first appearance since his return from Europe.
Musical director and conductor of " Martha," Max Maretzek.
Leader, Theodore Thomas.
The performance will conclude with the first act of Verdi's grand opera of
" LA TRAVIATA."

Violetta...Mme. Pauline Colson
Alfredo...Signor Errani
Musical director and conductor of " La Traviata," Signor Muzio.
Leader, Theodore Thomas.

The house was sold at increased prices many days before the appointed
night and the receipts were $7,000, which the treasurer employed by Kingsland
held subject to his orders. Mr. Jacob Grau and Frederick Rullmann had
by speculating in tickets about $3,000 ; Ullmann and Strakosch went there
with gleams of hope in their breasts, and the prospect of several more such
nights. But behold ! next morning the treasurer declared that every penny
had been paid out upon orders from New York, signed by Mr. Kingsland.
Nothing was left for the artists, chorus, orchestra and even for the supernumeraries, and I am witness myself that poor Mr. Ullmann and Maurice
Strakosch had that day not money enough left to pay their hotel bill
and to return to New York ! I take the liberty here to publish an extract
from a letter of Mr. William H. Paine, himself a stockholder of the Academy
of Music, New York, which he wrote to me after learning the news.

MAX MARETZEK, Esq. PARIS, November 1, 1860.
Dear Sir : I have your favor of Oct. 15. The news does not astonish me.
I told Strakosch when he showed me how useful and kind the stockholders were
(taking all monies and paying advances to artists) that in two months he would
be wound up. It was evident they were awaiting a chance for a grand *coup !*
The stockholders of the Academy of Music are, on the whole, a very good
set of fellows, but the control of the Academy has got into the hands of a set
of would-be gentlemen, but with the instinct of lackeys, so that it is impossible
to do anything there. I do not know any one better suited to deal with them
than Ullmann, and if he cannot get along with them, what chance is there
for an honest man ? Very truly yours, WM. H. PAINE.

Maurice Strakosch then took Adelina Patti on a concert tour and afterward to Europe and made a fortune there.
Bernard Ullmann tried a short season more in New York alone, but had to
give it up in despair and abject poverty. He was tendered a benefit in 1861,
and with the proceeds went to Europe, where he managed the concerts of
Adelina's sister, Carlotta Patti and others, and also became prosperous and rich,
but as for the Academy of Music in New York—once more Dante's verse :

Voi che qui entrate
Ogni speranza lasciate.

CHAPTER VI.

OPERA IN MEXICO.

About forty years ago the humble dwelling house, No. 96 East Tenth street, in New York, was occupied by Salvator Patti and his family, consisting of his wife, Madame Barili-Patti, three daughters, Amalia, Carlotta and Adelina, and one son Carlo. The next house, No. 94, was the abode of Rafael and Anna Maretzek, the parents of the writer, and their two daughters, Leontine and Rosa. Salvator Patti, formerly impresario, in partnership with Sanquirico, and lessee of Palmo's Opera House in Chambers street, had gone the way of all opera impresarios and failed in business, and being in reduced circumstances was engaged from 1849 to 1852 as second tenor, and his oldest daughter, Amalia, as comprimaria, at the Astor Place Opera House, then under my management. Mme. Barili-Patti used to sing occasionally, "Norma," "Gemma di Vergy" and other operas.

Carlotta and Adelina Patti were the schoolmates of their next neighbors, Rosa and Leontine Maretzek, and they could very often be seen together in the streets with other Bowery girls, playing, running, frolicking, skipping the rope, throwing snow-balls at the boys in winter and firecrackers in midsummer. The entire Patti family were born musicians, and the three daughters were gifted with beautiful voices, but Adelina had a wonderful ear in addition to her little silvery voice, and could repeat the songs of Jenny Lind and the arias of Theresa Parodi—the two vocal celebrities at that time in New York—after hearing them only a few times, in perfect time and tune. Often, after returning from school or from their play, did Adelina call, with my younger sister, at the office of the Astor Place Opera House and sing at my request the aria of " Ernani " or the melodies of Jenny Lind's Swedish songs, to the delight and astonishment of the singers and other persons present, and when rewarded with a half a dollar, the two girls could be seen rushing to the next apple stand or candy store and invest the money received. The pretty little child did not dream, then, to be once the worshiped diva of both hemispheres, and that nine thousand dollars would be paid to her for singing twice a week.

Adelina made her first appearance in public in February, 1852, in Tripler Hall, at a concert of Michael Hauser, assisted by Parodi and Badiali, under my direction. Afterward she appeared in two concerts given by her half-brother at John Brougham's Lyceum Theatre, on May 12 and June 8, 1852, on which occasion she sang the " Echo Song," by Eckert, and "Ah non giunge," from "Sonnambula." Her success was complete, but more one of wonder than admiration. After these brilliant debuts she made some concert tours with Moreau Gottschalk and others with Maurice Strakosch; and in November, 1859, she appeared for the first time on the operatic stage as *Lucia di Lammermoor*, at the Academy of Music in New York, under the management of Bernard Ullmann and Maurice Strakosch, as narrated in the previous chapter. She continued to sing in New York, Philadelphia and Boston for more than a year in different operas, until Ullmann and Strakosch separated, and Maurice Strakosch formed a new partnership with Salvator and Adelina Patti to give concerts and operas in the West and South of the United States. In February, 1861, Adelina Patti gave operatic performances in New Orleans.

About that time I contemplated a second tour with an opera company to Mexico. The Theatre Tacon, in Havana, had passed from the hands of Don

Pancho Marti, and became the property of a stock company, headed by Senor Ybannez, who was longing for the pleasures and relaxations which the occupation of an operatic impresario affords.

Don Francisco Marti, who sold the Tacon Theatre for $600,000, magnanimously accepted the half in cash and the other half in shares, and had obtained from me previous to concluding the sale the promise not to return to Havana with a company for two years. In return for my promise he offered me $10,000 in shares, or a loan of $25,000, if I needed money for carrying on my business elsewhere for two years. I understood immediately that Marti would depress the value of the stocks, and afterward buy up the shares of the Tacon Theatre Stock Company, and become within two years again proprietor of the premises. I refused the shares, therefore, and stipulated that in event of his again acquiring the Tacon Theatre he would furnish $25,000 and go into partnership with me. To this he agreed, and I concluded to go to Mexico, where I had been, so lucky eight years before, and where I supposed I should double the money to be invested in the enterprise.

I had already made conditional engagements with the celebrated contralto, Mme. D'Angri, the great basso, Biacchi, and with many others, but did not dare to make them conclusively binding till I had secured a star prima donna. For that object I dispatched my brother Albert to New Orleans, with instructions to negotiate with Adelina Patti and Strakosch, and if successful, to proceed at once to Mexico and to make the preliminary arrangements for our arrival.

In due time I received a telegram that Adelina Patti had agreed to go to Mexico, and by mail the following document:

(Copy.)

MEMORANDUM.

Adelina Patti agrees to go with Max Maretzek to Mexico, for three thousand ($3,000) dollars per month, to sing three times every week; or two thousand five hundred ($2,500) dollars per month, to sing eight times each month, and, if wanted, more than eight times per month, the extra pay for every evening to be stipulated hereafter. Traveling expenses from New Orleans to Mexico for three (3) persons. The engagement to last three (3) months, to begin on the 15th of April or 1st of May, with the privilege of Maretzek to continue, under the same conditions, for one, two, or three more months.

Adelina to have a full benefit, without cost, and, when advertised, to have first place on bills and posters. Payment always fifteen days in advance, and she to receive two thousand ($2,000) dollars before leaving, which sum to remain with her for the last fortnight's salary.

New Orleans, February 14th, 1861.
            (Signed)   Maurice Strakosch,
                                For Adelina Patti and her Father.

The next mail brought the letter hereby annexed:

            "New Orleans, La., February 15, 1861.

"To Max Maretzek, New York: *My Dear Max.*—I have sent you by mail the terms under which Adelina will come with you to Mexico. I recommend you, most earnestly, to accept them without the least hesitation.

"Adelina has made immense progress since she left New York. Her repertoire now is, 'Lucia,' 'Sonnambula,' 'Trovatore,' 'Rigoletto,' 'Huguenots,' 'Don Pasquale,' 'Martha,' 'Linda,' 'Traviata,' 'Mose,' 'Barbiere,' 'Daughter of the Regiment,' etc.

"If you go with Adelina, don't fear, and take anything you please. Only try to engage some reliable artists, who will not disappoint you by sickness. If anything is to be made in opera in Mexico you will make it with Adelina. I have proposals from London, but for private reasons I would come with Adelina and you to Mexico.

"If you take my advice take the Natalis with you.

"My dear Max, remember what I tell you—no other prima donñas but Adelina and Natalis. ' Your affectionate

"MAURICE STRAKOSCH."

Of course I accepted and received the following cablegram, dated New Orleans, February 27, 1861 :

"MAX MARETZEK, New York: Received letter, and all right. Telegraph immediately whether engagement commences 15th of April or 1st of May.

"MAURICE STRAKOSCH."

Relying on the good faith and old friendship of Patti and Strakosch, I concluded definitely all my engagements, paid the usual advance on salary to every one employed, bought new dresses for the operas to be performed, and engaged the passages to Vera Cruz, when the day before starting from New York I received

TELEGRAM NO. 2. "March 11, 1861.

"MAX MARETZEK, New York: Received news from Mexico. Papa and Adelina will on no consideration go there. Road to Mexico full of robbers.

"MAURICE STRAKOSCH."

ANSWER TO ABOVE TELEGRAM.

"March 11, 1861.

"MAURICE STRAKOSCH, St. Louis Hotel, New Orleans, La.: I am ready to postpone your departure till May 1, and send my brother Albert back to fetch you and have an escort for Adelina. If you then receive the news of my company's happy arrival and good prospects you cannot refuse coming. If, however, we get killed, I probably shall not insist. Answer to Havana.

"MAX MARETZEK."

Fully convinced that my telegraphic answer would dispel any groundless fears, I started next day for Havana, where I left instructions with Senor Marti to pay the advance to Adelina as agreed, and from there sailed for Vera Cruz, and soon arrived safe with the entire company in Mexico without the slightest accident to any of us. Maurice Strakosch answered my telegram to New York instead to Havana, as directed. His letter, after having been forwarded, reached me in Mexico, and reads as follows:

"NEW ORLEANS, March 18, 1861.

"To MAX MARETZEK, New York (Care of Don Francisco Marti y Torrens).

"*My Dear Max :* I cannot express to you how unhappy I am to cause you such great trouble, but I have done all that is possible to persuade Adelina to go to Mexico, but without success. * * * * * * * I will do anything in my power to indemnify you for the terrible injury inflicted upon you.

"Wishing you, from the innermost of my heart, happiness and success, I am forever your cousin, MAURICE STRAKOSCH."

"P. S.—Adelina and her papa send you their best regards."

My last hope was Don Francisco Marti, to whom I dispatched a messenger, and beseiged him to persuade Patti and Strakosch, in Havana, where they had announced two concerts, to keep their agreement, and to save me from ruin. Here is Marti's answer:

"HAVANA, April 15, 1861.

"MR. MAX MARETZEK:

"*My Dear Friend:* Your letter of the 1st inst. received. I regret that you had trouble about landing, as the steamer had not a clean bill of health.

"Patti, her father and Strakosch were in Havana, on their way to London, refusing to go to Mexico, as you know. I had already convinced Patti's father, by guaranteeing him, myself, the salary for three months, but on condition that she would have to sing three times a week for $3,500. She asked $4,000, as agreed upon with you, and, while these arrangements were pending, a vessel arrived in Vera Cruz, and they read in a newspaper that some passengers had been robbed on their way from the City of Mexico. Next day Strakosch came and told me that the Pattis had said that they would not go to Mexico for even $30,000, and on the 7th they took the English steamer for London. He said that if you need anything you should write him at London ; that he will make contracts with any artist you want; that if you ever want Patti she will come to you anywhere, excepting Mexico.   *

*   *   *   *   Your friend,

"DON FRANCISCO MARTI,
"y Torrens."

Imagine the feelings of a sea captain trying to make headway on a sailing vessel without a mast; the position of a general with his heavy guns cut off from the main army ; the endeavors of a prime minister to keep himself in power without a majority, or the agony of a tenor cast to sing *William Tell* without possessing a high C, and you will easily understand the dilemma in which I was placed in Mexico by the non-arrival of Adelina Patti.

The amount of subcription taken by my brother previous to my arrival indicated a willingness on the part of the Mexican public to support the opera in a liberal manner, and augured well for the success of the entire season; but no sooner was it known that Adelina Patti had not arrived with the rest of the company than all further subscriptions stopped at once, and when her refusal to keep her engagement was necessarily made public more than half of the money already paid in for subscription had to be refunded.

In the meantime Adelina Patti arrived in London, made her debut early in May, 1861, at Covent Garden, in the part of *Amina*, in "Sonnambula," and, according to Michel Mortier's authorized biography, she accepted an engagement with Mr. Gye for £100 ($500), per month, which sum, however, after her own success and the sudden death of Mme. Bosio, was raised voluntarily by Mr. Gye to £400. Mr. Mortier in his official biography, endorsed by Patti herself, says : "*That it must not be forgotten that her Manager (Mr. Gye) might have held her to the terms of her engagement, that is to say £100.*"

It is curious to know that Adelina Patti and her father and Mr. Strakosch at that time, when she went to London instead of Mexico, fully understood the value and the force of an engagement with a London manager, but still left me thousands of miles away from home with an opera company on my hands, but without a principal prima donna, and, after having forced me to announce her in glowing terms as the great particular "star" of the company, she appeared and shone brightly in the East instead of in the West.

The custom of calling popular singers "stars" is one of the curiosities of modern expression which merits some analytical investigation. Seen through the magnifying telescopes of interested managers and paid agents, the public may be deluded into the belief that a great singer is a real star on the musical horizon, but after closer observation the denomination "star" may be found a misnomer when applied to prima donnas.

It sounds like injustice and irony to call singers like Catalani, Jenny Lind, Patti and Nilsson, stars of the first magnitude in the musical firmament, and not a name to be given, and no place allotted to composers like Bach, Handel Mozart, Beethoven and others. It seems to me that the great composers ought to be called the major planets or fixed stars in the musical solar system, as they maintain the same position through ages, and the singers should be named only satellites of the composers, receiving from them the substance of their existence, and reflecting only the light of their genius; or, to judge from their eccentric and erratic courses, from their nebulous surroundings, from their doubtful ages, the uncertainty of their keeping the exact time of their appearance, their volatilization, prima donnas are only musical comets, who, after having reached their perihelion, take, with their long trains of gaseous followers, a downward course and disappear from public view.

But to return to the unfortunate opera company in Mexico. I seriously intended to refund all the subscription money and to return to the United States, but nearly all my available cash, the profits of two years of the Havana season, had already been expended in advances to the artists and in traveling expenses from New York to Mexico, and it is a long way and an expensive trip from there back to New York, and a very soft road to travel during the rainy season, which lasts from June to September in that country. But I went to work with a will, determined to use the material at hand to the best advantage and to fight our way back as soon as possible. "Martha," by Flotow, "The Prophete," by Meyerbeer, and "Attila," by Verdi—three operas never before heard in Mexico—formed the basis of our operations. The principal part of "The Prophete" being written for a mezzo-soprano or contralto, was sustained artistically by Mme. D'Angri, and the role of *Attila* by the famous basso Biachi; and any other possible shortcomings were covered by a splendid *mise-en-scène* never before witnessed in Mexico.

The principal success and attraction financially was the skating scene in the "Prophete" and the introduction of roller skates into Mexico. Skating was a new revelation to the majority of Mexicans, who knew it only from hearsay, and speedily became the rage. I remembered Mr. Niblo's advice and opinion about Meyerbeer's "Prophete," and to a certain extent acted upon it. Roller skates and skating lessons brought enormous prices; skating clubs were formed in every class of society, and each club in rotation asked, and paid for, the privilege of showing their skill during the performances of "Prophete" to their friends, who filled the house, and thus the "Gran Teatro Nacional," in Mexico, became a well-paying skating-hall, with the performance of Meyerbeer's "Prophete" thrown in as an additional entertainment for the price of admission. Finally, having learned that one of my double-bass players in the orchestra, by the name of Panyagua, had written a Mexican opera, I made that gentleman the happiest man in the world by accepting his opera, and produced it, appealing to the patriotism of the Mexican public to sustain their native composer and to encourage home-made operas. The entire population of Mexico responded to my appeal with an eagerness impossible to be met with in the United States, and if only the tenth part of the same encouragement should be extended toward a New York composer here that the Mexicans did toward their "Panyagua," many a bright talent might be brought to the surface and the importation of trashy operettas, which spoil the good taste of the public, would soon be stopped. In fact, while at the performances of Meyerbeer's "Prophete," the public came only to *see the skating scene*, they flocked to *hear the music* and *nothing but the music*, of Panyagua's "Catalina." After having called the composer out before the curtain each night about a dozen times, the public insisted that he should remain seated in an arm chair between the acts on the stage, exposed to the admiring gaze of his countrymen, and to receive their acclamations. The rainy season being over, the craze for skating having subsided, and the supply of Mexican operas having been exhausted with Panyagua's music of "Catalina," I thought it convenient and timely to make preparations for our return home.

The rumors of an approaching invasion and occupation of the country by France, Spain and England, in order to establish a strong government for Mexico, contributed to accelerate my departure from the capital. With the intention of giving a few performances in Puebla and other cities, I had sent the music and dresses of a few operas, and a portion of the company, with some chorus singers, in advance to Peubla, and early one fine autumn morning about three o'clock we left the city of Mexico.

The stage coach was occupied inside by seven of my company and two Mexican gentlemen, and outside by three chorus singers. We had hardly left the gates of the city when all my companions fell asleep, having been entertained by their friends at a farewell supper until the departure of the *diligence*.

The grandeur of the scenery on leaving Mexico, however, kept me awake. The reflection of the moon on the snow-capped volcanoes, the Izzwakhuatte on the left and the Popocatepetl on the right, and on the numerous lakelets on both sides of the road, lined with sycamores, balmy acacias and magueys (century plants), formed an *ensemble* of indescribable beauty, and produced a sensation of blissful contentment. The impression of such magnificent scenery can never be obliterated from the memory of its beholder.

After having feasted my eyes for some time, I reclined my head, closed my eyes and tried to think of the events since I left New York, regretting not to have accepted the $10,000 in shares of the Tacon Theatre, instead of losing borrowed money in Mexico, and wondering what Adelina Patti and her father would say when they learned that we had not been troubled even with the sight of a robber. Suddenly my reflections were interrupted by a whisper of the two Mexican gentlemen, who evidently believed me sound asleep with the rest of the company.

" I hope we will get through safe to Vera Cruz and accomplish our mission," said the first.

" No doubt; we have an escort of ten men behind us, and that number is enough to frighten any robbers," replied the other.

" I would not care for robbers—a few dollars will satisfy them. But President Juarez, when he handed me yesterday the dispatches to the governor of Vera Cruz, told me to be very careful about them, as he had received information that the guerilla chief, General Ordonnez, has been seen with a considerable force somewhere on the road between Puebla and Mexico."

" Bah! Ordonnez would hardly trouble opera singers, and we will ask Senor Maretzek, in case of accident, to say that we are chorus singers belonging to his company."

" Capital idea ! " retorted the other, " but if Ordonnez takes it into his head to search us all, and if he finds the dispatches of Juarez, what then ? "

" By the Holy Trinity and the immaculate Virgin, then we will be shot, every living body in this coach."

Very fine prospects for me and my company, I thought, but did not move a muscle. " Anyhow," resumed the first speaker, after a pause, " we ought to hide these confounded dispatches where they cannot be found ; or, if found, cannot be traced to us."

" Yes! Yes!—but where ? "

" Ah! there! this is a good place !"

And as noiselessly as possible he lifted the coach window from its socket and dropped an official envelope into the vacant slot.

It may not be improper to describe here in a few words the general state of political affairs of Mexico at that time. President Juarez and the Radicals had a short time before confiscated a great part of the church properties throughout the country and sold it at auction for the benefit of the government, causing considerable vexation to the clergy and monks of the convents, and as usually (and naturally) the property was not bought by poor Indians of the middle class, but by rich people for nominal prices, thus only changing hands without benefiting the masses. On the other side the clergy raised the price for reading masses, baptizing, marrying and burying the commoners and diminished the free soups and other hospitalities for the poor at the convents, and did not fail to denounce from the pulpit Juarez and the rich citizens as the oppressors of the poor, and sacrilegious robbers of the Holy Church; to instigate discontent and hatred against the government, and to create that powerful clerical party which fomented civil strife and caused the intervention of France and Spain, and eventually the tragic death of Maximilian of Austria. The government held the principal cities and fortified places in their grasp, but the villages and country places swarmed with guerillos, encouraged and even supported by the clergy.

About eight o'clock in the morning we arrived at Rio Frio, a small village situated in a valley between two steep hills, where the *diligence* (stage coach) usually halted for breakfast and change of horses.

The village tavern and post office was kept by a native of one of the Italian cantons of Switzerland, who, advised of our arrival, had a splendid breakfast prepared for us, considering Italian opera singers as his countrymen.

We were just enjoying the many good things which our landlord had spread before us, when a commotion in the street, and the cry of " Los Guerillos ! " startled us, and, in fact, by looking out of the window of the dining rooms, we could see on the hill of the Puebla road a troupe of about 100 horsemen approaching the village, while at the same time our escort, believing discretion the better part of valor, were running away on the opposite side on the road toward Mexico with all the speed their little mustangs could command.

" *Sauve qui peut !* There is the band of General Ordonnez coming !" screamed our landlord, and, following his own advice, vanished with his attendants to hide in the garret, leaving us alone in the room at the mercy of the guerillos.

At the mentioning of the name of General Ordonnez, the two Mexican bearers of dispatches jumped up terror-stricken, and in so doing nearly upset the table, and during the momentary panic several glasses and plates were broken and dishes upturned.

Believing that we ran less risk in remaining quietly together than in scattering separately in all directions, I peremptorily ordered the two Mexicans and all my company to resume their seats and to remain as unconcerned as possible at the table.

My next thought was how to save a purse of about twenty Mexican ounces in gold, which I carried for defraying expenses of the company. My eyes suddenly rested on an upturned large dish of salad, a portion of its oily contents oozing over the table. Quick as lightning I shoved the purse under the dish. I had hardly time to resume my seat when the guerillos arrived and surrounded the hotel and post office.

A coarse-looking individual with four guerillos immediately entered the room, placed his four men, with carbines pointed at us, at the door, and, pistol in hand, advanced to the table.

I was sitting at the head of the table; to my right the tenor, Signor Sbriglia, and to my left my wife and little daughter two years old. The valiant warrior approached Signor Sbriglia, put the pistol to his ear, and with rough voice exclaimed, " *Un reloj !* " (a watch). Sbriglia sank back speechless in his chair. Crick! Crick! the robber cocked his pistol and repeated, " A watch! —or——!!"

I had a watch, while Signor Sbriglia had sent his in advance safely to Puebla; so I stood up and with one hand I offered my watch, while with the other I gently pushed the pistol upward to the ceiling. " Here, my general!" I said, " is a watch and please put your pistol away. We, in sentiment, belong to your party and don't wish to offer any resistance to your demands."

Evidently flattered that I had promoted him to the rank of " general," he took the watch, put the pistol in his belt, and in a softer manner asked whether any other person had a watch.

One of the Mexican gentlemen handed his watch. " No more watches?" inquired the new-fledged general, addressing himself this time to Mme. Sbriglia. " We have no watches," she answered, " but I have two rings and a little money."

" Let everybody put his jewelry and money on the table before him!" he ordered, and then went around the table collecting the silver dollars and two or three more rings, the whole booty amounting in all to about $40. Coming around again toward me, I threw a few silver dollars cavalierly before me, which I had in my vest pocket, but it seems I had made a favorable impression on his generalship; for he left *one* dollar on the table and said:

" You may keep that for cigars !"

" Thank you, general, for your kindness ! Would you like to take something ? After your labors of the day you must be tired."

He surveyed the contents of the table, and my heart began to beat quicker when I thought of the upturned salad dish. Fortunately he was not used to salad prepared with oil, nor partial to vinegar, so in a disdainful manner he answered : " I see you only drink weak claret here ! Have you no cognac ? Hallo, waiter ! landlord ! A bottle of cognac !"

You might just as well have asked the king of the lower regions to bring you a bottle of holy water as try to lure the landlord from his retreat, so I went myself to the buffet, and finding a flask of brandy, I brought it and poured out a tumblerful, which I offered him.

" Oh, no !" he said, ironically. " That won't do, my good man. You drink first out of the same glass."

Guessing his suspicions, I took a big draught from the glass, and, having satisfied his scrutiny, he filled the glass to the brim and swallowed it at one gulp.

Having established such friendly relations with this Mexican hero, I asked him whether he would not allow us to pursue our journey to Puebla?

" Not yet !" he answered, we have some business with the stage coach from Puebla, and must have the road clear. It would not do that you reveal our arrival here to the travelers in the expected stage coach."

A few moments later the expected stage coach from Puebla appeared on the top of the hill, and immediately my new friend, with his men and others who were levying contributions in the village, joined a detachment of guerillos, stationed about 200 yards from the village and barring the highroad from Puebla.

No sooner had they left our room than I rushed for the salad-dish, and regained, amid the shouts of laughter from the company, my purse of Mexican ounces.

Natural curiosity urged our party to go outside to witness the coming events with the stage coach from Puebla, and we were more or less surprised to behold about a dozen half-bred Indian or Mexican women, followers of the guerillos, occupied in ransacking our trunks, valises and satchels, which had been left in our stage coach, and dividing the contents among themselves. They took everything they could lay their hands upon and said that whatever was of no use them to would be given to the church. "*Todo por dios.*" Goethe says "the church has a good digestion and can swallow anything." Some Indian women had just broken the case of a trombone, and taken out the beloved instrument belonging to Sig. Donizetti, a nephew of the composer of that name, a member of my orchestra. They looked at the instrument, looked through it, tried to make it shoot, and wondered what use could be made of it, when the owner of the trombone espied his pet in the hands of savage women. He could stand the loss of his dollars, the division of his wardrobe, the scattering of his music with heroic resignation, but his trombone was worth a fight! So he rushed into the crowd and snatched the end of his instrument. He pulled one side with all his strength, and the women at the other end, but as the trombone was of the old-fashioned pattern, composed of two sliding tubes, one portion remained with the women, and Donizetti, with the other half, landed safely on his back in the dust. Sig. Hyppolito, the baritone, went to the rescue of his friend Donizetti, but what could two Italian musicians do against half a dozen Indian viragos? The struggle was fierce, but short and decisive, and the Indian amazons not only carried away in triumph both parts of the trombone, but divested the two Italians also of their coats, hats and shoes, and left them in their shirt sleeves and stockings on the battle field. My wife at the same time had been pleading with a few other women, who had appropriated our linen, begging for the underwear of our baby only, as it could be of no use to them.

"*Es bueno para el nino della Santa Virgen de Gaudalupe ; Todo por dios*" was, however, the irrevocable answer she received, and, being a devoted Catholic, she seemed consoled in learning the destination of her baby's linen.

Our attention, however, was soon attracted toward the stage coach from Puebla, where the incidents took a more serious turn.

Approaching the village the stage coach was ordered to halt, the driver having already, as customary, lowered his sombrero (a broad-brimmed hat) to cover his eyes. This is usually done to prevent the driver recognizing the assailants, and thus unable to bear witness against them; but this time the driver covered not only his eyes but his entire face with his hat, in order not to be recognized himself.

The passengers were dragged out of the coach, placed under guard on one side of the road, and the interior of the vehicle rifled of its contents. Then the passengers, five men and two ladies, were searched for money, and probably not finding it in sufficient quantity, the coats, vests, shawls, were appropriated, and they were marched half-clad under escort to the village hotel, and consigned to a separate room.

In the meantime the commander-in-chief of the robber band, General (?) Ordonnez, himself ordered the driver to take off his hat.

"Ah, it is you, Pancho! The very man we want! Come down!"

Trembling like an aspen leaf the poor fellow obeyed.

"Kneel down under that tree!"

Two of the robbers helped him to reach the tree, and two others were placed about ten feet from the tree, with their carbines pointed toward the unlucky driver.

"Fire!" said the commander.

Two shots and the poor victim fell mortally wounded to the ground.

His bleeding and still breathing body was thrown in the coach, the horses were led by the robbers to the hotel, and the dying man deposited in the hall on the stone floor, just in front of our room, which we all had regained after the piteous spectacle enacted before us.

We were not long waiting for the reappearance of our former despoiler of watches, rings, and silver dollars, but this time with his four riflemen he only acted as a body guard to General Ordonnez, who himself bluntly entered the room.

"Have these gents all been registered?" he asked, in a gruff manner.

Not understanding clearly the sense of the word "*registrado*," on such an occasion, I believed he was asking whether we had been put under contribution, and I answered "yes, sir, and we have given already all we possessed."

"*Sin Verguenza*," he retorted, with a contemptuous look. "Do you take me for a robber? I want to know your names, your occupation, and your destination."

Somewhat ashamed, I told him that we were members of the Italian Opera Company from Mexico, on our way home to New York.

"All belonging to the same company?" he inquired, scrutinizing every one at the table, glancing from the left to the centre. "Who are those five men down at the end of the table? They don't look like foreigners," looking sternly at the three chorus singers and the two bearers of dispatches.

"Exactly, General, they are chorus singers from Mexico, and intend to return to the capital, after a few performances, which we are engaged to give in Puebla."

The two men, who were all the time trembling in their boots, sent a grateful look toward me for having anticipated their wishes, which they had no time to mention. The General continued his scrutiny, now toward the right of the table, where he beheld the beautiful figure of Mrs. Sbriglia, a young and blooming French lady. His expression changed suddenly from gruffness to agreeable surprise. He stared at her like a weary and thirsty traveler would at the unexpected sight of a tree laden with juicy oranges or luscious peaches, and, without much ado, he pushed Mr. Sbriglia off his chair and seated himself near the young woman. Mr. Sbriglia, who had not yet recovered from the shock of the first encounter, fell back with a loud and heavy groan on another chair.

"Who is that fool?" asked the General.

"That fool is my husband!" answered Mrs. Sbriglia, in a most bewitching French manner.

"Ah, your husband? You are married? Well, what is the matter with him, what ails him? He looks as if somebody had swallowed him and— could not digest him."

"One of your men," pointing to the very man, "held a pistol to his head, and that upset him."

"Ha! ha! ha! indeed! It upset him? Well, you have a valiant protector. If you were in MY care, I would have known how to shield you."

Here Mr. Sbriglia uttered another but this time a faint, half-suppressed groan.

"I hope my men have not molested you?" continued Senor Ordonnez.

"No, we gave them all our money, and do not regret it, but that man took one of my rings which I considered priceless as a keepsake."

" Keepsake from your husband ? "

" No, General," she answered, her face coloring with a crimson hue.

"All right, then! Hello, Captain," he addressed his aide-de-camp, "please return the ring which you *received as a present* from this lady."

The Captain obeyed with a forced smile, but ill-disguised expression of displeasure on his features.

Donizetti, who till now had been silently wailing over the loss of his trombone, picked up all his pluck and beseeched the General—whom he addressed as a noble hero and a kind-hearted philanthropist—to order the return of his beloved trombone.

Mme. Sbriglia had to narrate the battle of the Amazons for the possession of the trombone, and, as she joined Donizetti in his petition, the trombone was soon restored to the joyful owner.

Senorita Candelaria, a young Mexican woman, who had charge of our baby, perceiving the influence which Mme. Sbriglia began to exert over our captor, now told her she should implore the General to send for a priest and not to let the dying driver outside expire without the consolation of the last sacrament. Everybody with Mrs. Sbriglia requested the same favor, and soon after a priest was found and brought to poor Pancho. Before attending, however, to the luckless driver, the priest insisted on seeing the General, and when admitted, he asked humbly why Pancho had been shot.

" He was a renegade, a traitor, and carried letters and dispatches to the officials of Juarez. Therefore, I had him shot as a spy."

" *Ben hecho!* Well done! Served him right," said the priest, and, with one eye on the brandy-flask and the other on Mrs. Sbriglia, moved toward our table; Ordonnez, however, ordered him out to do his duty to Pancho.

" I go," said the priest, " but there is little hope of salvation for any traitor to our cause," and, with a reverence and a benediction to the General, he went out.

Had Ordonnez, instead of minding the priest and gazing at Mrs. Sbriglia, turned his head toward the two Mexican bearers of dispatches, he would have easily seen by their consternation that they were no chorus singers, and he might have ordered more executions; but he was too much occupied with Mrs. Sbriglia, and when the priest had left he asked her whether she was the prima donna of the company.

" No, I act the mimic parts in operas, like the dumb girl in ' Masaniello,' the *Abbess* in ' Robert le Diable,' and occasionally I dance, but my husband sings tenor, Mrs. Maretzek sings soprano, Sig. Hyppolito sings baritone, Sig. Donizetti plays the violin and the trombone."

" That is splendid," replied General Ordonnez, we shall have a fine concert and a jolly dance this afternoon and evening."

We all listened dumbfounded to that invitation to the dance and Mr. Sbriglia could not groan any more, but stretched his body on his chair, occasionally interrupted by a trembling fit.

Suddenly we were aroused from our gloom-foreboding thoughts and the General from his amorousness by the sound of bugles from the hills on the road from Mexico, and the alarm trumpets of the guerillos in the village.

" The Regulars are coming down the hill in large numbers," shouted the men outside through the windows, and in a moment the General and all his men were out and in the saddle—in fact our escort, who had fled at the approach of the guerillos had thought, like *Falstaff*, that who runs away now may be able to fight later, went only to the next military station on the road, to report the capture of the village of Rio Frio by Ordonnez and had been sent back with reinforcements, and they now in their turn tried to capture

the place.   A regular skirmish ensued just in front of the hotel.   The yelling
of the combatants, the blasting of bugles, and the pistol-shots made noise
enough to make the listener believe that thousands were fighting outside, but
although bullets flew in all directions—nobody was hurt.   The guerillos, however, still out-numbering the regular troops, began to out-flank the soldiers of
Juarez and they retreated, hotly pursued by Ordonnez.   On the top of the
hill, more reinforcements having arrived, the regulars made another stand and
the battle was renewed.   Seeing the coast clear for a time at least, I thought
this a good moment to escape.   I summoned all our party to go in search of
our landlord and his attendants, and specially of our driver.   By shouting
through the house and through the yard that "*the guerillos had left,*" they
emerged from the garret, the pigeon house, the corn-crib and our driver
peeped out cautiously from a hay-stack behind the stables.

No sooner had I espied him than I rushed at him and by promising him
one ounce of gold if he drove us safe to Puebla, and by frightening him that
he would be shot like poor Pancho if the guerillos should return and find him
here, he went for the horses, and all of us helping to harness them and put
them to the coach, in less than five minutes we were driven at a furious rate
up the hill toward Puebla.

Our trunks having been emptied and broken to pieces by the Amazons,
the vechile was light, and the driver, encouraged by the renewed promise of
an ounce in gold and the horses by the application of the whip, we were soon
out of the reach of the guerillos, even if they had intended to catch us
again.

"We escaped well," said one of the Mexican bearers of dispatches, "at
the price of a few dollars."

"Yes," I answered, "you had a very narrow escape."

"Not at all, we could save ourselves anyhow; all we had to do in case
of emergency was to tell the robbers how *you* robbed *them* of a purse of gold."

Shocked by such ingratitude on their part, after having saved their lives I
told them that they were entirely mistaken, and that I could save myself and
my party a great deal easier, by divulging the hiding place of some dispatches
inside this coach—(pointing at the same time with my finger toward the
spot where they had dropped the official papers entrusted to their care) and
that my experience of that day had taught me to consider them bigger rascals
than the robbers.

At every station, where the horses had to be changed, a crowd of people
has gathered to learn the cause of the delay of the stage coach, and the
lamentable death of poor Pancho was discussed and bewailed, especially by
the women, whose favorite he seemed to have been.

At last we arrived at the post-office and hotel in Puebla, where Sig. Errani,
Biacchi, Mme. De Angri and the rest of the opera company, under apprehension of some misfortune, had been anxiously waiting for us.

The news of our arrival and of our encounter with General Ordonnez spread
like wildfire through the town, and many visitors soon crowded our supper-
room, to congratulate us on our escape, by giving us medios (six-cent pieces)
according to Mexican custom.   Among the curious and eager crowd
one individual made himself conspicuous by his anxiety to learn all the
particulars, and the two Mexican bearers of dispatches, of course, had to
tell him how I *cheated* the robbers of a purse of gold.   He immediately
grasped my hands, complimented me for my presence of mind and shrewdness, introduced himself as Senor Don Jose de A——, and offered me his
services in anything and everything I should desire during our stay in
Puebla.   He soon proved to be a consummate master in the art of flattery

and obsequiousness, and I immediately took a dislike to his manners, and felt uncomfortable whenever he gazed at me with a kind of basilisk eyes. Without being asked he volunteered the opinion that the prospects for a successful opera season were not bright, that the streets in Puebla were all barricaded by the Government troops against the wishes of the inhabitants, who were sympathizing with the clerical party; that people disliked to go out in the evening to pass the barricades and to meet soldiers at each corner; that gold had entirely disappeared and silver was only seen in fractional currency, and that my only chance consisted in obtaining the patronage of the clerical party. He argued that wherever the clergy goes in the city of Puebla, there the women will go, and where the women go the men must follow. Knowing that Puebla is a city of prelates, priests, monks, and nuns of every denomination and every color, I did acquiesce in his opinion, and therefore I asked how the patronage could be obtained. After feigning a moment to think the matter over, he struck his forehead as if he had found suddenly the ways and means, and named Monsignor ——, the prelate of the —— Church, as the only person who could make the opera season prosperous, by his influence with the clergy and with "society" of which he is the acknowledged leader. At the same time he proposed to fetch me next day and to introduce me to His Excellency, whom he represented as an enlightened, social, and liberal man of the world. Seeing no harm in his proposal I agreed to be at his disposal at noon next morning.

"I hope we will be successful in spite of some drawback, one circumstance possibly working against you," he said in a very low tone.

"What can that be?" I answered.

"The circumstance of your robbing Ordonnez of a little bag of gold ounces," he whispered in my ear.

"What do you mean?" I asked astonished.

"It was very clever on your part, but it was a *mistake*. It ought to be compromised," he continued, still whispering lowly.

"Perhaps you wish me to send him the money back," I answered jokingly in an undertone.

"Not exactly that," he replied, but we will confer about it hereafter. "Be ready to-morrow by twelve o'clock; I will fetch you."

With these words he started, saluted the company in the most polite manner, and left the room.

Of all the strange events of that day, this occurrence seemed to me the strangest, and before retiring I went to the hotel-keeper and postmaster to seek information about Don Jose de A——.

"He is," said my host, "a kind of privileged character in Puebla. He seems to know everybody, and everybody's business, but nobody exactly knows him or his real occupation. Some say that he is an agent of General Miramon, who is now in Europe to instigate the invasion of Mexico by France, others say that he is the manager of a clerical syndicate from Quadalajara, still others pretend that he is on a secret diplomatic mission from Spain, which means a 'spy,' and a few shake their heads and believe him to be nothing but a chevalier of industry on his own account."

Worn out mentally and physically I went to bed and dreamed neither of robbers nor of Mexican bearers of dispatches, but of a vampire with the features of Don Jose fluttering over my head.

Next morning I heard that my tenor, Sig. Sbriglia, in consequence of his fright, had been stricken down with fever, and what was worse, that two doctors had already operated on him with leeches, cupping-glasses, after the fashion of Dr. Sangrado in "Gil Blas" I knew that, thanks to these doctors,

Sbriglia would not be able to sing for two or three weeks, but I still had the tenor Errani with me, upon whose good will and versatile talent I ever could fully rely.

Exactly at noon Don Jose appeared according to appointment to take me out and to present me to Monsignor ——. At every corner of a street we found a barricade with sentinels, and at every three or four blocks of each street a guard-house full of soldiers and women, who ostensibly offered holy images, small blessed figures of saints or relics from the Indian mound at Cholula, for sale, but who in reality acted like the "flying squadron" of Catharine of Medicis, by trying to seduce the soldiers from their allegiance to the established government. I could not help remarking the close remsemblance of the consecrated little statues to the relics of the Indian mounds, and concluded that they all must have been manufactured at the same laboratory.

On arriving at the church my attention was attracted in the vestibule by a very large picture representing the "Purgatory." A turbulent sea of fire! A lot of human beings, mostly women (without bathing dresses), swimming in that sea, and red-horned devils with lance-shaped tails stirring up the fires with tridents in their hands! Under the picture a strong box of solid silver was riveted to the wall, with the inscription: "Contributions for reading masses to save your relations from Purgatory." As a work of art the picture was a horrible daub, and Mr. Wanamaker would not have given $10 for it, but as a speculation I think it yielded more money by its public exhibition than all the pictures of Munkacsy and Millet combined ever did.

The church inside was crowded mostly with women kneeling on the bare stone floor, or waiting their turn at the confessionals, which were all occupied; priests officiated at the different altars, and everywhere one could observe evidences of a thriving business. Don Jose pointed out to me some marble statues of saints, who, from time to time, consented to perform miracles by healing rheumatism, making blind ones see and lame ones dance a fandango. One of the beadles of the church, who seemed to know Don Jose very well, led us through the vestry into Monsignor's home, where a young Mexican girl in Poblano costume (short dress and sleeves) ushered us into the library— to wait until the prelate had finished his lunch. A profusion of books in mahogany cases, and above them a number of pictures adorning the walls, comfortable old-fashioned arm-chairs and large morocco-covered tables, Indian potteries and Italian artistic marble works, filled the large, airy room. In looking around I discovered two fine copies of "Magdalenas in the wilderness," one after Corregio and the other after Salvator Rosa, a well executed picture of "Susanna in the bath" and another of "Samson and Delila," and others of this kind among a lot of portraits of eminent bishops, cardinals and martyrs. In the book-cases I espied, near grand folios of ecclesiastical works and biographies of saints—Balzac's "Cent nouvelles," Boccaccio's "Decameron," Brantome's "Dames galantes," Eugene Sue's "Juiferrant," and others. I concluded that our Monsignor must be like many other Catholic priests I have met—a clever fellow and a brilliant talker, when once allowed to divest himself safely of the official mask of hypocrisy, and therefore I made up my mind to address him as a private gentleman, without any allusions to his clerical dignity, at his entrance in the library.

After the usual ceremony of introduction, I expressed my pleasure of making the acquaintance of such a *connoisseur* and lover of arts.

"Who told you that I am a *dilletante?*" I pointed to his pictures, especially to "Magdalenas" and "Susanna in the bath." With a sly twinkle in his eye, he answered: "Oh, yes. Subjects from the Bible, you understand, and pretty well executed—— "

" Indeed, a great deal better pictures than that ' Purgatory ' in the vestibule of your church."

" I see," he said, "you are one of these reformers who think such an exhibition outrageous, or one of these modern philosophers who don't believe and consider that picture ridiculous, and perhaps I agree with you, but rest assured it contributes more than any police force could to keep order and peace in the city of Puebla."

" And that is not the only contribution it procures," I dared to remark.

" This is another false idea of yours," he answered. " The contributions from the poorer classes to the church are not the tenth part of the moneys which the clergy here contribute to keep them alive and comfortable. What would they do without us? There are about 4,000 ecclesiastics in Puebla. Each one, at least, gives employment to six men and to as many *women*." Here again he twinkled with his eyes, slapped with one hand his knees, and with the other poked the ribs of Don Jose. "You see 4,000 clergymen give bread to 48,000 persons, and their contributions to the church would hardly pay the interests of the money they receive."

" But how about their intellectual development and their spiritual welfare?" I queried.

" *We do* the thinking for them. We unlock the purgatory and open the gates of heaven for them. Our liberality is food for their bodies, and our *sermons food for their souls!* "

At this moment two well-dressed ladies entered the room without knocking at the door, and the elder one, a buxom woman of about thirty-five years of age, not caring for me nor for Don Jose, began lecturing His Excellency the Monsignor about some gossip which circulated in town about a certain French governess, who had been sent away from Mexico for having caused trouble in the family of the Es——s, and who, according to those gossips, now visits our Monsignor too often in his vestry for confession and absolution.

" If you don't care for your own reputation, Monsignor, you ought to consider mine, *your sister-in-law*, and of your *niece* here (pointing to the younger lady), just out of the convent. What will people think of *us*, who are living under the same roof with you."

Not in the least disconcerted, he burst out in a laughter which even Don Jose dared to join in.

" Don't you see," he remarked, " we are not alone here. Let me present to you Mr. Maretzek, the impresario of the opera."

" Ah! you are the gentleman who got the advantage over Ordonnez and his men ? " she exclaimed, with a smiling face.

" You know that already ? " I answered.

" I know everything that happens in Puebla or fifty miles around," and, turning toward the prelate she said:

" Of course, *papa*, you will subscribe for a box and take us every night to the opera, won't you ? "

" I will take a box for myself," he replied, " and you can go to the *tertullia* (ladies' gallery) whenever you like."

" What, you will not go with us ? " she flared up. " Perhaps you wish to go with the French governess. If I ever meet her alone I will change her appearance so that Mme. Es——, in Mexico, will have no more occasion to be jealous of her."

" Be calm," he replied, " I want a box for myself to invite friends and make propaganda for the opera."

" That seems to me a slow way of making propaganda," she answered. " You can't get all your friends in the box in one evening, and if they have to take turns, by that time the opera season will be finished. I have a better plan. *You* invite all your friends to dinner the day after to-morrow, Sunday, and you come too, Mr. Maretzek, and there we will get them all to subscribe at once; besides this, I will make my usual visits to-morrow among my friends, and when you come Sunday I am sure I will be able to present you with a big list of subscribers. You, Monsignor, can keep your box for yourself, and I shall take a separate one for my own use, and if you don't wish to escort us we can find plenty of others who will do it. I hope, after the opera season, you will put your mind to contrition, and let French women alone, and pray for forgiveness, and for the salvation of your soul," and, recommending me not to forget the private box for herself, she left the room with the niece. (?)

"What a fine preacher she would make!" he ejaculated, "if she were not plagiarizing my own sermons."

"It seems," I ventured to say, "that *her* sermons are not much food for *your* soul."

"Nor her liberality food for my body. *Et hinc illæ lacrimæ.*"

The conversation now turned to politics, and I remarked that the confiscation of church property by Juarez must be a heavy blow to the clergy.

"Nonsense!" he answered. "The diocese of Puebla, before the confiscation had mortgaged their property to the extent of $50,000,000, which the sale certainly would not bring in, and let them have just a few insignificant houses and farms. We treated them just as you treated Ordonnez, kept the gold and let them have the silver."

The dinner the following Sunday was splendid, and the guests were composed of dignitaries of the church, alcaldes, merchants, and, in fact, all the 400 of the town, and the sister-in-law (?) of the Monsignor proved to be the best theatrical agent I ever met, for the subscription collected by her filled half the house.

After dinner Don Jose proposed a game of cards and opened a bank of monte. He seemed to understand how to bridle Dame Fortune in dealing the cards, for he won lots of money, in fact every one else lost except the sister-in-law, to whom he dealt gently in order not to harass the presiding genius of the house.

The opera season of three weeks was tolerably successful, the Monsignor occupying a box with a communication to the stage, where, between the acts, he enjoyed his cigarettos and a bottle of Malaga, his position not allowing him to go outside "to see a man." And his sister-in-law (?) graced another box, in company with the niece (?) and two young and handsome canons of the church.

My only torment during our stay in Puebla was Don Jose, who every morning came to ask me to compromise the matter of the twenty ounces with Ordonnez—threatening me with his revenge the moment I should leave the gates of the city.

Impatient, I at length asked him point blank whether he was an authorized agent of Ordonnez, or a secret chief of the robbers.

"Supposing I was one or the other," he answered; "what could you do?"

"If you admit it," I answered, "I might first doubt your veracity; second, I would sue you for blackmail and denounce you to the authorities of the established government. What could *you* do then?"

"First," he retorted, "nobody would believe you, as my position is above suspicion; second, I could sue you for slander, and third, I wouldn't give one medio for your life."

"Then it is a game of bluff between us?"

" So it is," he answered.

" Well, what guarantee have I if I should compromise with you, that I shall not be attacked on the road ? "

" I'll furnish you with a safe conduct against all attacks by robbers from here to Perote," he said.   " Further than that my influence does not go."

In order to get rid of his daily importunities, and rather to recompense him for my introduction to monsignor, I agreed, after much bargaining, to give him six ounces in gold, and in return he handed me a letter directed to *Ad ustedes* (to you), sealed with an immense yellow seal of a cross surrounded by two swords and surmounted by a crown—after having taken my oath never to divulge his name.

On the road from Puebla to Perote, we never met with even the sight of a robber, but Mme. Angri seemed very anxious to make the acquaintance of some, and almost boisterously bragged that if she did meet any, they would never find what little money she might have, and in fact seemed to be fairly itching for the chance to show her cunning in hiding her valuables.   At the last station before Perote, we halted for refreshment and rest and Mme. Angri, who was a very large and heavy woman, summoned a waiter to assist her in alighting from the *diligence*, the step of which was high from the ground ; the waiter—a small, puny Mexican—went to her aid, but alas! found himself utterly unable to support the weight of the adipose fair one, and with a crash that shook the earth, they feel to the ground together.   The shock was so great that one of Madame's garters burst and out of her stocking rolled a gold ounce.   As she could not very well adjust her clothing before everybody, on regaining her feet she ran as quickly as possible into the house and at every step another ounce or half ounce rolled out from under her capacious skirts.

About fifteen minutes later, in the gathering twilight, I noticed across a little bridge, eight or ten mounted men in Mexican dress, skulking in a thicket.   Calling the driver, who had been promised a liberal tip if he gave timely notice of anything strange on the road, I asked him who these men were.

" Escort !" he replied ; " a private escort who hire themselves out, and I would advise you, Senor, to employ them ; it may save you some trouble," he added, with a significant wink.

" Go, then, to the chief," I replied, " and ask him to favor me with a few moments' private conversation on the middle of the bridge.   He must be alone and I also.

In a few minutes the interview was arranged, and on reaching the trysting place I found the gallant chief awaiting me.   With a flourish I produced my " safe conduct " and with a low bow, handed it to him, but to my dismay the draft was not honored.   The great man simply glanced at the formidable seal and without breaking it, handed it back to me.

"I know nothing of this paper, Senor," he said, " and as we are not ' Ustedes,' I will not open it.   My advice to you is, to hire us for your escort. The village people have seen the accident that happened a few minutes ago to that big woman and know that she has money, consequently you are almost sure to be attacked unless well guarded."

Knowing very well that he and his valuable escort were the villagers who would be almost certain to attack us, I closed a bargain with him to see us safely to Perote for the consideration of $8 for himself and $4 for each of his men, which bill I might say Mme. Angri was obliged to foot.

The distance from Topeyaguala, our last stopping place, to Perote is about fifteen English miles and the road, at first sandy or " salty " (known as the bottom of a dried up salt lake), ascends through cultivated fields lined with century plants and a great variety of vegetation, from an orange tree to forests of pine and oak. Our hired escorting cavaliers not only kept faithfully their agreement as guards, but acted also as scouts by exploring every suspicious looking bush of chapparal, and at nightfall tore down branches from pine trees, which they ignited and served as torch bearers in the dark. And still more remarkable, they did not exact the stipulated salary in advance, a feature which I recommended to the earnest consideration of my opera singers. They certainly made a very picturesque appearance with their broad brimmed sombreros, with silver snakes twisted around them, and their silver buttoned, crimson jackets, skillfully managing their swift mustangs.

Mme. D'Angri, although mourning the loss of $40, which this escort would cost her, admired the boys and especially their chief, a manly figure on a splendid charger, superior in beauty to the other small horses. She could not believe that they were common robbers, and inclined to be Don Quixottish. She insisted that they were sons of some gentlemen and their leader a nobleman in disguise, who escorted ladies as a pastime and diversion. Anxious, also, for a chance to tell her children and grand-children her experience and adventures in Mexico, she called the leader near the *diligence*, and asked him whether robbers would be so ungallant as to search ladies for hidden money.

" I don't know, Madame, for we are no robbers ; but I suppose if they were inclined to search them, they would begin just where you hid your ounces."

" But where should I hide them ? "

"*Under your wig*," he answered, "for no robber would be so ungallant as to drag a woman by the hair."

Somewhat disappointed, she continued, however, to ask, whether it was true that some robbers did forcibly abduct ladies and carried them off to the mountains.

" *You* need not be afraid of that," he said, " for no robber would be cruel enough to his horse to burden it with your weight, nor would he risk carrying you in his arms on foot, for if he should stumble and you should fall on him, you would make a *tortilla* (Mexican corn pancake) of him."

Mme. D'Angri no longer considered him to be a disguised nobleman, not even a chivalrous robber like *Fra Diavolo*, but a common thief. He, however, having entered into conversation with our party, now rode toward me and asked me more politely to tell him who gave me that pretended safe conduct with a yellow seal. I told him that I had given my word of honor never to divulge his name.

" Then I will not insist on knowing," he exclaimed. " It is so gratifying to find yet, in this wicked world, a gentleman like you, to whom a confiding robber can trust. But did he act for himself or for some other firm ? "

" He presumed to act for Ordonnez or his followers."

" Then he is a barefaced swindler," he interrupted me, " for if he were in the regular business he would have known that none of Ordonnez' men are now on this side of the road, and if he was a duly appointed agent he would not have dared to discredit his employer by raising money *under false pretenses.*"

" Then you do not belong to the guerrillos of Ordonnez ? " I asked.

" No, we do business on our own account by escorting travelers to Perote, and guarding the road against other intruders."

" And how is the travel from Perote to Vera Cruz ? Shall we have to again hire escorts for our protection ? " I inquired.

" Before and beyond Perote for a short distance you will have the regular government escort," he answered, "and afterward you will come to the lava lands of the extinct volcanoes, where robbers cannot find shelter nor stand the cold climate, and when you come to the valley of Jalapa there will be no danger whatever from robbers. The inhabitants there believe that their valley of Jalapa, being a region of such great beauty and with a soil so fertile that all the necessaries of life are produced without labor, is the original garden of Eden, which may be true, though you cannot find an apple tree in the whole place, and neither a tree nor any other vestige of knowledge. In fact, the people there are too lazy and too stupid to make successful robbers. After Jalapa, you may be attacked in the woody marshes or at Cerro Gordo; but once arrived at the Puente Nacional, you are safe until you reach Vera Cruz. As you, Senor, have acted so honorably and like a gentleman in not divulging the name of the person who gave you that 'safe conduct,' I will give you gratuitous advice how to save the expense of another escort. I see you have *two* stage coaches for your people; you would do well, after Jalapa, to take only *one* stage coach and put the rest of your men on horse-back. If any robbers see your party, they will then take your horsemen for an escort and are almost certain not to molest you."

By this time we were nearing Perote, when suddenly two of the escort, who had been acting as advance scouts, came rushing back and whispered something earnestly to the chief, who at once called to the driver of the stage coach to halt, and approaching me asked for his money. I paid him, and instantly the band like one man extinguished their torches and scattered in every direction, vanishing into the darkness like spirits; the next moment we were joined by the regular escort from Perote, who had come to meet us.

After having given two performances in Jalapa we started for Vera Cruz. I followed the advice of our whilom chief of escort by procuring horses for most of the men of the party and directing them to make the journey on horse-back in company with the stage coach. Travelers who took us for robbers and robbers who took us for "escort" all gave us a wide berth on the road.

On our arrival in Vera Cruz, Mr. Alfred Joel, our advance agent, informed me that the French and Spanish fleets, with the army of occupation, was daily expected in the harbor of Vera Cruz and advised me to leave as soon as possible, without stopping at that city. I unfortunately did not follow this advice, believing that the occupation of Vera Cruz would bring thousands of strangers to the city and make the amusement of opera desirable.

At the table d'hote of the principal hotel, "Hotel de Deligencias," the first persons my eyes rested upon were the two bearers of dispatches from Rio Frio, and the Secretary of the French Legation at the city of Mexico with them.

After dinner I entered into conversation with them, and at length one of them asked me whether I had any more adventures with robbers since the affair at the Rio Frio.

"Oh, yes!" I replied, "we have met them several times, but I had the good fortune while at Puebla to get a letter of safe conduct from a gentleman there, and every time we had the pleasure of meeting robbers, I produced the document and the effect was magical. They simply looked at the big seal—didn't even break the packet open, and here we all are safe and sound."

"What a piece of luck!" they exclaimed in chorus. "How did you manage to get such a valuable accommodation? and who was the man who has such power?" "And, by the way," continued one of them, eagerly, "as you are going to leave for New York in a few days and will not require it any more, why not let us have it, as we start in a day or two on the very same road that you have just come over?"

"That is very well," I replied, "but that letter cost me a heap of money; but I will tell you what I will do. As we are old fellow travelers, I will let you have it at half price—six ounces."

In a few minutes the bargain was settled, and I had six ounces in my pocket and they had the "safe conduct" in theirs.

Six months afterward, in New York, I met Monsieur de Saligny, the French Ambassador, with the Secretary, the same gentleman I had last seen in company with the dispatch bearers at Vera Cruz, who, the minute he saw me, not knowing, of course, the good reason I had to repay his friends for their intended treachery at Rio Frio, began to reproach me for having sold them such a worthless "safe conduct," and told me that they had been attacked between Rio Frio and Mexico by Ordonnez' men, and when they showed their "safe conduct" were first laughed at, then robbed, and then beaten into the bargain. The Secretary, however, said that by proving his identity by means of his official papers he was not in the slightest degree molested, as they considered France and Frenchmen as allies and friends.

Our first two nights in Vera Cruz were very successful, but on the third morning the French and Spanish fleets appeared in the harbor. All that day the streets of the city were entirely deserted—nobody being seen abroad, though one could notice a sort of suppressed excitement and hustle going on inside the houses. That night there was no one in the theatre and we played absolutely to empty seats.

The next morning we were awakened early by an unusual noise and confusion in the streets, and on looking out of the windows, what did we see but the whole population of the city swarming about on horseback, in wagons on foot, making a general exodus. Among the hurrying crowd, to my amazement, I even saw some of my chorus singers and orchestra, who, catching sight of me as I stood open-mouthed at the window, waved me a farewell. In a few hours, a few priests, the foreign consuls, my own party and our landlord were the only inhabitants left in the city. As I was thus the chief of the largest party in the place, I had not the slightest objection to surrendering the town to the fleet that lay at anchor in the harbor, but my amicable intentions were forestalled, as early in the afternoon the forces left their ships in small boats, landed, and took possession of the place.

Of course, opera without chorus or orchestra was out of the question, so in self defence we essayed a concert, but as the Spanish and French officers did not seem to care for it, and had come there evidently not very heavily freighted with gold, we hardly took in enough money to pay for the hall.

Here was a delightful prospect for me. No chance of making any money and no hope of getting away, as the port was now blockaded and open only to the English mail steamer, which was not due for three weeks. What I was to do till then with the company and expenses on my hands I did not know.

To add to the annoyances, as all outside communication was cut off, no food could be brought into the city, the soldiers being fed from their transport ships. For two or three days some few charitably disposed hens consented to lay an occasional egg, which could be bought for twenty-five cents apiece, but this source of supply was suddenly stopped by the soldiers, who amused themselves by catching the unlucky fowls by means of hooks and lines. We were therefore reduced to a steady diet of beans, and were regaled three times a day with black beans. To cap the climax, the landlord informed us that owing to the great difficulty of procuring food at all he would be compelled to raise the price from $3 to $4. As there was no help for us, I agreed to this, but begged him to try to give us a somewhat greater variety or the table, which he promised to do, and accordingly we feasted on black beans for breakfast only, while for dinner we had white beans, and for supper red beans.

But, worst of all, the dreaded pernicious fever broke out among the French soldiers, who were not so well acclimated as the Spaniards, who had come from Cuba, and who had, besides, encamped near the cemetery, which in their levity they had called the "Jardin d'Acclimatization," and in which they now were laid away by hundreds.

Worn out with anxieties and harrassed on every side, my money getting lower and lower, and no prospect of making any, I at length fell sick with the fever myself, and lay for days delirious, in which state I was bled by the doctor, the only treatment they seemed to have for fever patients. But one morning I came to my senses, weak and wretched, and suddenly my situation burst upon my mind. I could stand it no longer, and sick as I was I sprang out of bed, hurriedly dressed myself, and taking care not to be seen, emerged from a side-door of the hotel into the street. I hurried as fast as my tottering legs would carry me to the headquarters of General Gasser, who was in command of the troops in the city, and whom I had known in Havana, and on being admitted to his presence stated my case to him, and begged him for God's sake to get me and my company out of the city, as if no relief was forthcoming I felt that I should die there. The general was very kind, but said he was powerless to aid me in leaving the city, as that was in the hands of the admiral of the fleet, to whom he gave me a very warm letter of introduction, stating, among other things, that I was very well known in Havana, where I had given opera, also many performances for charity, and where, though not a Spaniard, I had been presented with the freedom of the city.

Thanking the general, I returned to the hotel armed with this letter, and there I met Errani and Alfred Joel, to whom I showed the letter, and prevailed on them to accompany me to the admiral. So off we started in a small boat to the flagship of the fleet.

On reaching her deck I found some two or three officers I had met in Havana, and by means of my letter and their good offices was speedily given an audience with the admiral. After consulting with his officers, who seemed to be giving me good recommendation, he sent for his quartermaster and inquired when a transport ship would sail for Havana.

"One will start in four days," answered the quartermaster, "but she is ready now. There is always one in readiness for any emergency that may arise."

Turning toward me, the admiral said, "*Ala disposicion de usted!*" "You can leave with your company when you like."

When I timidly murmured to him my thanks, and alluded to the low state of my finances and my probable inability to pay, after having settled my accounts at Vera Cruz, until my arrival in Havana, he smilingly answered:

"Her Majesty the Queen of Spain does not traffic in carrying passengers for money. I told you already, '*Ala disposicion de usted.*' You may pay the steward when you reach Havana for the actual cost of the food you and your company will have eaten, and no more."

His words did me more good than all the doctors in the world, and the next morning we embarked on the transport, and after five days' sail arrived safely in Havana, where I learned that Senor Ybannez had had enough of his experience as an opera manager, and had declined to renew his lease of the Tacon Theatre. A relapse of my fever, however, prevented me from attending to any negotiations in regard to opera there, and by the advice of a French doctor to leave the shores of the Island of Cuba as soon as possible, I made arrangements to carry my company and myself to New York.

Through the kindness of Senor Morales, the banker, and agent of the Spofford & Tileston line of steamers, I obtained passage for us all on credit by giving my obligation, paying at their New York office in thirty days.

After my previous Mexican trip I had reached home with my pockets full of money and drafts.   This time, when I set foot on the steamer's dock in West street, I had just exactly $6 in my pocket, and after paying my hotel bill that night I reached my home on Staten Island absolutely penniless—an unpleasant contrast.

I had hardly time for the welcome of my own family when Mr. Jacob Grau arrived at my humble cottage, and in a very patronizing manner, condoling warmly with my misfortunes, offered me an engagement from three to six years as conductor of his opera company.   Mr. Jacob Grau, who ten years before this time had been selling opera librettos for me outside Castle Garden, had worked his way to becoming manager himself, which was no difficult task after the departure of Strakosch and Ullmann for Europe, and during my absence in Mexico.

I respect any man who by his merit, or even by a stroke of fortune, betters his social position, and I do not think it any dishonor if a manager accepts a place as conductor or agent under adverse circumstances, any more than if a President of the United States, having returned to private life, and in practising law accepts a fee from one of his former employees; but I felt hurt at the manner in which the offer was made, as if it were a charity, when I knew well that only some necessity could have made him apply to me.   I would have refused, but the thought of paying my draft to Spofford & Tileston made me pliable, but instead of an engagement of six years, I offered my services for six weeks.

"Six weeks!" he said, with a contemptuous smile, "What can you do after that?   What do you intend to do?"

"I intend for next season to have the greatest and most complete opera company under my management," I replied.

He burst out laughing, but his incredulity changed into astonishment when six months later I reappeared on the scene with Mme. Medori, Mme. Charton Demeure, Miss Sulzer, Miss Kellogg, Signors Mazzoleni, Mimetti, Bellini, Biacchi, Vialletti, and others, under my banner.

CHAPTER VII.

MISCELLANEOUS.

On a fine summer evening in 1847, I received, in London, a note from Jullien to come without fail next morning to his house in Harley street, on important business.

Usually, Jullien, when desiring a selection from the latest successful opera arranged for orchestra for his promenade concerts, or something else for his music store, wrote or came himself to my modest dwelling near Golden Square, so when I received the summons on gilt-edged paper, with his monogram surmounted by a baronial crown, my curiosity was greatly excited, and I hastened early next morning to his mansion.

A footman, in a blue velvet, gold-buttoned dress coat, satin knee-breeches, silk stockings and buckled shoes, asked for my *carte-de-visite*, and, after having placed it in the entrance hall on a large silver salver, proceeded to the library of Monsieur Jullien, and soon after returned to open both folding doors and usher me into Jullien's presence.

"What is the matter, Jullien?" I exclaimed. "Why this ceremony?"

"Hush!" he returned, "*C'est la mise en scene!* Absolutely necessary in this country. But now we are alone, let us talk business."

"What do you desire and what can I do for you?"

"I will tell you. I have leased Drury Lane Theatre!"

"Will you give up your promenade concerts at Covent Garden?"

"Not at all, but I intend to establish English opera on an unprecedented scale at old Drury. I will make it the Royal English Academy of Music in London, just as the Grand Opera in Paris is the French Academy of Music!"

"But remember, Mr. Jullien, we have now already two Italian operas in London, with Jenny Lind and Lablache at Her Majesty's Theatre, and Grisi, Persiani, and Mario at Covent Garden! And do not forget that the Academy of Music in Paris is given to the manager, rent free, and with a subvention of about a million francs!"

"The Italian opera only plays here in summer, and I shall play in winter," he returned. "Nor do I care for subventions or millions."

"Very well. But what singers will you have?"

"I can and shall have Sims Reeves, a young tenor with a marvelous voice, who has just finished his studies and succeeded in several theatres in Italy. I have engaged Mme. Dorus-Gras, from Paris; Miss Dolby, the London favorite; I am in treaty with the great baritone, Pishek; I have Withworth, Weiss, and, perhaps, Staudigl as bassos; and I have Mlle. Fuoco, the great *danseuse*, from the Grand Opera in Paris, for the ballet!"

"All this sounds very well, but what do you want with me?"

"You shall take the same place you occupy now at Her Majesty's Theatre, as *Maestro al cembalo*, to study at the piano, with the soloists and chorus, and prepare the operas until they are ready for rehearsal with the orchestra.

"But, you know, Mr. Jullien, I am engaged by the year by Mr. Lumley, and draw my salary whether the theatre is opened or closed, and Mr. Lumley may send me to Italy or Germany during the winter, as he did last year."

"Never mind, Mr. Lumley will let you off for six months each year, to save your salary, and I will increase it further if you will write a new ballet, in two acts, for Mlle. Fuoco this season, and next year I shall have a libretto of an opera written expressly for you by Fitzball. You shall have a hundred guineas for the music of your ballet, besides your salary."

"This certainly is very tempting, but who will be your conductor of the orchestra? Have you Costa, Balfe, or Julius Benedict?"

"Neither of them," answered Julien; "but Balfe will write a new English opera for this season."

"Well, Mr. Jullien, I may be glad to serve under the direction of Balfe or Costa, as I did at Her Majesty's, or under Benedict, but I would not like to play second fiddle to Schira, Hatton, or other directors in London."

"I have better than any one of them," exclaimed Jullien with a laugh. "I have Hector Berlioz!"

He had hardly pronounced that magical name when I jumped up and rushed out saying: "All right, you shall have my answer in two hours!" And as fast as the nearest Hansom cab would carry me I went to Lumley, the manager of Her Majesty's Theatre, to tell him the news, and to ask him to change my engagement with him so as to enable me to accept Jullien's offer and study and improve myself under Berlioz' direction.

Mr. Lumley at first listened to my recital with some surprise, but soon after subsided into a stoical calm, and alternately looked into my eyes and at the ceiling of the room, without giving me any answer or expressing any opinion.

After several minutes of painful silence, he murmured to himself, entirely forgetting my presence (an habitual weakness with him), "So Jullien is trying opera!—it is nothing but a pretext!—I believed him in better circumstances."

"What do you say, sir?" I hazarded to observe.

"Oh, nothing!" he quickly answered. "I was thinking of something else. You desire to engage six months with Jullien in winter and six months with me in summer? I cannot do it. But you have worked faithfully for two years now, and I will give you two months' vacation, with permission to employ these two months with Jullien, and without deduction of your salary for the time of your vacation."

"But if Jullien wants me after those two months, what shall I do, sir?"

"Mr. Lumley burst out with an ironical laugh, and said:

"After two months with him, if you still desire to continue, write me at Hotel Vendome, Paris. Accept his offer, but insist that in engaging the chorus those from Her Majesty's Theatre shall have the preference over those from Covent Garden, and keep an eye on Sims Reeves. If he is good we must have him here with us and not allow him to go to Covent Garden."

"How about Berlioz?" I ventured to ask. "Could you not use him next summer? A well-sounding name on the prospectus!"

Mr. Lumley again looked at me and then at the ceiling, and after a minute's reflection, murmured to himself, "Berlioz!—not practical—Balfe—an Englishman very popular." Then turning to me, he dismissed me with the words, "Berlioz may do for some concerts, but there is plenty of time for that."

A few days after, Mr. Balfe met me at the stage door and inquired whether I had positively settled with Jullien, and upon my affirmative answer, took me under the collonade at the Haymarket, and told me that he had just agreed with his editors, Messrs. Chappell & Co., to furnish an opera in three acts to

Mr. Jullien for Drury Lane Theatre, but that he disliked to treat directly with Jullien, or to have to explain to Berlioz his ideas and his intentions concerning his new opera. He therefore had told Chappell that either Maretzek or Hatton would prepare his opera with the singers and chorus and when ready, he (Balfe) himself would come to preside at the last stage rehearsals.

"Why, Mr. Balfe, have you any particular objection to Jullien or Berlioz?" I asked with astonishment.

"None, whatever, as fellow-men, but as musicians and lunatics, I have. Jullien thinks his quadrilles as good as Beethoven's symphonies, and Berloiz labors under the delusion that he is the Michael-Angelo of music. He dislikes Donizetti, Verdi, and, of course, me, and two years ago he left not one spot in my opera, ' The Star of Seville,' when sung in Paris, in his criticism of it. And to avoid Jullien's friendly advices how to compose the opera, and the recommendations of Berloiz how not to compose it, I shall leave for Paris, write it there and send the score for rehearsal."

" But he will have to conduct your opera when it is ready?"

" He may conduct it, but I don't want him, or Mme. Dorus-Gras, or any Frenchman, to patronize it. Miss Dolby, Mr. Sims Reeves, Mr. and Mrs. Weiss and Withworth—all of them born on English soil—shall sing it, and they are good enough for me and the London public."

" Have you chosen your subject for your new opera?"

" Yes; it is to be called the ' Maid of Honor,' and is taken from the ballet 'Lady Henriette,' by M. St. Georges."

" But, dear sir!" I exclaimed, "this very same subject has been already used by Flotow in his successful opera, ' Martha.'"

" I know it and heard Flotow's ' Martha in Vienna last year. I like his music, but I prefer the libretto to the music, and wish to try my hand at it. I shall introduce an additional character in the plot, *Queen Betsey*, and have some military display; and anyhow, if Flotow's opera of ' Martha' ever passes the limits of its fatherland, and should reach London, I shall have the advantage of the first impression in my favor."

Genial and jovial Balfe did not then dream that in a few years he would have to conduct Flotow's " Martha" for Mme. Sontag and Giulini many, many times, while his own " Maid of Honor" would be nearly forgotten.

In due time, all the promised singers, with the exception of Pishek, who could not obtain the permission of the Court Theatre in Stuttgart, arrived, and also Hector Berloiz. I paid him my visit the first day of his arrival, and never before, and certainly never after, that day saw him in better humor and higher spirits. He looked toward a bright future and everything appeared to him in a rose-colored hue.

With a childish simplicity, he narrated how he had lately applied to Messrs. Roqueplan and Duponchel, the directors of the Grand Opera in Paris, for a place as one of the chorus masters, in order to save him from his embarrassed circumstances, and how with many expressions of regret they had refused him on the ground that he was not able to play the piano nor the fiddle, and it would be against the established custom and decorum to have the choruses rehearsed with accompaniment of a guitar or kettle-drum or flageolet, the only instruments he could practically make use of.

He remarked with joyful *abandon* that all now his troubles were over, that he had been engaged for six consecutive seasons by Jullien for operas, and for concerts of his own compositions; that dear Jullien had promised to make his (Berloiz') fortune, and that he had thought best to let another one undertake the job, as he was utterly unable to do it for himself. Finally, he said that Jullien had paid him one month's salary in advance, and that he had not seen so much money for a long time.

Poor, honest soul! he little thought that his first month's salary would also be his last, and that Jullien, if he could again make a fortune, would remember the maxim that " Charity begins at home."

Berlioz, in social intercourse, was the most honest, plain-forward, open-hearted and outspoken gentleman imaginable, but his sensitiveness often tried the patience of his most devoted friends. Any polite flattery he believed to the letter; any civility shown to him he accepted as a demonstration, and repeatedly spoke and wrote about it. While on the other side a slight remark about him or his music, even if addressed in the shape of an inquiry, would arouse his mistrust, and draw from him a bitter and sarcastic reply. Consequently he had plenty of enemies, and, although many admirers, only a few personal friends who could stand his varying humor and his fits of despondency, to which he was subject when disappointed.

However, we went on splendidly. At the piano rehearsals he stood behind my chair beating time and expressing his opinion about Donizetti's or Balfe's music in French, more realistic than ideal, which fortunately nobody but Mme. Dorus-Gras and I understood in its true sense. And after rehearsals I served him as cicerone to show him the sights of London and to amuse him generally.

In a short time I was not only his daily companion but also his confidential friend, to whom he would pour out his secret thoughts, and who would listen for hours to the stories of his endless disappointments in love and musical pursuits. His modesty, which sometimes nearly approached timidity, did not allow him even to ask for his *entrées* to the Italian opera, which certainly would have been courteously given to him, but he preferred to ask me or some other artist to procure him tickets when he desired to visit Her Majesty's Theatre. Here are some specimens of his requests:

LUNDI, 1st Mar.

Mon cher Maretzek:

Je n'ai jamais entendu Mlle. Lind au thèatre, voulez vous être assez bon pour faire quelque demarches en ma faveur et m'obtenir deux stalles d'orchestra *si fare si puo*, vous obligerez non seulement moi mais encore une dame de votre conaissance qui est ici depuis peu et qui espère que vous ferez l'impossible pour nous faire voir ensemble cette fameuse *Sonnambula*.

Tout à nous de cœur,

H. BERLIOZ.

26 Osnaburgh street, Regent's Park.

(Ne donnez pas mon address á des couchemar.)

[Translation.]

MONDAY, May 1.

MY DEAR MARETZEK: I never have heard Miss Lind in a theatre; would you be kind enough to make some endeavors in my favor to obtain two orchestra seats if possible; you would not only oblige me but also a lady of your acquaintance who arrived here lately, and who hopes that you will do the impossible even to make us see together that famous *Sonnambula*.

Entirely yours with my heart,

H. BERLIOZ,

26 Osnaburgh street, Regent's Park.

(Don't give my address to any incubus.)

Mon cher Maretzek:
Bouché m'avait promis une loge pour ce soir, il n'a pas pu sans doute me l'envoyer. Voyez donc ce qui'il en est et si Mr. Lumley pourrait m'en donner une. J'attends a la stage door, sous les arcades.

H. BERLIOZ.

[Translation.]

MY DEAR MARETZEK: Bouché had promised me a box for this evening, but undoubtedly he could not send it. See about it, and whether Mr. Lumley could give me one. I am waiting at the stage door, under the arcade.

H. BERLIOZ.

At last, in the early part of November, 1847, the grand English opera season a Drury Lane Theatre opened, with "Lucia di Lammermoor" and with a ballet, "Les Genies du Globe," by Maretzek.*

The performance opened with Beethoven's overture of "Leonore," No. 1. Berlioz was received with repeated acclamations, and conducted the entire performance. Sims Reeves carried off the honors. Mme. Dorus-Gras achieved a great success, and everything went off with flying colors until the middle of the third act of "Lucia," when an unfortunate occurrence nearly spoiled the favorable impression so far obtained.

Mr. Mapleson, a musical librarian, and the father of the present Colonel and Impresario Mapleson, had agreed to furnish to Mr. Jullien the necessary orchestra parts for the different operas, but not possessing enough copies for so large an orchestra (eighty performers), he had borrowed from different parties several string quartets of "Lucia," and it happened that the mad scene in the third act was written in different keys, according to abilities of different prima donnas who had sung it previously. Therefore, some were written in the original key in F and others were transposed to E or E flat. At the first orchestra rehearsal I, sitting on the stage near the prompter's box, called out that Mme. Dorus would sing the andante and cabaletta in F, and the intervening allegro in D flat, the original keys, which was sufficient, as every professor in the orchestra was familiar with the opera, and it went off to perfection.

On the evening of the first performance, however, Mme. Dorus-Gras, fatigued from rehearsals, oppressed by the heat, and suffering from the usual nervousness of a first appearance before a new audience, begged Mr. Berlioz to transpose (in the mad scene) the allegro after the andante and the following cabaletta, one-half note lower. Berlioz sent for Mr. Tolbegue, the first violin and leader, and inquired whether such a thing could be done and risked, to which Tolbegue answered, "We do this kind of thing nearly every night at Covent Garden or at Her Majesty's!" Whereupon he went down to notify the orchestra, but instead of naming the particular key in which they should play, he only ordered to attack the allegro, after the cadenza of *Lucia*, with the flute obligato, one-half note lower. They all did as requested, but naturally those who had their parts written in D flat played in C; those who had theirs in C played in B, and others even in B flat. The effect can sooner be imagined than described.

Berlioz could not explain in English what they should do, so Tolbegue rapped with his fiddle-bow on his music-stand, stopped the infernal charivari, and, after calling out the key in which to play, the orchestra resumed and the opera went on smoothly without further accidents. The enemies of Berlioz threw the blame on his shoulders, his friends pronounced it an intrigue against

---

* See notice "Biographique sur Hector Berlioz" by Daniel Bernard. Page 47. Paris imprimere Michel Levy.

him, but he seemed quite indifferent about it, remarking, after all. with the exception of the sextet in the second finale, it made no difference in what key " Lucia " was played and sung.

The first week " Lucia," or rather Sims Reeves, drew splendid houses, and everybody received his salary at the end of the week. The second week "Linda di Chamounix," without Sims Reeves and Dorus-Gras in the cast, was played to empty benches, and only the chorus and orchestra were paid. The third week Balfe's new opera, " The Maid of Honor," not being yet ready, Mr. Jullien ordered the revival of " Lucia," and went on a promenade concert tour of his own to Scotland, wherefrom he promised to send our salaries, and issued a writ appointing Sir Henry Bishop, Mr. Planché, Hector Berlioz, Max Maretzek and Frederick Gye a standing committee to carry on the grand English opera till his return.*

Sir Henry Bishop and Mr. Planché attended the first meeting of the committee after Jullien's departure, and upon learning the true state of financial affairs and ascertaining that the trouble and work of carrying on the the concern would far exceed the recompense in money or glory to be derived from it, gracefully slipped out by declaring that the institution could certainly not be in better hands than in those of the three remaining members.

Sir Henry Bishop, in retiring, hinted that a revival of one of his own operas could yet retrieve the fortunes of Jullien's enterprise ; while Mr. Planché regretted that Mr. Jullien had not thought of opening the season with "Oberon," and intrusted him (the author of the libretto) with the task of bringing it out properly.

Mr. Berlioz thereupon proposed to postpone the production of Balfe's opera, " The Maid of Honor," and to study Gluck's " Iphigénie in Tauris." Upon being informed that Balfe's opera could now be made ready for performance within eight or ten days, and that " Iphigenie " would take weeks to rehearse, that the promise to the public of a new opera by Balfe, and the agreement with the editor, Chappell, must be kept, and that a new opera, if successful, might replenish the empty treasury, Mr. Berlioz desisted. but followed the example of Bishop and Planché by declaring that he would conduct the orchestra, but would beg to be excused from participating in the management of the enterprise.

Not caring myself, at that time, for managerial honors and responsibilities, I promised to push rehearsals of Balfe's opera and " The Damnation of Faust," by Berlioz, and begged Mr. Frederick Gye to invest himself with full dictatorial powers. Mr. Gye, who had raised himself from the humble position of a lamplighter to be one of the agents of Jullien, and secretary of the Italian opera at Covent Garden, accepted with joy, foreseeing that this position might be conducive and useful as a stepping-stone to the realization of his ambitious plans for the future.

Mr. Balfe, who had expected that the season would be opened with his new opera, as can be seen by the annexed letter, no sooner learned the attempt of further delay than he left Paris and returned to London.

PARIS, 10 Octobre, 1847.

MON CHER AMI : Je vous prie de me tenir au courant de ce que vouz avez fait pour rompre les engagements de ceux engages a l'année. Il n'y que M. Lumley seul un monde qui pourrait bien faire cette affaire—je le crois au moins. Je travaille comme un ogre pour l'ouverture de Jullien. Ecrivez moi le plutot possible. Votre ami,

28 Rue St. Georges.   M. W. BALFE.

---

* " See Memoires de Hector Berlioz." Vol. II., page 315. Paris imprimere Michel Levy.

[Translation.]

PARIS, October 10, 1847.

Mr. MARETZEK, Her Majesty's Theatre, London :

My Dear Friend : I beg you to keep me informed about what you have done to cancel the engagements with these men, who were engaged by the year. It is only Mr. Lumley alone who could well accomplish this business; at least I believe so. I am working like an ogre for the opening of Jullien. Write me as soon as possible.   Your friend,

28 St. Georges street.   M. W. BALFE.

Soon after Mr. Balfe invited me to dinner, and to a little chat about his forthcoming opera. During the dinner he said : " I hear that Mr. Berlioz is poking fun at my music at rehearsals ! "

Of course I denied knowing anything about it. " Well," he continued, " you need not play the ignorant. Out of the hundred and twenty chorus singers, there are some men and plenty of women who understand enough French, and others who can read in his face the expression of pity at some passages of my opera, and you know that many of them are devoted to me and repeat his remarks."

I observed that all such telltales out of school are usually exaggerated, and that no importance should be attached to what they might say.

" Not the slightest," he replied. " On the contrary, I wish to satisfy him, if possible, and have composed a new piece for the second act, and wish you to hear it."

He handed me a roll of music to look at, opened the piano and played from memory a beautiful chorus, constructed in the shape of a motet of eight voices, and imitation of the style of Handel; the whole betraying a profound knowledge of the works of the ancient masters and of all the resources of musical science.

He told me to take the score home with me, and to rehearse it the next day with the chorus, recommending the division of the hundred and twenty singers into groups of fifteen each, and promising to send the chorus parts in time.

After a half hour's rehearsing the next day, Berlioz, who was reading some French papers in the lobby, rushed into the hall, asking :

" What are you rehearsing there ? "

" A new piece for ' Maid of Honor ' ! " I replied.

" Who wrote it ? "

" Balfe, of course."

Berlioz, with an incredulous look and a shrug of the shoulders, took the score from the piano, turned the pages, recognized Balfe's handwriting, but still doubting, said : " Please, try it again." His curiosity soon changed into a deep interest; his interest to a gratified satisfaction, little short of an excitement. He beat the time, admonished the minding of the shading and the coloring of the principal subject; placed the groups in different places to judge of the effect; corrected every wrong intonation himself, had it repeated several times and finally, turning toward me, said : *"Mais c'est un chef d'œuvre !"*

At that very moment, Balfe, who had probably listened outside, opened the door, and his appearance was the signal for an outburst of applause from the chorus, in which Berlioz joined.

The thanks which Balfe expressed to Berlioz, and the praises which Berlioz bestowed on Balfe, and their mutual protestations of friendship and admiration, were touching to the feelings of the cockney chorus singers, who cheered them both; but I could not help considering and enjoying the whole scene in a Pickwickian sense.

After repeating the chorus once more, Mr. Berlioz said: "I really congratulate you; this piece will be *the* success of the new opera, and your triumph is assured."

"Don't you think, sir," replied Balfe, "that the character of this chorus is not exactly in accordance with the rest of the music of the 'Maid of Honor?'"

"Never mind that," said Berlioz, honestly. "*This* will be the *piece de resistance;* the success of your opera, and will insure you the approbation of all critics and *connoisseurs.*"

With a sardonic smile, Balfe reached to the piano, took the score of the new piece, folded it and stuck it in the pocket of his overcoat; then addressing Berlioz, remarked:

"I am fully satisfied to have your approbation and don't care for the *connoisseurs*, and have decided to risk the new opera without this new piece. Good morning, ladies and gentlemen; many thanks for your good will."

At last, the long promised "Maid of Honor" was ushered before the footlights, and Balfe's music scored a *succes d'estime*, with the exception of a ballad in the last act, "In This Old Armchair," which created a genuine furore.

Sims Reeves, who had become an immense favorite, saved the opera and the season a few weeks longer. Chorus, orchestra and subordinates received their pay; the principal artists accepted small sums on account, but the *maestros*, as usual, were utterly ignored in the division of supplies. Berlioz reproached Balfe for having withdrawn his grand chorus in the second act, and Balfe retorted that if that chorus had been sung the audience would have left before hearing his ballad of the "Old Arm Chair."

Berlioz now grew morose and never pronounced the name of Jullien or of Balfe. The first one he used to call in conversation "My Salary," and the other "My Old Arm Chair," and it was really amusing to hear him say, with a grim humor, "I see by the papers that 'My Salary' had a big success in Leeds," or, "'My Salary' had a row in Glasgow with the musicians for not paying *their* salaries," or, "Have you heard any news from 'My Salary?'"

At other times he would say:

"My 'Old Arm Chair,' it seems, has no more attraction for the public than it has for me," or, "My 'Old Arm Chair' is getting played out, it needs a new frame, new elasticity and new coverings."

Once, early on a gloomy December morning, when the London fog was lying so thick in the streets that any one could cut off slices with a carving knife, Berlioz entered my room with a haggard face and threw himself on the lounge without saying a word for some time, but at last he broke out:

"Maretzek, have you some money?"

"Yes!" I answered, "I have about £50 of my economies at your disposal, and if that is not enough I may obtain an advance on my salary from Mr. Nugent, the treasurer of Her Majesty's Theatre."

"You are a lucky fellow to receive salary from Her Majesty's Theatre, without working at all, and I, working hard at Drury Lane every evening, have '*my salary*' running loose in Scotland. But you misunderstood me. I never borrow or accept money for my own use."

"But you accepted 20,000 francs from Paganini."

"Yes, and used it all for the production of my symphonies, and at the same time I often procured my breakfast at the expense of ten cents."

"Ten cents? How is that possible in Paris?"

"Very easy. A broiled pork chop from the corner pork shop, six cents;

fried potatoes, two cents; a roll of bread, two cents; making in all, ten cents. How often did I live on such fare!"

"I admire you more every day, but why do you ask me whether I have money, if you will not borrow any?"

"I will tell you frankly," he answered. "This is my birthday, and I just feel like drowning myself either in water or wine. I would prefer in wine, but three shillings is all that is left in my pocket, and ——"

"Well!" I interrupted hastily, "you shall not go out of this room till we have celebrated your birthday in good old-fashioned style. What wine do you like?"

"Send for two bottles of Burgundy, some sugar, cloves and cinnamon, and a tin pan!"

"I will send for an entire case of Burgundy and all that you desire!"

When the porter had brought all the required articles and opened the box, Berlioz changed the expression of his countenance, took off his coat, rolled up his shirt sleeves to his elbows, cleaned the tin pan and, turning toward me, said: "We shall now rehearse the wolf-glen scene from the 'Freischutz.' I will be *Caspar*, and you, of course, *Max!* Come nearer to the fire and learn the art of preparing hot Burgundy punch, so that you may know how to cook it yourself for me next time. First, two bottles of wine thrown in the kettle, then two handfuls of cinnamon, a half-pound of powdered sugar, a dozen of cloves—*Probatum est!*—now the benediction!"

Scarcely an hour has passed, and Berlioz, again in good humor, expressed a wish for some music paper, pen and ink, and there he sat, writing without eating anything the whole day, until it was time to dress and go to Drury Lane to conduct the opera. On the way there, he returned to his old hobby-horse and said: "We must now bring out 'Iphigénie' by Gluck. That is all I care for."

"Don't you care more for producing your 'Damnation of Faust'?"

"We can do that after 'Iphigenie'!"

"That is not certain. I have learned that Jullien has sold out his music store in Regent street, and transferred the lease of his house in Harley street, and if you don't insist on the immediate production of your 'Faust,' you may be too late. Anyhow, I shall begin the chorus rehearsals to-morrow."

I had about fifteen rehearsals with the chorus and soloists, and Berlioz five or six with the orchestra, and in the first week of February, 1848, the first representation of "The Damnation of Faust" was announced.

For two weeks previous to the appointed day, the chorus and orchestra had only received half salary, and on the very morning of the intended performance of Berlioz' masterwork Mr. Gye declared that no salary whatever could be paid for the past week, but if they would continue their work, a fraction of salary might be paid to each of them nightly, according to the receipts.

As is usual in such cases, the chorus organized meetings in the green room, the orchestra in the music room, some proposing to try for a few days longer, but the majority insisting on a general strike unless the salary of the past week was forthcoming, and poor Berlioz stood there, arguing, imploring, begging, till actually the tears began to run down his pale and furrowed cheeks.

At last I called another meeting of the chorus, and begged them as a personal favor not to persist in their resolution, hinted even that the engagements for the next season at Her Majesty's Theatre would be concluded within a few days, and that I should remember those who would sing at least for *that night*, the first performance of a masterwork of their own conductor, a stranger, who had worked for two months for nothing, and thus helped them

to get, so far, their own salaries, and if they desired it, I offered myself to be
responsible for that night's wages sooner than allow them to be blamed by the
public and the press for refusing their services on such an occasion.

They all, without further consultation, rushed on the stage, and declared
they would sing that night for Mr. Berlioz without compensation, and their
action soon decided the orchestra to fall into line, and the performance took
place the same evening.

Berlioz was the recipient of an ovation on the occasion of the first performance of his legend, " Damnation of Faust," from his friends and from a
sympathizing public, who, during the evening, had learned all the circumstances of the morning's proceedings.   But as a truthful witness, I cannot help
declaring that that masterwork which now is hailed with enthusiasm in every
European or American city whenever presented, did not make any profound
impression, nor was it able to attract a full house on its second performance.

The opinion of the London press, too, was divided; Davidson, Gruneisen
and Rosenberg doing justice to Berlioz, and showering praises and eulogies
on him, while others criticised severely ; and one (I believe it was Barnett)
even went so far as to say that Berlioz would ever be unsuccessful as a composer, but might distinguish himself as a critic !   Whereupon Berlioz answered
that Barnett would ever be a poor critic, but never a distinguished composer.

Things went from bad to worse ; Jullien returned, and called the Standing
Committee together again.   Bishop reiterated his opinion that one of his
operas would change the bad luck and fill the treasury.   Planché opiniated
that since " Oberon," no English opera season did, or could, succeed.   Gye
returned to Covent Garden, where he soon became sole lessee and manager,
Mme. Dorus Gras to Paris, Sims Reeves accepted an engagement from Lumley, and Jullien's enterprise collapsed, verifying Lumley's prediction that
Jullien's embarking in that opera speculation was only a pretext to find an
excuse for declaring himself bankrupt, and perhaps thus to save something
from the wreck of his former enterprises and extravagances.

Berlioz alone remained unprovided for, in want and misery, until July, 1848.

He applied to Lumley to give some concerts at Her Majesty's Theatre,
but that impresario, having engaged Verdi to come to London with a new
opera expressly composed for his theatre and for Jenny Lind (" I Masnadieri "), politely consoled Berlioz with promises for another year.   In vain
did he also try to obtain an opening at the Philharmonic of London.

The old fogies who composed and directed that society at that time
engaged Mr. Molique to play concertos on the violin, and chose symphonies
of Hesse in preference to " Damnation of Faust " or " Romeo and Juliet,"
by Berlioz.

Frederic Gye, who had pity for him, proposed to give a kind of a Shake-
spearian musical festival at Covent Garden, composed of Berlioz' music to
" King Lear," " Romeo and Juliet," the " Death of Ophelia," and fragments
from " Benvenuto Cellini; " but a clique of Italians who reigned supreme at
that time at Covent Garden prevented the success of that project.   Mr.
Berlioz himself, in his memories, accuses Mr. Costa as the instigator of all
opposition to his compositions at Covent Garden, but Berlioz very often
imagined enemies without real cause or reason.

Late in June, 1848, he succeeded in giving two concerts at Hanover
Square Rooms, on which occasion I again persuaded the chorus of Her
Majesty's Theatre to volunteer their services, which he acknowledged by the
following letters :

Mon Cher Maretzek : Voulez vous remercier de ma part Messieurs et Mesdames les choristes du Theatre de sa Majesté, et les prévenir que nous repeterons le choeur des Sylphes avec l'orchestre Mardi prochain 27 à midi à Hanover Square Rooms. Je compte sur votre bonne amitié pour venir mettre en ordre le choeur et le disposer comme il devra être disposé pour le jour du concert. Cela ne vous prendra que peu de temps. J'espère que Bouchè sera remis. Je le verrai d'icilà. Tout á vous avec amitié dêvouée,

H. Berlioz.

P. S.—N'oubliez pas la partition, ni les parties du choeur.

[Translation.]

My Dear Maretzek : Would you thank on my behalf the ladies and gentlemen of the chorus of Her Majesty's Theatre, and inform them that we shall rehearse the chorus of the " Sylphes " *next Tuesday*, the 27th, at *noon*, in Hanover Square Rooms. I count upon your obliging friendship to come and put in order and dispose the choruses as they ought to be on the day of the concert. It will take only a little of your time. I hope that Bouchè will have recovered. I shall see him; till then, entirely yours, with devoted friendship. H. Berlioz.

P. S.—Don't forget the full score, nor the chorus parts.

Mon Cher Maretzek : Voici la partition de " Faust " ou se trouve le morceau des "Sylphes," que nous executerons á mon concert. Veuillez le faire repeter dès que vous le pourrez car on doit l'avoir oublié. Vous avez aussi chez vous la partie de *Méphistopheles*, aves les paroles Anglaises. Veuillez la donner à M. Bouché, Il chantera le solo qui précede le choeur des " Sylphes."

Recevez mille remerciements et salutations amicales,

H. Berlioz.

[Translation.]

My Dear Maretzek : Hereby the score of " Faust " containing the piece of the " Sylphes," which we will execute at my concert. Please rehearse it as soon as you can, because they may have forgotten it. You have also with you the part of *Méphistopheles*, with the English words. Give it to- Bouché, who will sing the solo, which precedes the Chorus of the Sylphes.

With thousand thanks and friendship,

H. Berlioz.

The concerts did not yield much more than the expenses. Mr. Broadwood, the celebrated piano manufacturer and member of Parliament, started a subscription privately among his friends, the proceeds of which, amounting to 250 guineas, were handed to Berlioz by Mr. Beale under the guise of ordering two compositions from him, to avoid any possible refusal from the too sensitive and unlucky Berlioz.

MUSICAL GHOST STORIES.

By MAX MARETZEK,

Originally Written for and Published in "The American Musician,"
December 21, 1889.

"Hallo! is it you, Uncle Max? What a surprise! Merry Christmas to you!" exclaimed the colored girl, in answering my bell last Christmas day at a country mansion in a New England village.

"Are Mr. and Mrs. P—— at home?" I asked.

"No; they went around to the Christmas tree at the church, but they will be in presently to supper. Walk in; they will be so glad to see you."

I followed her lead into the dining-room, where she prepared the table for supper.

"Why didn't you come to dinner? We had such a splendid one—oysters! turkey! English plum pudding—just such pudding, with a bottle of rum burning all over it, which I held over my head so as not to let the flames burn my face; and the clerk of the silver factory here in town, who is sweet on Miss Ellen, said that I looked exactly like the Statue of Liberty, whatever that may mean, which made 'em all laugh, but made me feel so flurried that I nearly dropped the whole business on the floor."

"Well, I suppose he meant it as a compliment to you, Esther; but I couldn't come to dinner, as I dined in New York, and having some business early to-morrow morning in New Haven, I took an afternoon train and thought to pay my old friends here a visit for the evening."

"Oh! they'll be mighty glad to see you, as you've not been here since last February, just before the big blizzard. Oh, that horrid blizzard! Everything has changed since that time. We had no summer, and now we have a Christmas with green fields and sunshine instead of an old-fashioned snow-storm. And so many strange things have happened since the blizzard."

"Well, what has happened here, Esther?"

"Why, do you see, Uncle Titus, the old colored man, over seventy-five years of age, was sued for a breach of promise by a young white Dutch girl."

"Well, did she agree to marry old Uncle Titus?"

"Not a bit! He caught a cold in the blizzard and said that he was sure to die, and promised to leave his house and ground to any one who would nurse him during his sickness. Well, along comes this Dutch girl, who nursed him so well that he got well, and now she sues him for not having kept his promise to die.

"And then they had a fair last summer at the church in Sandy Ground, where Martha was to be *Rebekah at the Well*, and Tim to play the part of *Isaac*, and after the fair there was to be a concert, where Martha was to sing "The Birdling on the Tree," which she had studied for the last six months, and all the dresses were ready according to the pictures in the big Bible at the minister's house, and Isaac was to come on a real camel, for which they sent down to Bridgeport to Barnum's. But Mr. Barnum, instead of sending a camel, sent one of his trick donkeys, and when Tim came in on his donkey to court *Rebekah*, the beast turned around and kicked Tim over his head in the dust, and with his hind legs knocked the front teeth out of *Martha's* mouth.

"That spoiled the concert as far as 'the Birdling on the Tree' went, I suppose!"

"Not a bit! I came forward and sang instead 'The Old Folks at Home,' and don't you forget it, I took the cake.

"But that's not all. Mrs. Henney, who attended a Sunday singing school just the night before the blizzard, took home for supper the singing teacher who used to come every Sunday from Meriden, and on account of the blizzard he couldn't get home till the next Friday, and then didn't dare to go home to his wife, so they decided to send Mrs. Henney's husband down to Meriden to see her and tell her that her husband was sick, and would not be home for a day or two. But Mr. Henney didn't come back to this very day, nor did the singing teacher go home, and neither of the women will let the man she holds as a hostage go till her own man comes back! And then you remember little Mamie, that little colored one who used to be here last February to help me?"

"Well, what's the matter with her?"

"Well, she got a baby about a fortnight ago."

"What! That child got married?"

"Nonsense! Married! She was out in the blizzard."

By this time the family arrived, and we proceeded to supper in real New England style, with all the surroundings that can be seen in Denman Thompson's "Old Homestead."

But after supper came the reverse of the medal. The lady of the house invited us into the parlor to listen to a performance on the piano by her son and daughter, who played selections from Bellini's "Norma," and thus made me pay dearly for the supper.

Esther, who had been listening in the hall in raptures at the piano recital, then entered with a tray of ice cream, and ventured to remark that it was a splendid Christmas evening, but one thing was wanting.

"What is wanting, Esther?" queried the mistress of the house.

"Indeed, a Christmas without ghost stories is no Christmas," answered Esther.

All at once agreed that Esther's suggestion was a good one, and that we should have ghost stories. I know my warm desire for them being prompted by the hope of thereby escaping any further piano playing. After much urging, Aunt Melinda, an elderly and sedate lady, somewhat diffidently told the following as of her own experience:

"I was on my way to spend New Year's at my brother's house up in Massachusetts, a few years ago. The weather had been very bad for some days, and we were a long way behind time when I finally reached my destination, where, as it was nearly midnight, I was shortly shown to my room, and lost no time in retiring. Not, however, until I had spent a few minutes looking out of my window at the winter landscape, and the turbulent stream half choked with ice that rushed by a few yards from the house. At length, however, I got into bed and was fast falling asleep, when suddenly I seemed to hear the faint, sweet music of a violin; nearer and nearer came the strains, exquisitely played; surprised, as I knew none of my brother's family were musical, I sat up in bed, and then I found that the melody seemed to come from behind the headboard of the bed. My curiosity aroused, I sprang up, pushed the old-fashioned bedstead aside, and behind the headboard saw a heavy curtain hung against the wall. Pulling it to one side, a close inspection showed me a door imperfectly concealed beneath a thin coat of plaster.

As I looked, the music, which had been gradually getting fainter, ceased, and I returned to bed and fell asleep.

"The next norning at breakfast, on being asked how I had slept, I noticed glances being exchanged between the members of the family, and when I replied that with the exception of some beautiful music that had kept me awake for a short time, I had rested very well. I saw such significant looks on their faces, that I immediately concluded that there had been, and possibly still was, a little plot on hand to play a practical joke on me. The day passed pleasantly as only a New England New Year's Day can pass, and by eleven o'clock that night I was again in my room preparing to retire. As the clock struck twelve, and just as I had settled myself comfortably in bed, again I heard the distant playing of the violin. Quite awake this time, I lay quietly and listened in delight to the exquisite strains. Suddenly a loud knock on the door startled me, and the next instant, hearing a match struck on the outside of the door, I determined to catch the joker *inflagrante delicto*, and jumping out of bed I crossed the room with a bound, flung open the door and saw—nothing! Absolutely nothing! nobody could possibly have struck that match and then hidden themselves in the instant that had elapsed. The music had ceased, and there was an oppressive stillness in the house that made me feel queer creeps up my back, but pulling myself together, I grasped the door to close it again, when to my horror, my waist was grasped as if in a vice, by a large, muscular, but unseen hand; the pain of the grip was so great that I screamed aloud, and when the family came rushing from their various rooms in all sorts of improvised costumes, they found me fainting on the floor. However, I soon recovered my senses, and I told them my experience.

"' I am not surprised,' said my brother, ' at what you tell us—it has been the experience of every one who sieeps in that room, and had it not been the only one vacant we would never have put you there. There is a story connected with this house and particularly with this room that I may as well tell you now, as I am quite sure you won't sleep there again. Many years ago this place was bought by a wealthy gentleman, somewhat past his youth, and of an austere and severe character, who brought here his young and beautiful bride. The poor girl had lived a gay and brilliant life, and her existence here, after the novelty had worn off, was monotonous and tiresome to her, so that when one day it was advertised that an eminent virtuoso on the violin was to give a concert in the neighboring town, she hailed with delight her husband's expressed intention to invite the violinist to pass a few days at his house.

"' The virtuoso came, a young and strikingly handsome man. Agreeable and talented, he made such a good impression on his host that his intended visit of a few days lengthened into weeks. Suddenly the host, who had been gradually getting colder and more distant than ever in his manner, announced his intention of riding over to the town where he expected to be detained till the small hours of the morning. He set out on his blooded horse, but instead of going to the town, secreted himself in the grounds and at midnight made his way up the secret staircase, which opened into his wife's bedroom, and there found his worst suspicions verified. As his wretched wife instinctively covered her face with her hand he seized her with a grip of iron and hurled her across the room, and then clutching her paramour by the throat, choked him to death. When satisfied that his rival's guilty life was gone, he dashed the body down the staircase, left the house without a word to his miserable young wife and was never again heard of. The wife died in a lunatic asylum—and when finally the house was occupied again, years afterward, by outsiders who knew nothing of the tragedy that had been enacted there, the workmen, in repairing the foundations, were startled at finding at the bottom of a secret staircase the skeleton of a man and the remains of a broken violin. The sensation died out in time and the door and stairs were closed up and plastered over.'"

A buzz of conversation followed this story and, of course, for the time Aunt Melinda posed as a heroine, nobody attempting to explain the apparent mystery. I might have ventured to say that the occurrence of the first night was simply a vivid dream, the affair of the second night the result of an excited imagination, and the story of the brother either an invention of Aunt Melinda's own brain, concocted to give herself an importance, or a joke to amuse her listeners.

The horror of Aunt Melinda's story only whetted the appetite of the party for more of it, and they asked me if I hadn't experienced something of the kind during my many travels in both hemispheres.

In order to escape the more tangible horrors of a second performance on the piano, I consented to relate the story of the

SPECTRES THAT HAUNTED BELLINI.

Bellini, when a student at the Conservatory of Music in Naples, was introduced to the house of Signor Francesco Fumaroli, President of the Supreme Court, to whose beautiful and talented daughter, Maddalena, he gave lessons in singing, and naturally fell madly in love with his charming scholar, who fully reciprocated his passion. As usual in such cases, everybody knew the state of affairs except the father and mother of the love-sick girl.

After Bellini's first opera, "Adelson e Salvini," had been produced, with fair success, he, through a mutual friend, Sig. Marsigli by name, asked for the hand of Maddalena, and of course, as usual, the request was refused by the parents, who were surprised at his audacity, the refusal being accompanied by a decided prohibition of any further visits to the house. As usual, again in such case the lovers were in despair at first, and then exchanged mutual resolutions and vows never to belong to any one else.

" Before I shall have written ten operas, your parents will be only too glad to offer me your hand," said Bellini to Maddalena.

" It takes a long time to write ten operas," sighed poor Maddalena.

"Only a few years, and we are young and can wait," returned Bellini.

" Well, then, let us swear to be true to each other till then, and that we shall be united after your tenth opera, dead or alive," exclaimed the romantic and poetical Maddalena.

Bellini did swear.

His second opera, " Bianca e Fernando," had a great success and Bellini was called to Milan to write for the theatre of La Scala the opera " Il Pirata," which made a sensation and established Bellini's reputation through Europe.

The operas of " Straniera," " Zaira," " I Capuletti e Montecchi " followed in rapid succession, and " La Sonnambula " sealed Bellini's fame throughout the civilized world.

As Bellini had predicted, the parents of Maddalena Fumaroli did not wait till his tenth opera was finished, and after the enormous success of " La Sonnamula," he received a letter from his beloved Maddalena informing him that her father, yielding to her urgent entreaties, had given his consent to their union. This letter reached him when he was writing "Norma" for Mme. Pasta and Giula Grisi, but he who had formerly sent every day to Maddalena letters vowing everlasting fidelity, had lately become less enthusiastic in his visions of their mutual future bliss.

His great triumphs, which filled poor Maddalena's heart with hopes of the realization of her only desire in life, were, however, the very causes that undermined Bellini's early love for her.

Whether it was ambition or passion for glory, or Giulia Grisi that produced a change in his feelings, has never been decided, but Bellini answered in a lukewarm letter that he was then occupied in finishing the score of "Norma," and after its production he would go to Naples and decide about their union.

He never went!

Certain it is that Bellini could not resist the blandishments of Giula Grisi, and at her request interpolated that commonplace duet at the beginning of the second act of "Norma," which originally was not intended for the opera, and in doing so not only betrayed Maddalena Fumaroli, but his own muse.

Poor Maddalena soon after died of a broken heart, but in her last letter to Bellini conjured him not to forget that "after his tenth opera they must be united live or dead!"

Her death and last letter, however, made an everlasting impression on him, and a continual sadness took hold upon him, and, according to the general belief in Italy, he was haunted by the ghost of Maddalena, in the shape of a white dove, who fluttered nightly in his bedroom, and when after his opera of "Beatrice di Tenda," he composed his tenth opera, "I Puritani," the dove used to alight on the score of that opera, to gurgle ten sighs and to disappear.

Bellini died shortly after the first performance of "I Puritani," in his thirty-third year, in September, 1835.

It is a curious fact that nearly all biographers of Bellini mention that in his last years he had been persecuted by spectres like Socrates, Brutus and others. They only differ as to the appearance of the ghost. Instead of the dove, Sig. Cicconetti says the spectre was large, of a yellow hue, with green spectacles, who, after trying to magnetize Bellini, would retire with a bitter smile. According to Sig. Florimo, the ghost was tall, with a classical appearance and a bald head, who used to stare at Bellini with an ironical expression, and Sig. Scherillo said that Bellini was in his last years haunted in his sleep by a host of little imps, who kept up a continuous humming and buzzing in his ears.

After a performance of "Norma" in 1847, in London, when Jenny Lind had sung the principal part, a party of gentlemen met accidentally at a restaurant in Haymarket, among them Pugni, the composer of "Esmeralda" and "Salvator Rosa;" Hector Berlioz, Chòrley the critic, and several others. During the conversation at supper, the story about Bellini's spectres was mentioned. Pugni said that the dove was nothing but Bellini's own conscience that haunted him. Chòrley thought the large ghost with green spectacles was the spectre of musical pedantry, who sneered at the sweet melodies of Bellini. Berlioz sarcastically remarked that the tall spook with classical features and bald head was the ghost of Shakespeare, who laughed at the idea of Bellini's setting his "Romeo and Juliet" to music. And a young man of my acquaintance insisted that the humming and buzzing of imps were the microbes of the music of the future, who about that time were beginning to float in the air and settle in composers' heads. Meyerbeer could stand it; Berlioz could mould them; Wagner could create a new system out of the chaos, but poor Bellini's tender disposition and elegiac nature could not resist them. He died of unresolved dissonances on the brain.

INDEX.

Crotchets and Quavers/Sharps and Flats

Roman type indicates page numbers in *Crotchets and Quavers;* italic type indicates page numbers in *Sharps and Flats.* In the case where one reference appears in both books, the page numbers refer first to the entries in *Crotchets and Quavers,* followed by a slash (/), followed by the entries in *Sharps and Flats.*

534